# *The Mikado's Empire*

A History of Japan from the
Age of Gods to the Meiji Era
(660 BC–AD 1872)

# The Mikado's Empire

A History of Japan from the
Age of Gods to the Meiji Era
(660 BC–AD 1872)

William Elliot Griffis, A.M.
Formerly of the Imperial University of Tokio, Japan

STONE BRIDGE CLASSICS
Stone Bridge Press
Berkeley, California

YOHAN CLASSICS
IBC Publishing
Tokyo, Japan

Originally published in 1883 by Harper & Brothers, New York. This edition contains the text of *Book I: History of Japan from 660 B.C. to 1872 A.D.*, 8th edition, 1895.

Published simultaneously in the United States by Stone Bridge Press, P.O. Box 8208, Berkeley, California 94707, www.stonebridge.com, and in Japan by IBC Publishing, Akasaka Community Bldg 5F, 1-1-8 Moto-Akasaka, Minato-Ku, Tokyo 107-0051, www.ibcpub.co.jp.

Trade distribution in the United States and Canada by Consortium Book Sales and in Japan by Yohan, Inc.

For information on distribution  and purchase worldwide contact Stone Bridge Press at sbp@stonebridge.com, 510-524-8732 (tel), or 510-524-8711 (fax).

Cover and book design by Robert Goodman, Silvercat™, San Diego, California.

Printed in the United States of America.

2011  2010  2009  2008  2007  2006      10  9  8  7  6  5  4  3  2  1

ISBN 978-1-933330-18-1 (USA)
ISBN 978-4-89684-290-6 (Japan)

to

Japanese lovers of knowledge in every age:

the dead,
who first kindled the sacred fire, who passed on the torch;

the martyrs,
who suffered death for their loyalty, patriotism, devotion to
national unity, restoration, and regeneration;

the students,
who, in noble thirst for truth, found honored graves in alien soil;

the living,
with whom rests the future of their beautiful land,

this sketch of their country and people, made in the interest of
truth, and set down without extenuation or malice, is, with
fraternal regard, dedicated by their comrade and friend,

the author.

# Contents

# The Orthography and Pronunciation of Japanese Words

IT is impossible to represent Japanese words exactly by any foreign alphabet; but a knowledge of the sounds heard in Japan, and by using letters which have each one invariable value, will enable a foreigner to reproduce Japanese names with tolerable accuracy. When the native authors and grammarians do not agree, absolute unanimity among foreign scholars is not to be expected; but palpable absurdities, impossible combinations of letters, and mistakes arising out of pure ignorance of the language may be avoided. The system given below, and used throughout this work, is, at least, rational, and is based on the structure and laws of combination in the language itself. This system is substantially (the differences aiming to secure greater simplicity) that of Hepburn's Japanese-English and English-Japanese, and of Satow's English-Japanese dictionary; the Romanized version of the Scriptures, published by the American Bible Society; of the *American Cyclopaedia*; the revised editions of Worcester's, and Webster's, dictionary; in Brown's, Aston's, Satow's, Brinckley's, and Hepburn's grammar and works on the Japanese language; Monteith's, Mitchell's, Cornell's, Warren's, and Harper's (American), and the Student's (English) geography and atlas; Mitford's *Tales of Old Japan*; Adams's *History of Japan*; the official documents of the Japanese Government, Department of Education, schools, and colleges; the British and American Legations and Consulates; the Anglo-Japanese press, and almost all scholars and writers who make accuracy a matter of concern.

The standard language (not the local dialect) of Tôkiô—now the literary as well as the political capital of the nation—is taken as the basis, and the words are then transliterated from the katagana spelling, as given by the best native scholars. The vowels are sounded as follows:

| | |
|---|---|
| *a* | has the sound of *a* in father, arm; |
| *ai* | has the sound of *ai* in aisle, or *i* in bite; |
| *i* | has the sound of *i* in pique, machine; |
| *u* | has the sound of *u* in rule, or *oo* in boot; |
| *ua* | has the sound of *ua* in quarantine; |
| *e* | has the sound of *e* in prey, they; |
| *ei* | has the sound of *ay* in saying; |
| *o* | has the sound of *o* in bore, so. |

Long vowels are marked thus, ô, û.

The combination *uai* is sounded as *wai*; *iu* as *yu*; *E* or *é*, as e in *prey*; but *e*, as in *men*; *g* is always hard, and *s* surd, as in *sit*, *sap*.

*C* before a vowel, *g* as in *gin*, *gem*; *l*, *q*, *s* sonant; *x*, and the digraphs *ph* and *th*, are not used.

# Preface

Japan, once in the far-off Orient, is now our nearest Western neighbor. Her people walk our streets; her youth sit, peers and rivals of our students, in the class-room; her art adorns our homes, and has opened to us a new Gate Beautiful. The wise men from the West are, at this writing, opening their treasures of tea, silk, gold-lacquer, bronzes, and porcelain at the first centennial of our nation's birth.

We hail the brightness of the rising of this first among Asiatic nations to enter modern life, to win and hold a place among the foremost peoples of the earth. It is time that a writer treated Japan as something else than an Oriental puzzle, a nation of recluses, a land of fabulous wealth, of universal licentiousness or of Edenic purity, the fastness of a treacherous and fickle crew, a Paradise of guileless children, a Utopia of artists and poets. It is time to drop the license of exaggeration, and, with the light of common day, yet with sympathy and without prejudice, seek to know what Dai Nippon is and has been.

It has been well said by a literary critic and reader of all the books on the subject that to write a good history of Japan is difficult, not so much from lack of materials, but from the differences in psychology. This I realize. My endeavor, during eight years' living contact with these people, has been, from their language, books, life, and customs, to determine their mental parallax, and find out how they think and feel.

I have not made this book in libraries at home, but largely on the soil of the mikado's empire. I have slight obligation to acknowledge to foreign writers, except to those working scholars in Japan who have written during the last decade with knowledge of the language. To them I owe much; first and most of all to Mr. Ernest Satow, who, in the special department of historical research, stands leader. To Messrs. W. Dixon, Aston, Mitford, Hepburn, Brown, Blakiston, Von Brandt, and Parkes, I am also indebted. I am under many obligations to the editor of *The Japan Mail*. This scholarly paper, published in Yokohama, is a most valuable mirror of contemporaneous Japanese history, and a rich store-house of facts, especially the papers of the Asiatic Society of Japan. *The Japan Herald* and *The Japan Gazette* have also been of great service to me, for which I here thank the proprietors. The constant embarrassment in treating many subjects has been from wealth of material. I have been obliged to leave out several chapters on important subjects, and to treat others with mere passing allusions.

In the early summer of 1868, two Higo students, Isé and Numagawa, arrived in the United States. They were followed by retainers of the daimios of Satsuma and Echizen, and other feudal princes. I was surprised and delighted to find these earnest youth equals of American students in good-breeding, courtesy, and mental acumen. Some of them remained under my instruction two years, others for a shorter time. Among my friends or pupils in New Brunswick, New Jersey, are Mr. Yoshida Kiyonari, H. I. J. M. Minister Plenipotentiary at Washington; Mr. Takagi Samro, H. I. J. M. Vice-consul at San Francisco; Mr. Tomita Tetsunosuké, H. I. J. M. Consul at New York; Mr. Hatakéyama Yoshinari, President of the Imperial University of

Japan; Captain Matsumura Junzo, of the Japanese navy. Among others were the two sons of Iwakura Tomomi, Junior Prime Minister of Japan; and two young nobles of the Shimadzu family of Satsuma. I also met Prince Adzuma, nephew of the mikado, and many of the prominent men, ex-daimiôs, Tokugawa retainers, soldiers in the war of 1868, and representatives of every department of service under the old shôgunate and new National Government. Six white marble shafts in the cemetery at New Brunswick, New Jersey, mark the resting-place of Kusukabé Tarô, of Fukui, and his fellow-countrymen, whose devotion to study cost them their lives. I was invited by the Prince of Echizen, while Regent of the University, through the American superintendent, Rev. G. F. Verbeck, to go out to organize a scientific school on the American principle in Fukui, Echizen, and give instruction in the physical sciences. I arrived in Japan, December 29th, 1870, and remained until July 25th, 1874. During all my residence I enjoyed the society of cultivated scholars, artists, priests, antiquaries, and students, both in the provincial and national capitals. From the living I bore letters of introduction to the prominent men in the Japanese Government, and thus were given to me opportunities for research and observation not often afforded to foreigners. My facilities for regular and extended travel were limited only by my duties. Nothing Japanese was foreign to me, from palace to beggar's hut. I lived in Dai Nippon during four of the most pregnant years of the nation's history. Nearly one year was spent alone in a daimiô's capital far in the interior, away from Western influence, when feudalism was in its full bloom, and the old life in vogue. In the national capital, in the time well called "the flowering of the nation," as one of the instructors in the Imperial University, having picked students from all parts of the empire, I was a witness of the marvelous development, reforms, dangers, pageants, and changes of the epochal years 1872, 1873, and 1874. With pride I may say truly that I have felt the pulse and heart of New Japan.

I have studied economy in the matter of Japanese names and titles, risking the charge of monotony for the sake of clearness. The scholar will, I trust, pardon me for apparent anachronisms and omissions. For lack of space or literary skill, I have had, in some cases, to condense with a brevity painful to a lover of fairness and candor. The title justifies the emphasis of one idea that pervades the book.

In the department of illustrations, I claim no originality, except in their selection. Many are from photographs taken for me by natives in Japan. Those of my artist-friend, Ôzawa, were nearly all made from life at my suggestion. I have borrowed many fine sketches *from native books*, through Aimé Humbert, whose marvelously beautiful and painstaking work, *Japon Illustré*, is a mine of illustration. Few artists have excelled in spirit and truth Mr. A. Wirgman, the artist of *The London Illustrated News*, a painter of real genius, whose works in oil now adorn many home parlors of ex-residents in Japan and whose gems, fine gold, and dross fill the sprightly pages of *The Japan Punch*. Many of his sketches adorn Sir Rutherford Alcock's book on the vicissitudes of diplomatists, commonly called *The Capital of the Tycoon*, or *Three Years in Japan*. I am indebted both to this gentleman and to Mr. Laurence Oliphant, who wrote the charming volume, *Lord Elgin's Mission to China and Japan*, for many illustrations, chiefly from native sketches. Through the liberality of my publishers, I am permitted to use these from their stores of plates. I believe I have in no case reproduced old cuts without new or correct information that will assist the general reader or those who wish to study the various styles of the native artists, five of which are herein presented. Hokusai, the Dickens, and Kano, the Audubon of Japanese art, are well represented. The photographs of the living and of the renowned dead, from temples, statues, or old pictures, from the collections of daimiôs and nobles, are chiefly by Uchida, a native photographer of rare ability, skill, and enthusiasm, who unfortunately died in 1875. Four vignettes are copied from the steel-plate engravings on the greenbacks printed in New York for the Ono National Banking Company of Tôkiô, by the Continental Banknote Company of New York.

I gratefully acknowledge the assistance derived from native scholars in Fukui and Tôkiô, especially Messrs. Iwabuchi, Takakashi, and Ideura, my readers and helpers. To the members of the Mei Roku Sha, who have honored me with membership in their honorable body, I return my best thanks. This club of authors and reformers includes such men as Fukuzawa, Arinori Mori, Nakamura Masanawo, Kato Hiroyuki, Nishi Shiu, the Mitsukuri brothers, Shiuhei and Rinshô, Uchida Masawo, Hatakéyama Yoshinari, and others, all names of fame and honor, and earnest workers in the regeneration of their country. To my former students now in New York, who have kindly assisted me in proof-reading, and last and first of all to Mr. Tosui Imadaté, my friend and constant companion during the last six years, I return my thanks and obligations. I omit in this place the names of high officers in the Japanese Government, because the responsibility for any opinion advanced in this work rests on no native of Japan. That is all my own. To my sister, the companion, during two years, of several of my journeys and visits in the homes of the island empire, I owe many an idea and inspiration to research. To the publishers of the *North American Review*, *Appletons' Journal*, and *The Independent* my thanks are due for permission to print part of certain chapters first published in these periodicals.

I trust the tone of the work will not seem dogmatic. I submit with modesty what I have written on the Ainôs. I am inclined to believe that India is their original home; that the basic stock of the Japanese people is Ainô; and that in this fact lies the root of the marvelous difference in the psychology of the Japanese and their neighbors, the Chinese.

"Can a nation be born at once?" "With God all things are possible."

W. E. G.

*New York, May* 10th, 1876.

[The illustrations were almost omitted with regret in this edition. —The publisher.]

# Preface to the Second Edition

Anew issue of this work having been called for in a little over four months from the date of its publication, the author has endeavored to render the second edition more worthy than the first. This has been done by the addition of valuable matter in the appendix and foot-notes, and the recasting of a few pages, on which original has been substituted for compiled matter.

Critics have complained that in Book I, the line between the mythical, or legendary, and the historic period has not been clearly drawn. A writer in *The Japan Mail* of November 25th, 1876, says:

> After an introductory chapter on the physical features of the country, the author plunges into the dense mists of the historic and the prehistoric ages, where he completely loses his way for about a millennium and a half, until he at length strikes into the true path, under the guidance of the *Nihon Guai Shi*.

Did the critic read Chapter III? The author, before essaying the task, knew only too well the difficulties of the work before him. He made no attempt to do the work of a Niebuhr for Japan. His object was not to give an infallible record of absolute facts, nor has he pretended to do so. He merely sketched in outline a picture of what thirty-three millions of Japanese believe to be their ancient history. He relied on the intelligence of his readers, and even on that of the critics (who should not skip Chapter III), to appreciate the value of the narratives of the *Kojiki* and the *Nihongi*—the oldest extant books in the Japanese language, and on which all other accounts of the ancient period are based. He was not even afraid that any school-boy who had been graduated beyond his fairy tales would think the dragon-born Jimmu a character of equal historic reality with that of Cæsar or Charlemagne.

On the other hand, the author believes that history begins before writing, and that he who would brand the whole of Japanese tradition before the sixth century A.D. as "all but valueless" must demonstrate, and not merely affirm. The author preferred to introduce Jingu and Yamato Daké to Occidental readers, and let them take their chances before the light of research. Will this century see the scholar and historian capable of reeling off the thread of pure history, clear and without fracture, from the cocoon of Japanese myth, legend, and language? The author, even with his profound reverence for Anglo-Japanese scholarship, hopes for, yet doubts it.

In one point the author has been misapprehended. He nowhere attempts to explain whence came the dominant (Yamato) tribe or tribes to Japan. He believes the Japanese people are a mixed race, as stated on page 86; but where the original seats of that conquering people may have been on whom the light of written, undoubted history dawns in the seventh century, he has not stated. That these were in Mantchuria is probable, since their mythology is in some points but a transfiguration of Mantchu life. The writer left the question an open one. He is glad to add, without comment, the words of the *Mail* critic, who is, if he mistakes not, one of the most accomplished linguists in Japan, and the author of standard grammars of the written and spoken language of Japan:

As regards the position of the Japanese language, it gives no dubious response. Japanese has all the structural and syntactical peculiarities common to the Alatyan or Ural-Altaic group; and the evidence of the physiognomical tests points unmistakably to the same origin for the people. The short, round skull, the oblique eyes, the prominent cheek-bones, the dark-brown hair, and the scant beard, all proclaim the Mantchus and Coreans, as their nearest congeners. In fact, it is no longer rash to assert is certain that the Japanese are a Tungusic race, and their own traditions and the whole course of their history are incompatible with any other conclusion than that Corea is the route by which the immigrant tribes made their passage into Kiushiu from their ancestral Mantchurian seats.

The brevity of the chapter on the Ashikaga period, which has been complained of, arose, not from any lack of materials, but because the writer believed that this epoch deserved a special historian. Another reason that explains many omissions, notably, that of any detailed reference to Japanese art, is, that this volume is not an encyclopedia.

The author returns his hearty thanks to his Japanese friends, and to the critics whose scrutiny has enabled him in any way to improve the work.

W. E. G.
NEW YORK, *January* 10th, 1877

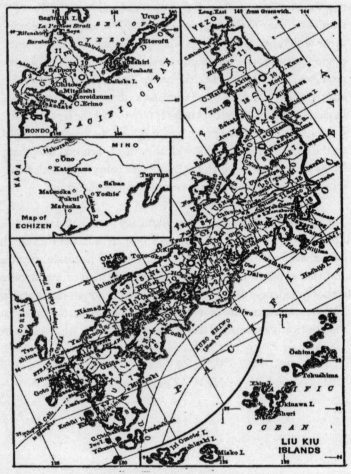

*Dai Nippon (the Empire of Japan)*

# I

# *The Background*

It is manifest that to understand a people and their national life, the physical conditions under which they live must be known. To enjoy the picture, we must study the background.

Dai Nippon, as the natives call their beautiful land, occupies a significant position on the globe. Lying in the Pacific Ocean, in the temperate zone, it bends like a crescent off the continent of Asia. In the extreme north, at the island of Saghalin, the distance from the main-land of Asia is so slight that the straits may be crossed easily in a canoe. From Kiushiu, with the island of Tsushima lying between, the distance from Corea is but one day's sail in a junk. For 4,000 miles eastward from the main island stretches the Pacific, shored in by the continent of America. From Yezo to Kamtchatka, the Kuriles stretch like the ruins of a causeway, prolonged by the Aleutian Islands, to Alaska. The configuration of the land is that resulting from the combined effects of volcanic action and the incessant motion of the corroding waves. The area of the empire is nearly equal to that of our Middle and New England States. Of the 150,000 square miles of surface, two-thirds consist of mountain land. The island of Saghalin (ceded to Russia in May, 1875) is one mountain chain; that of Yezo one mountain mass. On the main island,* a solid backbone of mountain-ous elevations runs continuously from Rikuoku to Shinano, whence it branches off into subordinate chains that are prolonged irregularly to Nagato and into Kiushiu and Shikoku. Speaking generally, the heights of the mountains gradually increase from the extremities to the centre. In Saghalin, they are low; in Yezo, they are higher: increas-ing gradually on the north of the main island, they culminate in the centre in the lofty ranges of Shinano, and the peaks of Nantaizan, Yatsugadaké, Hakuzan (nine thousand feet high), and Fuji, whose summit is over twelve thousand feet above the sea. Thence toward the south they gradually decrease in height. There are few high mountains along the sea-coast. The land slopes up gradually into hills, thence into lesser peaks, and finally into lofty ranges.

As Fuji, with his tall satellites, sweeps up from the land, so Japan itself rises up, peak-like, from the sea. From the shores the land plunges abruptly down into deep water. Japan is but an emerged crest of a submarine mountain—perhaps the edge of hard rock left by the submergence of the earth-crust which now floors the Sea of Japan and the Gulf of Tartary. There seems little reason to doubt that Saghalin, Yezo, Hondo, and Kiushiu were in geologic ages united together, forming one island. Surrounded on all sides by swift and variable currents, the islands everywhere on the sea-borders exhibit the effect of their action. At most points the continual detritus is such as to seri-ously encroach on the land area, and the belief holds among certain native sea-coast dwellers, strengthened by the traditional tales of past

* Dai Nippon, or Nihon, means Great Japan, and is the name of the entire empire, not of the main island. The foreign writers on Japan have almost unanimously blundered in calling the largest island "Niphon." Hondo is the name given to the main island in the *Military Geography of Japan* (Heiyo Nippon Chiri Yoshi, Tôkiô, 1872) published by the War Department, and which is used in this work throughout.

ravages, that in process of time the entire country, devoured by successive gnawings of the ocean, will finally sink into its insatiable maw.

The geological formations of the country—the natural foundations—
are not as yet accurately determined. Enough, however, is known to give
us a fair outline of fact, which future research and a thorough survey
must fill up.* Of the soil, more is known.

Even in a natural state, without artificial fertilization, most of the
tillable land produces good crops of grain or vegetables. On myriads

---

* Baron Richthofen, in a paper read before the Geological Society of Berlin,
June 4th, 1873, thus generalizes the geology of Japan: The west and east portion of the aggregate body of the Japanese islands is in every way the direct
continuation of the mountain system which occupies the south-eastern portion
of China, the axial chain of which extends from the frontier of Annam to the
island of Chusan, in the direction of W. 30° S.,E. 30° N. It is accompanied on
either side by a number of parallel chains. The prolongation of this group of
linear chains passes through the island of Kiushiu to the great bend of Japan
(Suruga and Shinano). Through Kiushiu and the southern part of the main
island, the structure of the hills and the rocks of which they are made up
(chiefly Silurian and Devonian strata, accompanied by granite) and the lines
of strike are the same as those observed in South-eastern China. This system
is intersected at either end by another, which runs S.S.W., N.N.E. On the
west it commences in Kiushiu, and extends southward in the direction of the
Liu Kiu Islands, while on the east it constitutes the northern branch of the
main island, and, with a slight deviation in its course, continues through the
islands of Yezo and Saghalin. A third system, which properly does not belong
to Japan, is indicated by the S.W. and N.E. line of the Kuriles.

The above outline throws light on the distribution of volcanoes. The first
system, where it occupies the breadth of the country for itself alone, is as free
from volcanoes, or any accumulation of volcanic rocks, as it is in South-eastern China. The second system is accompanied by volcanoes. But the greatest
accumulation of volcanic rocks, as well as of the extinct volcanoes, is found in
the places of interference, or those regions where the lines of the two systems
cross each other, and, besides, in that region where the third system branches
off from the second. To the same three regions the volcanoes which have been
active in historic times have been confined.

In the geological structure of Kiushiu, the longer axis is from N. to S., but
intersected by several solid bars made up of very ancient rocks, and following the

of rice-fields, which have yielded richly for ages, the fertility is easily maintained by irrigation and the ordinary application of manure, the natives being proficient in both these branches of practical husbandry.

The rivers on such narrow islands, where steep mountains and sharply excavated valleys predominate, are of necessity mainly useless for navigation. Ordinarily they are little more than brooks that flow lazily in narrow and shallow channels to the sea. After a storm, in rainy weather, or in winter, they become swollen torrents, often

---

strike of W. 30°S., E. 30°N. They form high mountain barriers, the most central of which, south of the provinces of Higo and Bungo, rises to over seven thousand feet, and is extremely wild and rugged. In Satsuma, the various families of volcanic rocks have arrived at the surface in exactly the same order of succession as in the case of Hungary, Mexico, and many other volcanic regions, viz., first, propylite, or trachytic greenstone; second, andesite; third, trachyte and rhyolite; fourth, the basaltic rocks. The third group was not visited by him. Thomas Antisell, M.D., and Professor Benjamin J. Lyman, M.E., and Henry S. Munroe, M.E., American geologists in Yezo, have also elucidated this interesting problem. From the first I quote. The mountain systems of Yezo and farther north are similar to those in the northern part of the main island. There are in Yezo two distinct systems of mountains. One, coming down directly from the north, is a continuation of the chain in Karafto (Saghalin), which, after passing down south along the west shore of Yezo, is found in Rikuoku, Ugo, Uzen, and farther south. The second enters Yezo from the Kuriles Islands and Kamtchatka, running N. 20–25°E., and S. 20–25°W., and crossing in places the first system. It is from the existence and crossing of these chains that Yezo derives its triangular form. The two systems possess very different mineral contents for their axes. The first has an essentially granitic and feldspathic axis, produced, perhaps, by shrinkage, and is slow of decomposition of its minerals forming the soils. The second has an axis, plutonic or volcanic, yielding basalts, traps, and diorites, decomposing readily, producing deep and rich soils. Hence the different kinds of vegetation on the two chains. Where the two chains cross, also, there is found a form of country closed up in the north and east by hills, the valleys opening to the south and west. This volcanic chain is secondary in the main island of Japan; but in Yezo and in Kiushiu it attains great prominence.

Professor Benjamin S. Lyman, an American geologist, has also made valuable surveys and explorations in Yezo, the results of which are given in the "Reports of Horace Capron and his Foreign Assistants," Tôkiô. 1875.

miles wide sweeping resistlessly over large tracts of land which they keep perpetually desolate—wildernesses of stones and gravel, where fruitful fields ought to be. The area of land kept permanently waste in Japan on this account is enormous. The traveler, who to-day crosses a clear brook on a plank, may to-morrow be terrified at a roaring flood of muddy water in which neither man, beast, nor boat can live a moment. There are, however, some large plains, and in those we must look to find the navigable rivers. In the mountains of Shinano and Kôdzuké are found the sources of most of the streams useful for navigation on the main island. On the plains of the Kuantô (from Suruga to Iwaki), Ôshiu (Rikuchiu and Rikuzen), Mino, and Echigo, are a few rivers on which one may travel in boats hundreds of miles. One may go by water from Tôkiô to Niigata by making a few portages, and from Ôzaka to the end of Lake Biwa by natural water. In the northern part of Hondo are several long rivers, notably the Kitagami and Sakata. In Yezo is the Ishikari. In Shikoku are several fine streams, which are large for the size of the islands. Kiushiu has but one or two of any importance. Almost every one of these rivers abounds in fish, affording, with the surrounding ocean, an inexhaustible and easily attainable supply of food of the best quality. Before their history began, the aboriginal islanders made this brain-nourishing food their chief diet, and through the recorded centuries to the quick-witted Japanese proper it has been the daily meat.

In the geologic ages volcanic action must have been extremely violent, as in historic time it has been almost continual. Hundreds, at least, of mountains, now quiet, were once blazing furnaces. The ever-greenery that decks them to-day reminds one of the ivy that mantles the ruins, or the flowers that overgrow the neglected cannon on the battle-field. Even within the memory of men now living have the most awful and deadly exhibitions of volcanic desolation been witnessed. The annals of Japan are replete with the records of these flame-and-lava-vomiting mountains, and the most harrowing tales of human life destroyed and human industry overwhelmed are truthfully portrayed by the pencil of the artist and the pen of the historian in the native literature. Even now the Japanese count over twenty active and hundreds of dormant volcanoes. As late as 1874, the volcano of Taromai, in Yezo, whose crater had long since congealed, leaving only a few puffing solfataras, exploded, blowing its rocky cap far up into the air, and scattering a rain of ashes as far as the sea-shore, many miles distant. Even the nearly perfect cone of Shiribéshi, in Yezo, is but one of many of nature's colossal ruins. Asama yama, never quiet, puffs off continual jets of steam, and at this moment of writing is groaning and quaking, to the terror of the people around it. Even the superb Fuji, that sits in lordly repose and looks down over the lesser peaks in thirteen provinces, owes its matchless form to volcanic action, being clothed by a garment of lava on a throne of granite. Hakuzan, on the west coast, which uprears its form above the clouds, nine thousand feet from the sea-level, and holds a lakelet of purest water in its bosom, once in fire and smoke belched out rocks and ulcered its crater jaws with floods of white and black lava. Not a few of these smoking furnaces by day are burning lamps by night to the mariner. Besides the masses and fields of scoria one everywhere meets, other evidences of the fierce unrest of the past are noticed. Beds of sulphur abound. Satsuma, Liu Kiu, and Yezo are noted for the large amount they easily produce. From the sides of Hakuzan huge crystals of sulphur are dug. Solfataras exist in active operation in many places. Sulphur-springs may be found in almost every province. Hot-springs abound, many of them highly impregnated with mineral salts, and famous for their geyser-like rhythm of ebb and flow. In Shinano and Echigo the people cook their food, and the farmer may work in his fields by night, lighted by the inflammable gas which issues from the ground, and is led through bamboo tubes.

Connected with volcanic are the seismic phenomena. The records of Japan from the earliest time make frequent mention of these devastating and terrifying visitations of subterranean disorder. Not only have villages, towns, and cities been shaken down or ingulfed, but in many neighborhoods tradition tells of mountains that have disappeared utter]y, or been leveled to earth. The local histories, so numerous in Japan, relate many such instances, and numerous gullies and depressions produced by the opening and partial closure of the earth-lips are pointed out. One, in the province of Echizen, is over a mile long, and resembles a great trench.

In addition to a good soil, Japan has been generously endowed by the Creator with mineral riches. Most of the useful varieties of stone are found throughout the empire. Granite and the harder rocks, through various degrees of softness, down to the easily carved or chipped sandstones and secondary formations useful for fortifications, buildings, tombs, walks, or walls, exist in almost every province.

Almost all the useful metals long known to man are found in this island empire. Gold and silver in workable quantities are found in many places. The island of Sado is a mass of gold-bearing quartz. Copper is very abundant, and of the purest kind. Lead, tin, antimony, and manganese abound. Of zinc and mercury there is but little. Iron is chiefly in the form of magnetic oxide. It occurs in the diluvium of rivers and along the sea-coast, lying in beds, often of great thickness. The first quality of iron may be extracted from it. Iron-stone and many other varieties of ore are also found. Petroleum issues from the ground in Echigo, Suruga, Echizen, Yezo, and in Saghalin; the ocean at some portions on the coast of the latter is said to be smeared with a floating scum of oil for miles.

The botanical wealth of Japan is very great. A considerable number of vegetable species have doubtless been introduced by human agency into

Japan from the Asiatic continent, but the indigenous plants and those imported by natural means are very numerous.

The timber of the main island, Kiushiu, and Shikoku is superb in appearance and growth, of great variety, beauty, and adaptability to the uses of man. Yezo is one vast boom and lumber yard. Thirty-six varieties of useful timber-trees, including true oak, are found there. The Kuriles also afford rich supplies, and are capable of becoming to the empire proper what forest-clad Norway is to England. Yamato, on the main-land, is also famous for its forests, ranging from tallest evergreen trees of great size, fineness of grain, and strength of fibre, to the soft and easily whittled pines; but the incessant demands for firing and carpentry make devastating inroads on the growing timber. Split wood for cooking, and charcoal for warmth, necessitate the system of forestry long in vogue in some parts of the empire requiring a tree to be planted for every one cut down; and nurseries of young forest trees are regularly set out, though the custom is not universal. Most of the trees and many of the plants are evergreen, thus keeping the islands clothed in perpetual verdure, and reducing the visual difference between winter and summer, in the southern half of Hondo, at least, to a nearly tropical minimum.

The various varieties of bamboo, graceful in appearance, and by its strength, symmetry, hollowness, and regularity of cleavage, adapted to an almost endless variety of uses, are almost omnipresent, from the scrub undergrowth in Yezo to that cultivated in luxuriant groves in Satsuma so as to be almost colossal in proportion. There is, however, as compared with our own country, a deficiency of fruit-trees and edible vegetables. The first use of most of the bread grains and plants is historic. In very ancient times it is nearly certain that the soil produced very little that could be used for food, except roots, nuts, and berries.

This is shown both by tradition and history, and also by the fact that the names of vegetables in Japan are mostly foreign.

The geographical position of the Japanese chain would lead us to expect a flora American, Asiatic, and semi-tropical in its character. The rapid variations of temperature, heavy and continuous rains, succeeded by scorching heats and the glare of an almost tropical sun, are accompanied and tempered by strong and constant winds. Hence we find semi-tropical vegetable forms in close contact with Northern temperate types. In general the predominant nature of the Japan flora is shrubby rather than herbaceous.*

The geographical position of Japan hardly explains the marked resemblance of its flora to that of Atlantic America,† on the one hand, and that of the Himalaya region, on the other. Such, however, is the fact:

---

* In the "Enumeratio Plantarum," which treats of all the known exogens and conifers in Japan, 1,699 species are enumerated, distributed in 643 genera, which are collocated in 122 orders. In other words, an imperfect botanical survey of the Nippon chain of islands shows that in it are represented nearly half the natural orders, ten percent of the genera, and nearly three percent of the species of dicotyledons known to exist on the surface of the globe. Future research must largely increase the number of species.

† Very large and splendidly illustrated works on botany exist in the Japanese language. The native botanists classify according to the Linnæan system. In their "Enumeratio Plantarum" (Paris, 1874), Drs. A. Franchet and L. Savatier have given a *résumé* of all the known dicotyledonous plants in Japan. It is a work of great research and conscientious accuracy. I have seen excellent and voluminous native works, richly illustrated, on ichthyology, conchology, zoölogy, entomology, reptilology, and mineralogy. Some of these works are in ninety volumes each. Ten thousand dollars were spent by a wealthy scholar in Mino in the publication of one of them. They would not satisfy the requirements of the exact science of this decade, but they constitute an invaluable thesaurus to the botanical investigator. I am indebted for most of the information concerning the Japanese flora to a paper in the *Japan Mail* of

the Japanese flora resembles that of Eastern North America more than
that of Western North America or Europe.‡

The fauna of the island is a very meagre one, and it is also quite
probable that the larger domestic animals have been imported. Of wild
beasts, the bear, deer, wolf, badger, fox, and monkey, and the smaller
ground animals, are most probably indigenous. So far as studied,
however, the types approach those of the remote American rather than
those of the near Asiatic continent.

It is most probable, and nearly certain, that prehistoric Japan did
not possess the cow, horse, sheep, or goat. Even in modern Japan, the
poverty of the fauna strikes the traveler with surprise. The birds are
mostly those of prey. Eagles and hawks are abundant. The crows, with
none to molest their ancient multitudinous reign, are now, as always
in the past, innumerable. The twittering of a noticeably small number of the smaller birds is occasionally heard; but bird-song seems to
have been omitted from the catalogue of natural glories of this island

---

September 25th, 1875, from the pen of a competent reviewer of Dr. Savatier's
great work.

‡ The results of Dr. Asa Gray's investigations of the herbarium brought to the
United States by the Perry expedition are summed up as follows:

48 percent had corresponding European representatives,
37 percent had corresponding Western North American representatives,
61 percent had corresponding Eastern North American representatives;

while

27 percent were identical with European species,
20 percent were identical with Western North American species,
23 percent were identical with Eastern North American species.

"Dr. Gray's report was drawn up in 1858, when Japanese botany was little
known, and considerable alteration might be made in his figures; but there
can be little doubt that the general result would be the same."

empire. Two birds, the stork and heron, now, as anciently, tread the fields in stately beauty, or strike admiration in the beholder as they sail in perfect grace in mid-air. The wild ducks and geese in flocks have, from time immemorial, summered in Yezo and wintered in Hondo.

The domestic fowls consist almost entirely of ducks and chickens. The others have, doubtless, been imported. Of sea-birds there are legions on the uninhabited coasts, and from the rocks the fishermen gather harvests of eggs.

Surrounding their land is the great reservoir of food, the ocean. The seas of Japan are probably unexcelled in the world for the multitude and variety of the choicest species of edible fish. The many bays and gulfs indenting the islands have been for ages the happy hunting-grounds of the fisherman. The rivers are well stocked with many varieties of fresh-water fish. In Yezo the finest salmon exist in inexhaustible supply, while almost every species of edible shell-fish, mollusca and crustacea, enlivens the shores of the islands, or fertilizes the soil with its catacombs. So abundant is fish that fish-manure is an article of standard manufacture, sale, and use. The variety and luxuriance of edible sea-weed are remarkable.

The aspects of nature in Japan, as in most volcanic countries, comprise a variety of savage hideousness, appalling destructiveness, and almost heavenly beauty. From the mountains burst volcanic eruptions; from the land come tremblings; from the ocean rises the tidal wave; over it blows the cyclone. Floods of rain in summer and autumn give rise to inundations and land-slides. During three months of the year the inevitable, dreaded typhoon may be expected; as the invisible agent of hideous ruin. Along the coast the winds and currents are very variable. Sunken and emerging rocks line the shore. All these make the dark side of nature to cloud the imagination of man, and to create the nightmare of superstition. But Nature's glory outshines her temporary gloom, and in presence of her cheering smiles the past

terrors are soon forgotten. The pomp of vegetation, the splendor of
the landscape, and the heavenly gentleness of air and climate come to
soothe and make vivacious the spirits of man. The seasons come and
go with well-nigh perfect regularity; the climate at times reaches the
perfection of that in a temperate zone—not too sultry in summer, nor
raw in winter. A majority of the inhabitants rarely see ice over an inch
thick, or snow more than twenty-four hours old. The average lowest
point in cold weather is probably 20° Fahrenheit.*

The surrounding ocean and the variable winds temper the climate
in summer; the Kuro Shiwo, the Gulf Stream of the Pacific, modifies
the cold of winter. A sky such as ever arches over the Mediterranean
bends above Japan, the ocean walls her in, and ever green and fertile
land is hers. With healthful air, fertile soil, temperate climate, a land
of mountains and valleys, with a coast-line indented with bays and
harbors, food in plenty, a country resplendent with natural beauty,
but liable at any moment to awful desolation and hideous ruin, what
influences had Nature in forming the physique and character of the
people who inhabit Japan?

---

* For statistics relating to nearly all the subjects treated of in this chapter, see
appendices at the end of this volume.

II

# The Aborigines*

In seeking the origin of the Japanese people, we must take into consideration the geographical position of their island chain, with reference to its proximity to the main-land, and its situation in the ocean currents. Japanese traditions and history may have much to tell us concerning the present people of Japan—whether they are exclusively an indigenous race, or the composite of several ethnic stocks. From a study, however imperfect, of the language, physiognomy, and bodily characteristics, survivals of ancient culture, historic geology, and the relics of man's struggle with nature in the early ages, and of the actual varieties of mankind now included within the mikado's dominions,† we may learn much of the ancestors of the present Japanese.

---

* I use the term "aborigines" for the sake of convenience, being by no means absolutely sure that those I so designate were the first people *in situ*. It has been conjectured and held by some native scholars that there was in Japan a pre-Ainô civilization; though of this there is scarcely a shadow of proof, as there is proof for an ancient Malay civilization higher than the present condition of the Malays. By the term "aborigines" I mean the people found on the soil at the dawn of history.

† In compiling this chapter I have used, in addition to my own material and that derived from Japanese books, students, and residents in Yezo, the careful notes of the English travelers, Captains Bridgeford and Blakiston, and Mr. Ernest Satow, and the reports and verbal accounts of the American

The horns of the crescent-shaped chain of Dai Nippon approach the Asiatic continent at the southern end of Corea and at Siberia. Nearly the whole of Saghalin is within easy reach of the continent by canoe. At the point called Norato, a little north of the fifty-second parallel, the opposite shore, but five miles distant, is easily seen. The water is here so shallow that junks can not cross it at low tide. After long prevalent favorable winds, the ground is left dry, and the natives can walk dry-shod into Asia. During three or four months in the year it is frozen over, so that, with dog-teams or on foot, communication is often a matter of a single hour. In Japanese atlases, on the map of Karafto, a sand-bank covered by very shallow water is figured as occupying the space between the island and the continent. A people even without canoes might make this place a gate of entrance into Saghalin. The people thus entering Japan from the north would have the attraction of richer supplies of food and more genial climate to tempt them southward. As matter of fact, communication is continually taking place between the Asiatic main-land and Saghalin.

Japan occupies a striking position in the ocean currents which flow up from the Indian Ocean and the Malay peninsula. That branch of the great equatorial current of the Pacific, called the Kuro Shiwo, or Black Stream, on account of its color, flows up in a westerly direction past Luzon, Formosa, and the Liu Kiu Islands, striking the south point of Kiushiu, and sometimes, in summer, sending a branch up the Sea of Japan. With great velocity it scours the east coast of Kiushiu, the south of Shikoku; thence, with diminished rapidity, enveloping both the group of islands south of the Bay of Yedo and Ôshima; and, at a point a little north of the latitude of Tôkiô, it leaves the coast of

engineers and geologists in the service of the Kai Taku Shi (Department for the Development of Yezo), organized in 1869 by the Imperial Government of Japan. Of these latter, I am especially indebted to Professors B. S. Lyman, Henry S. Munroe, and Thomas Antisell, M.D.

Japan, and flows north-east toward the shores of America. With the variable winds, cyclones, and sudden and violent storms continually arising, for which the coasts of Eastern Asia are notorious, it is easily seen that the drifting northward from the Malay Archipelago of boats and men, and sowing of the shores of Kiushiu, Shikoku, and the western shores of Hondo with people from the south and west, must have been a regular and continuous process. This is shown to be the fact in Japanese history, in both ancient and modern times, and is taking place nearly every year of the present century.

It seems most probable that the savages descended from the north, tempted south by richer fisheries and a warmer climate, or urged on by successive immigrations from the continent. There is abundant evidence from Japanese history of the habitation of the main island by the Ainôs, the savages whose descendants now occupy Yezo. Shikoku and Kiushiu were evidently peopled by mixed races, sprung of the waifs from the various shores of Southern Asia. When the conquerors landed in Kiushiu, or, in sacred Japanese phrase, "when our divine ancestors descended from heaven to the earth," they found the land peopled by savages, under tribal organizations, living in villages, each governed by a head-man. Conquering first the aborigines of Kiushiu and Shikoku, they advanced into the main island, fought and tranquilized the Ainôs, then called Ebisu, or barbarians, and fixed their capital not far from Kiôto. The Ainôs were not subjugated in a day, however, and continual military operations were necessary to keep them quiet. Only after centuries of fighting were they thoroughly subdued and tranquilized. The traveler to-day in the northern part of the main island may see the barrows of the Ainos' bones slain by Japanese armies more than a millennium ago. One of these mounds, near Morioka, in Rikuchiu, very large, and named "Yezo mori" (Ainô mound), is especially famous, containing the bones of the aborigines slaughtered, heaps upon heaps, by the Japanese shôgun (general),

Tamura, who was noted for being six feet high, and for his many bloody victories over the Ebisu.

For centuries more, the distinction between conquerors and conquered, as between Saxon and Norman in England, was kept up; but at length the fusion of races was complete, and the homogeneous Japanese people is the result. The remnants of Ainôs in Yezo, shut off by the straits of Tsugaru from Hondo, have preserved the aboriginal blood in purity.

The traditional origin of the Ainôs, said to be given by themselves, though I suspect the story to be an invention of the conquerors, or of the Japanese, is as follows: A certain prince, named Kamui, in one of the kingdoms in Asia, had three daughters. One of them having become the object of the incestuous passion of her father, by which her body became covered with hair, quit his palace in the middle of the night, and fled to the sea-shore. There she found a deserted canoe, on board which was only a large dog. The young girl resolutely embarked with her only companion to journey to some place in the East. After many months of travel, the young princess reached an uninhabited place in the mountains, and there gave birth to two children, a boy and a girl. These were the ancestors of the Ainô race. Their offspring in turn married, some among each other, others with the bears of the mountains. The fruits of this latter union were men of extraordinary valor, and nimble hunters, who, after a long life spent in the vicinity of their birth, departed to the far north, where they still live on the high and inaccessible table-lands above the mountains; and, being immortal, they direct, by their magical influences, the actions and the destiny of men, that is, the Ainôs.

The term "Ainô" is a comparatively modern epithet, applied by the Japanese. Its derivation, as given by several eminent native scholars whom I have consulted, is from *inu*, a dog. Others assert that it is an abbreviation of *ai no ko*, "offspring of the middle;" that is, a breed between man and beast. Or, if the Japanese were believers in a theory called of late years the "Darwinian," an idea by no means unknown in their speculations, the Ainôs would constitute the "missing link," or "intermediate" between man and the brutes. In the ancient Japanese literature, and until probably the twelfth century, the Ainôs were called Ebisu, or savages.

The proofs from language of the Ainô ancestry of the Japanese are very strong. So far as studied, the Ainô tongue and the Altai dialects are said to be very similar. The Ainô and Japanese languages differ no more than certain Chinese dialects do from each other. Ainôs and Japanese have little difficulty in learning to speak the language of each other. The most ancient specimens of the Japanese tongue are found to show as great a likeness to the Ainô as to modern Japanese.

Further proofs of the general habitation of Hondo by the Ainôs appear in the geographical names which linger upon the mountains and rivers. These names, musical in sound, and possessing, in their significance, a rude grandeur, have embalmed the life of a past race, as the sweet names of "Juniata" and "Altamaha," or the sonorous ono-matopes of "Niagara," "Katahdin," and "Tuscarora" echo the ancient glories of the well-nigh extinct aborigines of America, who indeed may be brethren of the Ainôs. These names abounding in the north, especially in the provinces north of the thirty-eighth parallel, are rare in the south, and in most cases have lost their exact ancient pronuncia-tion by being for centuries spoken by Japanese tongues.

The evidences of an aboriginal race are still to be found in the relics of the Stone Age in Japan. Flint, arrow and spear heads, ham-mers, chisels, scrapers, kitchen refuse, and various other trophies, are frequently excavated, or may be found in the museum or in homes of private persons. Though covered with the soil for centuries, they seem as though freshly brought from an Ainô hut in Yezo. In scores of striking instances, the very peculiar ideas, customs, and superstitions, of both Japanese and Ainô, are the same, or but slightly modified.

Amidst many variations, two distinctly marked types of features are found among the Japanese people. Among the upper classes, the fine, long, oval face, with prominent, well-chiseled features, deep-sunken eye-sockets, oblique eyes, long, drooping eyelids, elevated and arched eyebrows, high and narrow forehead, rounded nose, bud-like mouth, pointed chin, small hands and feet, contrast strikingly with the round, flattened face, less oblique eyes almost level with the face, and straight noses, expanded and upturned at the roots. The former type prevails among the higher classes—he nobility and gentry; the latter, among the agricultural and laboring classes. The one is the Ainô, or northern type; the other, the southern, or Yamato type. In the accompanying cut this difference is fairly shown in the strongly contrasting types of the Japanese lady and her servant, or child's nurse. The modern Ainôs are found inhabiting the islands of Yezo, Saghalin, the Kuriles, and a few of the outlying islands. They number less than twenty thousand in all.

As the Ainô of to-day is and lives, so Japanese art and traditions depict him in the dawn of history: of low stature, thick-set, full-bearded, bushy hair of a true black, eyes set at nearly right angles with the nose, which is short and thick, and chipped at the end, muscular in frame and limbs, with big hands and feet. His language, religion, dress, and general manner of life are the same as of old. He has no alphabet, no writing, no numbers above a thousand. His rice, tobacco, and pipe, cotton garments, and worship of Yoshitsuné, are of course later innovations—steps in the scale of civilization. Since the Restoration of 1868, a number of Ainôs of both sexes have been living in Tôkiô, under instruction of the Kai Taku Shi (Department for the

Colonization of Yezo). I have had frequent opportunities of studying their physical characteristics, language, and manners.

Their dwellings in Yezo are made of poles covered over with thick straw mats, with thatched roofs, the windows and doors being holes covered with the same material. The earth beaten down hard forms the floor, on which a few coarse mattings or rough boards are laid. Many of the huts are divided into two apartments, separated by a mud and wattle partition. The fire-place, with its pot-hooks, occupies the centre. There being no chimney, the interior walls become thickly varnished with creosote, densely packed with flakes of carbon, or festooned with masses of soot. They are adorned with the implements of the chase, and the skulls of animals taken in hunting. Scarcely any furniture except cooking-pots is visible. The empyreumatical odor and the stench of fish do not conspire to make the visit to an Ainô hut very pleasant.

Raised benches along two walls of the hut afford a sleeping or lounging place, doubtless the original of the *tokonoma* of the modern Japanese houses. They sit, like the Japanese, on their heels. Their food is mainly fish and sea-weed, with rice, beans, sweet-potatoes, millet, and barley, which, in Southern Yezo, they cultivate in small plots. They obtain rice, tobacco, saké, or rice-beer, an exhilarating beverage which they crave as the Indians do "fire-water," and cotton clothing from their masters, the Japanese. The women weave a coarse, strong, and durable cloth, ornamented in various colors, and ropes from the barks of trees. They make excellent dug-out canoes from elm-trees. Their dress consists of an under, and an upper garment having tight sleeves and reaching to the knees, very much like that of the Japanese. The woman's dress is longer, and the sleeves wider. They wear, also, straw leggings and straw shoes. Their hair, which is astonishingly thick, is clipped short in front, and falls in masses down the back and sides to the shoulders. It is of a true black, whereas the hair of the Japanese, when freed from unguents, is of a dark or reddish brown, and I have seen distinctly red hair among the latter. The beard and mustaches of the Ainôs are allowed to attain their fullest development, the former often reaching the length of twelve or fourteen inches. Hence, Ainôs take kindly to the "hairy foreigners," Englishmen and Americans, whose bearded faces the normal Japanese despise, while to a Japanese child, as I found out in Fukui, a man with mustaches appears to be only a dragon without wings or tail. Some, not all, of the older men, but very few of the younger, have their bodies and limbs covered with thick black hair, about an inch long. The term "hairy Kuriles," applied to them as a characteristic hairy race, is a mythical expression of book-makers, as the excessively hirsute covering supposed to be universal among the Ainôs is not to be found by the investigator on the ground. Their skin is brown, their eyes are horizontal, and their noses low, with the lobes well rounded out. The women are of proportionate stature to the men, but, unlike them, are very ugly. I never met with a handsome Ainô female, though I have seen many of the Yezo women. Their mouths seem like those of ogres, and to stretch from ear to ear. This arises from the fact that they tattoo a wide band of dirty blue, like the woad of the ancient Britons, around their lips, to the extent of three-quarters of an inch, and still longer at the tapering extremities. The tattooing is so completely done, that many persons mistake it for a daub of blue paint, like the artificial exaggeration of a circus clown's mouth. They increase their hideousness by joining their eyebrows over the nose by a fresh band of tattooing. This practice is resorted to in the case of married women and females who are of age, just as that of blackening the teeth and shaving the eyebrows is among the Japanese.

They are said to be faithful wives and laborious helpmates, their moral qualities compensating for their lack of physical charms. The women assist in hunting and fishing, often possessing equal skill with the men. They carry their babies pickapack, as the Japanese mothers, except that the strap passing under the child is put round the mother's forehead. Polygamy is permitted.

Their weapons are of the rudest form. The three-pronged spear is used for the salmon. The single-bladed lance is for the bear, their most terrible enemy, which they regard with superstitious reverence. Their bows are simply peeled boughs, three feet long. The arrows are one foot shorter, and, like those used by the tribes on the coast of Siberia and in Formosa, have no feather on the shaft. Their pipes are of the same form as those so common in Japan and China; and one obtained from an Ainô came from Santan, a place in Amurland.

The Ainôs possess dogs, which they use in hunting, understand the use of charcoal and candles, make excellent baskets and wicker-work of many kinds; and some of their fine bark-cloth and ornamented weapons for their chiefs show a skill and taste that compare very favorably with those exhibited by the North American Indians. Their oars, having handles fixed crosswise, or sculls made in two pieces, are almost exactly like those of the Japanese. Their river-canoes are dug out of a log, usually elm. Two men will fashion one in five days. For the sea-coast, they use a frame of wood, lacing on the sides with bark fibre. They are skillful canoe-men, using either pole or paddle.

The language of the Ainô is rude and poor, but much like the Japanese. It resembles it so closely, allowing for the fact that it is utterly unpolished and undeveloped, that it seems highly probable it is the original of the present Japanese tongue. They have no written character, no writing of any sort, no literature. A further study may possibly reveal valuable traditions held among them, which at present they are not known by me to have.

In character and morals, the Ainôs are stupid, good-natured, brave, honest, faithful, peaceful, and gentle. The American and English travelers in Yezo agree in ascribing to them these qualities. Their method of salutation is to raise the hands, with the palms upward, and stroke the beard. They understand the rudiments of politeness, as several of their verbal expressions and gestures indicate.

Their religion consists in the worship of kami, or spirits. They do not appear to have any special minister of religion or sacred structure.* They have festivals commemorative of certain events in the past, and they worship the spirit of Yoshitsuné, a Japanese hero, who is supposed to have lived among them in the twelfth century, and who taught them some of the arts of Japanese civilization.

The outward symbols of their religion are sticks of wood two or three feet long, which they whittle all around toward the end into shavings, until the smooth wand contains a mass of pendent curls.

---

* Some visitors to the Ainô villages in Yezo declare that they have noticed there the presence of the phallic shrines and symbols. It might be interesting if this assertion, and the worship of these symbols by the Ainôs, were clearly proved. It would help to settle definitely the question of the origin in Japan of this oldest form of fetich worship, the evidences of which are found all over the Nippon island-chain, including Yezo. I have noticed the prevalence of these shrines and symbols especially in Eastern and Northern Japan, having counted as many as a dozen, and these by the roadside, in a trip to Nikkô. The barren of both sexes worship them, or offer them *ex voto*. In Sagami, Kadzusa, and even in Tôkiô itself, they were visible as late as 1874, cut in stone and wood. Formerly the toy-shops, porcelain-shops, and itinerant venders of many wares were well supplied with them, made of various materials; they were to be seen in the cornucopia-banners at New-year's, paraded in the festivals, and at unexpected times and places disturbed the foreign spectator. It was like a glimpse of life in the antediluvian world, or of ancient India, whence doubtless they came, to see evidences of this once widely prevalent form of early religion. Buddhist priests whom I have consulted affirm, with some warmth, that they arose in the "wicked time of Ashikaga," though the majority of natives, learned and unlearned, say they are the relics of the ancient people, or aborigines. In 1872 the mikado's Government prohibited the sale or exposure of these emblems in any form or shape, together with the more artistic obscenities, pictures, books, carvings, and photographs, sent out from the studios of Paris and London.

They insert several of these in the ground at certain places, which they hold sacred. The Ainôs also deify mountains, the sea, which furnishes their daily food, bears, the forests, and other natural objects, which they believe to possess intelligence. These wands with the curled shavings are set up in every place of supposed danger or evil omen. The traveler in Yezo sees them on precipices, gorges of mountains, dangerous passes, and river banks.

When descending the rapids of a river in Yezo, he will notice that his Ainô boatmen from time to time will throw one of these wands into the river at every dangerous point or turning. The Ainôs pray raising their hands above their heads. The Buddhist bonzes have in vain attempted to convert them to Buddhism. They have rude songs, which they chant to their kami, or gods, and to the deified sea, forest, mountains, and bears, especially at the close of the hunting and fishing season, in all affairs of great importance, and at the end of the year. The following is given as a specimen:

> To the sea which nourishes us, to the forest that protects us, we present our grateful thanks. You are two mothers that nourish the same child; do not be angry if we leave one to go to the other.
> The Ainôs will always be the pride of the forest and the sea.

The inquirer into the origin of the Japanese must regret that as yet we know comparatively little of the Ainôs and their language. Any opinion hazarded on the subject may be pronounced rash. Yet, after a study of all the obtainable facts, I believe they unmistakably point to the Ainôs as the primal ancestors of the Japanese; that the mass of the Japanese people of to-day are substantially of Ainô stock. An infusion of foreign blood, the long effects of the daily hot baths and the warm climate of Southern Japan, of Chinese civilization, of agricultural instead of the hunter's method of life, have wrought the change between the Ainô and the Japanese.

It seems equally certain that almost all that the Japanese possess which is not of Chinese, Corean, or Tartar origin has descended from the Ainô, or has been developed or improved from an Ainô model. The Ainôs of Yezo hold politically the same relation to the Japanese as the North American Indians do to the white people of the United States; but ethnically they are, with probability bordering very closely on certainty, as the Saxons to the English.*

---

* I need scarcely, except to relieve, by borrowed humor, the dull weighing of facts, and the construction of an opinion void of all dogmatism, notice the assertion elaborated at length by some Americans, Scotchmen, and others too, for aught I know, that the Ainôs are the "ten lost tribes of Israel," or that they are the descendants of the sailors and gold-hunters sent out by King Solomon to gain spoil for his temple at Jerusalem. Really, this search after the "lost tribes"—or have they consolidated into the Wandering Jew?—is becoming absurd. They are the most discovered people known. They have been found in America, Britain, Persia, India, China, Japan, and in Yezo. I know of but one haystack left to find this needle in, and that is Corea. It will undoubtedly be found there. It has been kindly provided that there are more worlds for these Alexanders to conquer. It is now quite necessary for the archaeological respectability of a people that be the "lost tribes." To the inventory of wonders in Japan some would add that of her containing "the dispersed among the Gentiles," notwithstanding that the same claim has been made for a dozen other nations.

*The Ainô Arrow-poison.*—Dr. Stuart Eldredge, who has studied the properties of the Ainô arrow-poison, states that it is made by macerating and pounding the roots of one or more of the virulent species of aconite, mixing the mass into a paste, with (perhaps) inert ingredients, and burying it in the ground for some time. The stiff, dark, reddish-brown paste is then mixed with animal fat, and about ten grains' weight of the paste is applied to the bamboo arrow-tips which are used to set the bear-traps. The wounded animals are found dead near the trap, and their flesh is eaten with impunity, though the hunter cuts off the parts immediately near the wound. The Ainôs know of no antidote for the poison. (See "Transactions of the Asiatic Society of Japan, 1876.")

# III

# *Materials of History*

B efore attempting a brief sketch of Japanese history, it may be interesting to the reader to know something of the sources of such
history, and the character and amount of the materials. A dynasty of
rulers who ostentatiously boast of twenty-five centuries of unbroken
succession should have solid foundation of fact for their boast. The
august representatives of the mikado Mutsuhito,* the one hundred
and twenty-third of the imperial line of Dai Nippon, who, in the
presence of the President and Congress of the United States, and of
the sovereigns of Europe, claimed the immemorial antiquity of the
Japanese imperial rule, should have credentials to satisfy the foreigner
and silence the skeptic.

In this enlightened age, when all authority is challenged, and a
century after the moss of oblivion has covered the historic grave of

---

\* Mutsuhito ("meek man"), the present emperor, is the second son of the
mikado Komei (1847–1867), whom he succeeded, and the Empress Fujiwara
Asako. He was born November 3d, 1850. He succeeded his father February
3d, 1867; was crowned on the 28th day of the Eighth month, 1868; and was
married on the 28th of the Twelfth month, 1868, to Haruko, daughter of
Ichijô Tadaka, a noble of the second degree of the first rank. She was born
on the 17th of the Fourth month, 1850. The dowager-empress Asako, mother
of the emperor, is of the house of Kujô, and was born on the 14th day of the
Twelfth month, 1833.

the doctrine of divine right, the Japanese still cling to the divinity of
the mikado, not only making it the dogma of religion and the engine
of government, but accrediting their envoys as representatives of, and
asking of foreign diplomatists that they address his imperial Japanese
majesty as the King of Heaven (Tennô). A nation that has passed
through the successive stages of aboriginal migration, tribal government, conquest by invaders, pure monarchy, feudalism, anarchy, and
modern consolidated empire, should have secreted the material for
much interesting history. In the many lulls of peace, scholars would
arise, and opportunities would offer, to record the history which previous generations had made. The foreign historian who will bring the
necessary qualifications to the task of composing a complete history of
Japan, *i.e.*, knowledge of the languages and literature of Japan, China,
Corea, and the dialects of the Malay Archipelago, Siberia, and the
other islands of the North Pacific, historical insight, sympathy, and
judicial acumen, has before him a virgin field.

The body of native Japanese historical writings is rich and solid. It is
the largest and most important division of their voluminous literature.
It treats very fully the period between the rise of the noble families from
about the ninth century until the present time. The real history of the
period prior to the eighth century of the Christian era is very meagre.
It is nearly certain that the Japanese possessed no writing until the sixth
century A.D. Their oldest extant composition is the *Kojiki*, or "Book
of Ancient Traditions." It may be called the Bible of the Japanese.
It comprises three volumes, composed A.D. 711, 712. It is said to have
been preceded by two similar works, written respectively in A.D. 620
and A.D. 681; but neither of these has been preserved. The first volume
treats of the creation of the heavens and earth; the gods and goddesses,
called kami; and the events of the holy age, or mythological period. The

second and third give the history of the mikados* from the year 1 (660 B.C.) to the 1288th of the Japanese era. It was first printed during A.D. 1624–1642. The *Nihongi*, completed A.D. 720, also contains the Japanese cosmogony, records of the mythological period, and brings down the annals of the mikado to A.D. 699.

These are the oldest books in the language. Numerous and very valuable commentaries upon them have been written. They contain so much that is fabulous, mythical, or exaggerated, that their statements, especially in respect of dates, can not be accepted as true history. According to the Kojiki, Jimmu Tennô was the first emperor; yet it is extremely doubtful whether he was a historical personage. The best foreign scholars and critics regard him as a mythical character. The accounts of the first mikados are very meagre. The accession to the throne, marriage and death of the sovereign, with notices of occasional rebellions put down, tours made, and worship celebrated, are recorded, and interesting glimpses of the progress of civilization obtained.

---

* "The term 'mikado' is in general adhered to throughout this work. Other titles found in the native literature, and now or formerly in common use, are, Tenshi (Son of Heaven); Tennô, or Ten Ô (Heaven-king); Kotei (Sovereign Ruler of Nations); Kinri (The Forbidden Interior); Dairi (Imperial Palace); Chotei (Hall of Audience); Ô-ô, or Dai Ô (Great King); Ô Uji (The Great Family); Gosho (Palace). In using these titles, the common people add *sama*, a respectful term, after them. Several of them, as is evident, were used originally to denote places. It was quite common for the people in later time to speak of the mikado as Miako sama, or Uyé sama (Superior Lord), in distinction from the shôgun, whom they designated as Yedo sama. The Chinese characters employed to express the term 'mikado' mean Honorable Gate, an idea akin to the Turkish Sublime Porte. Satow, however, derives it from *mi*, great, august, awful; and *to* (*do* in composition), place; the notion being that the mikado is too far above ordinary mortals to be spoken of directly. Hence the Gate of the Palace is used as a figure for him. So, also, Ren-ka (Base of the Chariot, or Below the Palanquin); and Hei-ka (Foot of the Throne, or of the Steps leading to the Daïs), are used to denote the imperial person. A term anciently used was Nin Ô (King of Men)."

A number of works, containing what is evidently good history, illustrate the period between the eighth and eleventh centuries. A still richer collection of both original works and modern compilations treat of the mediæval period from the eleventh to the sixteenth century—the age of intestine strife and feudal war. The light which the stately prose of history casts upon the past is further heightened by the many poems, popular romances, founded on historic fact, and the classic compositions called *monogatari*, all of which help to make the perspective of by-gone centuries melt out into living pictures. That portion of the history which treats of the introduction, progress, and expulsion of Christianity in Japan has most interest to ourselves. Concerning it there is much deficiency of material, and that not of a kind to satisfy Occidental tastes. The profound peace which followed the victories of Iyéyasu, and which lasted from 1600–1868—the scholastic era of Japan—gave the peaceful leisure necessary for the study of ancient history, and the creation of a large library of historical literature, of which the magnificent works called the *Dai Nihon Shi* ("History of Great Japan"), and *Nihon Guai Shi* ("Japanese Outer, or Military History"), are the best examples.

Under the Tokugawa shôguns (1603–1868) liberty to explore, chronicle, and analyze the past in history was given; but the seal of silence, the ban of censorship, and the mandate forbidding all publication were put upon the production of contemporary history. Hence, the peaceful period, 1600 to 1853, is less known than others in earlier times. Several good native annalists have treated of the post-Perry period (1853–1872), and the events leading to the Restoration.

In the department of unwritten history, such as unearthed relics, coins, weapons, museums, memorial stones, tablets, temple records, etc., there is much valuable material. Scarcely a year passes but some rich trover is announced to delight the numerous native archæologists.

The Japanese are intensely proud of their history, and take great care in making and preserving records. Memorial-stones, keeping green the memory of some noted scholar, ruler, or benefactor, are among the most striking sights on the highways, or in the towns, villages, or temple-yards, betokening the desire to defy the ravages of oblivion and resist the inevitable tooth of Time.

Almost every large city has its published history; towns and villages have their annals written and preserved by local antiquarians; family records are faithfully copied from generation to generation; diaries, notes of journeys or events, dates of the erections of buildings, the names of the officiating priests, and many of the subscribing worshipers, are religiously kept in most of the large Buddhist temples and monasteries. The bonzes (Jap. *bôzu*) delight to write of the lives of their saintly predecessors and the mundane affairs of their patrons. Almost every province has its encyclopedic history, and every high-road its itineraries and guide-books, in which famous places and events are noted. Almost every neighborhood boasts its Old Mortality, or local antiquary, whose delight and occupation are to know the past. In the large cities professional story-tellers and readers gain a lucrative livelihood by narrating both the classic history and the legendary lore. The theatre, which in Japan draws its subjects for representation almost exclusively from the actual life, past or present, of the Japanese people, is often the most faithful mirror of actual history. Few people seem to be more thoroughly informed as to their own history: parents delight to instruct their children in their national lore; and there are hundreds of child's histories of Japan.

Besides the sober volumes of history, the number of books purporting to contain truth, but which are worthless for purposes of historical investigation, is legion. In addition to the motives, equally operative in other countries for the corruption or distortion of historical narrative, was the perpetual desire of the Buddhist monks, who were in many cases the writers, to glorify their patrons and helpers, and to damn their enemies. Hence their works are of little value. So plentiful are these garbled productions that the buyer of books always asked for *jitsu-roku*, or "true records," in order to avoid the "*zu-zan*," or "editions of Zu," so called from Zu, a noted Chinese forger of history.

In the chapters on the history of Japan, I shall occasionally quote from the text of some of the standard histories in literal translation. I shall feel only too happy if I can imitate the terse, vigorous, and luminous style of the Japanese annalists. The vividness and pictorial detail of the classic historians fascinate the reader who can analyze the closely massed syntax. Many of the pages of the *Nihon Guai Shi*, especially, are models of compression and elegance, and glow with the chastened eloquence that springs from clear discernment and conviction of truth, gained after patient sifting of facts, and groping through difficulties that lead to discovery. Many of its sentences are epigrams. To the student of Japanese it is a narrative of intensest interest.

The *Kojiki* and *Nihongi*, which give the only records of very ancient Japan, and on which all other works treating of this period are based, can not be accepted as sober history. Hence, in outlining the events prior to the second century of the Christian era, I head the chapters, not as the "Dawn of History," but the "Twilight of Fable." From these books, and the collections of ancient myths (*Koshi Seibun*), as well as the critical commentaries and explanations of the Japanese rationalists, which, by the assistance of native scholars, I have been able to consult, the two following chapters have been compiled.*

---

* In the following chapters, I use throughout the modern names of places and provinces, to avoid confusion. The ancient name of Kiushiu was Tsukushi, which was also applied to the then united provinces of Chikuzen and Chikugo. Buzen and Bungo were anciently one province, called Toyo. Higo and Hizen are modern divisions of Hi no kuni ("The Land of Fire"). Tamba, corrupted

from Taniwa, and Tango ("Back of Taniwa") were formerly one. Kadzusa and Shimôsa, contracted from Kami-tsu-fusa and Shimo-tsu-fusa (*kami*, upper; *shimo*, lower; *tsu*, ancient form of *no*; *fusa*, a proper name, tassel), were once united. Kôdzuke and Shimotsuké, formed like the preceding, were "Upper" and "Lower" Ké. All the region north of Echizen, known and unknown, including Echizen, Etchiu, Echigo, Kaga, Noto, Uzen, and Ugo, was included under the name Koshi no kuni. Later synonyms for Kiushiu are Saikoku (Western Provinces), or Chinzei in books. Chiugoku (Central Provinces) is applied to the region from Tamba to Nagato. Kamigata is a vague term for the country around and toward Kiôto.

*The Language.*—The apparatus for the study of the Japanese language and the critical examination of its texts is now, thanks to Anglo-Japanese scholars, both excellent and easily accessible. The following are such: GRAMMARS—W. G. Aston's *Grammar of the Spoken Language* (Nagasaki, 1869), and *Grammar of the Written Language of Japan, with a short Chrestomathy*; London, 1872: second edition, 1877. E. Satow's *Kuaiwa Hen, 25 Exercises in the Yedo Colloquial, for the Use of Students, with Notes*, 4 vols; Yokohama, 1873. J. J. Hoffman, *A Japanese Grammar*; Leiden, 1868: second edition, 1876. S. R. Brown, *Colloquial Japanese*; Shanghai, 1863. *Prendergast's Mastery System, adapted to the Study of Japanese or English*; Yokohama, 1875. DICTIONARIES—J. C. Hepburn, *Japanese-English and English-Japanese*; Shanghai, 1867: second edition, with grammatical introduction; Shanghai, 1872: pocket edition, New York, 1873. Satow and Ishibashi, *English-Japanese Dictionary of the Spoken Language*; London, 1876. See also valuable papers by Messrs. Satow, Aston, Dallas, Edkins, and Chamberlain, in the *Transactions of the Asiatic Society of Japan.*

# IV

# *Japanese Mythology*

In the beginning all things were in chaos. Heaven and earth were not separated. The world floated in the cosmic mass, like a fish in water, or the yolk in an egg. The ethereal matter sublimed and formed the heavens, the residuum became the present earth, from the warm mold of which a germ sprouted and became a self-animate being, called Kuni-toko-tachi no mikoto.* Two other beings of like genesis appeared. After them came four pairs of beings (*kami*). These were all single (*hitori-gami*, male, sexless, or self-begotten).

---

* It will be seen at once that the Japanese scheme of creation starts without a Creator, or any First Cause; and that the idea of space apart from matter is foreign to the Japanese philosophical system. *Mikoto* (masc.), *mikami* (fem.), mean "augustness." It is not the same term as mikado. *No* is the particle of.

The opening sentence of the *Kojiki* is as follows: At the time of the beginning of heaven and earth there existed three *hashira-gami* (pillar or chief *kami*, or gods). The name of one kami was *Amé-no-naka-nushi-no-kami* (Lord of the Middle of Heaven); next, *Taka-mi-musubi-no-kami* (High Ineffable Procreator); next, *Kami-musubi-no-kami* (Ineffable Procreator). These three, existing single, hid their bodies (died, or passed away, or became pure spirit [?]). Next, when the young land floated like oil moving about, there came into existence, sprouting upward like the *ashi* (rush) shoot, a kami named *Umaji-ashikabi-kikoji-no-kami* (Delightful Rush-sprout); next, *Amé-no-toko-tachi-no-kami*. These two chief kami, existing single, hid their bodies. Next, came into existence these three, *Kuni-no-toko-tachi-no-mikoto*, etc., etc.

Proceeding now to the work of creation, the kami separated the primordial substance into the five elements—wood, fire, metal, earth, and water—and ordained to each its properties and combination. As yet, the division into sexes had not taken place. In [Chinese] philosophical language, the male (*yo*) and female (*in*) principles that pervade all things had not yet appeared. The first manifestation of the male essence was *Izanagi*; of the female, *Izanami*. Standing together on the floating bridge of heaven, the male plunged his jeweled falchion, or spear, into the unstable waters beneath them, and withdrawing it, the trickling drops formed an island, upon which they descended. The creative pair, or divine man and woman, designing to make this island a pillar for a continent, separated—the male to the left, the female to the right— to make a journey round the island. At their meeting, the female spirit spoke first, "How joyful to meet a lovely man! " The male spirit, offended that the first use of the tongue had been by a woman, required the circuit to be repeated. On their second meeting, the man cried out, "How joyful to meet a lovely woman!" They were the first couple; and this was the beginning of the art of love, and of the human race. The island (Awaji), with seven

---

The *Nihongi* opens as follows: Of old, when heaven and earth were not yet separated, and the *in* (male, active, or positive principle) and the *yo* (female, passive, or negative principle) were not yet separated, chaos, enveloping all things, like a fowl's egg, contained within it a germ. The clear and ethereal substance expanding, became heaven; the heavy and thick substance agglutinating, became earth. The ethereal union of matter was easy, but the thickened substance hardened with difficulty. Therefore, heaven existed first; the earth was fixed afterward. Subsequently deity (*kami*) was born (*umaru*). Now, it is said that, "in the beginning of heaven and earth, the soil floated about like a fish floating on the top of the water," etc.

Evidently in the *Kojiki* we have the purely Japanese theory of creation, and in the *Nihongi* the same account, with Chinese philosophical ideas and terms added. In both, matter appears before mind, and the deities have no existence before matter.

other large, and many thousand small ones, became the Everlasting Great Japan.* At Izanami's first conception, the female essence in being more powerful, a female child was born, greatly to the chagrin of the father, who wished for male offspring. The child was named Ama-terasu ô mikami, or, the Heaven-illuminating Goddess. She shone beautifully, and lighted the heavens and the earth. Her father, therefore, transferred her from earth to heaven, and gave her the ethereal realm to rule over. At this time the earth was close to heaven,

---

* The various names of Japan which I have found in the native literature, or have heard in colloquial use, are as follows: 1. *Nihon*, or *Nippon*, compounded of the words *ni*, *nichi*, or *nitsu* (sun, day) and *hon* (root, origin, beginning); hence Sunrise, Dawn, or Dayspring. Japan is the foreigner's corruption of the Chinese Ji-pun, or Ji-puan. The name may have been given by the Chinese or Coreans to the land lying east of them, whence the sun rose, or by the conquerors coming from Manchuria, by way of Corea eastward. Or, it may have arisen anciently among the natives of the western provinces of Japan. It is found in Chinese books from the time of the Tang dynasty (618–905 A.D.). 2. *Dai Nihon Koku* (Country of Great Japan). 3. *Ô Yashima no Kuni* (Country of the Eight Great Islands), created by Izanagi and Izanami. 4. *Onogorojima* (Island of the Congealed Drops), which fell from the jeweled falchion or spear of Izanagi. 5. *Shiki Shima* (Outspread Islands), a name common in poetry, and referring to their being spread out like stepping-stones in a Japanese garden. 6. *Toyohara Akitsu Kuni* (Country between Heaven and Earth). 7. *Toyoakitsu Kuni* (Dragon-fly-shaped Country), from the resemblance to this insect with its wings outspread. 8. *Toyo Ashiwara Kuni* (Fertile Plain of Sweet Flags). 9. *Ô Yamato no Kuni* (Land of Great Peace). The same characters are read Wa Koku by the Chinese, and sometimes by the Japanese. 10. *Fuso Koku*. Fuso is the name of a tree which is fabled to petrify; hence, an emblem of national stability. 11. *On Koku* (Honorable Country). 12. *Shin Koku* (Land of the Holy Spirits). 13. *Kami no Kuni* (The God-land, or Land of the Gods). 14. *Horai no Kuni* (Land of the Elixir of Immortality), an allusion to the legend that a Chinese courtier came to Japan in search of the elixir of immortality. He brought a troop of young men and maidens with him. Dying in Japan, he was buried in Kii, and the young couples, marrying, colonized Japan. 15. *Ko Koku* (The Mikado's Empire), Land ruled by a Theocratic Dynasty. 16. *Tei Koku Nihon* (The Empire ruled by a Theocratic Dynasty, or, Japan, the Empire governed by Divine Rulers).

and the goddess easily mounted the pillar, on which heaven rested, to her kingdom.

The second child was also a female, and was called Tsuki no kami, and became the Goddess of the Moon. The third child, Hiruko (leech), was a male, but not well formed. When three years old, being still unable to stand, his parents made an ark of camphor-wood, and set him adrift at sea. He became the first fisherman, and was the God of the Sea and of Storms.

After two girls and a cripple had thus been born, the father was delighted with the next fruit of his spouse, a fine boy, whom they named Sosanoö no mikoto. Of him they entertained the highest hopes. He grew up, however, to be a most mischievous fellow, killing people, pulling up their trees, and trampling down their fields. He grew worse as he grew up. He was made ruler over the blue sea; but he never kept his kingdom in order. He let his beard grow down over his bosom. He cried constantly; and the land became a desert, the rivers and seas dried up, and human beings died in great numbers. His father, inquiring the reason of his surly behavior, was told that he wished to go to his mother, who was in the region under the earth. He then made his son ruler over the kingdom of night. The august scape-grace still continued his pranks, unable to refrain from mischief. One day, after his sister, the Sun-goddess, had planted a field with rice, he turned a wild horse loose, which trampled down and spoiled all her work. Again, having built a store-house for the new rice, he defiled it so that it could not be used. At another time, his sister was sitting at her loom, weaving. Sosanoö, having skinned a live horse by drawing its skin off from the tail to the head, flung the reeking hide over the loom, and the carcass in the room. The goddess was so frightened that she hurt herself with the shuttle, and, in her wrath, retired to a cave, closing the mouth with a large rock. Heaven, earth, and the four quarters became enshrouded in darkness, and the distinction between day and night ceased. Some of the turbulent and ill-mannered gods took advantage of the darkness to make a noise like the buzzing of flies, and the confusion was dreadful.

Then all the gods (eight hundred thousand in number) assembled on the heavenly river-plain of Yasu, to discuss what was to be done to appease the anger of the great goddess. The wisest of the gods was intrusted with the charge of thinking out a stratagem to entice her forth. The main part of the plan was to make an image of the self-imprisoned goddess, which was to be more beautiful than herself, and thus excite at once her curiosity and her jealousy. It was to be a round mirror like the sun.

A large rock from near the source of the river was taken to form an anvil. To make the bellows, they took the whole skin of a deer, and, with iron from the mines of heaven, the blacksmith-god made two mirrors, which successively failed to please the gods, being too small. The third was large and beautiful, like the sun.

The heavenly artisans now prepared to make the finest clothes and jewelry, and a splendid palace for the Sun-goddess, when she should come out. Two gods planted the paper-mulberry and hemp, and prepared bark and fibre; while three other gods wove them into coarse, striped, and fine cloth, to deck her dainty limbs. Two gods, the first carpenters, dug holes in the ground with a spade, erected posts, and built a palace. Another deity, the first jeweler, made a string of *magatama* (curved jewels), the material for a necklace, hair-pins, and bracelets. Two other gods held in their hands the sacred wands, called *tama-gushi*.

Two gods were then appointed to find out, by divination, whether the goddess was likely to appear. They caught a buck, tore out a bone from one of its forelegs, and set it free again. The bone was placed in a fire of cherry-bark, and the crack produced by the heat in the blade of the bone was considered a satisfactory omen.

A sakaki-tree was then pulled up by the roots. To the upper branches was hung the necklace of jewels, to the middle was attached the mirror, and from the lower branches depended the coarse and fine cloth. This was called a *gohei*. A large number of perpetually crowing cocks was obtained from (what had been) the region of perpetual day. These irrepressible chanticleers were set before the cave, and began to crow lustily in concert. The God of Invincibly Strong Hands was placed in concealment near the rocky door, ready to pull the goddess out at her first peering forth. A goddess with a countenance of heavenly glossiness, named Uzume, was appointed manager of the dance. She first bound up her flowing sleeves close to her body, under the armpits, by a creeping plant, called *masaki*, and donned a headdress made of long moss. While she blew a bamboo tube, with holes pierced in it between the joints, the other deities kept time to the music with two flat, hard pieces of wood, which they clapped together. Another kami took six bows, and, from the long moss hanging from the pine-trees on the high hills, she strung the bows, and made the harp called the *koto*. His son made music on this instrument by drawing across the strings grass and rushes, which he held in both hands. Bonfires were now lighted before the door of the cavern, and the orchestra of fifes, drums, cymbals, and harp began. The goddess Uzumé now mounted the circular box, having a bâton of twigs of bamboo grass in one hand, with a spear of bamboo twined with grass, on which small bells tinkled. As she danced, the drum-like box prepared for her resounded, and she, becoming possessed by a spirit of folly, sung a song in verses of six syllables each, which some interpret as the numerals, 1, 2, 3, 4, 5, 6, 7, 8, 9, 10, 100, 1,000, 10,000. The goddess, as she danced, loosened her dress, exposing her nude charms. All this was caused by the spirit which possessed her. It so excited the mirth of the gods that they laughed so loudly that heaven shook. The song and its interpretations are:

| Hito, futa, miyo | One, two, three, four, |
|---|---|
| Itsu, muyu, nana | Five, six, seven, |
| Ya, koko-no, tari | Eight, nine, ten, |
| Momo, chi, yorodzu | Hundred, thousand, ten thousand. |

Ye gods, behold the cavern doors!
Majesty appears—hurra!
Our hearts are quite satisfied;
Behold my charms.

or,

Gods, behold the door!
Lo! the majesty of the goddess!
Shall we not be filled with rapture?
Are not my charms excellent?

The Sun-goddess within, unable to account for the ill-timed mirth, since heaven and earth were in darkness, rose, and approaching the rocky door, listened to the honeyed words of one of the gods, who was praising her. Impelled further by curiosity, she opened the door slightly, and asked why Uzumé danced and the gods laughed? Uzumé replied, "I dance because there is an honorable deity who surpasses your glory." As she said this, the exceedingly beauteous god Futodama showed the mirror. The Sun-goddess within, astonished at her own loveliness, which she now first beheld in the reflection, stepped out a little further to gratify her curiosity. The God of Invincibly Strong Hands, who stood concealed, pulled the rock door open, caught her by the hand, and dragged her forth. The wisest of the gods, who superintended the whole proceedings, took a rope of twisted rice-straw, passed it behind her, and said, "Do not go behind this." They then removed the Sun-goddess to her new palace, and put a straw rope around it to keep off evil gods. Her wicked brother was punished by having each particular hair of his head pulled out, and his finger and toe nails extracted. He was then banished.

Izanami's fifth child, the last in whose conception the two gods shared, was a son, called the God of Wild Fire. In bringing him forth the goddess suffered great pain; and from the matter which she vomited in her agony sprung the God and Goddess of Metal. She afterward created the gods of Clay and Fresh Water, who were to pacify the God of Fire when inclined to be turbulent. Izanami had enjoined her consort not to look at her during her retirement, but he disregarded her wish. She fled from him, and departed to the nether regions. Izanagi, incensed at the God of Fire, clove him in three pieces with his sword. From these fragments sprung the gods of Thunder, of Mountains, and of Rain. He then descended into the region of night to induce Izanami to come back to the earth. There he met his consort, who would not return. He found the region to be one of perpetual and indescribable foulness, and, before he left, he saw the body of his wife had become a mass of putrefaction. Escaping into the upper world, he washed himself in the sea, and, in the act of escape and purification, many gods were created. According to one version, Amaterasu was produced out of his left eye, and Sosanoo out of his nose. Those deities created out of the filth from which he cleansed himself became the wicked gods, who now war against the good gods and trouble mankind. The God of Clay and the Goddess of Fresh Water married. Their offspring was Naka musubi. From his head grew the mulberry and silk-worm, and from his navel sprung the five cereals, rice, wheat, beans, millet, and sorghum.

Another legend, changing the sex of Sosanoö, says the Sun-goddess spoke to Sosanoö (the Moon-goddess), who reigned jointly with her over the high plain of heaven, and said, "I have heard that there is a food-possessing goddess in the central country of luxuriant reedy moors (Japan). Go and see." Descending from heaven, he came to the august abode of the Goddess of Food, and asked for refreshment. The goddess, creating various forms of food, such as boiled rice from the land, fish from the sea, beasts, with coarse and fine hair, from the hills, set them on a banqueting-table before Sosanoö, who, enraged at the manner of the creation of the food, killed her.

Reporting the matter in heaven, Amaterasu was angry at Sosanoö, and degraded her (the Moon-goddess) from joint rule, and condemned her to appear only at night, while she, the Sun-goddess, slept. Amaterasu then sent a messenger the second time to see whether the Food-goddess was really dead. This was found to be the case. Out of the dead body were growing, millet on the forehead; silk-worms and a mulberry-tree on the eyebrows; grass on the eyes; on the belly, rice, barley, and large and small beans. The head finally changed into a cow and horse. The messenger took them all, and presented them to Amaterasu. The Sun-goddess rejoiced, and ordained that these should be the food of human beings, setting apart rice as the seed of the watery fields, and the other cereals as the seed of the dry fields. She appointed lords of the villages of heaven, and began for the first time to plant the rice-seeds. In the autumn the drooping ears ripened in luxuriant abundance. She planted the mulberry-trees on the fragrant hills of heaven, and rearing silk-worms, and chewing cocoons in her mouth, spun thread. Thus began the arts of agriculture, silk-worm rearing, and weaving.

When Sosanoö was in banishment, there was a huge eight-headed dragon that had devastated the land and eaten up all the fair virgins. Sosanoö enticed the monster to partake of an intoxicating liquor set in eight jars, and then slew him while in stupor. In the tail of the dragon he found a sword of marvelous temper, which he presented to Amaterasu. This sword, called "Cloud-cluster," afterward became one of the three sacred emblems constituting the regalia of the Japanese sovereigns. In these last days of commerce, Sosanoö's exploit is pictured on the national paper money. He is also said to have invented poetry. Being as irregularly amorous as the Jupiter of another mythology, he was the father of many children by various mothers. One of the most illustrious of his offspring was Daikoku, now worshiped in every household as the God of Fortune. In the later stages of the mythology, heaven and earth are found peopled with myriads of kami, some of whom have inhabited heaven from the beginning, while those on the earth have been ruling or contending together from an indefinite period. Finally, before ushering in the third or final stage of the mythical history, there are general war and confusion among the gods on earth, and Amaterasu resolves to bring order out of the troubles, and to subdue and develop the land for herself.

She desired to make a son of her own a ruler over the terrestrial world. One had been produced from her necklace, called Oshi-ho-mi no mikoto, who married Tamayori himé no mikoto, one of the granddaughters of Izanagi and Izanami. Their offspring was Ninigi no mikoto. After much delay, caused by the dispatch and failure of envoys to the gods of the earth, he prepared to descend from heaven to his realm on earth. The Sun-goddess gave her grandson various treasures, chief of which were the mirror, emblem of her own soul, and now worshiped at Isé, the sword Cloud-cluster, taken by Sosanoö from the dragon's tail, and a stone or seal. Concerning the mirror she said. "Look upon this mirror as my spirit; keep it in the same house and on the same floor with yourself, and worship it as if you were worshiping my actual presence."

Another version of this divine investiture is given in these words:

For centuries upon centuries shall thy followers rule this kingdom. Herewith receive from me the succession and the three crown talismans. Should you at any future time desire to see me, look in this mirror. Govern this country with the pure lustre that radiates from its surface. Deal with thy subjects with the gentleness which the smooth rounding of the stone typifies. Combat the enemies of thy kingdom with this sword, and slay them on the edge of it.

Accompanied by a number of inferior gods of both sexes, he descended on the floating bridge of heaven, on which the first pair had stood when separating the dry land from the water, to the mountain of Kirishima, between Hiuga and Ôzumi, in Kiushiu. After his descent, the sun and earth, which had already receded from each other to a considerable distance, became further separated, and communication by the floating bridge of heaven ceased. According to the commentators on the sacred books, as Japan lay directly opposite to the sun when it separated from the earth, it is clear (to a devout Japanese) that Japan lies on the summit of the globe. As it was created first, it is especially the Land of the Gods, the Holy Land, the Country of the Divine Spirits. All other countries were formed later by the spontaneous consolidation of the foam and mud of the sea. All foreign countries were of course created by the power of the heavenly gods, but they were not begotten by Izanagi and Izanami, nor did they give birth to the Sun-goddess, which is the cause of their inferiority. Japan is superior to all the world for the reasons given above. The traditions current in other countries as to the origin of the world are of course incorrect, since, being so far from the sources of truth, they can not be accurate, and must be greatly distorted. From the fact of the divine descent of the Japanese people proceeds their immeasurable superiority to the natives of other countries in courage and intelligence. This opinion, long held by Japanese in general, still lingers among the fanatical Shintô scholars, and helps to explain the intense hatred and contempt manifested toward foreigners as late as within the last decade.

Ninigi no mikoto descended on Kirishima yama, and was received with due honors by one of the kami of the place. He had a son, who lived five hundred and eighty years. This son married a sea-monster, who appeared to him in the form of a woman, and by her he had a son, who became ruler, and was succeeded by a son born of an aunt. Ninigi, the heavenly descendant, was thus the great-grandfather of Jimmu Tennô, the first emperor of Japan.

It is not easy to weave into a continuous and consistent whole the various versions of the Japanese accounts of creation and the acts of the gods, or to be always safe in deciding their origin, sex, or relations to each other; for these spirits act like Milton's, and "as they please, they limb themselves." These myths arising among the primitive Japanese people of various localities, who never attempted to formulate them, are frequently at hopeless variance with each other; and the ingenuity and ability of the learned native commentators on the sacred books, especially the *Nihongi* and *Kojiki*, are exercised to the highest degree to reconcile them.

One author devotes twenty volumes of comment to two of the text of the *Kojiki* in these earnest efforts, making his works a rich mine to the student of Japanese antiquities. Translated into English, in the spirit of a devout Japanese, an exalted Biblical or Miltonic style should be used. Mr. Aston thus renders a passage from the *Nakatomi no harai*, one of the most ancient monuments of the language, describing the descent of the god Ninigi to the earth (Japan): "They caused him to thrust from him heaven's eternal throne, to fling open heaven's eternal doors, to cleave with might his way from out heaven's many piled clouds, and then to descend from heaven."

A literal, or even free, translation into plain English could not, however, be made in a book to be read, unexpurgated, in the family circle. Many physiological details, and not a few references probably, pure to the native pure, would not be suffered by the tastes or moral codes in vogue among the mass of readers in Europe or America. Like the mythology of Greece, that of Japan is full of beauty, pathos, poetic fancy, charming story, and valorous exploit. Like that, it forms the soil of the national art, whether expressed in bronze, porcelain, colors; or poetry, song, picture, the dance, pantomime, romance, symbolism; or the æsthetics of religion.

In spite of Buddhism, rationalism, and skeptical philosophy, it has entered as fully into the life and art and faith of the people of Japan as the mythology of the Aryan nations has entered into the life and art of Europe. Like that of the nations classic to us, the Japanese mythology, when criticised in the light of morals, and as divorced from art, looked at by one of alien clime, race, and faith, contains much that is hideous, absurd, impure, and even revolting. Judged as the growth and creation of the imagination, faith, and intellect of the primitive inhabitants of Japan, influenced by natural surroundings, it is a faithful mirror of their country, and condition and character, before these were greatly modified by outside religion or philosophy. Judged as a religious influence upon the descendants of the ancient Nihonese—the Japanese, as we know them—it may be fairly held responsible for much of the peculiar moral traits of their character, both good and evil. The Japanese mythology is the doctrinal basis of their ancient and indigenous religion, called Kami no michi, or Shintô (way or doctrine of the gods, or, by literal rendering, theology).

One of the greatest pleasures to a student of Japanese art, antiquities, and the life as seen in the Japan of to-day, is to discover the survivals of primitive culture among the natives, or to trace in their customs the fashions and ceremonies current tens of centuries ago, whose genesis is to be sought in the age of the gods. Beneath the poetic and mythical costume are many beautiful truths.

One of the many Japanese rationalistic writers explains the hiding of Amaterasu in the cave as an eclipse of the sun. Ebisu, the third child of the first pair, is now worshiped as the God of Daily Food, fish being the staple of Japanese diet. He is usually represented as a jolly angler, with a red fish (*tai*) under one fat arm, and a rod and line under the other. One need not go far from Kiôto to find the identical spots of common earth which the fertile imagination of the children of Nippon has transfigured into celestial regions. Thus, the prototype of "the dry bed of the river Ame no yasu" is now to be seen in front of the city of Kiôto, where the people still gather for pleasure or public ceremony. The "land of roots," to which Sosanoö was banished, is a region evidently situated a few miles north-west of Kiôto. The dancing of Suzumé before the cavern is imitated in the pantomimic dance still seen in every Japanese village and city street. The mirror made from iron in the mines of heaven by the Blacksmith god was the original of the burnished disks before which the Japanese beauty of to-day, sitting for hours on knee and heels, and nude to the waist, heightens her charms. A mask of Suzumé, representing the laughing face of a fat girl, with narrow forehead, having the imperial spots of sable, and with black hair in rifts on her forehead, cheeks puffed out, and dimpled chin, adorns the walls of many a modern Japanese house, and notably on certain festival days, and on their many occasions of mirth. The stranger, ignorant of its symbolic import, could, without entering the palace, find its prototype in five minutes, by looking around him, from one of the jolly fat girls at the well or the rice-bucket. The *magatama* jewels, curved and perforated pieces of soapstone occasionally dug up in various parts of Japan, show the work of the finger of man, and ancient pictures depict the chiefs of tribes decked with these adornments. In the preparations made to attract forth the Sun-goddess, we see the origin of the arts of music by wind and stringed instruments, dancing, divination, adornment, weaving, and carpentry. To this day, when the Japanese female is about to sweep, draw water, or perform household duties, she binds up her sleeves to her armpits, with a string twisted over her shoulders, like the sleeve-binder of the dancing goddess. Before Shintô shrines, trees sacred to the kami, at New-year's-day before gates and doors, and often in children's plays, one sees stretched the twisted ropes of rice-straw. In the month of August especially, but often at the fairs, festivals, and on holidays, the wand of waving jewels, made by suspending colored paper and trinkets to a branch of bamboo, and something like a Christmas-tree, is a frequent sight. The *gohei* is still the characteristic emblem seen on a Shintô shrine. All these relics, trivial and void of meaning to the hasty tourist, or the alien, whose only motive for dwelling on the island is purely sordid, are, in the eye of the native, and the intelligent foreigner, ancient, sacred, and productive of innocent joy, and to the latter, sources of fresh surprise and enjoyment of a people in themselves intensely interesting.

# V

# *The Twilight of Fable*

Between the long night of the unknown ages that preceded the advent of the conquerors, and the morning of what may be called real history, there lies the twilight of mythology and fabulous narration.

The mythology of Nippon, though in essence Chinese, is Japanese in form and coloring, and bears the true flavor of the soil from whence it sprung. The patriotic native or the devout Shintôist may accept the statements of the *Kojiki* as genuine history; but in the cold, clear eye of an alien they are the inventions of men shaped to exalt the imperial family. They are a living and luxurious growth of fancy around the ruins of facts that in the slow decay of time have lost the shape by which recognition is possible. Chinese history does indeed, at certain points, corroborate what the Japanese traditions declare, and thus gives us some sure light; but for a clear understanding of the period antedating the second century of the Christian era, the native mythology and the fabulous narrations of the *Kojiki* are but as moonlight.

Jimmu Tenno, the first mikado, was the fifth in descent from the Sun-goddess. His original name was Kan Yamato Iware Hiko no mikoto. The title Jimmu Tennô, meaning "spirit of war," was posthumously applied to him many centuries afterward. When the *Kojiki* was compiled, pure Japanese names only were in use. Hence, in that book we meet with many very long quaint names and titles which, when written in the Chinese equivalents, are greatly abbreviated. The introduction of the written characters of China at a later period enabled the Japanese to express almost all their own words, whether names, objects, or abstract ideas, in Chinese as well as Japanese. Thus, in the literature of Japan two languages exist side by side, or imbedded in each other. This applies to the words only. Japanese syntax, being incoercible, has preserved itself almost entirely unchanged.

The *Kojiki* states that Jimmu was fifty years old when he set out upon his conquests. He was accompanied by his brothers and a few retainers, all of whom are spoken of as kami, or gods. The country of Japan was already populated by an aboriginal people dwelling in villages, each under a head-man, and it is interesting to notice how the inventors of the *Kojiki* account for their origin. They declare, and the Japanese popularly believe, that these aboriginal savages were the progeny of the same gods (Izanagi and Izanami) from whom Jimmu sprung; but they were wicked, while Jimmu was righteous.

The interpretation doubtless is, that a band of foreign invaders landed in Hiuga, in Kiushiu, or they were perhaps colonists, who had occupied this part of the country for some time previous. The territory of Hiuga could never satisfy a restless, warlike people. It is mountainous, volcanic, and one of the least productive parts of Japan.

At the foot of the famous mountain of Kirishima, which lies on the boundary between Hiuga and Ôzumi, is the spot where Jimmu resided, and whence he took his departure.

Izanagi and Izanami first, and afterward Ninigi, the fourth ancestor of Jimmu, had descended from this same height to the earth. Every Japanese child who lives within sight of this mountain gazes with reverent wonder upon its summit, far above the sailing clouds and within the blue sky, believing that here the gods came down from heaven.

The story of Jimmu's march is detailed in the *Kojiki*, and the numerous popular books based upon it. A great many wonderful creatures

and men that resembled colossal spiders were encountered and overcome. Even wicked gods had to be fought or circumvented. His path
was to Usa, in Buzen; thence to Okada; thence by ship through the
windings of the Suwo Nada, a part of the Inland Sea,* landing in Aki.
Here he built a palace, and remained seven years. He then went to
the region of Bizen, and, after dwelling there eight years, he sailed
to the East. The waves were very rough and rapid at the spot near the

---

* The "Inland Sea" (Séto Uchi) is a name which has been given by foreigners, and
adopted by the Japanese, who until modern times had no special name for it as a
whole. Indeed, the whole system of Japanese geographical nomenclature proves
that the generalizations made by foreigners were absent from their conceptions.
The large bays have not a name which unifies all their parts and limbs into one
body. The long rivers possess each, not one name, but many local appellations
along their length. The main island was nameless, so were Shikoku and Kiushiu
for many centuries. Yezo, to the native, is a region, not an island. Even for the
same street in a city a single name, as a rule, is not in use, each block receiving
a name by itself. This was quite a natural proceeding when the universe, or "all
beneath heaven," meant Japan. The Séto Uchi has been in Japanese history what
the Mediterranean was to the course of empire in Europe, due allowance being
made for proportions, both physical and moral. It extends nearly east and west two
hundred and forty miles, with a breadth varying from ten to thirty miles, with
many narrow passages. It has six divisions (*nada*), taking their names from the
provinces whose shores they wash. It contains a vast number of islands, but few
known dangers, and has a sea-board of seven hundred miles, densely populated,
abounding with safe and convenient anchorages, dotted with many large towns
and provincial capitals and castled cities, and noted for the active trade of its
inhabitants. It communicates with the Pacific by the channels of Kii on the east,
Bungo on the south, and by the Straits of Shimonoséki ("the Gibraltar of Japan"),
half a mile wide, on the west. It can be navigated safely at all seasons of the year
by day, and now, under ordinary circumstances, by night, thanks to the system of
light-houses thoroughly equipped with the latest instruments of optical science,
including dioptric and catoptric, fixed and revolving, white and colored lights, in
earthquake-proof towers, erected by English engineers in the service of the mikado's Government. The tides and currents of the Séto Uchi are not as yet perfectly
known, but are found to be regular at the east and west entrances, the tide-
waves coming from the Pacific. In many parts they run with great velocity. The

present site of Ôzaka,† where he finally succeeded in landing, and he gave the spot the name *Nami Haya* (swift waves). This afterward became, in the colloquial, and in poetry, Naniwa.

Hitherto the career of the invaders had been one of victory and easy conquest, but they now received their first repulse. After severe fighting, Jimmu was defeated, and one of his brothers was wounded. A council of war was held, and sacred ceremonies celebrated to discover the cause of the defeat. The solemn verdict was that as children of the Sun-goddess they had acted with irreverence and presumption in journeying in opposition to the course of the sun from west to east, instead of moving, as the sun moves, from east to west. Thereupon they resolved to turn to the south, and advance westward. Leaving the ill-omened shores, they coasted round the southern point of Kii, and landed at Arasaka. Here a peaceful triumph awaited them, for the chief surrendered, and presented Jimmu with a sword. A representation of this scene, engraved on steel, now adorns the greenback of one of the denominations of the national bank-notes issued in 1872. The steps of the conqueror were now bent toward Yamato. The mountain-passes

---

cut on page 57 shows one of these narrow passages where the eddying currents rush past a rock in mid-channel, scouring the shores, and leaving just enough room for the passage of a large steamer. (The cut was omitted in this edition.)

A very destructive species of mollusk inhabits the Inland Sea, which perforates timber, making holes one-third of an inch in diameter. Sailing-vessels bound to Nagasaki sometimes find it better in winter to work through the Inland Sea rather than to beat round Cape Chichakoff against the Kuro Shiwo. This latter feat is so difficult that sailors are apt to drop the *o* from the Japanese name (Satano) of this cape (*misaki*) and turn it into an English or Hebrew word. Those who are trying to prove that the Japanese are the "lost tribes" might make one of their best arguments from this fact. Kaempfer, it may be stated, derived the Japanese, by rapid transit, from the Tower of Babel, across Siberia to the islands.

† The spelling of Ôzaka (accent on the ô) is in accordance with the requirements of Japanese rules of orthography, and the usage of the people in Ôzaka and Kiôto.

were difficult, and the way unknown; but by act of one of the gods, Michi no Omi no mikoto, who interposed for their guidance, a gigantic crow, having wings eight feet long, went before the host, and led the warriors into the rich land of Yamato. Here they were not permitted to rest, for the natives fought stoutly for their soil.

On one occasion the clouds lowered, and thick darkness brooded over the battle-field, so that neither of the hosts could discern each other, and the conflict staved. Suddenly the gloom was cleft by the descent from heaven of a bird like a hawk, which, hovering in a flood of golden effulgence, perched upon the bow of Jimmu. His adversaries, dazzled to blindness by the awful light, fled in dismay. Jimmu, being now complete victor, proceeded to make his permanent abode, and fixed the *miako*, or capital, at Kashiwabara, some miles distant from the present site of Kiôto. Here he set up his government, and began to rule over all the lands which he had conquered. Peace was celebrated with rejoicings, and religious ceremonies of imposing magnificence. He distributed rewards to his soldiers and officers, and chose his chief captains to be rulers over provinces, apportioning them lands, to be held in return for military service. It will be noticed that this primal form of general government was a species of feudalism. Such a political system was of the most rudimentary kind; only a little better than the Council of the Six Nations of the Iroquois, or was similar to that of the Aztecs of Mexico.

The country being now tranquilized, weapons were laid aside, and attention was given to the arts of peace. Among the first things accomplished was the solemn deposit of the three sacred emblems —mirror, sword, and ball—in the palace. Sacrifices were offered to the Sun-goddess on Torimino yama.

Jimmu married the princess Tatara, the most beautiful woman in Japan, and daughter of one of his captains. During his life-time his chief energies were spent in consolidating his power, and civilizing his subjects. Several rebellions had to be put down. After choosing an heir, he died leaving three children, at the age of one hundred and twenty-seven years, according to the *Nihongi*, and of one hundred and thirty-seven, according to the *Kojiki*.

It is by no means certain that Jimmu was a historical character. The only books describing him are but collections of myths and fables, in which exists, perhaps, a mere skeleton of history. Even the Japanese writers, as, for instance, the author of a popular history (*Dai Nihon Koku Kai Biaku Yuraii Ki*), interpret the narratives in a rationalistic manner. Thus, the "eight-headed serpents" in the *Kojiki* are explained to be persistent arch-rebels, or valorous enemies; the "ground-spiders," to be rebels of lesser note; and the "spider-pits or holes," the rebels' lurking-places. The gigantic crow, with wings eight feet long, that led the host into Yamato was probably, says the native writer, a famous captain whose name was Karasu (crow), who led the advance-guard into Yamato, with such valor, directness, and rapidity, that it seemed miraculous. The myth of ascribing the guidance of the army to a crow was probably invented later. A large number of the incidents related in the *Kojiki* have all the characteristics of the myth.

Chinese tradition ascribes the peopling of Japan to the following causes: The grandfather (Taiko) of the first emperor (Buwo) of the Shu dynasty (thirty-seven emperors, eight hundred and seventy-two years, B.C. 1120–249) in China, having three sons, wished to bequeath his titles and estates to his youngest son, notwithstanding that law and custom required him to endow the eldest. The younger son refused to receive the inheritance; but the elder, knowing that his father Taiko would persist in his determination, and unwilling to cause trouble, secretly left his father's house and dominions, and sailed away to the South of China. Thence he is supposed to have gone to Japan and founded a colony in Hiuga. His name was Taihaku Ki. From this legend the Chinese frequently apply the name Kishi Koku, or "country of the Ki family," to Japan.

Whatever may be the actual facts, Jimmu Tennô is popularly believed to have been a real person, and the first emperor of Japan. He is deified in the Shintô religion, and in thousands of shrines dedicated to him the people worship his spirit. In the official list of mikados, he is named as the first. The reigning emperor refers to him as his ancestor from whom he claims unbroken descent. The 7th day of the Fourth month (April 7th) is fixed as the anniversary of his ascension to the throne, and that day is a national holiday, on which the iron-clad navy of modern Japan fires salutes, from Krupp and Armstrong guns, in his honor, and the military, in French uniforms, from Snider and Remington rifles, burn *in memoriam* powder.

The era of Jimmu is the starting-point of Japanese chronology, and the year 1 of the Japanese era is that upon which he ascended the throne at Kashiwabara.* A large number of Japanese students and educated men who have been abroad, or who, though remaining at home, have shed their old beliefs, and imbibed the modern spirit of nihilism, regard Jimmu as a myth. The majority, however, cling to their old belief that the name Jimmu represents a historical verity, and hold it as the sheet-anchor of their shifting faith. A young Japanese, fresh from several years' residence in Europe, was recently rallied concerning his belief in the divinity of the mikado and in the truth of the *Kojiki*. His final answer was, "It is my duty to believe in them."

---

* Dr. J. J. Hoffman, who has written the best Japanese grammar yet published, in expressing the exact date given in the *Kojiki*, in terms of the Julian style, says the 19th of February (660 B.C.) was the day of Jimmu's ascension. Professor F. Kaiser has found out by calculation that at eight A.M. on that day of the said year there was a new moon at the *miako*. "Therefore," says this grammarian, leaping on the wings of his own logic to a tremendous conclusion, and settling down into assured satisfaction, "the correctness of the Japanese chronology may not be called in question." (See page 173, and note of *A Japanese Grammar,*" J. J. Hoffman, Leyden, 1868.)

# VI

# *Sûjin, the Civilizer*

From the death of Jimmu Tennô to that of Kimmei, in whose reign Buddhism was introduced (A.D. 571), there were, according to the *Dai Nihon Shi*, thirty-one mikados. During this period of twelve hundred and thirty-six years, believed to be historic by most Japanese, the most interesting subjects to be noted are the reforms of Sûjin Tennô, the military expeditions to Eastern Japan by Yamato Dake, the invasion of Corea by the Empress Jingu Kôgô, and the introduction of Chinese civilization and of Buddhism.

The *Nihongi* details the history and exploits of these ancient rulers with a minuteness and exactness of circumstance that are very suspicious. It gives the precise birthdays and ages of the emperors, who in those days attained an incredible longevity. Takénouchi, the Japanese Methusaleh, lived to be over three hundred and fifty years old, and served as prime minister to five successive emperors. Twelve mikados lived to be over one hundred years old. One of them ruled one hundred and one years. The reigns of the first seventeen averaged over sixty-one years. From the seventeenth to the thirty-first, the average reign is little over twelve years. In the list there are many whose deeds, though exaggerated in the mirage of fable, are, in the main, most probably historic.

Sûjin, also called Shûjin or Sunin (B.C. 97–30), was, according to
the *Dai Nihon Shi*, a man of intense earnestness and piety. The traits
of courage and energy which characterized his youth gave him in
manhood signal fitness for his chosen task of elevating his people.
He mourned over their wickedness, and called upon them to forsake
their sins, and turn their minds to the worship of the gods. A great
pestilence having broken out, and the people being still unrepentant,
the pious monarch rose early in the morning, fasted, and purified his
body with water, and called on the kami to stay the plague. After
solemn public worship the gods answered him, and the plague abated.
A revival of religious feeling and worship followed. In his reign dates
the building of special shrines for the adoration of the gods. Hitherto
the sacred ceremonies had been celebrated in the open air. Further,
the three holy regalia (mirror, sword, and ball) had hitherto been
kept in the palace of the mikado. It was believed that the efficacy
of the spirit was so great that the mikado dwelling with the spirit
was, as it were, equal to a god. These three emblems had been placed
within the palace, that it might be said that where they were dwelt
the divine power. A rebellion having broken out during his reign, he
was led to believe that this was a mark of the disfavor of the gods,
and in consequence of his keeping the emblems under his own roof.
Reverencing the majesty of the divine symbols, and fearing that they
might be defiled by too close proximity to his carnal body, he removed
them from his dwelling, and dedicated them in a temple erected for
the purpose at Kasanui, a village in Yamato. He appointed his own
daughter priestess of the shrine and custodian of the symbols—a
custom which has continued to the present time.

The shrines of Uji, in Isé, which now hold these precious relics of the
divine age, are always in charge of a virgin princess of imperial blood.
Later, being warned by the goddess Amaterasu to do so, she carried
the mirror from province to province, seeking a suitable locality; but

having grown old in their search, Yamato himé* continued it, and finally, after many changes, they were deposited in their present place A.D. 4. Copies of the mirror and sword were, however, made by Sûjin, and placed in a separate building within the palace called the "place of reverence." This was the origin of the chapel still connected with the mikado's imperial palace.

From the most early time the dwelling and surroundings of the mikado were characterized by the most austere simplicity, quite like the Shintô temples themselves, and the name *miya* was applied to both. In imagining the imperial palace in Japan, the reader on this side the Pacific must dissolve the view projected on his mind at the mention of the term "palace." Little of the stateliness of architecture or the splendor and magnificence of the interior of a European palace belongs to the Japanese imperial residence. A simple structure, larger than an ordinary first-class dwelling, but quite like a temple in outward appearance, and destitute of all meretricious or artistic ornamentation within, marks the presence of royalty, or semi-divinity, in Japan. Even in Kiôto, for centuries, the palace, except for its size and slightly greater elevation, could not be distinguished from the residences of the nobles, or from a temple. All this was in keeping with the sacredness of the personage enshrined within. For vain mortals, sprung from inferior or wicked gods, for upstart generals, or low traders bloated with wealth, luxury and display were quite seemly. Divinity needed no material show. The circumstances and attributes of deity were enough. The indulgence in gaudy display was opposed to the attributes and character of the living representative of the Heavenly Line. This rigid simplicity was carried out even after death.

---

* The suffix *himé* after female proper names means "princess." It is still used by the ladies of the imperial family, and by the daughters of the court nobles. *Maye*, with *no*, was also added to names of ladies of rank.

In striking contrast with the royal burial customs of the nations of Asia are those of Japan. All over the East, the tombs of dead dynasties are edifices of all others the most magnificent. The durable splendor of the homes of the departed far exceed that of the palaces of the living. But in Japan, in place of the gorgeous mausoleums and the colossal masterpieces of mortuary architecture of continental Asia, the sepulchres of the mikados seem monuments of chaste poverty. Nearly all of the imperial tombs are within the three provinces of Yamato, Yamashiro, and Settsu. A simple base of stone, surmounted by a low shaft, set upon a hillock, surrounded by a trench, and inclosed with a neat railing of timber, marks the resting-places of the dead emperors. All this is in accordance with the precepts of Shintô.

The whole life of Sûjin was one long effort to civilize his half-savage subjects. He ordained certain days when persons of both sexes must lay aside their regular employment, and give the Government his or her quantum of labor. The term for the labor of the men means "bow-point," and of the women "hand-point," implying that in the one case military service was the chief requirement, and in the other that of the loom or the field. He endeavored, in order to secure just taxation, to inaugurate a regular periodical census, and to reform the methods of dividing and recording time.* He encouraged the building of boats, in order to increase the means of transportation, promote commerce, and to bring

---

* The twenty-four divisions of the solar year (according to the lunar calendar), by which the Japanese farmers have for centuries regulated their labors, are as follows:

| | | | |
|---|---|---|---|
| Beginning of Spring | February 3 | Beginning of Autumn | August 7 |
| Rainwater | February 19 | Local Heat | August 23 |
| Awakening of the Insects | March 5 | White Dew | September 8 |
| Middle of the Spring | March 20 | Middle of Autumn | September 23 |
| Clear Weather | April 5 | Cold Dew | October 8 |

the people at the extremities of the country in contact with each other. Communication between Corea and Kiushiu was rendered not only possible, but promised to be regular and profitable. We read that, during his reign, an envoy, bringing presents, arrived from Mimana, in Corea, B.C. 33. Six years later, it is recorded that the prince, a chief of Shiraki, in Corea, came to Japan to live. It is evident that these Coreans would tell much of what they had seen in their own country, and that many useful ideas and appliances would be introduced under the patronage of this enlightened monarch. Sûjin may be also called the father of Japanese agriculture, since he encouraged it by edict and example, ordering canals to be dug, water-courses provided, and irrigation to be extensively carried on. Water is the first necessity of the rice-farmer of Asia. It is to him as precious a commodity as it is to the miner of California. Rice must be sown, transplanted, and grown under water. Hence, in a country where this cereal is the staple crop, immense areas of irrigated fields are necessary. One of the unique forms of theft in rice-countries, which, in popular judgment, equals in iniquity the stealing of ore at the mines, or horses on the prairies, is the drawing off water from a neighbor's field. In those old rude times, the Japanese water-thief, when detected, received but little more mercy than the horse-robber in the West. The immense labor necessary to obtain the requisite water-supply can only be appreciated by one who has studied the flumes of California, the tanks

| | | | |
|---|---|---|---|
| Seed Rain | April 20 | Fall of Hoar-frost | October 23 |
| Beginning of Summer | May 5 | Beginning of Winter | November 7 |
| Little Plenty | May 20 | Little Snow | November 22 |
| Transplanting the Rice | June 5 | Great Snow | December 7 |
| Height of the Summer | June 21 | Height of the Winter | December 22 |
| Little Heat | July 6 | Little Frost | January 6 |
| Great Heat | July 23 | Great Frost | January 20 |

of India, or the various appliances in Southern Asia. In Japan, it is very common to terrace, with great labor, the mountain gulches, and utilize the stream in irrigating the platforms, thus changing a noisy, foaming stream into a silent and useful servant. In many cases, the water is led for miles along artificial canals, or ditches, to the fertile soil which needs it. On flat lands, at the base of mountains, huge reservoirs are excavated, and tapped as often as desired. In the bosom of the Hakoné Mountains, between Sagami and Suruga, is a deep lake of pure cold water, over five thousand feet above the sea-level. On the plain below are few or no natural streams. Centuries ago, but long after Sûjin's time, the mountain wall was breached and tunneled by manual labor, and now through the rocky sluices flows a flood sufficient to enrich the millions of acres of Suruga province. The work begun by Sûjin was followed up vigorously by his successor, as we read that, in the year A.D. 6, a proclamation was issued ordering canals and sluices to be dug in over eight hundred places.

The emperor had two sons, whom he loved equally. Unable to determine which of them should succeed him, he one day told them to tell him their dreams the next morning, and he should decide the issue by interpretation. The young princes accordingly washed their bodies, changed their garments, and slept. Next day the elder son said, "I dreamed that I climbed up a mountain, and, facing the east, I cut with the sword and thrust with the spear eight times." The younger said, "I climbed the same mountain, and, stretching snares of cords on every side, tried to catch the sparrows that destroy the grain." The emperor then interpreted the dream, "You, my son," said he to the elder, "looked in one direction. You will go to the East, and become its governor." "You, my son," said he to the younger, "looked in every direction. You will govern on all sides. You will become my heir." It happened as the father had said. The younger became emperor, and a peaceful ruler. The elder became the governor of, and a warrior in, the East.

The story is interesting as illustrating the method of succession to the throne. Usually it was by primogeniture, but often it depended upon the will or whim of the father, the councils of his chiefs, or the intrigues of courtiers.

The energies of this pious mikado were further exerted in devising and executing a national military system, whereby his peaceably disposed subjects could be protected and the extremities of his dominions extended. The eastern and northern frontiers were exposed to the assaults of the wild tribes of Ainôs who were yet unsubdued. Between the peaceful agricultural inhabitants who owned the sway of the ruler in Yamato, and the untamed savages who gloried in their freedom, a continual border-war existed. The military division of the empire into four departments was made, and a shôgun, or general, was appointed over each. These departments were the Tô, Nan, and Sai kai dô, and Hokurikudô, or the East, South, and West-sea Circuits, and the Northern-land Circuit. The strict division of the empire into ô, or circuits, according with the natural features and partitions of the country, which is still recognized, was of later time; but already, B.C. 25, it seems to have been foreshadowed by Sûjin.

One of these shôguns, or generals, named Obiko, who was assigned to the Northern Department, lying north of Yamato and along the west coast, holds a high place of renown among the long list of famous Japanese warriors. It is said that when, just after he had started to join his command, he heard of a conspiracy against the mikado, returning quickly, he killed the traitor, restored order, and then resumed his duties in the camp at the North. His son held command in the East. In the following reign, it is written that military arsenals and magazines were established, so that weapons and rations were ready at any moment for a military expedition to repel incursions from the wild tribes on the border, or to suppress insurrections within the pale of the empire. The half-subdued inhabitants in the extremes of the realm needed constant watching, and seem to have been as restless and treacherous as the Indians on our own frontiers. The whole history of the extension and development of the mikado's empire is one of war and blood, rivaling, if not exceeding, that of our own country in its early struggles with the Indians. This constant military action and life in the camp resulted, in the course of time, in the creation of a powerful and numerous military class, who made war professional and hereditary. It developed that military genius and character which so distinguish the modern Japanese, and mark them in such strong contrast with other nations of Eastern Asia. The long-sustained military operations also served to consolidate the empire. In these ancient days, however, there was no regular army, no special class of warriors, as in later times. Until the eighth century, the armies were extemporized from the farmers and people generally, as occasion demanded. The war over, they returned to their daily employments. The mikados were military chiefs, and led their armies, or gave to their sons or near relatives only, the charge of expeditions.

It is not my purpose to follow in detail the long series of battles, or even court conspiracies and intrigues, which fill the Japanese histories, and lead some readers to suppose that war was the normal condition of the palace and empire. I prefer to show the condition of the people, their methods of life, customs, ideas, and beliefs. Although wars without and intrigues within were frequent, these by no means made up the life of the nation. Peace had its victories, no less renowned than those of war. A study of the life of the people, showing their progress from barbarism to civilization, will, I think, be of more interest to the reader than details concerning imperial rebels, poisoners, or stabbers.

In the Japanese histories, and in official language, literature, and etiquette of later days, there exists the conception of two great spheres of activity and of two kinds of transactions, requiring two methods of treatment. They are the *nai* and *guai*, the inner and the outer, the interior and exterior of the palace, or the throne and the empire. Thus the *Nihon Guai Shi*, by Rai Sanyô, or "External History of Japan," treats of the events, chiefly military, outside the palace. His other work, *Nihon Seiki*, treats rather of the affairs of the "forbidden interior" of the palace. In those early days this conception had not been elaborated.

The mikado from ancient times has had two crests, answering to the coats of arms in European heraldry. One is a representation of a chrysanthemum (kiku), and is used for government purposes outside the palace. It is embroidered on flags and banners, and printed on official documents. Since the Restoration, in 1868, the soldiers of the imperial army wear it as a frontlet on their caps. The other crest, representing a blossom and leaves of the *Paulownia imperialis* (kiri), is used in business personal to the mikado and his family. The ancient golden chrysanthemum has, since 1868, burst into new bloom, like the flowering of the nation itself, and has everywhere displaced the trefoil of the parvenus of later feudalism —the Tokugawas, the only military vassals of the mikado who ever assumed the preposterous title of "Tycoon."

## VII

# *Yamato-dakê,*
# *the Conqueror of the Kuantô**

A new hero appears in the second century, whose personality seems so marked that it is impossible to doubt that within the shell of fabulous narration is a rich kernel of history. This hero, a son of the twelfth emperor, Keikô (71–130 A.D.), is pictured as of fair mien, manly and graceful carriage. In his youth he led an army to put down a rebellion in Kiushiu; and, wishing to enter the enemy's camp, he disguised himself as a dancing-girl, and presented himself before the sentinel, who, dazed by the beauty and voluptuous figure of the supposed damsel, and hoping for a rich reward from his chief, admitted her to the arch-rebel's tent. After dancing before him and his carousing guests,

---

* Kuantô (east of the barrier). The term Kuantô was, probably as early as the ninth century, applied to that part of Japan lying east of the guard-gate, or barrier, at Ôzaka, a small village on the borders of Yamashiro and Ômi. It included thirty-three provinces. The remaining thirty-three provinces were called Kuansei (west of the barrier). In modern times and at present, the term Kuantô (written also Kantô) is applied to the eight provinces (Kuan-has-shiu) east of the Hakoné range, consisting of Sagami, Musashi, Kôdzuké, Shimotsuké, Kadzusa, Awa, Shimôsa, and Hitachi. Sometimes Idzu, Kai, and the provinces of Hondo north of the thirty-eighth parallel, formerly called Mutsu and Déwa, are also included.

the delighted voluptuary drew his prize by the hand into his own tent. Instead of a yielding girl, he found more than his match in the heroic youth, who seized him, held him powerless, and took his life. For this valorous effort he received the name Yamato-Daké, or, the Warlike. Thirteen years after this victory, A.D. 110, the tribes in eastern Japan revolted, and Yamato-Daké went to subdue them. He stopped at the shrine of the Sun-goddess in Isé, and, leaving his own sword under a pine-tree, he obtained from the priestess the sacred sword, one of the holy emblems enshrined by Sûjin. Armed with this palladium, he penetrated into the wilds of Suruga, to fight the Ainôs, who fled before him from the plains into the woods and mountain fastnesses. The Ainô method of warfare, like that of our North American Indians, was to avoid an encounter in the open field, and to fight in ambush from behind trees, rocks, or in the rank undergrowth, using every artifice by which, as pursued, they could inflict the greatest damage upon an enemy with the least loss and danger to themselves. In the lore of the forest they were so well read that they felt at home in the most tangled wilds. They were able to take advantage of every sound and sign. They were accustomed to disguise themselves in bear-skins, and thus act as spies and scouts. Fire was one of their chief means of attack. On a certain occasion they kindled the underbrush, which is still seen so densely covering the uncleared portions of the base of Fuji. The flames, urged by the wind, threatened to surround and destroy the Japanese army—a sight which the Ainôs beheld with yells of delight. The Sun-goddess then appeared to Yamato-Daké, who, drawing the divinely bestowed sword—Murakumo, or "Cloud-cluster"—cut the grass around him. So invincible was the blade that the flames ceased advancing and turned toward his enemies, who were consumed, or fled defeated. Yamato-Daké then gratefully acknowledging to the gods the victory vouchsafed to him, changed the name of the sword to Kusanagi (Grass-mower).

Crossing the Hakoné Mountains, he descended into the great plain of the East, in later days called the Kuantô, which stretches from the base of the central ranges and table-land of Hondo to the shores of the Pacific, and from Sagami to Iwaki. On reaching the Bay of Yedo at about Kamizaki, near Uraga, off which Commodore Perry anchored with his steamers in 1853, the hills of the opposite peninsula of Awa seemed so very close at hand, that Yamato-Dake supposed it would be a trifling matter to cross the intervening channel. He did not know what we know so well now, that at these narrows of the bay the winds, tides, currents, and weather are most treacherous. Having embarked with his host, a terrific storm arose, and the waves tossed the boat so helplessly about that death seemed inevitable. Then the frightened monarch understood that the Sea-god, insulted by his disparaging remark, had raised the storm to punish him. The only way to appease the wrath of the deity was by the sacrifice of a victim. Who would offer? One was ready. In the boat with her lord was his wife, Tachibana himé. Bidding him farewell, she leaped into the mad waves. The blinding tempest drove on the helpless boat, and the victim and the saved were parted. But the sacrifice was accepted. Soon the storm ceased, the sky cleared, the lovely landscape unveiled in serene repose. Yamato-Daké landed in Kadzusa, and subdued the tribes. At the head of the peninsula, at a site still pointed out within the limits of modern Tôkiô, he found the perfumed wooden comb of his wife, which had floated ashore. Erecting an altar, he dedicated the precious relic as a votive offering to the gods. A Shintô shrine still occupies the site where her spirit and that of Yamato-Daké are worshiped by the fishermen and sailors, whose junks fill the Bay of Yedo with animation and picturesque beauty. As usual, a pine-tree stands near the shrine. The artist has put Mount Fuji in the distance, a beautiful view of which is had from the strand. Yamato-Daké then advanced northward, through Shimôsa, sailing along the coast in boats to the border, as the Japanese claimed it to be, between the empire proper and the savages, which lay at or near the thirty-eighth parallel. The two greatest chiefs of the Ainôs, apprised of his coming, collected a great army to overwhelm the invader. Seeing his fleet approaching, and awed at the sight, they were struck with consternation, and said, "These ships must be from the gods. If so, and we draw bow against them, we shall be destroyed." No sooner had Yamato-Daké landed than they came to the strand and surrendered. The hero kept the leaders as hostages, and having tranquilized the tribes, exacting promise of tribute, he set out on the homeward journey. His long absence from the capital in the wilds of the East doubtless disposed him to return gladly. He passed through Hitachi and Shimôsa, resting temporarily at Sakura, then through Musashi and Kai. Here he is said to have invented the distich, or thirty-one-syllable poem, so much used at the present day. After his army had been refreshed by their halt, he sent one of his generals into Echizen and Echigo to tranquilize the North-west and meet him in Yamato. He himself marched into Shinano. Hitherto, since crossing the Hakoné range, he had carried on his operations on the plains. Shinano is a great table-land averaging twenty-five hundred, and rising in many places over five thousand, feet above the sea-level, surrounded and intersected by the loftiest peaks and mountain ranges in Japan. Ninety-five miles north-west of Tôkiô is the famous mountain pass of Usui Tôgé, the ascent of which from Sakamoto, on the high plain below, is a toilsome task. At this point, twenty-six hundred feet above Sakamoto, unrolls before the spectator a magnificent view of the Bay of Yedo and the plain below, one of the most beautiful and impressive in Japan. Here Yamato stood and gazed at the land and water, draperied in the azure of distance, and, recalling the memory of his beloved wife, who had sacrificed her life for him, he murmured, sadly, "Adzuma, adzuma" (My wife, my wife). The plain of Yedo is still, in poetry, called Adzuma. One of the princes of the blood uses Adzuma as his surname; and the ex-Confederate iron-clad ram *Stone-wall*, now of the Japanese navy, is christened Adzuma-kuan.

To cross the then almost unknown mountains of Shinano was a bold undertaking, which only a chief of stout heart would essay.* To travel in the thinly populated mountainous portions of Japan even at the present time, at least to one accustomed to the comfort of the palace-cars of civilization, is not pleasant. In those days, roads in the Kuantô were unknown. The march of an army up the slippery ascents, through rocky defiles, over lava-beds and river torrents, required as much nerve and caution as muscle and valor. To their superstitious fancies, every mountain was the abode of a god, every cave and defile the lurking-place of spirits. Air and water and solid earth were populous with the creatures of their imagination. Every calamity was the manifestation of the wrath of the local gods; every success a proof that the good kami were specially favoring them and their leaders. The clouds and fogs were the discomfiting snares of evil deities to cause them to lose their path. The asphyxiating exhalations from

---

* The cold in winter in the high mountain regions of Shinano is severe, and fires are needed in the depth of summer. Heavy falls of snow in winter make traveling tedious and difficult. I went over this part of Yamato-Daké's journey in 1873, completing a tour of nine hundred miles. As I have gone on foot over the mountain *tôgés* (passes) from Takata, in Echigo, to Tôkiô, in Musashi, and likewise have been a pedestrian up and over the pass of St. Bernard, I think, all things considered, the achievement of Yamato-Daké fully equal in courage, skill, daring, patience, and romantic interest to that of Napoleon. The tourist to-day who makes the trip over this route is rewarded with the most inspiring views of Fuji, Asama yama, Yatsugadaké, and other monarchs in this throne-room of nature in Japan. In the lowlands of Kôdzuké also is the richest silk district in all Japan, the golden cocoons, from which is spun silver thread, covering the floors of almost every house during two summer months, while the deft fingers of Japanese maidens, pretty and otherwise, may be seen busily engaged in unraveling the shroud of the worm, illustrating the living proverb, "With time and patience even the mulberry-leaf becomes silk."

volcanoes, or from the earth, which to this day jet out inflammable gas, were the poisonous breath of the mountain gods, insulted by the daring intrusion into their sacred domain. On one occasion the god of the mountain came to Yamato-Daké, in the form of a white deer, to trouble him. Yamato-Daké, suspecting the animal, threw some wild garlic in its eye, causing it to smart so violently that the deer died. Immediately the mountain was shrouded in mist and fog, and the path disappeared. In the terror and dismay, a white dog—a good kami in disguise—appeared, and led the way safely to the plains of Mino.

Again the host were stricken by the spirit of the white deer. All the men and animals of the camp were unable to stand, stupefied by the mephitic gas discharged among them by the wicked kami. Happily, some one bethought him of the wild garlic, ate it, and gave to the men and animals, and all recovered. At the present day in Japan, partly in commemoration of this incident, but chiefly for the purpose of warding off infectious or malarious diseases, garlic is hung up before gates and doors in time of epidemic, when an attack of disease is apprehended. Thousands of people believe it to be fully as efficacious as a horseshoe against witches, or camphor against contagion. Descending to the plains of Mino, and crossing through it, he came to Ibuki yama, a mountain shaped like a truncated sugar-loaf, which rears its colossal flat head in awful majesty above the clouds. Yamato-Daké attempted to subdue the kami that dwelt on this mountain. Leaving his sword, "Grass-mower," at the foot of the mountain, he advanced unarmed. The god transformed himself into a serpent, and barred his progress. The hero leaped over him. Suddenly the heavens darkened. Losing the path, Yamato-Daké swooned and fell. On drinking of a spring by the way, he was able to lift up his head. Henceforward it was called Samé no idzumi, or the Fountain of Recovery. Reaching Ôtsu, in Isé, though still feeble, he found, under the pine-tree, the sword which he had taken off before, and forthwith composed a poem: "O pine, were you a man, I should give you this sword to wear for your fidelity." He had been absent in the Kuantô three years. He recounted before the gods his adventures, difficulties, and victories, made votive offerings of his weapons and prisoners, and gave solemn thanks for the deliverance vouchsafed him. He then reported his transactions to his father, the mikado, and, being weak and nigh to death, he begged to see him. The parent sent a messenger to comfort his son. When he arrived, Yamato-Daké was dead. He was buried at Nobono, in Isé. From his tomb a white bird flew up; and on opening it, only the chaplet and robes of the dead hero were found. Those who followed the bird saw it alight at Koto-hiki hara (Plain of the Koto-players) in Yamato, which was henceforth called Misazaki Shiratori (Imperial Tomb of the White Bird). His death took place A.D. 113, at the age of thirty-six. Many temples in the Kuantô and in various parts of Japan are dedicated to him.

I have given so full an account of Yamato-Daké to show the style and quality of ancient Japanese tradition, and exhibit the state of Eastern Japan at that time, and because under the narration there is good history of one who extended the real boundaries of the early empire.* Yamato-Daké was one of the partly historic and partly ideal heroes that are equally the cause and the effect of the Japanese military spirit. It may be that the future historians of Japan may consider this chapter as literary trash, and put Yamato-Daké and all his deeds in the same limbo with Romulus and his wolf-nurse, William Tell

---

* The Names of the various provinces of Japan are given below. Each name of Japanese origin has likewise a synonym compounded of the Chinese word *shiu* (province), affixed to the pronunciation of the Chinese character with which the first syllable of the native word is written. In some cases the Chinese form is most in use, in which case it is italicized. In a few cases, both forms are current.

and his apple; but I consider him to have been a historical personage, and his deeds a part of genuine history.

Go Kinai (Five Home Provinces)
*Yamashiro*, or Joshiu
*Yamato*, or Washiu
*Kawachi*, or Kashiu
Idzumi, or *Senshiu*
Settsu, or Sesshiu

Tôkaidô (Eastern-sea Region)
*Iga*, or Ishiu
*Isé*, or *Seishiu*
*Shima*, or Shishiu
*Owari*, or *Bishiu*
Mikawa, or *Sanshiu*
Tôtômi, or *Enshiu*
Suruga, or *Sunshiu*
*Idzu*, or Dzushiu
Kai, or *Kôshiu*
*Sagami*, or *Sôshiu*
Musashi, or *Bushiu*
Awa, or *Bôshiu*
*Kadzusa*, or Sôshiu
*Shimôsa*, or Sôshiu
*Hitachi*, or Jôshiu

Tôzandô (Eastern-mountain Region)
Ômi, or *Gôshiu*
*Mino*, or Noshiu
*Hida*, or Hishiu
Shinano, or *Shinshiu*
Kôdzuké, or *Jôshiu*
Shimotsuké, or *Yashiu*
Iwashi, or Ôshiu
Iwashiro, or Ôshiu
Rikuzen, or Ôshiu

Rikuchiu, or Ôshiu
Michinoku, or Ôshiu
Uzen, or Ushiu
Ugo, or Ushiu

Hokurikudô (Northern-land Region)
Wakasa, or *Jakushiu*
*Echizen*, or Esshiu
*Kaga*, or *Kashiu*
*Noto*, or Nôshiu
*Etchiu*, or Esshiu
*Echigo*, or Esshiu
*Sado* (island), or Sashiu

Sanindô (Mountain-back Region)
*Tamba*, or Tanshiu
*Tango*, or Tanshiu
*Tajima*, or Tanshiu
Inaba, or *Inshiu*
*Hôki*, or Hakushiu
Idzumo, or *Unshiu*
Iwami, or Sekishiu
*Oki* (islands)

Sanyôdô (Mountain-front Region)
Harima, or *Banshiu*
Mimasaka, or *Sakushiu*
*Bizen*, or Bishiu.
*Bitchiu*, or Bishiu
*Bingo*, or Bishiu
Aki, or Geishiu
*Suwô*, or Bôshiu
Nagato, or Chôshiu

Nankaidô (Southern-sea Region)
    Kii, or Kishiu
    *Awaji* (island), or Tanshiu
    Awa, or *Ashiu*
    *Sanuki*, or Sanshiu
    *Iyo*, or Yoshiu
    *Tosa*, or *Toshiu*

Saikaidô (Western-sea Region)
    *Chikuzen*, or Chikushiu
    *Chikugo*, or Chikushiu

*Buzen*, or Hôshiu
*Bungo*, or Hôshiu
*Hizen*, or Hishiu
*Higo*, or Hishiu
*Hiuga*, or Nisshiu
*Ôzumi*, or Gushiu
Satsuma, or Sasshiu

The "Two Islands"
    Tsushima, or *Taishiu*
    *Iki*, or Ishiu.

# VIII

# *The Introduction of Continental Civilization*

If Japan is to Asia what Great Britain is to Europe—according to the comparison so often made by the modern Japanese—then Corea was to Dai Nippon what Norman France was to Saxon England. Through this peninsula, and not directly from China, flowed the influences whose confluence with the elements of Japanese life produced the civilization which for twelve centuries has run its course in the island empire. The comparison is not perfect, inasmuch as Japan sent the conqueror to Corea, whereas Normandy sent William across the Channel. In the moral and æsthetic conquest of Rome by Greece, though vanquished by Roman arms, we may perhaps find a closer resemblance to the events of the second triad of the Christian centuries in the history of Japan.

Is it true among historic nations that anciently the position of woman was higher than in later times? It has been pointed out by more than one writer on Greece "that in the former and ruder period women had undoubtedly the higher place, and their type exhibited the highest perfection." This is certainly the case in Japan. The women of the early centuries were, according to Japanese history, possessed of more intellectual and physical vigor, filling the offices of state, religion, and household honors, and approaching more nearly the ideal cherished in those countries in which the relation of the sexes is that of professed or real equality. Certain it is that, whereas there are many instances of ancient Japanese women reaching a high plane of social dignity and public honor, in later ages the virtuous woman dwelt in seclusion; exemplars of ability were rare; and the courtesan became the most splendid type of womanhood. This must be more than the fancy of poets. As in the Greece of Homer and the tragedians, so in early Nippon, woman's abilities and possibilities far surpassed those that were hers in the later days of luxury and civilization. To a woman is awarded the glory of the conquest of Corea, whence came letters, religion, and civilization to Japan.

In all Japanese tradition or history, there is no greater female character than the empress Jingu (godlike exploit). Her name was Okinaga Tarashi himé, but she is better known by her posthumous title of Jingu Kôgô, or Jingu, the wife or spouse of the mikado. She was equally renowned for her beauty, piety, intelligence, energy, and martial valor. She was not only very obedient to the gods, but they delighted to honor her by their inspiration. She feared neither the waves of the sea, the arrows of the battle-field, nor the difficulties that wait on all great enterprises. Great as she was in her own person, she is greater in the Japanese eyes as the mother of the god of war.

In the year 193 a rebellion broke out at Kumaso, in Kiushiu. The mikado Chiuai (191–200) headed his army, and marched to subdue the rebels. Jingu Kôgô, or Jingu, the empress, followed him by ship, embarking from Tsuruga, in Echizen—a port a few miles north-west of the head of Lake Biwa—meeting her husband at Toyo no ura, near the modern Shimonoséki, of indemnity fame. While worshiping on one of the islands of the Inland Sea, the god spoke to her, and said, "Why are you so deeply concerned to conquer Kumaso? It is but a poor, sparse region, not worth conquering with an army. There is a much larger and richer country, as sweet and lovely as the face of a fair virgin. It is dazzling bright with gold, silver, and fine colors, and every kind of rich treasures is to be found in Shiraki (in Corea). Worship me, and I will give you power to conquer the country without bloodshed; and by my help, and the glory of your conquest, Kumaso shall be straightway subdued." The emperor, hearing this from his wife, which she declared was the message of the gods, doubted, and, climbing to the summit of a high mountain, looked over the sea, and seeing no land to the westward, answered her: "I looked everywhere and saw water, but no land. Is there a country in the sky? If not, you deceived me. My ancestors worshiped all the gods: is there any whom they did not worship?"

The gods, answering through the inspired empress, made reply: "If you believe only your doubts, and say there is no country when I have declared there is one, you blaspheme, and you shall not go thither; but the empress, your wife, has conceived, and the child within her shall conquer the country." Nevertheless, the emperor doubted, and advanced against Kumaso, but was worsted by the rebels. While in camp, he took sick and died suddenly. According to another tradition, he was slain in battle by an arrow. His minister, Takénouchi, concealed his death from the soldiers, and carried the corpse back to Toyo no ura, in Nagato. The brave Jingu, with the aid of Takénouchi, suppressed the rebellion, and then longed for conquest beyond the sea.

While in Hizen, in order to obtain a sign from the gods she went down to the sea-shore, and baited a hook with a grain of boiled rice, to catch a fish. "Now," said she, "I shall conquer a rich country if a fish be caught with this grain of rice." The bait took. A fish was caught, and Jingu exultingly accepted the success of her venture as a token of celestial approval of her design. "Médzurashiki mono!" (wonderful thing), exclaimed the royal lady. The place of the omen is still called Matsura, corrupted from the words she used. In further commemoration, the women of that section, every year, in the first part of the Fourth month, go fishing, no males being allowed the privilege on that day. The pious Jingu prepared to invade Corea; but wishing another indication of the will of the kami, she on one occasion immersed her hair in water, saying that, if the gods approved of her enterprise, her tresses would become dry, and be parted into two divisions. It was as she desired. Her luxuriant black hair came from the water dry, and parted in two. Her mind was now fixed. She ordered her generals and captains to collect troops, build ships, and be ready to embark. Addressing them, she said: "The safety or destruction of our country depends upon this enterprise. I intrust the details to you. It will be your fault if they are not carried out. I am a woman, and young; I shall disguise myself as a man, and undertake this gallant expedition, trusting to the gods, and to my troops and captains. We shall acquire a wealthy country. The glory is yours, if we succeed; if we fail, the guilt and disgrace shall be mine." Her captains, with unanimity and enthusiasm, promised to support her and carry out her plans. The enterprise was a colossal one for Japan at that time. Although the recruiting went on in the various provinces, and the ships were built, the army formed slowly. Chafing at the delay, but not discouraged, again she had recourse to the efficacy of worship and an appeal to the gods. Erecting a tabernacle of purification, with prayers and lustrations and sacrifices she prayed the kami to grant her speedy embarkation and success. The gods were propitious. Troops came in. The army soon assembled, and all was ready, A.D. 201.

Before starting, Jingu issued orders to her soldiers, as follows:

"No loot.

"Neither despise a few enemies nor fear many.

"Give mercy to those who yield, but no quarter to the stubborn.

"Rewards shall be apportioned to the victors; punishments shall be meted to the deserters."

Then the words of the gods came, saying, "The Spirit of Peace will always guide you and protect your life. The Spirit of War will go before you and lead your ships."

Jingu again returned thanks for these fresh exhibitions of divine favor, and made her final preparations to start, when a new impediment threatened to delay hopelessly the expedition, or to rob it of its soul and leader, the Amazonian chief. She discovered that she was pregnant. Again the good favor of the gods enabled her to triumph over the obstacles which nature, or the fate of her sex, might throw in the path of her towering ambition. She found a stone which, being placed in her girdle, delayed her accouchement until her return from Corea.

It does not seem to have been perfectly clear in the minds of those ancient filibusters where Corea was, or for what particular point of the horizon they were to steer. They had no chart or compass. The sun, stars, and the flight of birds were their guides. In a storm they would be helpless. One fisherman had been sent to sail westward and report. He came back declaring there was no land to be seen. Another man was dispatched, and returned, having seen the mountains on the main-land. The fleet sailed in the Tenth month. Winds, waves, and currents were all favorable. The gods watched over the fleet, and sent shoals of huge fishes to urge on the waves that by their impact lifted the sterns and made the prows leap as though alive. The ships beached safely in Southern Corea, the Japanese army landed in the glory of sunlight and the grandeur of war in splendid array. The king of this part of Corea had heard from his messengers of the coming of a strange fleet from the East, and, terrified, exclaimed, "We never knew there was any country outside of us. Have our gods forsaken us!" The invaders had no fighting to do as they expected. It was a bloodless invasion. The Coreans came, holding white flags, and surrendered, offering to give up their treasures. They took an oath that they would be tributary to Japan, that they would never cause their conquerors to dispatch another expedition, and that they would send hostages to Japan. The rivers might flow backward, or the pebbles in their beds leap up to the stars, yet would they not break their oath. Jingu set up weapons before the gate of the king in token of peace. By his order eighty ships well laden with gold and silver, articles of wealth, silk and precious goods of all kinds, and eighty hostages, men of high families, were put on board.

The stay of the Japanese army in Corea was very brief, and the troops returned in the Twelfth month. Jingu was, on her arrival, delivered of a son, who, in the popular estimation of gods and mortals, holds even a higher place of honor than his mother, who is believed to have conquered Southern Corea through the power of her yet unborn illustrious offspring. After leaving her couch, the queen-regent erected in Nagato (Chôshiu) a shrine, and in it dedicated the Spirit of War that had guided her army. She then attended to the funeral rites of her deceased husband, and returned to the capital.

The conquest of Corea, more correctly a naval raid into one of the southern provinces, took place A.D. 203. The motive which induced the invasion seems to have been the same as that carried out by Hideyoshi in 1583, and contemplated in 1873—mere love of war and conquest. The Japanese refer with great pride to this their initial exploit on foreign soil. It was the first time they had ever gone in ships to a foreign country to fight. For the first time it gave them the opportunity of displaying their valor in making "the arms of Japan shine beyond the seas"—a pet phrase which occurs in many documents in Japan, even in this 2536th year of the Japanese empire, and of our Lord 1876. Nevertheless, the honor of the exploit is given to the unborn son on whom dwelt the Spirit of War, rather than to the mother who bore him.

The queen-mother is worshiped in many temples as Kashii dai miô jin. The son, Ôjin, afterward a great warrior, was, at his death, 313 A.D., deified as the god of war; and down through the centuries he has been worshiped by all classes of people, especially by soldiers, who offer their prayers, pay their vows, and raise their votive offerings to him. Many of the troops, before taking steamer for Formosa, in 1874, implored his protection. In his honor some of the most magnificent temples in Japan have been erected, and almost every town and village, as well as many a rural grove and hill, has its shrine erected to this Japanese Mars. He is usually represented in his images as of frightful, scowling countenance, holding, with arms akimbo, a broad two-edged sword. One of the favorite subjects of Japanese artists of all periods is the group of figures consisting of the snowy-bearded Takénouchi, in civil dress, holding the infant of Jingu Kôgô in his arms, the mother standing by in martial robes. Jingu is the heroine and model for boys, not of the girls. In the collection of pictures, images, and dolls which in Japanese households on the 5th of May, every year, teach to the children the names and deeds of the national heroes, and instill the lessons taught by their example, this warrior-woman is placed among the male, and not among the female, groups.

Nine empresses in all have sat upon the throne of Japan as rulers, four of whom reigned at the capital, Nara. None have won such martial renown as Jingu. It is not probable, however, that military enterprise will ever again give the nation another ideal woman like the conqueror of Corea. It is now, in modern days, given to the Empress of Japan to elevate the condition of her female subjects by graciously encouraging the education of the girls, and setting a noble example, not only of womanly character and of active deeds of benevolence, but also in discarding the foolish and barbarous customs of past ages; notably that of blacking the teeth and shaving off the eyebrows. This the present empress, Haruko, has done. Already this chief lady of the empire has accomplished great reforms in social customs and fashions, and, both by the encouragement of her presence and by gifts from her private purse, has greatly stimulated the cause of the education and the elevation of woman in Japan. Haply, it may come to pass that this lady in peaceful life may do more for the good and glory of the empire than even the renowned queen-regent, Jingu Kôgô.

The early centuries of the Christian era, from the third to the eighth, mark that period in Japanese history during which the future development and character of the nation were mightily influenced by the introduction, from the continent of Asia, of the most potent factors in any civilization. They were letters, religion, philosophy, literature, laws, ethics, medicine, science, and art. Heretofore the first unfoldings of the Japanese intellect in the composition of sacred hymns, odes, poems, myths, and tradition had no prop upon which to train, and no shield against oblivion but the unassisted memory. The Japanese were now to have records. Heretofore religion was simply the rude offspring of human imagination, fear, and aspiration, without doctrinal systems, moral codes, elaborate temples, or sacerdotal caste. Henceforth the Japanese were to be led, guided, and developed in morals, intellect, and worship by a religion that had already brought the nations of Asia under its sway—a strong, overpowering, and aggressive faith, that was destined to add Japan to its conquests. Buddhism, bringing new and greater sanctions, penalties, motives, and a positive theology and code of morals, was to develop and broaden the whole nature of the individual man, and to lead the entire nation forward. Chinese philosophy and Confucian morals were to form the basis of the education and culture of the Japanese statesman, scholar, and noble, to modify Shintô, and with it to create new ideals of government, of codes, laws, personal honor, and household ordering. Under their influence, and that of circumstances, have been shaped the unique ideals of the *samurai*; and by it a healthy skepticism, amidst dense superstition, has been maintained. The coming of many immigrants brought new blood, ideas, opinions, methods, improvements in labor, husbandry, social organization.

Japan received from China, through Corea, what she is now receiving from America and Europe—a new civilization.

For nearly a century after the birth of Ôjin, the record of events is blank. In 249 A.D. a Japanese general, Arata, was sent to assist one state of Corea against another. Occasional notices of tribute-bearers arriving from Corea occur. In 283 a number of tailors, in 284 excellent horses, were sent over to Japan. In 285, Wani, a Corean scholar, came over to Japan, and, residing some time at the court, gave the mikado's son instruction in writing. If the *Nihongi*—the authority for the date of Wani's arrival in Japan—could be trusted in its chronology, the introduction of Chinese writing, and probably of Buddhism, would date from this time; but the probabilities are against positive certainty on this point. If it be true, it shows that the first missionary conquest of this nation was the work of four centuries instead of as many decades. Wani died in Japan, and his tomb stands near Ôzaka. In A.D. 403 a court annalist was chosen. Envoys and tribute-bearers came, and presents were exchanged. In 462 mulberry-trees were planted—evidently brought, together with the silk-worm, for whose sustenance they were intended—from China or Corea. Again, tailors in 471, and architects in 493, and learned men in 512, arrived. An envoy from China came in 522. The arrival of fresh immigrants and presents from Corea in 543 is noted. In 551, during a famine in Corea, several thousand bushels of barley were dispatched thither by Japan. In 552, a company of doctors, diviners, astronomers, and mathematicians from Corea came to live at the Japanese court. With them came Buddhist missionaries. This may be called the introduction of continental civilization. Beginning with Jingu, there seems to have poured into the island empire a stream of immigrants, skilled artisans, scholars, and teachers, bringing arts, sciences, letters and written literature, and the Buddhist religion. This was the first of three great waves of foreign civilization in Japan. The first was from

China, through Corea in the sixth; the second from Western Europe, in the fifteenth century; the third was from America, Europe, and the world, in the decade following the advent of Commodore Perry. These innovations were destined to leaven mightily the whole Japanese nation as a lump. Of these none was so powerful and far-reaching in effects as that in the sixth century, and no one element as Buddhism. This mighty force was destined to exert a resistless and unifying influence on the whole people. Nothing, among all the elements that make up Japanese civilization, has been so potent in forming the Japanese character as the religion of Buddha. That the work of these new civilizers may be fully appreciated, let us glance at life in Dai Nippon before their appearance.*

---

* The Empress Jingu, after her return, made a very important change in the divisions of the empire. Seimu Tennô (A.D. 131–190) had divided the empire into provinces, the number of which was thirty-two in all, the land above the thirty-eighth parallel being still unknown, and inhabited by the wild tribes of Ainôs. Jingu, imitating the Corean arrangement, divided the empire into five home provinces, and seven *do*, or circuits, naming them in relation to their direction from the capital. These are analogous to our "Eastern," "Middle," "Southern," "Western," "Trans-Mississippi," and "Pacific-coast" divisions of States. The "five home provinces" (Go Kinai) are Yamashiro, Yamato, Kawachi, Idzumi, and Settsu. The Tôkaidô, or Eastern-sea Circuit, comprised the provinces skirting the Pacific Ocean from Iga to Hitachi, including Kai.

The Tôzandô, or Eastern-mountain Circuit, included those provinces from Ômi to the end of the main island, not on the Sea of Japan, nor included within the Tôkaidô.

The Hokurikudô, or Northern-land Circuit, comprised the provinces from Wakasa to Echigo inclusive, bordering on the Sea of Japan, and Sado Island.

The Sanindô, or Mountain-back Circuit, comprised with the Oki group of islands the provinces from Tamba to Iwami, bordering on the Sea of Japan.

The Sanyôdô, or Mountain-front Circuit, comprised the provinces from Harima to Nagato (or Chôshiu) bordering the Inland Sea.

The Saikaidô, or Western-sea Circuit, comprises nine provinces of Kiushiu (*kiu*, nine; *shiu*, province).

The "two islands" are Iki and Tsushima.

This division accords with the physical features of the country, and has ever since been retained, with slight modifications as to provinces. It is very probable that in the time of Jingu, the Japanese did not know that Hondo was an island. A foreigner looking at the map of the empire, or a globe representing the world, could hardly imagine that the Japanese have no special and universally used name for the main island. Yet such is the fact, that neither they nor their books popularly apply any particular name to the main island. It may be even doubted whether the people in general ever think of the main island as being a particular division requiring a name, as the foreigner conceives it, and thus feels a name to be a necessity. This necessity has given rise to the error of applying the term "Niphon" (Nihon, Nippon, or Nifon), first done by Kaempfer. The Japanese had no more necessity to apply a special name to the main island than the early American colonists had to give a name to the region beyond the Mississippi. Even now we have no name in general use for that now well-known part of our country. To foreigners, the absence of a name for the largest island seems an anomaly. In the Japanese mind it never existed. He rarely spoke even of Kiushiu or Shikoku as names of islands, always using the names of the *do*, or circuits, just as an American speaks of the New England or the Eastern States. In modern times, native scholars who have, from their study, comparisons and foreign methods of thought, felt the need of a distinctive name, have used Hondo (main continent or division), Honjima (main island) or Honjiu (main country). Of these, Hondo seems to be the best; and as it is used in the official geography recently issued by the War Department, I have made use of it. Nippon is not, nor ever was, the name of the main island, as Kaempfer first asserted. Nippon, or Dai Nippon, is the name of the whole empire. The word is Chinese, and must have been applied in very ancient times, as the *Nihongi* contains the three characters with which the name is written. The very name of the book, *Nippongi*, or, more elegantly, *Nihongi*, shows that the use of the term Nippon antedates the eighth century. Tenchi Tennô, in A.D. 670, first officially declared Nippon to be the name of Japan. It has been asserted that the use of Dai (Great) before Nippon is quite recent, and that the motive of the modern natives of Japan in thus designating their empire is "from a desire to imitate what they mistake for the pride or vainglory of Great Britain, not knowing that the term Great was used there to distinguish it from a smaller French province of the same name." To this remarkable statement it is sufficient to answer, that one of the most ancient names of Japan is Ô Yamato, the word *o* meaning great, and the Japanese equivalent of the Chinese word *tai* or *dai*. When Chinese writing was introduced, the Japanese, in seeking an equivalent for Ô Yamato, found it in Dai Nippon, as may be seen in the *Nihongi*. The Chinese have always been in the habit of prefixing *dai* or *tai* to whatever relates to their country, government, or any thing which they in their pride consider very superior. Anciently they called China Dai Tô, and they now call it Dai Tsin (or Dai Chin), Great China. The Japanese have done the same analogous thing for at least twelve, probably for fifteen, centuries. That the use of Dai (Great) before Nippon is not the fashion of the present century is proved by the fact that the Japanese encyclopedia *San Sai Dzu Ye*, finished in 1712, contains the name with the pronunciation as now used, and that it is found in the very name *Dai Nihon Shi*, a book completed in 1715. The use of Nippon (or Niphon, or Nipon), applied to the main island, is altogether unwarrantable and confusing. The Japanese have very properly protested against this improper naming of their chief island, and, notwithstanding the long use of the name in Europe and America, I believe it should be expunged. The Japanese have some geographical rights which we are bound to respect.

*Map of Japan.*—The best map of Japan is that by Mr. R. Henry Brunton, C.E., F.R.G.S., late Engineer-in-chief of the Light-house Department of the Japanese Government. It is five feet by four, and drawn to a scale of twenty miles to the inch. It is well engraved, and gives also rules of pronunciation, explanation of terms, Japanese lineal measures, railways, highways, by-roads, telegraph lines, light-houses, depths of water along the coast, steamer routes, lists of principal mountains, rivers, islands, promontories, lakes, open ports, classes of population, provinces, *fu*, *ken*, and a comparative scale of English miles and Japanese *ri*.

## IX

# *Life in Ancient Japan*

The comparatively profound peace from the era of Sûjin Tennô to the introduction of Chinese civilization was occasionally interrupted by insurrections in the southern and western parts of the empire, or by the incursions of the unsubdued aborigines in the North and East.

During these centuries there continued that welding of races— the Ainô, Malay, Nigrito, Corean, and Yamato—into one ethnic composite—the Japanese—and the development of the national temperament, molded by nature, circumstances, and original bent, which have produced the unique Japanese character. Although, in later centuries, Japan borrowed largely from China, blood, language, religion, letters, education, laws, politics, science, art, and the accumulated treasures of Chinese civilization, her children are to-day, as they have ever been, a people distinct from the Chinese, ethnologically, physically, and morally.

Though frequent fighting was necessary, and many of the aborigines were slaughtered, the great mass of them were tranquilized. To rude men, in a state of savagery whose existence is mainly animal, it matters little who are their masters, so long as they are not treated with intolerable cruelty. The aborigines attached to the land roamed over it to hunt, or remained upon it to till it, and, along the watercourses and

sea-coast, to fish. With a soil that repaid generously the rude agriculture of that day, an ample food-supply in the sea, without severe labor,
or exorbitant tribute to pay, the conquered tribes, when once quieted,
lived in happiness, content, and peace. The government of them was
the easiest possible. The invaders from the very beginning practiced
that system of concubinage which is practical polygamy, and filled
their harems with the most attractive of the young native females. The
daughter of the former chief shared the couch of the conqueror, and
the peasant became the wife of the soldier, securing that admixture
of races that the merest tyro in ethnology notices in modern Japan.
In certain portions, as in the extreme north of Hondo, the Ainô type
of face and head and the general physical characteristics of skin, hair,
eyes, and form, have suffered the least modification, owing to later
conquest and less mixture of foreign blood. In Southern and Central
Japan, where the fusion of the races was more perfect, the oval face,
oblique eyes, aquiline nose, prominent features, and light skin prevail. Yet even here are found comparatively pure specimens of the
Malay and even Nigrito races, besides the Ainô and Corean types.
The clod-hopper, with his flat, round face, upturned nose, expanded
at the roots and wide and sunken at the bridge, nostrils round, and
gaping like the muzzle of a proboscidian, bears in his veins the nearly
pure blood of his aboriginal ancestors. Intellectually and physically,
he is the developed and improved Ainô—the resultant of the action
upon the original stock of the soil, food, climate, and agricultural life,
prolonged for more than twenty centuries.

In the imperial family, and among the kugé, or court-nobles, are
to be oftener found the nearest approach to the ideal Japanese of
high birth. Yet even among these, who claim twenty-five centuries
of semi-divine succession, and notably among the daimiôs, or territorial nobles—the parvenus of feudalism—the grossly sensual cast,
the animal features, the beastly expression, the low type, the plebeian

face of some peasant ancestor re-appear to plague the descendant, and to imbitter his cup of power and luxury. This phenomenon is made abundant capital of by the native fiction-writers, caricaturists, and dramatists. The diversity of the two types is shown, especially by the artists, in strongly marked contrast. In the pictures illustrative of legendary or historic lore, and notably on the Japanese fans, now so fashionably common among us, the noble hero, the chivalrous knight, or the doughty warrior, is delineated with oblique eyes, high eyebrows, rounded nose, oval face, and smooth skin; while the peasant, boor, vanquished ruffian, or general scape-goat, is invariably a man of round, flat face, upturned and depressed nose, gaping nostrils, horizontal eyes, and low eyebrows. In painting the faces of actors, singing-girls, and those public characters who, though the popular idols, are of low birth and blood, the fan-artist exaggerates the marks of beauty to the delight of his native, and to the disgust of his foreign patrons. What depreciates the value of his wares in the eyes of the latter enhances it in those of the natives.

All savages worship heroes, and look upon their conquerors, who have been able apparently to overcome not only themselves, but even the gods in whom they trusted, if not as gods themselves, at least as imbued with divine power. The Ainôs of Yezo to this day adore the warrior Yoshitsune. Their fathers doubtless considered Jimmu and his followers as gods or men divinely assisted. The conquerors were not slow in cultivating such a belief for their own benefit, and thus what was once the fancy of savages became the dogma of religion and the tool of the magistrate. The reverence and obedience of the people were still further secured by making the government purely theocratic, and its general procedure and ceremonial identical with those of worship. The forms of local authority among the once independent tribes were but little interfered with, and the government exercised over them consisted at first chiefly in the exaction of tribute. The floating legends, local traditions, and religious ideas of the aborigines, gathered up, amplified by the dominant race, transformed and made coherent by the dogmatics of a theocracy, became the basis of Shintô, upon which a modified Chinese cosmogony and abstract philosophical ideas were afterward grafted. It was this background that has made the resultant form of Shintô different from what is most probably its prototype, the ante-Confucian Chinese religion. In its origin, Shintô is from the main-land of Asia. In growth and development it is "a genuine product of Japanese soil." As yet, before the advent of Buddhism and Chinese philosophy, there were no moral codes, no systems of abstract doctrines, no priestly caste. These were all later developments. There were then no colossal temples with their great belfries and immense bells whose notes quivered the air into leagues of liquid melody; no sacred courtyards decked with palm-trees; no costly shrines decked out in the gaudy magnificence characteristic of Buddhism, or impure Shintô. No extensive monasteries, from which floated on the breeze the chanting of priests or the droning hum of students, were then built. No crimson pagodas peeped out from camphor groves, or cordons of fire-warding firs and keyaki-trees. No splendid vestments, gorgeous ritual, waves of incense, blazing lights, antiphonal responses, were seen or heard in the thatched huts which served as shrines of the kami. No idols decked the altars. No wayside images dotted the mountain or the meadow paths. No huge portals (*torii*) of stone or red-lacquered timber stood fronting or opening the path to holy edifices.

On the hill-top, or river-side, or forest grove, the people assembled when invocations were offered and thanksgiving rendered to the gods. Confession of sin was made, and the wrath of the kami, therefore, was deprecated. The priest, after fasting and lustrations, purified himself and, robed in white, made offerings of the fruits of the earth or the trophies of the net and the chase.

At the court, a shrine of the Sun-goddess had been set up and sacrifices offered. Gradually in the towns and villages similar shrines were erected, and temples built; but for long centuries among the mountains, along the rivers and sea-coasts, the child of the soil set up his fetich, made the water-worn stone, the gnarled tree, or the storm-cloud his god. Wherever evil was supposed to lurk, or malignity reside, there were the emblems of the Ainô religion. On precipice, in gorge, in that primeval landscape, stood the plume of curled shavings to ward off the evil influences. In agony of terror in presence of the awful phenomenon of nature, earthquake, typhoon, flood, or tidal wave, the savage could but supplicate deified Nature to cease from wrath and tumult, and restore her face in peace of sunshine and calm.

The houses of the ancient Japanese were oblong huts, made by placing poles of young trees, with the bark on, upright in the ground, with transverse poles to make the frame, and fastened together with ropes made of rushes or vines. The walls were of matted grass, boughs, or rushes, the rafters of bamboo, and the sloping roof of grass-thatch, fastened down by heavy ridge-poles. The two larger rafters at each end projected and crossed each other, like two bayonets in a stack of guns. Across the ridge-pole, and beneath it and another heavy tree laid lengthwise on top of the thatch, projected at right angles on either side short, heavy logs, which by their weight, and from being firmly bound by withes running under the ridge-pole, kept the thatch firmly in its place. This primeval hut is the model of the architecture of a pure Shintô temple. A short study of one easily reveals the fact. The floor, of hardened earth, had the fire in the centre; the doors and windows were holes covered at times with mats—in short, the Aino hut of to-day. The modern Japanese dwelling is simply an improvement upon that ancient model.

The clothing of that period consisted of skins of animals, coarsely woven stuff of straw, grass, bark, palm-fibre, and in some cases of asbestos. Silk and cotton fabrics were of later invention and use. It is evident, even from modern proof, as exhibited in the normal Japanese of to-day, that the wearing of many garments was not congenial to the ancient people. As for straw and grass, these materials are even now universally used in town and country for hats, rain-coats, leggings, sandals, and a great variety of wearing apparel. A long loose garment, with the breech, or loin-cloth, and girdle, leggings, and sandals of straw, comprised a suit of ancient Japanese clothing. The food of the people consisted chiefly of fish, roots, and the flesh of animals. They ate venison, bear-meat, and other flesh, with untroubled consciences, until Buddhism came with its injunctions. The conquerors evidently brought cereals with them, and taught their cultivation; but the main reliance of the masses was upon the spoils of the rivers and sea. Even now the great centres and lines of the population are rivers and the sea-coast. Roots, sea-weed, and edible wild vegetables were, as at present, an important portion of native diet.

The landscape of modern Japan is one of minute prettiness. It is one continued succession of mountains and valleys. The irregularities of the surface render it picturesque, and the labors of centuries have brought almost every inch of the cultivable soil in the populous districts into a state of high agricultural finish. The peasant of to-day is in many cases the direct descendant of the man who first plunged mattock and hoe into the rooty soil, and led the water from a distance of miles to his new-made fields. The gullies, gorges, and valleys are everywhere terraced for the growth of rice. Millions of irrigated fields without fences or live-stock, bounded by water-courses, and animate with unharmed and harmless wild-fowl, the snowy heron, and the crane, and whose fertility astonishes the stranger, and the elaborate system of reservoirs, ditches, and flumes, are the harvest of twenty centuries of toil. The face of nature has been smoothed; the unkempt luxuriance of forest and undergrowth has been sobered; the courses of rivers have been bridled; the once inaccessible sides of mountains graded, and their summits crossed by the paths of the traveler or pilgrim. The earth has been honey-combed by miners in quest of its metallic wealth.

In the primeval landscape of Japan there were no meadows, hedges, cattle, horses, prairies of ripening rice, irrigated fields, and terraced gulches. Then also, as now, the landscape was nude of domestic animal life. Instead of castled cities, fortified hills, gardens, and hedges, were only thatched villages, or semi-subterranean huts. There were no roads, no dikes. No water-courses had been altered, no slopes or hills denuded of timber. The plethora of nature was unpruned; the scrub bamboo, wild flowers, or grass covered the hills. The great plains of the East and North were luxuriant moors, covered with grass, reeds, or bamboo, populous with wild animal life. No laden junks moved up the rivers. The mulberry and tea plantations had not yet been set out. The conquerors found a virgin soil and a land of enrapturing beauty. They brought with them, doubtless, a knowledge of agriculture and metals. Gradually the face of nature changed. The hunter became a farmer. The women learned to spin and weave cotton and hemp. Division of labor began. The artisan and merchant appeared. Arts, sciences, skilled agriculture, changed the face of the land. Society emerged from its savage state, and civilization began.

As yet there was no writing. All communications were oral, all teachings handed down from father to son. Memory was the only treasury of thought. There is, indeed, shown in Japan at the present day a so-called ancient Japanese alphabet—the kami, or god, letters —which it is asserted the ancient Japanese used. This assertion is voided of truth by the testimony of the best native scholars to the contrary. No books or ancient inscriptions exist in this character. I have myself sought in vain, in the grave-yards of Kioto and other ancient places, to discover any of these characters upon the old tombs. The best authorities, scholars who have investigated the subject, pronounce the so-called god-letters a forgery, that reveals their artificial and modern character upon a slight examination. They consist almost entirely of a system of straight lines and circles, which has, doubtless, either been borrowed from Corea, or invented by some person in modern times. Yet the morning of litera-ture had dawned before writing was known. Poems, odes to the gods, prayers, fragments of the Shintô liturgy, which still exist in the *Kojiki* and *Nihongi*, had been composed. From these fragments we may pre-sume that a much larger unwritten literature existed, which was enjoyed by the men who, in those early days, by thought and reflection, attained to a certain degree of culture above their fellows. The early sovereigns worshiped the gods in person, and prayed that their people might enjoy a sufficiency of food, clothing, and shelter from the elements; and twice a year, in the Sixth and Twelfth months, the people assembled at the river-side, and, by washings and prayer, celebrated the festival of General Purification, by which the whole nation was purged of offenses and pollutions. This was the most characteristic of Shintô festivals, and the liturgy used in celebrating it is still in vogue at the present day. Time was measured by the phases of the moon, and the summer and winter solstices. The division of months and years was in use. The ancient laws and punishments were exceedingly severe. Besides the wager of battle to decide a quarrel, the ordeal still in use among the Ainôs was then availed of. The persons involved immersed their hands in boiling water. He whose hand was scalded most was the guilty one. The wholly innocent escaped without scath, or was so slightly injured that his hand rapidly healed.

Japanese art had its birth in mercy, about the time of Christ's advent on earth. A custom long adhered to among the noble classes was the burial of the living with the dead (*jun-shi*, dying with the master).

The wife, and one or more servants, of the deceased lord committed suicide, and were inhumed with him. The mikado Suinin, son of Sûjin, attempted (B.C. 2) to abolish the cruel rite by imperial edict. Yet the old fashion was not immediately abandoned. In A.D. 3, the empress died. Nomi no Tsukuné, a courtier, having made some clay images, succeeded in having these substituted for the living victims. This was the birth of Japanese art. Henceforth these first products of man's unfolding genius stood vicarious for the breathing beings they simulated. For this reform, the originator was given the honorable designation, Haji (*ha*, clay; *shi*, *ji*, teacher = clay-image teacher, or artist).

The domestic life and morals of those days deserve notice. There were no family names. The institution of marriage, if such it may be called, was upon the same basis as that among the modern Ainôs or North American Indians. Polygamy was common. Marriage between those whom we consider brothers and sisters was frequent, and a thing not to be condemned. Children of the same fathers by different mothers were not considered fraternally related to each other, and hence could marry; but marriage between a brother and sister born of the same mother was prohibited as immoral.

The annexed illustration is taken from a native work, and represents a chief or nobleman in ancient Japan. It will be noticed that beards and mustaches were worn in those days. The artist has depicted his subject with a well-wrinkled face to make him appear venerable, and with protruding cheeks to show his lusty physique, recalling the ideals of Chinese art, in which the men are always portly and massive, while the women are invariably frail and slender. His pose, expression, folded arms, and dress of figured material (consisting of one long loose robe with flowing sleeves, and a second garment, like very wide trousers, girded at the waist with straps of the same material) are all to be seen, though in modified forms, in modern Japan. The fashions of twenty centuries have changed but slightly. Suspended from his girdle may be seen the *magatama* chatelaine, evidently symbolizing his rank. The *magatama* are perforated and polished pieces of soapstone or cornelian, of various colors, shaped something like a curved seed-pod. They were strung together like beads. Other ornaments of this age were the *kudatama*, jewels of gold, silver, or iron. The ancient sword was a straight, double-edged blade, about three feet long.

Buddhists and Confucianists assert that there existed no words in their language for benevolence, justice, propriety, sagacity, and truth. Doubtless these virtues existed, though not as necessary principles, to be taught, formulated, and incorporated into daily life. Chastity and restraint among the unmarried were not reckoned as necessary virtues; and the most ancient Japanese literature, to say nothing of their mythology, proves that marriage was a flimsy bar against the excursions of irregular passion. Great feasts and drinking-bouts, in which excessive eating was practiced, were common. They were fond of the chase, and hunting-parties were frequent from the most ancient times. Among the commendable features of their life were the habit of daily bathing and other methods of cleanliness. They treated their women with comparative kindness and respect. They loved the beautiful in Nature, and seemed to have been ever susceptible to her charms. In brief, they had neither the virtues nor vices of high civilization.

The arts were in the rudest state. Painting, carving, and sculpture were scarcely known. No theatre existed. Sacred dancing with masks, at the holy festivals, was practiced as part of the public worship, with music from both wind and stringed instruments.

Until the seventh century of our era, when the Chinese centralized system was adopted, the government of the Japanese empire was a species of feudalism. The invaders, on conquering the land, divided it into fiefs that were held sometimes by direct followers of Jimmu, or by the original Ainô chiefs, or nobles of mixed blood, on their rendition of homage or tribute to the conqueror. The frequent defection of these native or semi-Japanese chiefs was the cause of the numerous rebellions, the accounts of which enter so largely into the history of the first centuries of the empire. The mikado himself ruled over what is now called the Kinai, or Five Home Provinces, a space of country included between Lake Biwa and the bays of Ôzaka and Owari. The provinces in Shikoku, Kiushiu, and the circuits west, north, and east, were ruled by tributary chiefs who paid homage to the mikado as their suzerain, but most probably allowed him to interfere to a slight extent in the details of the administration of their lands. In cases of dispute between them, the mikado doubtless acted as umpire, his geographical position, superior power, and the sacredness of person insuring his supremacy at all times, even in the height of turbulence and riot so often prevailing.

In the ancient mikadoate, called by the Japanese the Ôsei era, or the government of monarchs, there were several features tending to increase the power of the suzerain, or central chief. The first was the essentially theocratic form of the government. The sovereign was the centre of that superstitious awe, as well as of loyalty and personal reverence, which still exists. There grew into being that prestige, that sense of hedging divinity and super-mortal supremacy of the mikado that still forms the most striking trait of the Japanese character, and the mightiest political, as it is a great religious and moral, force in Japan, overshadowing even the tremendous power of Buddhism, which is, as Shintô is not, armed with the terrors of eternity. In both a theological and political sense, in him dwelt the fullness of the gods bodily. He was their hypostasis. He was not only their chosen servant, but was himself a god, and the vicegerent of all the gods. His celestial fathers had created the very ground on which they dwelt. His wrath could destroy, his favor appease, celestial anger, and bring them fortune and prosperity. He was their preserver and benefactor. In his custody were the three sacred symbols. It was by superior intellect and the dogmatism of religion, as well as with superior valor, weapons, and skill, that a handful of invaders conquered and kept a land populated by millions of savages.

To the eye of a foreigner and a native of Japan, this imperfect picture of primitive Japan which I have given appears in very different lights. The native who looks at this far-off morning of Great Japan, the Holy Country, sees his ancestors only through the atmosphere in which he has lived and breathed. The dim religious light of reverent teaching of mother, nurse, father, or book falls on every object to reveal beauty and conceal defects. The rose-tints which innocent childhood casts upon every object here makes all things lovely. Heaven lies about his country's infancy. The precepts of his religion make the story sacred, and forbid the prying eye and the sandaled foot. The native loves, with passionate devotion, the land that nursed his holy ancestors, and thrills at the oft-told story of their prowess and their holy lives. He makes them his model of conduct.

The foreigner, in cold blood and with critical eye, patiently seeks the truth beneath, and, regarding not the dogma which claims to rest upon it, looks through dry light. To the one Nippon is the Land of the Gods, and the primal ages were holy. To the other, Japan is merely a geographical division of the earth, and its beginnings were from barbarism.

# X

# *The Ancient Religion*

The ancient religion of the Japanese is called *Kami no michi* (way or doctrine of the gods; *i.e.*, theology). The Chinese form of the same is Shintô. Foreigners call it Shintôism, or Sintooism. Almost all the foreign writers* who have professed to treat of Shinto have described only the impure form which has resulted from the contact with it of Buddhism and Chinese philosophy, and as known to them since the sixteenth century. My purpose in this chapter is to give a mere outline of ancient Shintô in its purity. A sketch of its traditional and doctrinal basis has been given. Only a very few Shintô temples, called *miya*, have preserved the ancient purity of the rites and dogmas during the overshadowing influences of Buddhism.

In Japanese mythology the universe is Japan, the legends relating to Japan exclusively. All the deities, with perhaps a few exceptions, are historical personages; and the conclusion of the whole matter of cosmogony and celestial genealogy is that the mikado is the descen-

---

* By far the best writing on Shintô, based on profound researches, is the long article of Mr. Ernest Satow, entitled "The Revival of Pure Shintô," in the *Japan Mail*, 1874, and contained in the "Proceedings of the Asiatic Society of Japan" for the same year. Also on *The Shintô Temples of Isé,* by the same writer. A scholarly article, by Mr. P. Kemperman, secretary to the German legation in Japan, was published in the *Japan Mail* of August 26th, 1874.

dant and representative of the gods who created the heavens and earth (Japan). Hence, the imperative duty of all Japanese is to obey him. Its principles, as summed up by the Department of Religion, and promulgated throughout the empire so late as 1872, are expressed in the following commandments;

1. Thou shalt honor the Gods, and love thy country
2. Thou shalt clearly understand the principles of Heaven and the duty of man
3. Thou shalt revere the Mikado as thy sovereign, and obey the will of his court

The chief characteristic, which is preserved in various manifestations, is the worship of ancestors, and the deification of emperors, heroes, and scholars. The adoration of the personified forces of nature enters largely into it. It employs no idols, images, or effigies in its worship. Its symbols are the mirror and the *gohei*— strips of notched white paper depending from a wand of wood. It teaches no doctrine of the immortality of the soul, though it is easy to see that such a dogma may be developed from it, since all men (Japanese) are descended from the immortal gods. The native derivation of the term for man is *hito* ("light-bearer"); and the ancient title of the mikado's heir-apparent was "light-inheritor." Fire and light (sun) have from earliest ages been the objects of veneration.

Shintô has no moral code, no accurately defined system of ethics or belief. The leading principle of its adherents is imitation of the illustrious deeds of their ancestors, and they are to prove themselves worthy of their descent by the purity of their lives. A number of salient points in their mythology are recognized as maxims for their guidance. It expresses great detestation of all forms of uncleanness, and is remarkable for the fullness of its ceremonies for bodily purification. Birth and death are especially polluting. Anciently, the corpse and the lying-in woman were assigned to buildings set apart, which were afterward burned. The priest must bathe and don clean garments before officiating, and bind a slip of paper over his mouth, lest his breath should pollute the offerings. Many special festivals were observed for purification, the ground dedicated for the purpose being first sprinkled with salt. The house and ground were defiled by death, and those who attended a funeral must also free themselves from contamination by the use of salt. The ancient emperors and priests in the provinces performed the actual ablution of the people, or made public lustrations. Later on, twice a year, at the festivals of purification, paper figures representing the people were thrown into the river, allegorical of the cleansing of the nation from the sins of the past six months. Still later, the mikado deputized the chief minister of religion at Kiôto to perform the symbolical act for the people of the whole country.

After death, the members of a family in which death had occurred must exclude themselves from all intercourse with the world, attend no religious services, and, if in official position, do no work for a specified number of days.

Thanksgiving, supplication, penance, and praise are all represented in the prayers to the gods, which are offered by both sexes. The emperor and nobles often met in the temple gardens to compose hymns or sacred poems to the gods. Usually in prayer the hands are clapped twice, the head or the knees bowed, and the petition made in silence. The worshiper does not enter the temple, but stands before it, and first pulls a rope dangling down over a double gong, like a huge sleigh-bell, with which he calls the attention of the deity. The kami are believed to hear the prayer when as yet but in thought, before it rises to the lips. Not being intended for human ears, eloquence is not needed. The mikado in his palace daily offers up petitions for all his people, which are more effectual than those of his subjects. Washing the hands and rinsing out the mouth, the worshiper repeats prayers, of which the following is an example: "O God, that dwellest in the high plain of heaven, who art divine in substance and in intellect, and able to give protection from guilt and its penalties, to banish impurity, and to cleanse us from uncleanness—hosts of gods, give ear and listen to these our petitions." Or this: "I say with awe, deign to bless me by correcting the unwitting faults which, seen and heard by you, I have committed; by blowing off and clearing away the calamities which evil gods might inflict; by causing me to live long, like the hard and lasting rock; and by repeating to the gods of heavenly origin, and to the gods of earthly origin, the petitions which I present every day, along with your breath, that they may hear with the sharp-earedness of the forth-galloping colt."

The offerings, most commonly laid with great ceremony by the priest, in white robes, before the gods, were fruit and vegetables in season, fish and venison. At night they were removed, and became the property of the priest. Game and fowls were offered up as an act of worship, but with the peculiarity that their lives were not sacrificed. They were hung up by the legs before the temple for some time, and then permitted to escape, and, being regarded as sacred to the gods, were exempt from harm. The new rice and the products furnished by the silk-worm and the cotton-plant were also dedicated.

Before each temple stood a *torii*, or bird-rest. This was made of two upright tree-trunks. On the top of these rested a smoother tree, with ends slightly projecting, and underneath this a smaller horizontal beam. On this perched the fowls offered up to the gods, not as food, but as chanticleers to give notice of day-break. In later centuries the meaning of the *torii* was forgotten, and it was supposed to be a gateway. The Buddhists attached tablets to its cross-beam, painted or coppered its posts, curved its top-piece, made it of stone or bronze, and otherwise altered its character. Resembling two crosses with their ends joined, the *torii* is a conspicuous object in the landscape, and a purely original work of Japanese architecture.

All the *miyas* were characterized by rigid simplicity, constructed of pure wood, and thatched. No paint, lacquer, gilding, or any meretricious ornaments were ever allowed to adorn or defile the sacred structure, and the use of metal was avoided. Within, only the *gohei* and the daily offerings were visible. Within a closet of purest wood is a case of wood containing the "august spirit-substitute," or "gods'-seed," in which the deity enshrined in the particular temple is believed to reside. This spirit-substitute is usually a mirror, which in some temples is exposed to view. The principal Shintô temples are at Isé, in which the mirror given by Amaterasu to Ninigi, and brought down from heaven, was enshrined. Some native writers assert that the mirror was the goddess herself; others, that it merely represented her. All others in Japan are imitations or copies of this original.

The priests of Shintô are designated according to their rank. They are called *kannushi* (shrine-keepers). Sometimes they receive titles from the emperor, and the higher ranks of the priesthood are court nobles. They are, in the strictest sense of the word, Government officials. The office of chief minister of religion was hereditary in the Nakatomi family. Ordinarily they dress like other people, but are robed in white when officiating, or in court-dress when at court. They marry, rear families, and do not shave their heads. The office is usually hereditary. Virgin priestesses also minister at the shrines.

After all the research of foreign scholars who have examined the claims of Shintô on the soil, and by the aid of the language, and the sacred books and commentators, many hesitate to decide whether Shintô is "a genuine product of Japanese soil," or whether it is not closely allied with the ancient religion of China, which existed before the period of Confucius. The weight of opinion inclines to the latter belief. Certain it is that many of the Japanese myths are almost exactly like those of China, while many parts of the cosmogony can be found unaltered in older Chinese works. The *Kojiki* (the Bible of the Japanese believers in Shintô) is full of narrations; but it lays down no precepts, teaches no morals or doctrines, prescribes no ritual. Shintô has very few of the characteristics of a religion, as understood by us. The most learned native commentators and exponents of Shintô expressly maintain the view, that Shintô has no moral code. Motoöri, the great modern revivalist of Shintô, teaches, with polemic emphasis, that morals were invented by the Chinese because they were an immoral people; but in Japan there was no necessity for any system of morals, as every Japanese acted aright if he only consulted his own heart. The duty of a good Japanese consists in obeying the commands of the mikado without questioning whether these commands are right or wrong. It was only immoral people, like the Chinese, who presumed to discuss the character of their sovereigns. Among the ancient Japanese, government and religion were the same.*

---

* In this chapter, I have carefully endeavored to exclude mere opinions and conjectures, and to give the facts only. I append below the views held by gentlemen of cosmopolitan culture, and earnest students of shinto on the soil, whose researches and candor entitle them to be heard.

"Shintô, as expounded by Motoöri, is nothing else than an engine for reducing the people to a condition of mental slavery."—ERNEST SATOW, *English, the foremost living Japanese scholar, and a special student of Shintô.*

"There is good evidence that Shinto resembles very closely the ancient religion of the Chinese." "A distinction should be drawn between the Shinto of ancient times and the doctrine as developed by writers at the court of the mikado in modern times." "The sword and dragon, the thyrsus staff and ivy, the staff of Æsculapius and snakes, most probably had the same significance as the Japanese *gohei*; and, as Siebold has remarked, it symbolized the union of the two elements, male and female. The history of the creation of the world, as given by the Japanese, bore the closest resemblance to the myths of China and India; while little doubt existed that these (symbol and myth) were imported from the West, the difficulty being to fix the date. Little was known of Shintô that might give it the character of a religion as understood by Western nations."—J. A. Von Brandt, *German, late minister of the German empire to Japan, and now to Peking, a student of Japanese archaeology, and founder of the German Asiatic Society of Japan.*

"Japanese, in general, are at a loss to describe what Shintô is; but this circumstance is intelligible if what was once an indigenous faith had been turned in later days, into a political engine." "Infallibility on the part of the head of the state, which was naturally attributed to rulers claiming divine descent, was a convenient doctrine for political purposes in China or Japan, as elsewhere." "We must look to early times for the meaning of Shintô." "Its origin is closely allied to the early religion of the Chinese." "The practice of putting up sticks with shavings or paper attached, in order to attract the attention of the spirits, is observable among certain hill tribes of India, as well as among the Ainôs of Yezo. The Hindoos, Burmese, and Chinese have converted these sticks into flags, or streamers." "If Shintô had ever worked great results, or had taken deep hold on the Japanese people, it would scarcely have been superseded so completely as it had been by Buddhism."—Sir Harry S. Parkes, *British minister plenipotentiary in Japan, a fine scholar, and long resident in both China and Japan.*

"The leading idea of Shinto is a reverential feeling toward the dead." "As to the political use of it, the state is quite right in turning it to account in support of the absolute government which exists in Japan." "The early records of Japan are by no means reliable."—Arinori Mori, *Japanese, formerly chargé d'affaires of Japan at Washington, U. S. A., now Vice-Minister of Foreign Affairs in Japan.*

# XI

# The Throne and the Noble Families

From the beginning of the Japanese empire, until the century after the introduction of Buddhism, the mikados were the real rulers of their people, having no hedge of division between them and their subjects. The palace was not secluded from the outer world. No screen hid the face of the monarch from the gaze of his subjects. No bureaucracy rose, like a wall of division, between ruler and ruled. No hedge or net of officialdom hindered free passage of remonstrance or petition. The mikado, active in word and deed, was a real ruler, leading his armies, directing his Government. Those early days of comparative national poverty when the mikado was the warrior-chief of a conquering tribe; and, later, when he ruled a little kingdom in Central Japan, holding the distant portions of his quasi-empire in tribute; and, still later, when he was the head of an undivided empire—mark the era of his personal importance and energy. Then, in the mikado dwelt a manly soul, and a strong mind in a strong body. This era was the golden age of the imperial power. He was the true executive of the nation, initiating and carrying out the enterprises of peace or war. As yet, no military class had arisen to make themselves the arbiters of the throne; as yet, that throne was under no proprietorship; as yet, there was but one capital and centre of authority.

Gradually, however, there arose families of nobility who shared and dictated the power, and developed the two official castes of civilian and military officials, widening the distance between the sovereign and his subjects, and rendering him more and more inaccessible to his people. Then followed in succession the decay of his power, the creation of a dual system of government, with two capitals and centres of authority; the domination of the military classes; the centuries of anarchy; the progress of feudalism; the rending of the empire into hundreds of petty provinces, baronies, and feudal tenures. Within the time of European knowledge of Japan, true national unity has scarcely been known. The political system has been ever in a state of unstable equilibrium, and the nation but a conglomeration of units, in which the forces of repulsion ever threatened to overcome the forces of cohesion. Two rulers in two capitals gave to foreigners the impression that there were two "emperors" in Japan—an idea that has been incorporated into most of the text-books and cyclopedias of Christendom. Let it be clearly understood, however, that there never was but one emperor in Japan, the mikado, who is and always was the only sovereign, though his measure of power has been very different at various times. Until the rise and domination of the military classes, he was in fact, as well as by law, supreme. How the mikado's actual power ebbed away shall form the subject of this and the following chapter.

From the death of Nintoku Tenno, the last of the long-lived mikados, to Kimmei (540–571), in whose time continental civilization was introduced, a period of one hundred and forty-one years, fourteen emperors ruled, averaging a little over ten years each. From Kimmei to Gotoba (A.D. 1198) fifty-three emperors reigned, averaging eleven years each. (See list of emperors, p. 138.)

In A.D. 603, the first attempt to create orders of nobility for the nobles, already numerously existing, was made by the Empress Suiko.

Twelve orders were instituted, with symbolic names, after the Chinese custom—such as Virtue, Humanity, Propriety, etc.—distinguished by the colors of the caps worn. In 649, this system was changed for that having nine ranks, with two divisions. In each of the last six were two subdivisions, thus in reality making thirty grades. The first grade was a posthumous reward, given only to those who in life had held the second. Every officer, from the prime minister to the official clerks, had a rank attached to his office, which was independent of birth or age. All officers were presented, and all questions of precedence were settled, in accordance with this rank.

The court officials, at first, had been very few, as might be imagined in this simple state of society without writing. The Jin Gi Kuan, which had existed from very ancient times, supervised the ceremonies of religion, the positions being chiefly held by members of the Nakatomi family. This was the highest division of the Government. In A.D. 603, with the introduction of orders of nobility, the form of government was changed from simple feudalism to centralized monarchy, with eight ministries, or departments of state, as follows:

1. Nakatsukasa no Shô (Department of the Imperial Palace)
2. Shiki bu Shô (Department of Civil Office and Education)
3. Ji bu Shô (Department of Etiquette and Ceremonies)
4. Mim bu Shô (Department of Revenue and Census)
5. Hiô bu Shô (Department of War)
6. Giô bu Shô (Department of Justice)
7. O kura Shô (Department of Treasury)
8. Ku nai Shô (Department of Imperial Household)

The Jin Gi Kuan (Council of Religion; literally, Council of the Gods of Heaven and Earth), though anciently outranking the Dai Jô Kuan (Great Government Council), lost its prestige after the introduction of

Buddhism. The Dai Jô Kuan, created A.D. 786, superintended the eight boards and ruled the empire by means of local governors appointed from the capital. In it were four ministers:

1. Dai Jô Dai Jin (Great Minister of the Great Government)
2. Sa Dai Jin (Great Minister of the Left)
3. U Dai Jin (Great Minister of the Right)
4. Nai Dai Jin (Inner Great Minister)

Of the eight departments, that of War ultimately became the most important. A special department was necessary to attend to the public manners and forms of society, etiquette being more than morals, and equal to literary education. The foreign relations of the empire were then of so little importance that they were assigned to a bureau of the above department. The treasury consisted of imperial store-houses and granaries, as money was not then in general use. Rice was the standard of value, and all taxes were paid in this grain.

The introduction of these orders of nobility and departments of state from China brought about the change from the species of feudalism hitherto existing to centralized monarchy, the rise of the noble families, and the fixing of official castes composed, not, as in most ancient countries, of the priestly and warrior classes, but, as in China, of the civilian and military.

The seeds of the mediæval and modern complex feudalism, which lasted until 1872, were planted about this time. A division of all the able-bodied males into three classes was now made, one of which was to consist of regular soldiers permanently in service. This was the "military class," from which the legions kept as garrisons in the remote provinces were recruited. The unit of combination was the *go*, consisting of five men. Two *go* formed a *kua*, five *kua* a *tai*, two *tai* a *rio*, ten *rio* a *dan*. These terms may be translated "file," "squad," "company," "battalion," "regiment." The *dan*, or regiment, could also be regularly divided into four detachments. The generals who commanded the army in the field were in many cases civil officials, who were more or less conversant with the rude military science of the day. In their time, success in war depended more on disciplined numbers and personal valor, and was not so much a problem of weight, mathematics, machinery, and money as in our day. The expeditions were led by a shôgun, or general, who, if he commanded three regiments, was called a tai-shôgun, or generalissimo. The vice-commanders were called fuku-shôgun. Thus it will be seen that the term "shôgun" is merely the Japanese word for "general." All generals were shôguns, and even the effete figure-head of the great usurpation at Yedo, with whom Commodore Perry and those who followed him made treaties, supposing him to be the "secular emperor" was nothing more.

Muster-rolls were kept of the number of men in the two remaining classes that could be sent in the field on an emergency; and whenever an insurrection broke out, and a military expedition was determined upon, orders were sent to the provinces along the line of march to be ready to obey the imperial command, and compare the quota required with the local muster-rolls. An army would thus be quickly assembled at the capital, or, starting thence, could be re-enforced on the route to the rebellious province. All that was necessary were the orders of the emperor. When war was over, the army was dissolved, and the army corps, regiments, and companies were mustered out of service into their units of combination, *go* of five men. The general, doffing helmet, made his votive offering to the gods, and returned to garrison duty.

Until about the twelfth century, the Japanese empire, like the old Roman, was a centre of civilization surrounded by barbarism, or, rather, like a wave advancing ever farther northward. The numerous revolts in Kiushiu, Shikoku, and even in the North and East of Hondo, show that the subjugation of these provinces was by no means complete on their first pacification. The Kuantô needed continual military care, as well as civil government; while the northern provinces were in a chronic state of riot and disorder, being now peaceful and loyally obedient, and anon in rebellion against the mikado. To keep the remote provinces in order, to defend their boundaries, and to collect tribute, military occupation became a necessity; and, accordingly, in each of the distant provinces, especially those next to the frontier, beyond which were the still unconquered savages, an army was permanently encamped. This, in the remote provinces, was the permanent military force. Throughout the country was a reserve militia, or latent army; and in the capital was the regular army, consisting of the generals and "the Six Guards," or household troops, who formed the regular garrison of Kiôto in peace, and in war became the nucleus of the army of chastisement.

This system worked well at first, but time showed its defects, and wherein it could be improved. Among that third of the population classed as soldiers, some naturally proved themselves brave, apt, and skillful; others were worthless in war, while in the remaining two-thirds many who were able and willing could not enter the army. About the end of the eighth century a reform was instituted, and a new division of the people made. The court decided that all those among the rich peasants who had capacity, and were skilled in archery and horsemanship, should compose the military class, and that the remainder, the weak and feeble, should continue to till the soil and apply themselves to agriculture. The above was one of the most significant of all the changes in the history of Japan. Its fruits are seen to-day in the social constitution of the Japanese people. Though there are many classes, there are but two great divisions of the Japanese, the military and the agricultural. It wrought the complete severance of the soldier and the farmer. It lifted up one part of the people to a plane of life on which travel, adventure, the profession and the pursuit of arms, letters, and the cultivation of honor and chivalry were possible, and by which that brightest type of the Japanese man, the *samurai*, was produced. This is the class which for centuries has monopolized arms, polite learning, patriotism, and intellect of Japan. They are the men whose minds have been ever open to learn, from whom sprung the ideas that once made, and which later overthrew, the feudal system, which wrought the mighty reforms that swept away the shôgunate in 1868, restored the mikado to ancient power, who introduced those ideas that now rule Japan, and sent their sons abroad to study the civilization of the West. To the samurai Japan looks to-day for safety in war, and progress in peace. The samurai is the soul of the nation. In other lands the priestly and the military castes were formed. In Japan one and the same class held the sword and the pen—liberal learning and secular culture. The other class—the agricultural—remained unchanged. Left to the soil to till it, to live and die upon it, the Japanese farmer has remained the same to-day as he was then. Like the wheat that for successive ages is planted as wheat, sprouts, beards, and fills as wheat, the peasant, with his horizon bounded by his rice-fields, his water-courses, or the timbered hills, his intellect laid away for safe-keeping in the priests' hands, is the son of the soil; caring little who rules him, unless he is taxed beyond the power of flesh and blood to bear, or an overmeddlesome officialdom touches his land to transfer, sell, or re-divide it: then he rises as a rebel. In time of war, he is a disinterested and a passive spectator, and he does not fight. He changes masters with apparent unconcern. Amidst all the ferment of ideas induced by the contact of Western civilization with Asiatic within the last two decades, the farmer stolidly remains conservative: he knows not, nor cares to hear, of it, and hates it because of the heavier taxes it imposes upon him.

To support the military, a certain portion of rice was set apart permanently as revenue, and given as wages to the soldiers. This is the

*A Japanese Farmer (seed beds of rice protected
from the birds by strings and slips of wood)**

origin of the pensions still enjoyed by the samurai, and the burden of
the Government and people, which in 1876, after repeated reductions,
amounts to nearly $18,000,000.

Let us notice how the noble families originated. To this hour
these same families, numbering one hundred and fifty-five in all,
dwell in Tôkiô or Kiôto, intensely proud of their high descent from
the mikados and the heavenly gods, glorying in their pedigree more

---

* In the above sketch by Hokusai, the farmer, well advanced in life, bent
and bald is looking dubiously over a piece of newly tilled land, perhaps just
reclaimed, which he defends from the birds by the device of strings holding
strips of thin wood and bamboo stretched from a pole. With his ever-present
bath-towel and headkerchief on his shoulders, his pipe held behind him, he
stands in meditative attitude, in his old rice-straw sandals, run down and out
at the heels, his well-worn cotton coat, darned crosswise for durability and
economy, wondering whether he will see a full crop before he dies, or whether
he can pay his taxes, and fill his children's mouths with rice. The writing at
side is a proverb which has two meanings: it may be read, "A new field gives a
small crop," or "Human life is but fifty years." In either case, it has pregnant
significance to the farmer. The pathos and humor are irresistible to one who
knows the life of these sons of toil.

than the autochthons of Greece gloried in their native soil. The existence of this feeling of superiority to all mankind among some of the highest officials under the present mikado's government has been the cause of bitter quarrels, leading almost to civil war. Under the altered circumstances of the national life since 1868, the officials of ancient lineage, either unable to conceal, or desirous of manifesting their pride of birth, have on various occasions stung to rage the rising young men who have reached power by sheer force of merit. Between these self-made men, whose minds have been expanded by contact with the outer world, and the high nobles nursed in the atmosphere of immemorial antiquity, and claiming descent from the gods, an estrangement that at times seems irreconcilable has grown. As the chasm between the forms and spirit of the past and the present widens, as the modern claims jostle the ancient traditions, as vigorous parvenuism challenges effete antiquity, the difficulty of harmonizing these tendencies becomes apparent, adding another to the catalogue of problems awaiting solution in Japan. I have heard even high officers under the Government make the complaint I have indicated against their superiors; but I doubt not that native patience and patriotism will heal the wound, though the body politic must suffer long.

The *kugé*, or court nobles, sprung from mikados. From the first, polygamy was common among both aborigines and conquerors. The emperor had his harem of many beauties who shared his couch. In very ancient times, as early as Jimmu, it was the custom to choose one woman, called kôgô, who was wife or empress in the sense of receiving special honor, and of having her offspring most likely to succeed to the throne. In addition to the wife, the mikado had twelve concubines, whose offspring might fill the throne in case of failure of issue by the wife. To guard still further against desinence, four families of imperial descent were afterward set apart, from which an heir to the throne or a husband of the mikado's daughter might be sought. In either case the chosen one became mikado. Only those sons, brothers, or grandsons of the sovereign, to whom the title was specially granted by patent, were called princes of the blood. There were five grades of these. Surnames were anciently unknown in Japan; individuals only having distinguishing appellatives. In 415, families were first distinguished by special names, usually after those of places. Younger sons of mikados took surnames and founded cadet families. The most famous in the Japanese peerage are given below. By long custom it came to pass that each particular family held the monopoly of some one high office as its prerogative. The Nakatomi family was formerly charged with the ceremonies of Shintô, and religious offices became hereditary in that family. The Fujiwara (Wistaria meadow) family is the most illustrious in all Japan. It was founded by Kamatari, who was regent of the empire (A.D. 645–649), who was said to have been descended from Amé no ko yané no mikoto, the servant of the grandfather of Jimmu. The influence of this family on the destinies of Japan, and the prominent part it has played in history, will be fully seen. At present ninety-five of the one hundred and fifty-five families of *kugé* are of Fujiwara name and descent. The office of Kuambaku, or Regent, the highest to which a subject could attain, was held by members of this family exclusively. The Sugawara family, of which six families of *kugé* are descendants, is nearly as old as the Fujiwara. Its members have been noted for scholarship and learning, and as teachers and lecturers on religion.

The Taira family was founded by Takamochi, great grandson of the Emperor Kuammu (A.D. 782–805), and became prominent as the great military vassals of the mikado. But five *kugé* families claim descent from the survivors.

The Minamoto family was founded by Tsunémoto, grandson of the Emperor Seiwa (839–880). They were the rivals of the Taira. Seventeen families of *kugé* are descended from this old stock. The office of Sei-i

Tai Shôgun, or Barbarian-chastising Great General, was monopolized by the Minamoto, and, later, by other branches of the stock, named Ashikaga and Tokugawa.

Though so many offices were created in the seventh century, the *kugé* were sufficiently numerous to fill them. The members of the Fujiwara family gradually absorbed the majority, until almost all of the important ones at court, and the governorships of many provinces, were filled by them. When vacancies occurred, no question was raised as to this or that man's fitness for the position: it was simply one of high descent, and a man of Fujiwara blood was sure to get the appointment, whether he had abilities or not. This family, in spite of its illustrious name and deeds, are to be credited with the formation of a "ring" around the mikado, which his people could not break, and with the creation of one of the most accursed systems of nepotism ever seen in any country. Proceeding step by step, with craft and signal ability, they gradually obtained the administration of the government in the mikado's name. Formerly it had been the privilege of every subject to petition the sovereign. The Fujiwara ministers gradually assumed the right to open all such petitions, and decide upon them. They also secured the appointment of younger sons, brothers, nephews, and kinsmen to all the important positions. They based their hold on the throne itself by marrying their daughters to the mikado, whose will was thus bent to their own designs. For centuries the empresses were chiefly of Fujiwara blood. In this way, having completely isolated the sovereign, they became the virtual rulers of the country and the proprietors of the throne, and dictated as to who should be made emperor. Every new office, as fast as created, was filled by them. In the year 888, the title of Kuambaku (literally, "the bolt inside the gate," but meaning "to represent to the mikado") was first used and bestowed on a Fujiwara noble. The Kuambaku was the highest subject in the empire. He was regent during the minority of the emperor, or when an empress filled the throne. The office of Kuambaku, first filled by Fujiwara Mototsuné, became hereditary in the family, thus making them all powerful. In time the Fujiwaras, who had increased to the proportions of a great clan, were divided into five branches called the Sekké, or Regent families, named Konoyé, Kujô, Nijô, Ichijô and Takadzukasa.

So long as the succession to the throne was so indefinite, and on such a wide basis, it was easy for this powerful family to choose the heir whenever the throne was empty, as it was in their power to make it empty when it so suited them, by compelling the mikado to abdicate.

In A.D. 794 the capital was removed to Kiôto, seven miles from Lake Biwa, and there permanently located. Before that time it was at Kashiwabara, at Nara,* or at some place in the Home Provinces (*kinai*) of Yamato, Yamashiro, or Settsu. So long as the course of empire was identified with that of a central military chief, who was the ruler of a few provinces and suzerain of tributaries, requiring him

---

* The ancient town of Nara, one of the most interesting in all Japan, lies about twenty miles due east of Ôzaka, in Yamato. The town and neighborhood abound with antiquities, mikado's tombs, grand old temples, and colossal images of Buddha. Seven sovereigns, of whom four were females, ruled at Nara from A.D. 708–782. Their reigns were prosperous and glorious, and were distinguished for the cultivation of the arts, literature, and religion. Here, in 711, the *Kojiki* was written and in 713, by orders of the imperial court, sent to all the governors of provinces; a book, in sixty-six volumes, descriptive of the provinces, cities, mountains, rivers, valleys, and plains, plants, trees, birds, and quadrupeds, was begun, and finished in 1634. Only fragments of this fine work are now extant. In the period 708–715 copper was discovered. In 739, the colossal gilded copper image of Buddha, fifty-three feet high, was cast and set up. Many envoys from China, and Buddhist priests from Siam, India, and China, visited Nara, one of the latter bringing a library of five thousand volumes of Buddhist literature. In 749 it was forbidden by imperial edict to slaughter animals in Japan. A large collection of the personal and household articles in the possession of the mikados of the eighth century was exhibited at Nara in June, 1875, the inventories made at that ancient period being accessible for comparison.

to be often in camp or on the march, government was by the sword rather than by the sceptre, and the permanent location of a capital was unnecessary. As the area of dominion increased and became more settled the government business grew apace, in amount and complexity, and division of labor was imperative, and a permanent capital was of prime importance. The choice was most felicitous. The ancient city of Heianjô, seven miles south-west of the southern end of Lake Biwa, was chosen. The Japanese word meaning capital, or large city, is *miako*, of which *kiô* or *kiôto* is the Chinese equivalent. The name Heianjo soon fell into disuse, the people speaking of the city as the miako. Even this term gave way in popular usage to Kiôto. Miako is now chiefly used in poetry, while the name most generally applied has been and is Kiôto, the *miako* by excellence. Kiôto remained the capital of Japan until 1868, when the miako was removed to Yedo, which city having become the kio, was renamed Tôkiô, or Eastern capital. The name Yedo is no longer in use among the Japanese. No more eligible site could have been chosen for the purpose. Kiôto lies not mathematically, but geographically and practically in respect of the distribution of population and habitable area, in the centre of Japan. It is nearly in the middle of the narrowest neck of land between the Sea of Japan and the Pacific Ocean. It lies at the foot, and stands like a gate between the great mountain ranges, diverging north and south, or east and west. Its situation at the base of the great central lake of Biwa, or Ômi, forty miles from whose northern point is the harbor and sea-port of Tsuruga, makes it accessible to the ships coming from the entire west coast and from Yezo. On the west and east the natural mountain roads and passes slope down and open toward it. Forty miles to the south are the great harbors lining the bay of Ôzaka, the haven of all ships from northern or southern points of the eastern coast. Easy river communications connect Ôzaka with Kiôto.

The miako is beautiful for situation, the joy of the whole empire of Japan. The tone of reverential tenderness, of exulting joy, the sparkling of the eyes with which Japanese invariably speak of Kiôto, witness to the fact of its natural beauty, its sacred and classic associations, and its place in the affections of the people. The city stands on an elliptical plain walled in on all sides by evergreen hills and mountains, like the floor of a huge flattened crater no longer choked with lava, but mantled with flowers. On the south the river Kamo, and on the north, east, and west, flowing in crystal clearness, the affluents of Kamo curve around the city, nearly encircle it, uniting at the south-west to form the Yodo River. Through the centre and in several of the streets the branches of the river flow, giving a feeling of grateful coolness in the heats of summer, and is the source of the cleanliness characteristic of Kiôto. The streets run parallel and cross at right angles, and the whole plan of the city is excellent. The mikado's palace is situated in the north-eastern quarter. Art and nature are wedded in beauty. The monotony of the clean squares is broken by numerous groves, temples, monasteries, and cemeteries. On the mountain overlooking the city peep out pagodas and shrines. The hill-slopes blossom with gardens. The suburbs are places of delight and loveliness. The blue Lake of Biwa, the tea-plantations of Uji, the thousand chosen resorts of picnic groups in the adjacent shady hills, the resorts for ramblers the leafy walks for the poet, the groves for the meditative student or the pious monk, the thousand historical and holy associations invest Kiôto with an interest attaching to no other place in Japan. Here, or in its vicinity, have dwelt for seventeen centuries the mikados of Japan.

As the children and descendants of the mikados increased at the capital there was formed the material for classes of nobility. It was to the interest of these nobles to cherish with pride their traditions of divine descent. Their studied exaltation of the mikado as their head was the natural consequence. The respect and deference of distant tributary princes wishing to obtain and preserve favor at court served only to increase the honor of these nobles of the capital. The fealty of the distant princes was measured not only by their tribute and military assistance, but by their close conformity to the customs of the miako, which naturally became the centre of learning and civilization.

Previous to the era of Sûjin, the observance of the time of beginning the new year, as well as the celebration of the sacred festivals to the gods, was not the same throughout the provinces. The acceptance of a uniform calendar promulgated from the capital was then, as now, a sign of loyalty of far greater significance than would appear to us at first sight. This was forcibly shown in Yokohama, as late as 1872, after the mikado had abolished the lunar, and ordered the use of the solar, or Gregorian, calendar in his dominions. The resident Chinese, in an incendiary document, which was audaciously posted on the gates of the Japanese magistrate's office, denounced the Japanese for having thus signified, by the adoption of the barbarians' time, that they had yielded themselves up to be the slaves of the "foreign devils."

The mikado has no family name. He needs none, because his dynasty never changes. Being above ordinary mortals, no name is necessary to distinguish him from men. He need be personally distinguished only from the gods. When he dies, he will enter the company of the gods. He is deified under some name, with Tennô (son, or king, of heaven) affixed. It was not proper (until 1872, when the custom was abrogated) for ordinary people to pronounce the name of the living mikado aloud, or to write it in full: a stroke should be left out of each of the characters.

Previous to the general use of Chinese writing, the mikados, about fifty in all, had long names ending in "mikoto," a term of respect equivalent to "augustness," and quite similar to those applied to the gods. These extremely long names, now so unmanageable to foreign, and even to modern native, tongues, gave place in popular use to the greatly abbreviated Chinese equivalents. A complete calendar of the names of the gods and goddesses, mikados and empresses and heroes, was made out in Chinese characters. It is so much more convenient to use these, that I have inserted them in the text, even though to do so seems in many an instance an anachronism. The difference in learned length and thundering sound of the Japanese and the Chinese form of some of these names will be easily seen and fully appreciated after a glance, by the Occidental reader who is terrified at the uncouthness of both, or who fears to trust his vocal organs to attempt their pronunciation. Amaterasu ô mikami becomes Ten Shô Dai Jin; Okinaga Tarashi Himé becomes Jingu Kôgô.

After the Chinese writing became fashionable, the term mikoto was dropped. The mikados after death received a different name from that used when living: thus Kan Yamato Iware hiko no mikoto became, posthumously, Jimmu Tenno.

The Golden Age of the mikado's power ceased after the introduction of Buddhism and the Chinese system of officialdom. The decadence of his personal power began, and steadily continued. Many of the high ministers at court became Buddhists, as well as the mikados. It now began to be a custom for the emperors to abdicate after short reigns, shave off their hair in token of renunciation of the world, become monks, and retire from active life, taking the title Hô-ô (*ho*, law of Buddha; *ô*, mikado = cloistered emperor). During the eighth century, while priests were multiplying, and monasteries were everywhere being established, the court was the chief propaganda. The courtiers vied with each other in holy zeal and study of the sacred books of India, while the minds of the empresses and boy-emperors were occupied with schemes for the advancement of Buddhism. In 741, the erection of two great temples, and of a seven-storied pagoda in each province, was ordered. The abdication after short reigns made the mikados mere puppets of the ministers and courtiers. Instead of warriors braving discomforts of the camp, leading armies in battle, or fighting savages, the chief rulers of the empire abdicated, after short reigns, to retire into monasteries, or give themselves up to license. This evil state of affairs continued, until, in later centuries, effeminate men, steeped in sensual delights, or silly boys, who droned away their lives in empty pomp and idle luxury, or became the tools of monks, filled the throne. Meanwhile the administration of the empire from the capital declined, while the influence of the military classes increased. As the mikado's actual power grew weaker, his nominal importance increased. He was surrounded by a hedge of etiquette that secluded him from the outer world. He never appeared in public. His subjects, except his wife and concubines and highest ministers, never saw his face. He sat on a throne of mats behind a curtain. His feet were never allowed to touch the earth. When he went abroad in the city, he rode in a car closely curtained, and drawn by bullocks. The relation of emperor and subject thus grew mythical, and the way was paved for some bold usurper to seize the actuality of power, while the name remained sacred and inviolate.

# XII

# *The Beginning of Military Domination*

With rank, place, and power as the prizes, there were not wanting rival contestants to dispute the monopoly of the Fujiwara. The prosperity and domineering pride of the scions of this ancient house, instead of overawing those of younger families that were forming in the capital, served only as spurs to their pride and determination to share the highest gifts of the sovereign. It may be easily supposed that the Fujiwara did not attain the summit of their power without the sacrifice of many a rival aspirant. The looseness of the marriage tie, the intensity of ambition, the greatness of the prize—he throne itself—made the court ever the fruitful soil of intrigue, jealousies, proscription, and even the use of poison and the dagger. The fate of many a noble victim thus sacrificed on the altars of jealousy and revenge forms the subject of the most pathetic passages of the Japanese historians, and the tear-compelling scenes of the romance and the drama. The increase of families was the increase of feuds. Arrogance and pride were matched by craft and subtlety that finally led to quarrels which rent the nation, to civil war, and to the almost utter extinction of one of the great families.

The Sugawara were the most ancient rivals of the Fujiwara. The most illustrious victim of court intrigue bearing this name was Sugawara Michizané. This polished courtier, the Beauclerc of his age, had, by the force of his talents and learning, risen to the position of inner great minister. As a scholar, he ranked among the highest of his age. At different periods of his life he wrote, or compiled, from the oldest records various histories, some of which are still extant. His industry and ability did not, however, exempt him from the jealous annoyances of the Fujiwara courtiers, who imbittered his life by poisoning the minds of the emperor and courtiers against him. One of them, Tokihira, secured an edict banishing him to Kiushiu. Here, in the horrors of poverty and exile, he endeavored to get a petition to the mikado, but failed to do so, and starved to death, on the 25th day of the Second month, 903. Michizané is now known by his posthumous name of Tenjin. Many temples have been erected in his honor, and students worship his spirit, as the patron god of letters and literature. Children at school pray to him that they may become good writers, and win success in study. Some of his descendants are still living.

When Michizané died, the Sugawara were no longer to be dreaded as a rival family. Another brood were springing up, who were destined to become the most formidable rivals of the Fujiwara. More than a century before, one of the concubines, or extra wives, of the Emperor Kuammu had borne a son, who, having talents as well as imperial blood, rose to be head of the Board of Civil Office, and master of court ceremonies—an office similar to the lord high chamberlain of England.* To his grandson Takamochi was given the surname of Taira in 889—one hundred and one years before the banishment of Michizané.

The civil offices being already monopolized by the Fujiwara, the members of the family of Taira early showed a fondness and special,

---

* Princes of the blood were eligible to the following offices: Minister of the imperial household, lord high chamberlain, minister of war, president, of the censorate, and the governorships of Kôdzuké, Kadzusa, and Hitachi. The actual duties of the office were, however, performed by inferior officials.

fitness for military life, which, with their experience, made them most eligible to the commands of military expeditions. The Fujiwara had become wholly wedded to palace life, and preferred the ease and luxury of the court to the discomforts of the camp and the dangers of the battle-field. Hence the shoguns, or generals, were invariably appointed among sons of the Taira or the Minamoto, both of which families became the military vassals of the crown. While the men led the armies, fought the foe, and returned in triumph, the mothers at home fired the minds of their sons with the recital of the deeds of their fathers. Thus bred to arms, inured to war, and living chiefly in the camp, a hardy race of warriors grew up and formed the military caste. So long as the Taira or Minamoto leaders were content with war and its glory, there was no reason for the Fujiwara to fear danger from them as rivals at court. But in times of peace and inaction, the minds of these men of war longed to share in the spoils of peace; or, having no more enemies to conquer, their energies were turned against their fellows. The peculiar basis of the imperial succession opened an equally wide field for the play of female ambition; and while Taira and Minamoto generals lusted after the high offices held by Fujiwara courtiers, Taira and Minamoto ladies aspired to become empresses, or at least imperial concubines, where they might, for the glory of their family, beard the dragon of power in his own den. They had so far increased in influence at court, that in 1008, the wife of the boy-emperor, Ichijô, was chosen from the house of Minamoto.

The Minamoto family, or, as the Chinese characters express the name, Genji, was founded by Tsunémoto, the grandson of Seiwa (859–880) and son of the minister of war. His great-grandson Yoriyoshi became a shôgun, and was sent to fight the Ainôs; and the half-breeds, or rebels of mixed Ainô and Japanese blood, in the east and extreme north of Hondo. Yoriyoshi's son, Yoshiiyé, followed an his father in arms, and was likewise made a shôgun. So terrible was Yoshiiyé in battle that he was called Hachiman Tarô. The name Tarô is given to the first-born son. Hachiman is the Buddhist form of Ôjin, the deified son of Jingu Kôgô, and the patron of warriors, or god of war. After long years of fighting, he completely tranquilized the provinces of the Kuantô. His great-grandson Yoshitomo* became the greatest rival of the Taira, and the father of Yoritomo, one of the ablest men in Japanese history. The star of Minamoto was in the ascendant.

Meanwhile the Taira shôguns, who had the military oversight of the South and West, achieved a succession of brilliant victories. As a reward for his services, the court bestowed the island of Tsushima on Tadamori, the head of the house. It being a time of peace, Tadamori came to Kiôto to live, and while at court had a *liaison* with one of the palace lady attendants, whom he afterward married. The fruit of this union was a son, who grew to be a man of stout physique. In boyhood he gave equal indications of his future greatness and his future arrogance. He wore unusually high clogs—the Japanese equivalent

---

* The family name (*uji*) precedes the personal, or what we call the baptismal or Christian name. Thus the full name of the boy Kotarô, son of Mr. Ota, would be Ota Kotarô. Family names nearly always have a topographical meaning, having been taken from names of streets, villages, districts, rivers, mountains, etc. The following are specimens, taken from the register of my students in the Imperial College in Tôkiô, many of whom are descendants of the illustrious personages mentioned in this book, or in Japanese history. The great bulk of the Samurai claim descent from less than a hundred original families: Plain-village, Crane-slope, Hill-village, Middle-mountain, Mountain-foot, Grove-entrance, High-bridge, East-river, River-point, Garden-mountain, River-meadow, Pine-village, Great-tree, Pine-well, Shrine-promontory, Cherry-well, Cedar-bay, Lower-field, Stone-pine, Front-field, Bamboo-bridge, Large-island, Happy-field, Shrine-plain, Temple-island, Hand-island, North-village, etc., etc. It was not the custom to have godparents, or name-sakes, in our sense of these words. Middle names were not given or used, each person having but a family and a personal name. Neither could there be a senior and junior of exactly the same name in the same family, as with us. The father usually bestowed on his son half of his name; that is, he gave him one of the Chinese characters with which his own was written. Thus,

for "riding a high horse." His fellows gave the strutting roisterer the nickname of *kohéda* ("high clogs"). Being the son of a soldier, he had abundant opportunity to display his valor. At this time the seas swarmed with pirates, who ravaged the coasts and were the scourge of Corea as well as Japan. Kiyomori, a boy full of fire and energy, thirsting for fame, asked to be sent against the pirates. At the age of eighteen he cruised in the Sea of Iyo, or the Suwo Nada, which is part of the Inland Sea, a sheet of water extremely beautiful in itself, and worthy, in a high degree, to be called the Mediterranean of Japan. While on shipboard, he made himself a name by attacking and capturing a ship full of the most desperate villains, and by destroying their lurking-place. His early manhood was spent alternately in the capital and in service in the South. In 1153, at the age of thirty-six, he succeeded his father as minister of justice. The two families of Minamoto and Taira, who had together emerged from comparative obscurity to fame, place, and honor, had dwelt peacefully together in Kiôto, or had been friendly rivals as soldiers in a common cause on distant battle-fields, until the year 1156, from which time they became

---

Yoriyoshi named his first-born son Yoshiiyé, *i.e.*, Yoshi (*good*) and iyé (*house* or *family*). Yoshiiye had six sons, named, respectively, Yoshimune, Yoshichika, Yoshikuni, Yoshitada, Yoshitoki, and Yoshitaka. The Taira nobles retained the *mori* in Tadamori, in their own personal names. Female names were borrowed from those of beautiful and attractive objects or of auspicious omens, and were usually not changed at marriage or throughout life. Males made use during life of a number of appellations given them, or assumed on the occasions of birth, reaching adult age, official promotion, change of life; or on account of special events, entering a monastery, and after death. This custom as a police measure, as well as for other reasons, was abolished in 1872. Often a superior rewarded an inferior by bestowing upon him a new name, or by allowing him to incorporate one of the syllables expressed vividly to the eye by a Chinese character, of the superior's name. It was never the custom to name children after great men, as we do after our national heroes. Formerly the genitive particle *no* (of) was used; as Minamoto no Yoritomo means Yoritomo of the Minamoto family. In 1872, the peasantry were allowed to have family as well as individual names.

implacable enemies. In that year the first battle was fought between the adherents of two rival claimants of the throne. The Taira party was successful, and obtained possession of the imperial palace, which gave them the supreme advantage and prestige which have ever since been possessed by the leader or party in whose hands the mikado is. The whole administration of the empire was now at Kiyomori's disposal. The emperor, who thus owed his elevation to the Taira, made them the executors of his policy. This was the beginning of the domination of the military classes that lasted until 1868. The ambition of Kiyomori was now not only to advance himself to the highest position possible for a subject to occupy, but also to raise the influence and power of his family to the highest pitch. He further determined to exterminate the only rivals whom he feared—the Minamoto. Not content with exercising the military power, he filled the offices at court with his own relatives, carrying the policy of nepotism to a point equal to that of his rivals, the Fujiwara. In 1167, at the age of fifty years, having, by his energy and cunning, made himself the military chief of the empire, having crushed not only the enemies of the imperial court, but also his own, and having tremendous influence with the emperor and court, he received the appointment of Dai Jô Dai Jin.

Kiyomori was thus, virtually, the ruler of Japan. In all his measures he was assisted, if not often instigated to originate them by the ex-emperor, Go-Shirakawa, who ascended the throne in 1156, and abdicated in 1159, but was the chief manager of affairs during the reigns of his son and two grandsons. This mikado was a very immoral man, and the evident reason of his resigning was that he might abandon himself to debauchery, and wield even more actual power than when on the throne. In 1169, he abdicated, shaved off his hair, and took the title of Hô-ô, or "cloistered emperor," and became a Buddhist monk, professing to retire from the world. In industrious seclusion, he granted the ranks and titles created by his predecessor in lavish profusion. He thus exercised, as a monk, even more influence than when in actual office. The head of the Taira hesitated not to use all these rewards for his own and his family's private ends. In him several offices were held by one person. He argued that as others who had done no great services for court or emperor had held high offices, he who had done so much should get all he could. Finally, neither court nor emperor could control him, and he banished *kugé*, and even moved the capital and court at his pleasure. In 1168, the power of the Taira family was paramount. Sixty men of the house held high offices at court, and the lands from which they enjoyed revenue extended over thirty provinces. They had splendid palaces in Kiôto and at Fukuwara, where the modern treaty-port of Hiôgo now stands overlooking the splendid scenery of the Inland Sea. Hesitating at nothing that would add to his glory or power, Kiyomori, in 1171, imitating his predecessors, made his daughter the concubine, and afterward the wife, of the Emperor Takakura, a boy eleven years old. Of his children one was now empress, and his two sons were generals of highest rank. His cup of power was full.

The fortunes of the Fujiwara and Minamoto were under hopeless eclipse, the former having no military power, the latter being scattered in exile. Yoshitomo, his rival, had been killed, while in his bath, by Osada, his own traitorous retainer, who was bribed by Kiyomori to do the deed. The head of Yoshitomo's eldest son had fallen under the sword at Kiôto, and his younger sons—the last of the Minamoto, as he supposed—were in banishment, or immured in monasteries.

The most famous archer, Minamoto Tamétomo, took part in many of the struggles of the two rival families. His great strength, equal to that of many men (fifty, according to the legends), and the fact that his right arm was shorter than his left, enabled him to draw a bow which four ordinary warriors could not bend, and send a shaft five feet long, with enormous bolt-head. The court, influenced by the Taira, banished him, in a cage, to Idzu (after cutting the muscles of his arm), under a guard. He escaped, and fled to the islands of Ôshima and Hachijô, and the chain south of the Bay of Yedo. His arm having healed, he ruled over the people, ordering them not to send tribute to Idzu or Kiôto. A fleet of boats was sent against him. Tamétomo, on the strand of Ôshima, sped a shaft at one of the approaching vessels that pierced the thin gunwale and sunk it. He then, after a shout of defiance, shut himself up, set the house on fire, and killed himself. Another account declares that he fled to the Liu Kiu Islands, ruled over them, and founded the family of Liu Kiu kings, being the father of Sunten, the first historical ruler of this group of islands. A picture of this doughty warrior has been chosen to adorn the greenback currency of the banks of modern Japan.

"Woe unto thee, O land, when thy king is a child!" The mikados* during the Taira period were nearly all children. Toba began to reign

* For convenience of reference, the following chronological list of the sovereigns of Japan is here appended. It is based on the list given in the *Nihon Riyaku Shi* (Abridgment of Japanese History), Tôkiô, 1874—a book from which I have drawn freely in this work. The dates of their reigns, in terms of the Gregorian calendar, are obtained chiefly from a comparative almanac of Chinese, Japanese, and Western dates, compiled by a learned native scholar, who brings down this invaluable chronological harmony to the third day of the Twelfth month of Meiji (January 1st, 1874), when the solar or Gregorian calendar was adopted in Japan. The year dates approximate to within a few weeks of exactness. The names in italics denote female sovereigns. In two instances (37 and 39, 48 and 50), one empress reigned twice, and has two posthumous titles. I have put the name of Jingu Kôgô in the list, though the *Dai Nihon Shi* does not admit it, she having never been crowned or formally declared empress by investiture with the regalia of sovereignty. In several cases the duration of the reign was lees than a year. The five "false emperors," printed in black spaces, are omitted from this list. Only the posthumous titles under which the mikados were apotheosized are here given, though their living names, and those of their parents, are printed in the *Nihon Riyaku Shi*. Including Jingu, there were 123 sovereigns. The average length of the reigns of 122 was nearly twenty-one years. There has been but one dynasty in Japan. In comparison, the present emperor of China is the 273d, and the dynasty the 23d or 24th.

at six, abdicating at seventeen in behalf of his son Shiutoku, four years old; who at twenty-four resigned in favor of Konoyé, then four years old. The latter died at the age of sixteen, and was succeeded by Go-Shirakawa, who abdicated after three years in favor of Nijô, sixteen years old, who died after six years, when Rokujô, one year old, succeeded. After three years, Takakura, eight years old, ruled thirteen years, resigning to Antoku, then three years of age. It is easily seen that the real power lay not with these boys and babies, but with the august wire-pullers behind the throne.

The *Heiké Monogatari*, or the "Historic Romance of the Taira," is one of the most popular of the many classic works of fiction read by all classes of people in Japan. In this book the chief events in the lives, and even the manners and personal appearance, of the principal actors of the times of the Taira are seen, so that they become more than shadows of names, and seem to live before us, men of yesterday. The terms Heiké and Genji, though Chinese forms of the names Taira and Minamoto, were, from their brevity, popularly used in preference to the pure native, but longer, forms of Taira and Minamoto.

---

Chronological List of Japanese Emperors

| Posthumous Title (Age at Death) | Date of Reign | Posthumous Title (Age at Death) | Date of Reign |
|---|---|---|---|
| 1. Jimmu (127) | B.C. 660–585 | 10. Sûjin (119) | 97–30 |
| 2. Suisei (84) | 581–549 | 11. Suinin (141) | 29 B.C.–70 A.D. |
| 3. Annei (57) | 548–511 | 12. Keikô (143) | 71–130 |
| 4. Itoku (77) | 510–477 | 13. Seimu (108) | 131–191 |
| 5. Kôshô (114) | 475–393 | 14. Chiuai (52) | 192–200 |
| 6. Kôan (137) | 392–291 | 15. Jingu Kôgô (100) | 201–269 |
| 7. Kôrei (128) | 290–215 | 16. Ojin (111) | 270–310 |
| 8. Kôgen (116) | 214–158 | 17. Nintoku (110) | 313–399 |
| 9. Kuaika (115) | 157–98 | 18. Richiu (77) | 400–405 |

| Posthumous Title (Age at Death) | Date of Reign | Posthumous Title (Age at Death) | Date of Reign |
|---|---|---|---|
| 19. Hanshô (60) | 406–411 | 58. Yôzei (82) | 877-884 |
| 20. Inkiô (80) | 412–453 | 59. Kôkô (58) | 885-887 |
| 21. Ankô (50) | 454–456 | 60. Uda (65) | 888-897 |
| 22. Yuriyaku (62) | 457–479 | 61. Daigo (46) | 898-930 |
| 23. Seinei (41) | 480–484 | 62. Shunjaku (30) | 931-946 |
| 24. Kensô (38) | 485–487 | 63. Murakami (42) | 947-967 |
| 25. Ninken (51) | 488–498 | 64. Reizei (62) | 968-969 |
| 26. Buretsu (57) | 499–506 | 65. Enniu (33) | 970-984 |
| 27. Keitai (82) | 507–531 | 66. Kuasan (41) | 985-986 |
| 28. Ankan (70) | 534–535 | 67. Ichijô (32) | 987-1011 |
| 29. Senkua (73) | 536–539 | 68. Sanjô (43) | 1012-1016 |
| 30. Kimmei (63) | 540–571 | 69. Go-Ichijô (29) | 1017-1036 |
| 31. Bidatsu (48) | 572–585 | 70. Go-Shujaku (37) | 1037-1046 |
| 32. Yômei (69) | 586–587 | 71. Go-Reizei (44) | 1047-1068 |
| 33. Sujun (73) | 588–592 | 72. Go-Sanjô (40) | 1069-1072 |
| 34. *Suiko* (75) | 593–628 | 73. Shirakawa (77) | 1073-1086 |
| 35. Jomei (49) | 629–641 | 74. Horikawa (29) | 1087-1107 |
| 36. *Kôgioku* (68) | 642–644 | 75. Toba (55) | 1108-1123 |
| 37. Kôtoku (59) | 645–654 | 76. Shiutoku (46) | 1124-1141 |
| 38. *Saimei* (..) | 655–661 | 77. Konoyé (17) | 1142-1155 |
| 39. Tenchi (58) | 668–672 | 78. Go-Shirakawa (66) | 1156-1158 |
| 40. Kôbun (25) | 672–672 | 79. Nijô (23) | 1159-1165 |
| 41. Temmu (65) | 673–686 | 80. Rokujô (13) | 1166-1168 |
| 42. *Jitô* (58) | 690–696 | 81. Takakura (21) | 1169-1180 |
| 43. Mommu (25) | 697–707 | 82. Antoku (8) | 1181-1185 |
| 44. *Gemmiô* (61) | 708–714 | 83. Go-Toba (60) | 1184-1198 |
| 45. *Genshô* (69) | 715–723 | 84. Tsuchimikado (37) | 1199-1210 |
| 46. Shômu (56) | 724–748 | 85. Juntoku (46) | 1211-1221 |
| 47. *Kôken* (53) | 749–758 | 86. Chiukiô (17) | 1222-1222 |
| 48. Junnin (33) | 759–764 | 87. Go-Horikawa (23) | 1222-1232 |
| 49. *Shôtoku* (..) | 765–769 | 88. Shijô (12) | 1233-1242 |
| 50. Kônin (73) | 770–781 | 89. Go-Saga (53) | 1243-1246 |
| 51. Kuammu (70) | 782–805 | 90. Go-Fukakusa (62) | 1247-1259 |
| 52. Heijô (51) | 806–809 | 91. Kaméyama (57) | 1260-1274 |
| 53. Saga (57) | 810-823 | 92. Go-Uda (58) | 1275-1287 |
| 54. Junwa (55) | 824–833 | 93. Fushimi (53) | 1288-1298 |
| 55. Nimmiô (41) | 834–850 | 94. Go-Fushimi (49) | 1299-1301 |
| 56. Montoku (32) | 851–858 | 95. Go-Nijô (24) | 1302-1307 |
| 57. Seiwa (31) | 859–876 | 96. Hanazono (52) | 1308-1318 |

| Posthumous Title (Age at Death) | Date of Reign | Posthumous Title (Age at Death) | Date of Reign |
|---|---|---|---|
| 97. Go-Daigo (52) | 1319-1338 | 110. *Miôjô* (74) | 1630-1643 |
| 98. Go-Murakami (41) | 1339-1367 | 111. Go-Kômiô (22) | 1644-1654 |
| 99. Chôkei (..) | 1368-1383 | 112. Gosai (49) | 1655-1662 |
| 100. Go-Kaméyama (78) | 1383-1392 | 113. Reigen (79) | 1663-1686 |
| 101. Go-Komatsu (57) | 1393-1412 | 114. Higashiyama (35) | 1687-1709 |
| 102. Shôkô (28) | 1413-1428 | 115. Nakanomikado (37) | 1710-1735 |
| 103. Go-Hanazono (52) | 1429-1464 | 116. Sakuramachi (31) | 1736-1746 |
| 104. Go-Tsuchimikado (59) | 1465-1500 | 117. Momozono (22) | 1747-1762 |
| 105. Go-Kashiwara (63) | 1501-1526 | 118. *Go-Sakuramachi* (74) | 1763-1770 |
| 106. Go-Nara (62) | 1527-1557 | 119. Go-Momozono (22) | 1747-1762 |
| 107. Ôgimachi (75) | 1558-1586 | 120. Kokaku (70) | 1780-1816 |
| 108. Go-Yôzei (47) | 1587-1611 | 121. Ninkô (47) | 1817-1846 |
| 109. Go-Miwo (85) | 1612-1629 | 122. Kômei (37) | 1847-1866 |
| | | 123. Mutsuhito (..) | 1867 |

# XIII

# *Yoritomo and the Minamoto Family*

Next to portraying the beauties of nature, there is no class of subjects in which the native artists delight more than in the historical events related in their classics. Among these there are none treated with more frequency and spirit than the flight of Yoshitomo's concubine, Tokiwa, after the death of her lord at the hands of bribed traitors. After the fight with the Taira in Kiôto, in 1159, he fled eastward, and was killed in a bath-room by three hired assassins at Utsumi, in Owari. Tokiwa was a young peasant-girl of surpassing beauty, whom Yoshitomo had made his concubine, and who bore him three children. She fled, to escape the minions of Taira. Her flight was in winter, and snow lay on the ground. She knew neither where to go nor how to subsist; but, clasping her babe to her bosom, her two little sons on her right, one holding his mother's hand, the other carrying his father's sword, trudged on. That babe at her breast was Yoshitsuné—a name that awakens in the breast of a Japanese youth emotions that kindle his enthusiasm to emulate a character that was the mirror of chivalrous valor and knightly conduct, and that saddens him at the thought of one who suffered cruel death at the hands of a jealous brother. Yoshitsuné, the youngest son of Yoshitomo, lives, and will live, immortal in the minds of Japanese youth as the Bayard of Japan.

Kiyomori, intoxicated with success, conceived the plan of exterminating the Minamoto family root and branch. Not knowing where Tokiwa and her children had fled, he seized her mother, and had her brought to Kiôto. In Japan, as in China, filial piety is the highest duty of man, filial affection the strongest tie. Kiyomori well knew that Tokiwa's sense of a daughter's duty would prevail over that of a mother's love or womanly fear. He expected Tokiwa to come to Kiôto to save her mother.

Meanwhile the daughter, nearly frozen and half starved, was met in her flight by a Taira soldier, who, pitying her and her children, gave her shelter, and fed her with his own rations. Tokiwa heard of her mother's durance at Kiôto. Then came the struggle between maternal and filial love. To enter the palace would be the salvation of her mother, but the death of her children. What should she do? Her wit showed her the way of escape. Her resolution was taken to go to the capital, and trust to her beauty to melt the heart of Kiyomori. Thus she would save her mother and the lives of her sons.

Her success was complete. Appearing in the presence of the dreaded enemy of her children, Kiyomori was dazed by her beauty, and wished to make her his concubine. At first she utterly refused; but her mother, weeping floods of tears, represented to her the misery of disobedience, and the happiness in store for her, and Tokiwa was obliged to yield. She consented on condition of his sparing her offspring.

Kiyomori's retainers insisted that these young Minamotos should be put to death; but by the pleadings of the beautiful mother, backed by the intercession of Kiyomori's aunt, their lives were spared. The babe grew to be a healthy, rosy-cheeked boy, small in stature, with a ruddy face and slightly protruding teeth. In spirit he was fiery and impetuous. All three of the boys, when grown, were sent to a monastery near Kiôto, to be made priests: their fine black hair was shaved, and they put on the robes of Buddhist neophytes. Two of them remained so, but Yoshitsuné gave little promise of becoming a grave and reverend bonze, who would honor his crape, and inspire respect by his bald crown and embroidered collar. He refused to have his hair shaved off, and in the monastery was irrepressibly merry, lively, and self-willed. The task of managing this young ox (Ushi-waka, he was then called) gave the holy brethren much trouble, and greatly scandalized their reverences. Yoshitsuné, chafing at his dull life, and longing to take part in a more active one, and especially in the wars in the North, of which he could not but hear, determined to escape. How to do it was the question.

Among the outside lay-folk who visited the monastery for trade or business was an iron-merchant, who made frequent journeys from Kiôto to the north of Hondo. In those days, as now, the mines of Oshiu were celebrated for yielding the best iron for swords and other cutting implements. This iron, being smelted from the magnetic oxide and reduced by the use of charcoal as fuel, gave a steel of singular purity and temper which has never been rivaled in modern times.

Yoshitsuné begged the merchant to take him to Mutsu. He, being afraid of offending the priest, would not at first consent. Yoshitsuné persuaded him by saying that the priests would be only too glad to be rid of such a troublesome boy. The point was won, and Yoshitsune went off. The boy's surmises were correct. The priest thought it excellent riddance to very bad rubbish.

While in the East, they stopped some time in Kadzusa, then infested with robbers. Here Yoshitsuné gave signal proof of his mettle. Among other exploits, he, on one occasion, single-handed and unarmed, seized a bold robber, and, on another, assisted a rich man to defend his house, killing five of the ruffians with his own hand. Yorishigé, his companion and bosom-friend, begged him not to indulge in any unnecessary displays of courage, lest the Taira would surely hear of him, and know he was a Minamoto, and so destroy him.

They finally reached their destination, and Yoshitsuné was taken to live with Hidéhira, a nobleman of the Fujiwara, who was prince of Mutsu. Here he grew to manhood, spending his time most congenially, in the chase, in manly sports, and in military exercises. At the age of twenty-one, he had won a reputation as a soldier of peerless valor and consummate skill, and the exponent of the loftiest code of Japanese chivalry. He became to Yoritomo, his brother, as Ney to Napoleon. Nor can the splendor of the marshal's courage outshine that of the young Japanese shogun's.

Yoritomo, the third son of Yoshitomo, was born in the year 1146, and consequently was twelve years old when his brother Yoshitsuné was a baby. After the defeat of his father, he, in the retreat, was separated from his companions, and finally fell into the hands of a Taira officer. On his way through a village called Awohaka, in Ômi, a girl, the child of the daughter of the head-man whom Yoshitomo had once loved, hearing this, said, "I will follow my brother and die with him." Her people stopped her as she was about to follow Yoshitomo, but she afterward went out alone and drowned herself. The Taira officer brought his prize to Kiôto, where his execution was ordered, and the day fixed; but there, again, woman's tender heart and supplications saved the life of one destined for greater things. The boy's captor had asked him if he would like to live. He answered, "Yes; both my father and brother are dead; who but I can pray for their happiness in the next world?" Struck by this filial answer, the officer went to Kiyomori's stepmother, who was a Buddhist nun, having become so after the death of her husband, Tadamori. Becoming interested in him, her heart was deeply touched; the chambers of her memory were unlocked when the officer said, "Yoritomo resembles Prince Uma." She had borne one son of great promise, on whom she had lavished her affection, and who had been named Uma. The mother's bosom heaved under the robes of the nun, and, pitying Yoritomo, she resolved to entreat Kiyomori to spare him. After importunate pleadings, the reluctant son yielded to his mother's prayer, but condemned the youth to distant exile—a punishment one degree less than death, and Yoritomo was banished to the province of Idzu. He was advised by his former retainers to shave off his hair, enter a monastery, and become a priest; but Morinaga, one of his faithful servants, advised him to keep his hair, and with a brave heart await the future. Even the few that still called themselves vassals of Minamoto did not dare to hold any communication with him, as he was under the charge of two officers who were responsible to the Taira for the care of their ward. Yoritomo was a shrewd, self-reliant boy, gifted with high self-control, restraining his feelings so as to express neither joy nor grief nor anger in his face, patient, and capable of great endurance, winning the love and respect of all. He was as "Prince Hal." He afterward became as "bluff King Harry," barring the latter's bad eminence as a marrier of many wives.

Such was the condition of the Minamoto family. No longer in power and place, with an empress and ministers at court, but scattered, in poverty and exile, their lives scarcely their own. Yoritomo was fortunate in his courtship and marriage, the story of which is one of great romantic interest.* His wife, Masago, is one of the many female characters famous in Japanese history. She contributed not a little to the success of her husband and the splendor of the Kamakura court,

---

* Yoritomo had inquired which of the daughters of Hôjô Tokimasa was most beautiful. He was told the eldest was most noted for personal charms, but the second, the child of a second wife, was homely. Yoritomo, afraid of a step-mother's jealousy (though fearing neither spear nor sword), deemed it prudent to pay his addresses to the homely daughter, and thus win the mother's favor also. He sent her a letter by the hand of Morinaga, his retainer, who, however, thought his master's affection for the plain girl would not lasts; so he destroyed his master's letter, and, writing another one to Masago, the eldest, sent it to her. It so happened that on the previous night the homely daughter dreamed that a pigeon came to her, carrying a golden box in her beak. On awaking,

during her life, as wife and widow. She outlived her husband many years. Her father, Hôjô Tokimasa, an able man, in whose veins ran imperial blood, made and fulfilled a solemn oath to assist Yoritomo, and the Hôjô family subsequently rose to be a leading one in Japan.

The tyranny and insolence of Kiyomori at Kiôto had by this time (1180), one year before his death, become so galling and outrageous that one of the royal princes, determining to kill the usurper, conspired with the Minamoto men to overthrow him. Letters were sent to the clansmen, and especially to Yoritomo, who wrote to Yoshitsuné and to his friends to join him and take up arms. Among the former retainers of his father and grandfather were many members of the Miura family. Morinaga personally secured the fealty of many men of mark in the Kuantô; but among those who refused to rise against the Taira was one, Tsunetoshi, who laughed scornfully, and said, "For an exile to plot against the Heishi [Taira] is like a mouse plotting against a cat."

At the head of the peninsula of Idzu is a range of mountains, the outjutting spurs of the chain that trends upward to the table-lands of Shinano, and thus divides Eastern from Western Japan. This range

---

she told her dream to her sister, who was so interested in it that, after eager consideration, she resolved "to buy her sister's dream," and, as a price, gave her toilet mirror to her sister, saying, as the Japanese always do on similar occasions, "The price I pay is little." The homely sister, perhaps thinking some of Masago's beauty might be reflected to hers, gladly bartered her unsubstantial happiness. Scarcely had she done this, than Yoritomo's (Morinaga's) letter came, asking her to be his bride. It turned out to be a true love-match. Masago was then twenty-one years of age—it being no ungallantry to state the age of a Japanese lady, living or dead. Masago's father, on his way home from Kiôto, not knowing of the betrothal of the young couple, promised Masago to Kanetaka, a Taira officer. On coming home, *he* would not break *his* word, and so married her to Kanétaka. But early on the wedding night Masago eloped with Yoritomo, who was at hand. Kanétaka searched in vain for the pair. Tokimasa outwardly professed to be very angry with Yoritomo, but really loved him.

is called Hakoné, and is famous not only as classic ground in history; but also as a casket enshrining the choicest gems of nature. It is well known to the foreign residents; who resort hither in summer to enjoy the pure air of its altitudes. Its inspiring scenery embraces a lake of intensely cold pure water, and of great depth and elevation above the sea-level, groves of aromatic pines of colossal size, savage gorges, sublime mountain heights, overcrowned by cloud-excelling Fuji, foaming cataracts, and boiling springs of intermittent and rhythmic flow, surrounded by infernal vistas of melted sulphur enveloped in clouds of poisonous steam, or incrusted with myriad glistening crystals of the same mineral. Over these mountains there is a narrow pass, which is the key of the Kuantô. Near the pass, above the village of Yumoto, is Ishi Bashi Yama (Stone-bridge Mountain), and here Yoritomo's second battle was fought, and his first defeat experienced. "Every time his bowstring twanged an enemy fell," but finally he was obliged to flee. He barely escaped with his life, and fortunately eluded pursuit, secreting himself in a hollow log, having first sent his father-in-law to call out all his retainers and meet again. He afterward hid in the priest's wardrobe, in one of the rooms of a temple. Finally, reaching the sea-shore, he took ship and sailed across the bay to Awa. "At this time the sea and land were covered with his enemies." Fortune favored the brave. Yoritomo, defeated, but not discouraged, while on the water met a company of soldiers, all equipped, belonging to the Miura clan, who became his friends, and offered to assist him. Landing in Awa, he sent out letters to all the Minamoto adherents to bring soldiers and join him. He met with encouraging and substantial response, for many hated Kiyomori and the Taira; and as Yoritomo's father and grandfather had given protection and secured quiet in the Kuantô, the prestige of the Minamoto party still remained. The local military chieftains had fought under Yoritomo's father, and were now glad to join the son of their old leader. He chose Kamakura as a place of retreat and permanent residence, it having been an old seat of the Minamoto family. Yoriyoshi had, in 1063, built the shrine of Hachiman at Tsurugaöka, near the village, in gratitude for his victories. Yoritomo now organized his troops, appointed his officers, and made arrangements to establish a fixed commissariat. The latter was a comparatively easy thing to do in a fertile country covered with irrigated rice-fields and girdled with teeming seas, and where the daily food of soldier, as of laborer, was rice and fish. Marching up around the country at the head of the Bay of Yedo through Kadzusa, Shimôsa, Musashi, and Sagami, crossing, on his way, the Sumida River, which flows through the modern Tôkiô, many men of rank, with their followers and horses, joined him. His father-in-law also brought an army from Kai. In a few months he had raised large forces, with many noted generals. He awakened new life in the Minamoto clan, and completely turned the tide of success. Many courtiers from Kiôto, disappointed in their schemes at court, or in any way chagrined at the Taira, flocked to Yoritomo as his power rose, and thus brought to him a fund of experience and ability which he was not slow to utilize for his own benefit. Meanwhile the Taira had not been idle. A large army was dispatched to the East, reaching the Fuji River, in Suruga, about the same time that the Minamoto, headed by Yoritomo, appeared on the other side. The Taira were surprised to see such a host in arms. Both armies encamped on opposite banks, and glared at each other, eager for the fight, but neither attempting to cross the torrent. This is not to be wondered at. The Fujikawa bears the just reputation of being the swiftest stream in Japan. It rises in the northern part of Kai, on the precipitous side of the group of mountains called Yatsu daké, or "eight peaks," and, winding around the western base of the lordly Fuji, collecting into its own volume a host of impetuous tributaries born from the snows of lofty summits, it traverses the rich province of Suruga in steep gradient, plunging across the Tokaidô, in arrowy celerity and volcanic force, into the sea near the lordly mountain which it encircles. To cross it at any time in good boats is a feat requiring coolness and skill; in a flood, impossibility; in the face of a hostile attack, sure annihilation. Though supremely eager to measure swords, neither party cared to cross to the attack, and the wager of battle was postponed. Both armies retired, the Taira retreating first.

It is said that one of the Taira men, foreseeing that the tide would turn in favor of Yoritomo, went to the river flats at night, and scared up the flocks of wild fowl; and the Taira, hearing the great noise, imagined the Minamoto host was attacking them, and fled, panic-stricken. Yoritomo returned to Kamakura, and began in earnest to found a city that ultimately rivaled Kiôto in magnificence, as it excelled it in power. He gathered together and set to work an army of laborers, carpenters, and armorers. In a few months a city sprung up where once had been only timbered hills and valleys, matted with the perennial luxuriance of reeds or scrub bamboo, starred and fragrant with the tall lilies that still abound. The town lay in a valley surrounded by hills on every side, opening only on the glorious sea. The wall of hills was soon breached by cuttings which served as gate-ways, giving easy access to friends, and safe defense against enemies. While the laborers delved and graded, the carpenters plied axe, hooked adze, and chisel, and the sword-makers and armorers sounded a war chorus on their anvils by day, and lighted up the hills by their forges at night. The streets marked out were soon lined with shops; and merchants came to sell, bringing gold, copper, and iron, silk, cotton, and hemp, and raw material for food and clothing, war and display. Store-houses of rice were built and filled; boats were constructed and launched; temples were erected. In process of time, the wealth of the Kuantô centred at Kamakura. While the old Taira chief lay dying in Kiôto, praying for Yoritomo's head to be laid on his new tomb, this same head, safely settled on vigorous shoulders, was devising the schemes, and seeing them executed, of fixing the Minamoto power permanently at Kamakura, and of wiping the name of Taira from the earth.

The long night of exile, of defeat, and defensive waiting of the Minamoto had broken, and their day had dawned with sudden and unexpected splendor. Henceforward they took the initiative. While Yoritomo carried on the enterprises of peace and the operations of war from his sustained stronghold, his uncle, Yukiiyé, his cousin, Yoshinaka, and his brother, Yoshitsuné, led the armies in the field.

Meanwhile, in 1181, Kiyomori fell sick at Kiôto. He had been a monk, as well as a prime minister. His death was not that of a saint. He did not pray for his enemies. The *Nihon Guai Shi* thus describes the scene in the chamber where the chief of the Taira lay dying: In the Second leap-month, his sickness having increased, his family and high officers assembled round his bedside, and asked him what he would say. Sighing deeply, he said, "He that is born must necessarily die, and not I alone. Since the period of Heiji (1159), I have served the imperial house. I have ruled under heaven (the empire) absolutely. I have attained the highest rank possible to a subject. I am the grandfather of the emperor on his mother's side. Is there still a regret? My regret is only that I am dying, and have not yet seen the head of Yoritomo of the Minamoto. After my decease, do not make offerings to Buddha on my behalf; do not read the sacred books. Only cut off the head of Yoritomo of the Minamoto, and hang it on my tomb. Let all my sons and grandsons, retainers and servants, each and every one, follow out my commands, and on no account neglect them." So saying, Kiyomori died at the age of sixty-four. His tomb, near Hiôgo, is marked by an upright monolith and railing of granite. Munémori, his son, became head of the Taira house. Strange words from a death-bed; yet such as these were more than once used by dying Japanese warriors. Yoritomo's head was on his body when, eighteen years afterward, in 1199, he died peacefully in his bed.

Nevertheless, while in Kamakura, his bed-chamber was nightly guarded by chosen warriors, lest treachery might cut off the hopes of the Minamoto. The flames of war were now lighted throughout the whole empire. From Kamakura forces were sent into the provinces of Hitachi, in the East, and of Echizen and Kaga, North and West, destroying the authority of the Kiôto bureaucracy. Victory and increase made the army of the rising clan invincible. After numerous bloody skirmishes, the victors advanced through Ômi, and swooped on the chief prize, and Kiôto, the coveted capital, was in their hands. The captors of the city were Yukiiyé and Yoshinaka, the uncle and cousin of Yoritomo respectively. The Taira, with the young mikado, Antoku, and his wife, Kiyomori's daughter, fled. Go-Toba, his brother, was proclaimed mikado in his stead, and the estates and treasures of the Taira were confiscated, and divided among the victors.

Yoshinaka was called the Asahi shôgun (Morning-sun General), on account of the suddenness and brilliancy of his rising. Being now in command of a victorious army at the capital, swollen with pride, and intoxicated with sudden success, and with the actual power then in his hands, he seems to have lost his head. He was elevated to high rank, and given the title and office of governor of Echigo; but having been bred in the country, he could not endure the cap and dress of ceremony, and was the subject of ridicule to the people of Kiôto. He became jealous of his superior, Yoritomo, who was in Kamakura, two hundred miles away. He acted in such an arbitrary and over-bearing spirit that the wrath of the cloistered emperor Go-Shirakawa was roused against him. Being able to command no military forces, he incited the monks of the immense monasteries of Hiyeizan and Miidera, near the city, to obstruct his authority. Before they could execute any schemes, Yoshinaka, with a military force, seized them, put the ex-mikado in prison, beheaded the abbots, and deprived the high officers of state of their honors and titles. He then wrested from the court the title of Sei-i Shôgun (Barbarian-subjugating General). His exercise of power was of brief duration, for Yoshitsuné was invested with the command of the forces in the West, and, sent against him, he was defeated and killed,* and the ex-mikado was released, and the reigning emperor set free from the terrorism under which he had been put.

Meanwhile the Taira men, in their fortified palace at Fukuwara, were planning to recover their lost power, and assembling a great army in the South and West. The Minamoto, on the other hand, were

---

* The details of this struggle are graphically portrayed in the *Nihon Guai Shi.* Yoshinaka had married the lady Fujiwara, daughter of the court noble, Motofusa. When the Kamakura army was approaching Kiôto, and quite near the city, he left his troops, and called at the palace to take leave of his wife. A Long while having elapsed before he appeared, and every moment being critical, two of his samurai, grieved at his unseasonable delay, remonstrated with him, and then committed suicide. This hastened his movements. He attempted to carry off the cloistered emperor, but was repulsed by Yoshitsuné in person, and fled. His horse, falling into a quagmire in a rice-field, fell, and he, turning around to look at Kanéhira, his faithful vassal, was hit by an arrow in the forehead and fell dead. He was thirty-one years old. Kanéhira, having but eight arrows left in his quiver, shot down eight of the enemy's horsemen; and then, hearing a cry among the enemy that his lord was dead, said, "My business is done," and, putting his sword in his mouth, fell skillfully from his horse so that the blade should pierce him, and died. His beautiful sister, Tomoyé, was a concubine of Yoshinaka; and being of great personal strength, constantly followed her lord in battle, sheathed in armor and riding a swift horse. In this last battle she fought in the van, and, among other exploits, cut off the head of Iyéyoshi, one of Yoshitsuné's best men. When her lord fled, she asked to be allowed to die with him. He refused to allow her, and, in spite of her tears, persisted in his refusal. Doffing her armor, she reached Shinano by private paths, and thence retired into Echigo, shaved off her hair, became a nun, and spent the remainder of her life praying for the eternal happiness of Yoshinaka.

expending all their energies to destroy them. The bitter animosity of the two great families had reached such a pitch that the extermination of one or the other seemed inevitable. In 1184, Yoshitsuné laid siege to the Fukuwara palace, and, after a short time, set it on fire. The son of Kiyomori and his chief followers fled to Sanuki, in Shikoku. Thither, as with the winged feet of an avenger, Yoshitsuné followed, besieged them at the castle of Yashima, burned it, and drove his enemies, like scattered sheep, to the Straits of Shimonoséki.

Both armies now prepared a fleet of junks, for the contest was to be upon the water. In the Fourth month of the year 1185, all was ready for the struggle. The battle was fought at Dan no ura, near the modern town of Shimonoseki, where, in 1863, the combined squadrons of England, France, Holland, and the United States bombarded the batteries of the Chôshiu clansmen. In the latter instance the foreigner demonstrated the superiority of his artillery and discipline, and, for the sake of trade and gain, wreaked his vengeance as savage and unjust as any that stains the record of native war.

In 1185, nearly seven centuries before, the contest was between men of a common country. It was the slaughter of brother by brother. The guerdon of ambition was supremacy. The Taira clan were at bay, driven, pursued, and hunted to the sea-shore. Like a wounded stag that turns upon its pursuers, the clan were about to give final battle; by its wager they were to decide their future destiny — a grave in a bloody sea, or peace under victory. They had collected five hundred vessels. They hurried on board their aged fathers and mothers, their wives and children. Among them were gentle ladies from the palace, whose silken robes seemed sadly out of place in the crowded junks. There were mothers, with babes at breast, and little children, too young to know the awful passions that kindle man against man. Among the crowd were the widow and daughter of Kiyomori, the former a nun, the latter the empress-dowager, with the dethroned mikado, a child six years old. With them were the sacred insignia of imperial power, the sword and ball.

The Minamoto host was almost entirely composed of men, unincumbered with women or families. They had seven hundred junks. Both fleets were gayly fluttering with flags and streamers. The Taira pennant was red, the Minamoto white, with two black bars near the top. The junks, though clumsy, were excellent vessels for fighting purposes—fully equal to the old war-galleys of Actium.

On one side were brave men flushed with victory, with passions kindled by hate and the memory of awful wrongs. On the other side were brave men nerved with the courage of despair, resolved to die only in honor, scorning life and country, wounds and death.

Tho battle began. With impetuosity and despair, the Taira drove their junks hard against the Minamoto, and gained a temporary advantage by the suddenness of their onset. Seeing this, Yoshitsuné, ever fearless, cried out and encouraged his soldiers. Then came a lull in the combat. Wada, a noted archer of the Minamoto, shot an arrow, and struck the junk of a Taira leader. "Shoot it back!" cried the chief. An archer immediately plucked it out of the gunwale, and, fitting it to his bow before the gaze of the crews of the hostile fleet, let fly. The arrow sped. It grazed the helmet of one, and pierced another warrior. The Minamoto were ashamed. "Shoot it back!" thundered Yoshitsuné. The archer, plucking it out and coolly examining it, said, "It is short and weak." Drawing from his quiver an arrow of fourteen fists' length, and fitting it to the string, he shot it. The five-feet length of shaft leaped through the air, and, piercing the armor and flesh of the Taira bowman who reshot the first arrow, fell, spent, into the sea beyond. Elated with the lucky stroke, Yoshitsuné emptied his quiver, shooting with such celerity and skill that many Taira fell. The Minamoto, encouraged, and roused to the highest pitch of enthusiasm, redoubled their exertions with oar and arrow, and the tide of victory turned.

The white flag triumphed. Yet the Taira might have won the day had not treachery aided the foe. The pages of Japanese history teem with instances of the destruction of friends by traitors. Perhaps the annals of no other country are richer in the recitals of results gained by treachery. The Arnold of the Taira army was Shigéyoshi, friend to Yoshitsuné. He had agreed upon a signal, by which the prize could be seen, and when seen could be surrounded and captured. Yoshitsuné, eagerly scanning the Taira fleet, finally caught sight of the preconcerted signal, and ordered the captains of a number of his junks to surround the particular one of the Taira. In a trice the junks of the white pennant shot along-side the devoted ship, and her decks were boarded by armed men. Seeing this, a Taira man leaped from his own boat to kill Yoshitsuné in close combat. Yoshitsuné jumped into another junk. His enemy, thus foiled, drowned himself. In the hand-to-hand fight with swords, Tomomori and six other Taira leaders were slain.

Seeing the hopeless state of affairs, and resolving not to be captured alive, the nun, Kiyomori's widow, holding her grandson, the child emperor, in her arms, leaped into the sea. Taigo, the emperor's mother, vainly tried to save her child. Both were drowned. Munémori, head of the Taira house, and many nobles, gentlemen, and ladies, were made prisoners.

The combat deepened. The Minamoto loved fighting. The Taira scorned to surrender. Revenge lent its maddening intoxication. Life, robbed of all its charms, gladly welcomed glorious death. The whizzing of arrows, the clash of two-handed swords, the clanging of armor, the sweep of churning oars, the crash of colliding junks, the wild song of the rowers, the shouts of the warriors, made the storm-chorus of battle. One after another the Taira ships, crushed by the prows of their opponents, or scuttled by the iron bolt-heads of the Minamoto archers, sunk beneath the bubbling waters, leaving red whirlpools of blood. Those that were boarded were swept with sword and spear of their human freight. The dead bodies clogged the decks, on which the mimic tides of blood ebbed and flowed and splashed with the motion of the waves, while the scuppers ran red like the spouts of an abattoir. The warriors who leaped into the sea became targets for the avenger's arrows. Noble and peasant, woman and babe, rower and archer, lifting imploring arms, or sullenly spurning mercy, perished by hundred.

That May morning looked upon a blue sea laughing with unnumbered ripples, and glinting with the steel of warriors decked in all the glory of battle-array, and flaunting with the gay pennants of the fleet which it seemed proud to bear. At night, heaving crimson like the vat of a dyer, defiled by floating corpses, and spewing its foul corruption for miles along the strand, it bore awful though transient witness to the hate of man.

The Taira, driven off the face of the earth, were buried with war's red burial beneath the sea, that soon forgot its stain, and laughed again in purity of golden gleam and deep-blue wave. The humble fisherman casting his nets, or trudging along the shore, in astonishment saw the delicate corpses of the court lady and the tiny babe, and the sun-bronzed bodies of rowers, cast upon the shore. The child who waded in the surf to pick up shells was frightened at the wave-rolled carcass of the dead warrior, from whose breast the feathered arrow or the broken spear-stock protruded. The peasant, for many a day after, burned or consigned to the burial flames many a fair child whose silken dress and light skin told of higher birth and gentler blood than their own rude brood.

Among a superstitious people dwelling by and on the sea, such an awful ingulfing of human life made a profound impression. The presence of so many thousand souls of dead heroes was overpowering. For years, nay, for centuries afterward, the ghosts of the Taira found naught but unrest in the sea in which their mortal bodies sunk. The sailor by day hurried with bated breath past the scene of slaughter and unsubstantial life. The mariner by night, unable to anchor, and driven by wind, spent the hours of darkness in prayer, while his vivid imagination converted the dancing phosphorescence into the white hosts of the Taira dead. Even to-day the Chôshiu peasant fancies he sees the ghostly armies baling out the sea with bottomless dippers, condemned thus to cleanse the ocean of the stain of centuries ago.

A few of the Taira escaped and fled to Kiushiu. There, secluded in the fastnesses of deep valleys and high mountains, their descendants, who have kept themselves apart from their countrymen for nearly seven hundred years, a few hundred in number, still live in poverty and pride. Their lurking-place was discovered only within the last century. Of the women spared from the massacre, some married their conquerors, some killed themselves, and others kept life in their defiled bodies by plying the trade in which beauty ever finds ready customers. At the present day, in Shimonoséki,* the courtesans descended from the Taira ladies claim, and are accorded, special privileges.

The vengeance of the Minamoto did not stop at the sea. They searched every hill and valley to exterminate every male of the doomed

---

*Shimonoséki is a town of great commercial importance, from its position at the entrance of the Inland Sea. It consists chiefly of one long street of two miles, at the base of a range of low steep hills. It lies four miles from the western entrance of Hayato no séto, or strait of Shimonoséki. The strait is from two thousand to five thousand feet wide, and about seven miles long. Mutsuré Island (incorrectly printed as "Rockuren" on foreign charts) lies near the entrance. On Hiku Island, and at the eastern end of the strait, are lighthouses equipped according to modern scientific requirements. Four beacons, also, light the passage at night. The current is very strong. A submarine telegraphic cable now connects the electric wires of Nagasaki, from Siberia to St. Petersburg; and of Shanghae (China) to London and New York, with those of Tôkiô and Hakodaté. On a ledge of rocks in the channel is a monument in honor of Antoku, the young emperor who perished here in the arms of his grandmother, Tokiko, the *Nii no ama*, a title composed of *Nii*, noble of the second rank, and *ama*, nun, equal to "the noble nun of the second rank."

clan. In Kiôto many boys and infant sons of the Taira family were living. All that were found were put to death. The Herod of Kamakura sent his father-in-law to attend to the bloody business.

In the Fourth month the army of Kamakura returned to Kiôto, enjoying a public triumph, with their spoils and prisoners, retainers of the Taira. They had also recovered the sacred emblems. For days the streets of the capital were gay with processions and festivals, and the coffers of the temples were enriched with the pious offerings of the victors, and their walls with votive tablets of gratitude.

Munémori was sent to Kamakura, where he saw the man whose head his father had charged him on his death-bed to cut off and hang on his tomb. His own head was shortly afterward severed from his body by the guards who were conducting him to Kiôto.

## XIV

# Creation of the Dual System of Government

Meanwhile Yoritomo was strengthening his power at Kamakura and initiating that dual system of government which has puzzled so many modern writers on Japan, and has given rise to the supposition that Japan had "two emperors, one temporal, the other spiritual."

The country at this time was distracted with the disturbances of the past few years; robbers were numerous, and the Buddhist monasteries were often nests of soldiers. Possessed of wealth, arms, and military equipments, the bonzes were ever ready to side with the party that pleased them. The presence of such men and institutions rendered it difficult for any one ruler to preserve tranquillity, since it was never known at what moment these professedly peaceful men would turn out as trained bands of military warriors. To restore order, prosperity, revenue, and firm government was now the professed wish of Yoritomo. He left the name and honor of government at Kiôto. He kept the reality in Kamakura in his own hands, and for his own family.

In 1184, while his capital was rapidly becoming a magnificent city, he created the Mandokoro, or Council of State, at which all the government affairs of the Kuantô were discussed, and through which the administration of the government was carried on. The officers of the Internal Revenue Department in Kiôto, seeing which way the tide of power was flowing, had previously come to Kamakura bringing the records of the department, and became subject to Yoritomo's orders. Thus the first necessity, revenue, was obtained. A criminal tribunal was also established, especially for the trial of the numerous robbers, as well as for ordinary cases. He permitted all who had objections to make or improvements to suggest to send in their petitions. He requested permission of the mikado to reward all who had performed meritorious actions, and to disarm the priests, and to confiscate their war materials. These requests, urged on the emperor in the interest of good government, were no sooner granted, and the plans executed, than the news of the destruction of the Taira family at Dan no ura was received. Then Yoritomo prayed the mikado that five men of his family name might be made governors of provinces. The petition was granted, and Yoshitsuné was made governor of Iyo by special decree.

Here may be distinctly seen the first great step toward the military government that lasted nearly seven centuries.

The name of the shôgun's government, and used especially by its opposers, was *bakufu*—literally, curtain government, because anciently in China, as in Japan, a curtain (*baku*) surrounded the tent or head-quarters of the commanding general. *Bakufu*, like most technical military terms in Japan, is a Chinese word.

The appointing of five military men as governors of provinces was a profound innovation in Japanese governmental affairs. Hitherto it had been the custom to appoint only civilians from the court to those offices. It does not appear, however, that Yoritomo at first intended to seize the military control of the whole empire; but his chief minister, Ôyé no Hiromoto, president of the Council of State, conceived another plan which, when carried out, as it afterward was, threw all real power in Yoritomo's hands. As the Kuantô was tranquil and prosperous under vigorous government, and as the Kuantô troops were used to put down rebels elsewhere, he proposed that in all the circuits and provinces of the empire a special tax should be levied for the support of troops in those places. By this means a permanent force could be kept, by which the peace of the empire could be maintained without the expense and trouble of calling out the Eastern army. Also—and here was another step to military government and feudalism—that a *shiugo*—a military chief, should be placed in each province, dividing the authority with the *kokushiu*, or civil governor, and a *jitô*, to be appointed from Kamakura, should rule jointly with rulers of small districts, called *shôyen*. Still further—another step in feudalism—he proposed that *his own relations* who had performed meritorious service in battle should fill these offices, and that they should all be under his control from Kamakura. This was done, and Yoritomo thus acquired the governing power of all Japan.

It seems, at first sight, strange that the mikado and his court should grant these propositions; yet they did so. They saw the Kuantô—half the empire—tranquil under the strong military government of Yoritomo. Hôjô, his father-in-law, was commanding the garrison at Kiôto. The mikado, Gotoba, may be said to have owed his throne to Yoritomo, whose ancestors had conquered, almost added to the realm, all the extreme Northern and Eastern parts of Japan. This portion, merely tributary before, was now actually settled and governed like the older parts of the empire.

In 1180, Yoritomo made a campaign in that part of Japan north of the thirty-seventh parallel, then called Mutsu and Déwa. On his return, being now all-victorious, he visited the court at Kiôto. The quondam exile was now the foremost subject in the empire. His reception and treatment by the reigning and cloistered emperors were in the highest possible scale of magnificence. The splendor of his own retinue astonished even the old courtiers, accustomed to the gay pageants of the capital. They could scarcely believe that such wealth existed and such knowledge of the art of display was cultivated in the Kuantô. Military shows, athletic games, and banquets were held for many days, and the costliest presents exchanged, many of which are still shown at Kamakura and Kiôto. Yoritomo returned, clothed with the highest honor, and with vastly greater jurisdiction than had ever been intrusted to a subject. With all the civil functions ever held by the once rival Fujiwara, he united in himself more military power than a Taira had ever wielded.

In 1192, he attained to the climax of honor, when the mikado appointed him Sei-i Tai Shôgun (Barbarian-subjugating Great General), a title and office that existed until 1868. Henceforth the term shôgun came to have a new significance. Anciently all generals were called shôguns; but, with new emphasis added to the name, *the* shôgun acquired more and more power, until foreigners supposed him to be a sovereign. Yet this subordinate from first to last—from 1194 until 1868—was a general only, and a military vassal of the emperor. Though he governed the country with a strong military hand, he did it as a vassal, in the name and for the sake of the mikado at Kiôto.

Peace now reigned in Japan. The soldier-ruler at Kamakura spent the prime of his life in consolidating his power, expecting to found a family that should rule for many generations. He encouraged hunting on Mount Fuji, and sports calculated to foster a martial spirit in the enervating times of peace. In 1195, he made another visit to Kiôto, staying four months. Toward the end of 1198, he had a fall from his horse, and died early in 1199. He was fifty-three years old, and had ruled fifteen years.

Yoritomo is looked upon as one of the ablest rulers and greatest generals that ever lived in Japan. Yet, while all acknowledge his consummate ability, many regard him as a cruel tyrant, and a heartless and selfish man. His treatment of his two brothers, Noriyori and Yoshitsuné, are evidences that this opinion is too well founded. Certain it is that the splendor of Yoritomo's career has never blinded the minds of posterity to his selfishness and cruelty; and though, like

Napoleon, he has had his eulogists, yet the example held up for the imitation of youth is that of Yoshitsuné, and not Yoritomo. Mori says of the latter: "He encouraged each of his followers to believe himself the sole confidant of his leader's schemes, and in this cunning manner separated their interests, and made them his own. Nearly all of those around him who became possible rivals in power or popularity were cruelly handled when he had exhausted the benefit of their service." His simple tomb stands at the top of a knoll on the slope of hills a few hundred yards distant from the great temple at Kamakura, overlooking the fields on which a mighty city once rose, when called into being by his genius and energy, which flourished for centuries, and disappeared, to allow luxuriant Nature to again assert her sway. The rice-swamps and the millet-fields now cover the former sites of his proudest palaces. Where metropolitan splendor and luxury once predominated, the irreverent tourist bandies his jests, or the toiling farmer stands knee-deep in the fertile ooze, to win from classic soil his taxes and his daily food.

The victory over the Taira was even greater than Yoritomo had supposed possible. Though exulting in the results, he burned with jealousy that Yoshitsuné had the real claim to the honor of victory. While in this mood, there were not wanting men to poison his mind, and fan the suspicions into fires of hate. There was one Kajiwara, who had been a military adviser to the expedition to destroy the Taira. On one occasion, Yoshitsuné advised a night attack in full force on the enemy. Kajiwara opposed the project, and hindered it. Yoshitsuné, with only fifty men, carried out his plan, and, to the chagrin and disgrace of Kajiwara, he won a brilliant victory. This man, incensed at his rival, and consuming with wrath, hied to Yoritomo with tales and slanders, which the jealous brother too willingly believed. Yoshitsuné, returning as a victor, and with the spoils for his brother, received peremptory orders not to enter Kamakura, but to remain in the village of Koshigoyé, opposite the isle of Enoshima. While there, he wrote a touching letter, recounting all his toils and dangers while pursuing the Taira, and appealing for clearance of his name from slander and suspicion. It was sent to Ôyé no Hiromoto, chief councilor of Yoritomo, whom Yoshitsuné begged to intercede to his brother for him. This letter, still extant, and considered a model of filial and fraternal affection, is taught by parents to their children. It is among the most pathetic writings in Japanese literature, and is found in one of the many popular collections of famous letters.

Wearying of waiting in the suburbs of the city, Yoshitsuné went to Kiôto. Yoritomo's troops, obeying orders, attacked his house to kill him. He fled, with sixteen retainers, into Yamato. There he was again attacked, but escaped and fled. He now determined to go to Ôshiu, to his old friend Hidéhira. He took the route along the west coast, through Echizen, Kaga, and Echigo, and found a refuge, as he supposed, with Hidéhira. The spies of his brother soon discovered his lurking-place, and ordered him to be put to death. The son of Hidéhira attacked him. According to popular belief, Yoshitsuné, after killing his wife and children with his own hands, committed *hara-kiri*. His head, preserved in saké, was sent to Kamakura.

The exact truth concerning the death of Yoshitsuné is by no means yet ascertained. It is declared by some that he escaped and fled to Yezo, where he lived among the Ainôs for many years, and died among them, either naturally or by *hara-kiri*. The Ainos have a great reverence for his deeds, and to this day worship his spirit, and over his grave in Hitaka they have erected a shrine. Others assert that he fled to Asia, and became the great conqueror, Genghis Khan.*

---

* In a Chinese book called *Seppu*, a collection of legends and historical miscellanies, published in China, it is stated that Genghis Khan was one Yoshitsuné, who came from Japan. The Chinese form of Minamoto Yoshitsuné is Gen Gike. He was also called, after his reputed death, Temujin (or Tenjin). As is

Concerning this last, a Japanese student once remarked, "Nothing but the extraordinary vanity of the Japanese people could originate such a report."

Nevertheless, the immortality of Yoshitsuné is secured. Worshiped as a god by the Ainôs, honored and beloved by every Japanese youth as an ideal hero of chivalry, his features pictured on boys' kites, his mien and form represented in household effigies displayed annually at the boys' great festival of flags, glorified in art, song, and story, Yoshitsuné, the hero warrior and martyr, will live in unfading memory so long as the ideals of the warlike Japanese stand unshattered or their traditions are preserved.*

---

well known, the Mongol conqueror's name was originally, on his first appearance, Temujin. The Japanese Ainôs have also apotheosized Yoshitsuné under the title Hanguan Dai Miô Jin—Great Illustrious Lawgiver. Yoshitsuné was born in 1159; he was thirty years old at the time of his reputed death. Genghis Khan was born, according to the usually received data, in 1160, and died 1227. If Gen Giké and Genghis Khan, or Gengis Kan, were identical, the hero had thirty-eight years for his achievements. Genghis Khan was born, it is said, with his hand full of blood. Obeying the words of a *shaman* (inspired seer), he took the name Genghis (greatest), and called his people Mongols (bold). The conquest of the whole earth was promised him. He and his sons subjugated China and Corea, overthrew the caliphate of Bagdad, and extended the Mongolian empire as far as the Oder and the Danube. They attempted to conquer Japan, as we shall see in the chapter headed "The Invasion of the Mongol Tartars."

* The struggles of the rival houses of Gen and Hei form an inexhaustible mine of incidents to the playwright, author, poet, and artist. I can not resist the temptation of giving one of these in this place. The artist's representation of it adorns many a Japanese house. At the siege of Ichinotani, a famous captain, named Naozané, who fought under the white flag, while in camp one day investing the Taira forces, saw a boat approach the beach fronting the fort. Shortly after, a Taira soldier rode out of the castle-gate into the waves to embark. Naozané saw, by the splendid crimson armor and golden helmet of the rider, that he was a Taira noble. Here was a prize indeed, the capture of which would make the Kuantô captain a general. Naozané thundered out

the challenge: "Do my eyes deceive me? Is he a Taira leader; and is he such a coward that he shows his back to the eye of his enemy? Come back and fight!" The rider was indeed a Taira noble, young Atsumori, only sixteen years of age, of high and gentle birth, and had been reared in the palace. Naozané was a bronzed veteran of forty years. Both charged each other on horseback, with swords drawn. After a few passes, Naozané flung away his sword, and, unarmed, rushed to grasp his foe. Not yet to be outdone in gallantry, Atsumori did the same. Both clinched while in the saddle, and fell to the sand, the old campaigner uppermost. He tore off the golden helmet, and, to his amazement, saw the pale, smooth face and noble mien of a noble boy that looked just like his own beloved son of the same age. The father was more than the soldier. The victor trembled with emotion. "How wretched the life of a warrior to have to kill such a lovely boy! How miserable will those parents be who find their darling is in an enemy's hand! Wretched me, that I thought to destroy this life for the sake of reward!" He then resolved to let his enemy go secretly away, and make his escape. At that moment a loud voice shouted angrily, "Naozané is double-hearted: he captures an enemy, and then thinks to let him escape." Thus compelled, Naozané steeled his heart, took up his sword, and cut off Atsumori's head. He carried the bloody trophy to Yoshitsuné, and, while all stood admiring and ready to applaud, Naozané refused all reward, and, to the amazement of his chief and the whole camp, begged leave to resign. Doffing helmet, armor, and sword, he shaved off his hair, and became a disciple of the holy bonze Hônen, learned the doctrines of Buddha, and becoming profoundly versed in the sacred lore, he resolved to spend the remnant of his days in a monastery. He set out for the Kuantô, riding with his face to the tail of the animal, but in the direction of paradise. Some one asked him why he rode thus. He replied,

"In the Clear Land, perchance they're me reputing
A warrior brave,
Because I turn my back, refusing
Fame, once so dear."

## XV

# *The Glory and the Fall of the Hôjô Family*

Though there may be some slight justification of Yoritomo's setting up a dual system of government to control and check the intrigues of courtiers at Kiôto, yet at best it was a usurpation of the power belonging only to the mikado. The creation of a duarchy was the swift and sure result of Japan having no foreign enemies.

So long as the peace or existence of the empire was threatened by the savages on the frontier, or by invading fleets on the sea-coast, there was an impelling cause to bind together the throne and people; but when the barbarians were tranquilized, China and Corea gave no signs of war; and especially when the nobility were divided into the civil and military classes, and the mikado was no longer a man of physical and mental vigor, a division of the governing power naturally arose.

From the opening of the thirteenth century, the course of Japanese history flows in two streams. There were now two capitals, Kiôto and Kamakura, and two centres of authority: one, the lawful but overawed emperor and the imperial court; the other, the military vassal, and a government based on the power of arms. It must never be forgotten, however, that the fountain of authority was in Kiôto, the ultimate seat of power in the ancient constitution. Throughout the centuries the prestige of the mikado's person never declined. The only conditions under which it was possible for this division of political power to exist was the absence of foreigners from the soil of Japan. So soon as Japan entered into political relations with outside nations, which would naturally seek the real source of power, the duarchy was doomed.

When Yoritomo died, all men wondered whether the power would remain at Kamakura, the country rest peaceful, and his successors reign with ability. The Japanese have a proverb conveying a bitter truth, learned from oft-repeated experience, *"Taishô ni tané ga nashi"* (The general has no child, or, There is no seed to a great man). The spectacle of a great house decaying through the inanity or supineness of sons is constantly repeated in their history. The theme also forms the basis of their standard novels. Yoritomo's sons, not inheriting their father's ability, failed to wield his personal power of administration. From the day of his death, it may be said that the glory of the Minamoto family declined, while that of the Hôjô began.

Yet it seemed strange that the proverb should be verified in this case. Yoritomo had married no ordinary female. His wife, Masago, was a woman of uncommon intellectual ability, who had borne him a son, Yoriiyé. This young man, who was eighteen years old at his father's death, was immediately appointed chief of all the military officers in the empire, and it was expected he would equal his father in military prowess and administrative skill. His mother, Masago, though a shorn nun, who had professed retirement from the world, continued to take a very active part in the government.

The parental authority and influence in Japan, as in China, is often far greater than that of any other. Not even death or the marriage relation weakens, to any great extent, the hold of a father on a child. With affection on the one hand, and cunning on the other, an unscrupulous father may do what he will. We have seen how the Fujiwara and Taira families controlled court, throne, and emperor, by marrying their daughters to infant or boy mikados. We shall now find the Hôjô dispensing the power at Kamakura by means of a crafty woman willing to minister to her father's rather than to her son's aggrandizement.

Hôjô Tokimasa was the father of Masago, wife of Yoritomo. The latter always had great confidence in and respect for the abilities of his father-in-law. At his death, Tokimasa became chief of the council of state. Instead of assisting and training Yoriiyé in government affairs, giving him the benefit of his experience, and thus enabling the son to tread in his father's footsteps, he would not allow Yoriiyé to hear cases in person, or to take active share in public business. When the youth plunged into dissipation and idleness, which terminated in a vicious course of life, his mother often reproved him, while Tokimasa, doubtless rejoicing over the fact, pretended to know nothing of the matter. All this time, however, he was filling the offices of government, not with the Minamoto adherents, but with his own kindred and partisans. Nepotism in Japan is a science; but cursed as the Japanese have been, probably none exceeded in this subtle craft the master, Tokimasa; though Yoriiyé, receiving his father's office, had been appointed Sei-i Tai Shôgun, with the rank ju-ni-i (second division of the second rank), his grandfather still kept the real power. When twenty-two years of age, while he was suffering from sickness—probably the result of his manner of life -- his mother and Tokimasa, who instigated her, attempted to compel him to resign his office, and to give the superintendency of the provincial governors to his infant son, and set over the Kuansei, or Western Japan, his younger brother, aged twelve years. This was the old trick of setting up boys and babies on the nominal seat of power, in order that crafty subordinates might rule.

Yoriiyé heard of this plan, and resolved to avert its execution. He failed, and, as is usual in such cases, was compelled to shave off his hair, as a sign that his interest in political affairs had ceased. He was exiled to a temple in Idzu. There he was strangled, while in his bath, by the hired assassins sent by Tokimasa.

Sanétomo, brother of Yoriiyé, succeeded in office. The boy was but twelve years old, and very unlike his father. He cared nothing for hunting or military exercises. His chief occupation was in playing foot-ball—a very mild game, compared with that played in this country—and composing poetry. His time was spent with fair girls and women, of whom he had as many as he wished. All this was in accordance with the desire and plans of the Hôjô family, who meanwhile wielded all power. Sanétomo lived his luxuriant life in the harem, the bath, and the garden, until twenty-eight years old. Meanwhile, Kugiô, the son of Yoriiyé, who had been made a priest, grew up, and had always looked upon Sanétomo, instead of Tokimasa, as his father's murderer. One night as Sanétomo was returning from worship at the famous shrine of Tsurugaōka—the unusual hour of nine having been chosen by the diviners—Kugio leaped out from behind a staircase, cut off Sanétomo's head, and made off with it, but was himself beheaded by a soldier sent after him. The main line of the Minamoto family was now extinct. Thus, in the very origin and foundation of the line of shoguns, the same fate befell them as in the case of the emperors—the power wielded by an illustrious ancestor, when transferred to descendants, was lost. A nominal ruler sat on the throne, while a wire-puller behind directed every movement. This is the history of every line of shôguns that ruled from the first, in 1196, until the last, in 1868.

The usurpation of the Hôjô was a double usurpation. Properly, they were vassals of the shôgun, who was himself a vassal of the mikado. It must not be supposed that the emperor at Kiôto calmly looked on, caring for none of these things at Kamakura. The meshes of the Minamoto had been woven completely round the imperial authority. Now the

Hôjô, like a new spider, was spinning a more fatal thread, sucking from the emperor, as from a helpless fly, the lifeblood of power.

The Hôjô family traced their descent from the mikado Kuammu (782–805) through Sadamori, a Taira noble, from whom Tokimasa was the seventh in descent. Their ancestors had settled at Hôjô, in Idzu, whence they took their name. While the Minamoto rose to power, the Hôjô assisted them, and, by intermarriage, the two clans had become closely attached to each other.

The names of the twelve rulers, usually reckoned as seven generations, were: Tokimasa, Yoshitoki, Yasutoki, Tsunétoki, Tokiyori, Masatoki, Tokimuné, Sadatoki, Morotoki, Hirotoki, Takatoki, and Moritoki. Of these, the third, fourth, and fifth were the ablest, and most devoted to public business. It was on the strength of their merit and fame that their successors were so long able to hold power. Yasutoki established two councils, the one with legislative and executive, and the other with judicial powers. Both were representative of the wishes of the people. He promulgated sixty regulations in respect to the method of judicature. This judicial record is of great value to the historian; and long afterward, in 1534, an edition of Yasutoki's laws, in one volume, with a commentary, was published. In later times it has been in popular use as a copy-book for children. He also took an oath before the assembly to maintain the same with equity, swearing by the gods of Japan, saying, "We stand as judges of the whole country; if we be partial in our judgments, may the Heavenly Gods punish us." In his private life he was self-abnegative and benevolent, a polite and accomplished scholar, loving the society of the learned. Tsunétoki faithfully executed the laws, and carried out the policy of his predecessor. Tokiyori, before he became regent, traveled, usually in disguise, all over the empire, to examine into the details of local administration, and to pick out able men, so as to put them in office

when he should need their services. In his choice he made no distinction of rank. Among the upright men he elevated to the judges'
bench was the Awodo, who, for conscientious reasons, never wore silk
garments, nor a lacquered scabbard to his sword, nor ever held a bribe
in his hand. He was the terror of venal officials, injustice and bribery
being known to him as if by sorcery; while every detected culprit was
sure to be disgracefully cashiered. Hôjô Akitoki established a library,
consisting of Chinese, Confucian, Buddhistic, and native literature, at
Kanazawa, in Sagami. Here scholars gathered, and students flocked,
to hear their lectures and to study the classics, or the tenets of the
faith, nearly all the learned men of this period being priests. While
the writer of the *Guai Shi* attacks the Hôjô for their usurpations, he
applauds them for their abilities and excellent administration.

The line of shôguns who nominally ruled from 1199 to 1333 were
merely their creatures; and that period of one hundred and forty
years, including seven generations, may be called the period of the
Hôjô. The political history of these years is but that of a monotonous
recurrence of the exaltation of boys and babies of noble blood, to
whom was given the semblance of power, who were sprinkled with
titles, and deposed as soon as they were old enough to be troublesome.
None of the Hôjô ever seized the office of Shôgun, but in reality they
wielded all and more of the power attaching to the office, under the
title of *shikken*. It was an august game of state-craft, in which little
children with colossal names were set up like nine-pins, and bowled
down as suited the playful fancies of subordinates who declined name
and titles, and kept the reality of power. The counters were neglected,
while the prize was won.

After the line of Yoritomo became extinct, Yoritomo's widow,
Masago, requested of the imperial court at Kiôto that Yoritsuné, a
Fujiwara baby two years old, should be made shôgun. The Fujiwara
nobles were glad to have even a child of their blood elevated to a

position in which, when grown, he might have power. The baby came to Kamakura. He cast the shadow of authority twenty-five years, when he was made to resign, in 1244, in favor of his own baby boy, Yoshitsugu, six years old. This boy-shôgun when fourteen years old, in 1252, was deposed by Hôjô Tokiyori, and sent back to Kiôto. Tired of the Fujiwara scions, the latter then obtained as shôgun a more august victim, the boy Munétaka, a son of the emperor Go-Saga, who after fourteen years fell ill, in 1266, with that very common Japanese disease—official illness. He was probably compelled to feign disease. His infant son, three years of age, was then set up, and, when twenty-three years of age (1289), was bowled down by Hôjô Sadatoki, who sent him in disgrace, heels upward, in a palanquin to Kiôto. Hisaakira, the third son of the emperor Go-Fukakusa, was set up as shogun in 1289. The Hôjô bowled down this fresh dummy in 1308, and put up Morikuni, his eldest son. This was the last shôgun of imperial blood. The game of the players was now nearly over.

The ex-emperor, Go-Toba, made a desperate effort to drive the usurping Hôjô from power. A small and gallant army was raised; fighting took place; but the handful of imperial troops was defeated by the overwhelming hosts sent from Kamakura. Their victory riveted the chains upon the imperial family. To the arrogant insolence of the usurper was now added the cruelty of the conscious tyrant.

Never before had such outrageous deeds been committed, or such insults been heaped upon the sovereigns as were done by these upstarts at Kamakura. Drunk with blood and exultation, the Hôjô wreaked their vengeance on sovereign and subject alike. Banishment and confiscation were the order of their day. The ex-emperor was compelled to shave off his hair, and was exiled to the island of Oki. The reigning mikado was deposed, and sent to Sado. Two princes of the blood were banished to Tajima and Bizen. The ex-emperor Tsuchimikado—there were now three living emperors—not willing to dwell in palace luxury while his brethren were in exile, expressed a wish to share their fate. He was sent to Awa. To complete the victory and the theft of power, the Hôjô chief Yasutoki confiscated the estates of all who had fought on the emperor's side, and distributed them among his own minions. Over three thousand fiefs were thus disposed of. No camp-followers ever stripped a dead hero's body worse than these human vultures tore from the lawful sovereign the last fragment of authority. All over Japan the patriots heard, with groans of despair, the slaughter of the loyal army, and the pitiful fate of their emperors. The imperial exile died in Sado of a broken heart. A nominal mikado at Kiôto, and a nominal shogun at Kamakura, were set up, but the Hôjô were the keepers of both.

The later days of the Hôjô present a spectacle of tyranny and mis-government such as would disgrace the worst Asiatic bureaucracy. The distinguished and able men such as at first shed lustre on the name of this family were no more. The last of them were given to luxury and carousal, and the neglect of public business. A horde of rapacious officials sucked the life-blood and paralyzed the energies of the people. To obtain means to support themselves in luxury, they increased the weight of taxes, that ever crushes the spirit of the Asiatic peasant. Their triple oppression, of mikado, shôgun and people, became intolerable. The handwriting was on the wall. Their days were numbered.

In 1327, Moriyoshi, son of the Emperor Go-Daigo, began to mature plans for the recovery of imperial power. By means of the ubiquitous spies, and through treachery, his schemes were revealed, and he was only saved from punishment from Hôjô by being ordered by his father to retire into a Buddhist monastery. This was ostensibly to show that he had given up all interest in worldly affairs. In reality, however, he assisted his father in planning the destruction of Hôjô. He lived at Ôtô, and was called, by the people, Ôtô no miya. The Emperor

Go-Daigo, though himself put on the throne by the king-makers at Kamakura, chafed under the galling dictatorship of those who were by right his vassals. He resolved to risk life, and all that was dear to him, to overthrow the dual system, and establish the original splendor and prestige of the mikadoate. He knew the reverence of the people for the throne would sustain him, could he but raise sufficient military force to reduce the Hôjô.

He secured the aid of the Buddhist priests and, in, 1330, fortified Kasagi, in Yamato. Kusunoki Masashigé about the same time arose in Kawachi, making it the aim of his life to restore the mikadoate. The next year Hôjô sent an army against Kasagi, attacked and burned it. The emperor was taken prisoner, and banished to Oki. Kusunoki, though twice besieged, escaped, and lived to win immortal fame.

Connected with this mikado's sad fate is one incident of great dramatic interest, which has been enshrined in Japanese art, besides finding worthy record in history. While Go-Daigo was on his way to banishment, borne in a palanquin, under guard of the soldiers of Hôjô, Kojima Takanori attempted to rescue his sovereign. This young nobleman was the third son of the lord of Bingo, who occupied his hereditary possessions in Bizen. Setting out with a band of retainers to intercept the convoy and to release the imperial prisoner, at the hill of Funasaka he waited patiently for the train to approach, finding, when too late, that he had occupied the wrong pass. Hastening to the rear range of hills, they learned that the objects of their search had already gone by. Kojima's followers, being now disheartened, returned, leaving him alone. He, however, cautious, followed on, and for several days attempted in vain to approach the palanquin and whisper a word of hope in the ear of the imperial exile. The vigilance of the Hôjô vassals rendering all succor hopeless, Kojima hit upon a plan that baffled his enemies and lighted hope in the bosom of the captive. Secretly entering the garden of the inn at which the party was resting at night, Kojima scraped off the bark of a cherry-tree, and wrote in ink, on the inner white membrane, this poetic stanza,

*"Ten Kôsen wo horobosu nakaré*
*Toki ni Hanrei naki ni shimo aradzu."*
(O Heaven! destroy not Kôsen,
While Hanrei still lives.)

The allusion, couched in delicate phrase, is to Kôsen, an ancient king in China, who was dethroned and made prisoner, but was afterward restored to honor and power by the faithfulness and valor of his retainer, Hanrei.

The next morning, the attention of the soldiers was excited by the fresh handwriting on the tree. As none of them were able to read, they showed it to the Emperor Go-Daigo, who read the writing, and its significance, in a moment. Concealing his joy, he went to banishment, keeping hope alive during his loneliness. He knew that he was not forgotten by his faithful vassals. Kojima afterward fought to restore the mikado, and perished on the battle-field. The illustration given above is borrowed from a picture by a native artist, which now adorns the national-bank notes issued under the reign of the present mikado.

This darkest hour of the mikado's fortune preceded the dawn. Already a hero was emerging from obscurity who was destined to be the destroyer of Kamakura and the Hôjô. This was Nitta Yoshisada.

The third son of Minamoto Yoshiiyé, born A.D. 1057, had two sons. The elder son succeeded his father to the fief of Nitta, in the province of Kôdzuké. The second inherited from his adopted father. Tawara, the fief of Ashikaga, in Shimotsuké. Both these sons founded families which took their name from their place of hereditary possession. At this period, four hundred years later, their illustrious descendants became conspicuous. Nitta Yoshisada, a captain in the army of Hôjô, had been sent to besiege Kusunoki, one of the mikado's faithful vassals; but, refusing to fight against the imperial forces, Nitta deserted with his command. He sent his retainer to Ôtô no miya, son of the emperor, then hiding in the mountains, who gave him a commission in the name of his exiled father. Nitta immediately returned to his native place, collected all his retainers, and before the shrine of the village raised the standard of revolt against Hôjô. His banner was a long white pennant, crossed near the top by two black bars, beneath which was a circle bisected with a black zone. Adopting the plan of attack proposed by his brother, and marching down into Sagami, he appeared at Inamura Saki, on the outskirts of Kamakura, in thirteen days after raising his banner as the mikado's vassal.

At this point, where the road from Kamakura to Enoshima strikes the beach, a splendid panorama breaks upon the vision of the beholder. In front is the ocean, with its rolling waves and refreshing salt breeze. To the south, in imposing proportions, and clothed in the blue of distance, is the island of Ôshima; and farther on are the mountains of the peninsula of Idzu. To the right emerges, fair and lovely, in perpetual green, the island of Enoshima. Landward is the peak of Ôyama, with its satellites; but, above all, in full magnificence of proportion, stands Fuji, the lordly mountain. Here Nitta performed an act that has become immortal in song and poem, and the artist's colors.

On the eve before the attack, Nitta, assembling his host at the edge of the strand, and removing his helmet, thus addressed his warriors: "Our heavenly son (mikado) has been deposed by his traitorous subject, and is now in distant exile in the Western Sea. I, Yoshisada, being unable to look upon this act unmoved, have raised an army to punish the thieves yonder. I humbly pray thee, O God of the Sea, to look into my loyal heart; command the tide to ebb and open a path." Thus saying, he bowed reverently, and then, as Rai says, with his head bare (though the artist has overlooked the statement), and in the sight of heaven cast his sword into the waves as a prayer-offering to the gods that the waves might recede, in token of their righteous favor. The golden hilt gleamed for a moment in the air, and the sword sunk from sight. The next morning the tide had ebbed, the strand was dry, and the army, headed by the chief whom the soldiers now looked upon as the chosen favorite of Heaven, marched resistlessly on. Kamakura was attacked from three sides. The fighting was severe and bloody, but victory everywhere deserted the banners of the traitors, and rested upon the pennons of the loyal. Nitta, after performing great feats of valor in person, finally set the city on fire, and in a few hours Kamakura was a waste of ashes.

Just before the final destruction of the city, a noble named Andô, vassal of the house of Hôjô, on seeing the ruin around him, the soldiers slaughtered, and the palaces burned, remarking that for a hundred years no instance of a retainer dying for his lord had been known, resolved to commit *hara-kiri*. The wife of Nitta was his niece. Just as he was about to plunge his dirk into his body, a servant handed him a letter from her, begging him to surrender. The old man indignantly exclaimed: "My niece is the daughter of a samurai house. Why did she make so shameless a request? And Nitta, her husband, is a samurai Why did he allow her to do so?" He then took the letter, wrapped it round his sword, which he plunged into his body, and died. A great number of vassals of Hôjô did likewise.

While Nitta was fighting at Kamakura, and thus overthrowing the Hôjô power in the East, Ashikaga Takauji had drawn sword in Kiôto, and with Kusunoki re-established the imperial rule in the West. The number of the doomed clan who were slain in battle, or who committed *hara-kiri*, as defeated soldiers, in accordance with the code of honor already established, is set down at six thousand eight hundred.

All over the empire the people rose up against their oppressors and massacred them. The Hôjô domination, which had been paramount for nearly one hundred and fifty years, was utterly broken.

From A.D. 1219 until 1333, the mikados at Kiôto were:

| | |
|---|---|
| Juntoku | 1211–1221 |
| Chiukiô (reigned four months) | 1222 |
| Go-Horikawa | 1222–1232 |
| Shijô | 1233–1242 |
| Go-Saga | 1243–1246 |
| Go-Fukakusa | 1247–1259 |
| Kaméyama | 1260–1274 |
| Go-Uda | 1275–1287 |
| Fushimi | 1288–1298 |
| Go-Fushimi | 1299–1301 |
| Go-Nijô | 1302–1307 |
| Hanazono | 1308–1318 |
| Go-Daigo | 1319 –1338 |

From the establishment of Kamakura as military capital, the shô-guns were:

### MINAMOTO

| | |
|---|---|
| Yoritomo | 1185–1199 |
| Yoriiyé | 1201–1203 |
| Sanetomo | 1203–1219 |

### FUJIWARA

| | |
|---|---|
| Yoritsuné | 1220–1243 |
| Yoritsugu | 1244–1251 |

EMPEROR'S SONS

| | |
|---|---|
| Munétaka | 1252–1265 |
| Koréyasu | 1266–1289 |
| Hisaakira | 1289–1307 |
| Morikuni | 1308–1333 |

The Hôjô have never been forgiven for their arbitrary treatment of the mikados. The author of the *Nihon Guai Shi* terms them "serpents, fiends, beasts," etc. To this day, historian, dramatist, novelist, and story-teller delight to load them with vilest obloquy. Even the peasants keep alive the memory of the past. One of the most voracious and destructive insects is still called the "Hôjô bug." A great annual ceremony of extermination of these pests keeps alive the hated recollection of their human namesakes. The memory of the wrongs suffered by the imperial family goaded on the soldiers in the revolution of 1868, who wreaked their vengeance on the Tokugawas, as successors of the Hôjô. In fighting to abolish forever the hated usurpation of six hundred years, and to restore the mikado to his ancient rightful and supreme authority, they remembered well the deeds of the Hôjô, which the *Nihon Guai Shi* so eloquently told. In 1873, envoys sent out from the imperial court in Tôkiô, proceeded to the island of Sado, and solemnly removing the remains of the banished emperor, who had died of a broken heart, buried them, with due pomp, in the sacred soil of Yamato, where sleep so many of the dead mikados.

I have given a picture of the Hôjô rule and rulers, which is but the reflection of the Japanese popular sentiment, and the opinion of native scholars. There is, however, another side to the story. It must be conceded that the Hôjô were able rulers, and kept order and peace in the empire for over a century. They encouraged literature, and the cultivation of the arts and sciences. During their period, the resources of the country were developed, and some branches of useful handicraft and fine arts were brought to a perfection never since surpassed. To this time belong the famous image-carver, sculptor, and architect, Unkei, and the lacquer-artists, who are the "old masters" in this branch of art. The military spirit of the people was kept alive, tactics were improved, and the methods of governmental administration simplified. During this period of splendid temples, monasteries, pagodas, colossal images, and other monuments of holy zeal, Hôjô Sadatoki erected a monument over the grave of Kiyomori at Hiôgo. Hôjô Tokimuné raised and kept in readiness a permanent war-fund, so that the military expenses might not interfere with the revenue reserved for ordinary government expenses. To his invincible courage, patriotic pride, and indomitable energy are due the vindication of the national honor and the repulse of the Tartar invasion.

# XVI

# *Buddhism in Japan*

The religion founded by Buddha, which is older by six centuries than that founded by Christ, which is professed by nearly one-third of the human race, which has a literature perhaps larger than all other religious literatures combined, I shall not attempt to treat of except in the broadest terms. My object in this chapter is to portray the entrance and development of Buddhism in Japan, to outline its rise and progress, and to show its status in that now fermenting nation in which its latest fruits are found.

Christians must surely be interested in knowing of the faith they are endeavoring to destroy, or, at least, to displace. When it is considered that Buddhist temples are already erected upon American soil, that a new development of this ancient faith may yet set itself up as a rival of Christianity in the Western part of our country, that it has already won admirers, if not professors, in Boston, London, and Berlin, the subject will be seen to possess an immediate interest.

Buddhism originated as a pure atheistic humanitarianism, with a lofty philosophy and a code of morals higher, perhaps, than any heathen religion had reached before, or has since attained. Its three great distinguishing characteristics are atheism, metempsychosis, and absence of caste. First preached in a land accursed by secular and spiritual oppression, it acknowledged no caste, and declared all men equally sinful and miserable, and all equally capable of being freed from sin and misery through knowledge. It taught that the souls of all men had lived in a previous state of existence, and that all the sorrows of this life are punishments for sins committed in a previous state. Each human soul has whirled through countless eddies of existence, and has still to pass through a long succession of birth, pain, and death. All is fleeting. Nothing is real. This life is all a delusion. After death, the soul must migrate for ages through stages of life, inferior or superior, until, perchance, it arrives at last in Nirvana, or absorption in Buddha.

The total extinction of being, personality, and consciousness is the aspiration of the vast majority of true believers, as it should be of every suffering soul, *i.e.*, of all mankind. The true estate of the human soul, according to the Buddhist of the Buddhists, is blissful annihilation. The morals of Buddhism are superior to its metaphysics. Its commandments are the dictates of the most refined morality. Besides the cardinal prohibitions against murder, stealing, adultery, lying, drunkenness, and unchastity, "every shade of vice, hypocrisy, anger, pride, suspicion, greediness, gossiping, cruelty to animals, is guarded against by special precepts. Among the virtues recommended, we find not only reverence of parents, care of children, submission to authority, gratitude, moderation in time of prosperity, submission in time of trial, equanimity at all times; but virtues such as the duty of forgiving insults, and not rewarding evil with evil." Whatever the *practice* of the people may be, they are taught, as laid down in their sacred books, the rules thus summarized above.

Such, we may glean, was Buddhism in its early purity. Besides its moral code and philosophical doctrines, it had almost nothing. An "ecclesiastical system" it was not in any sense. Its progress was rapid and remarkable. Though finally driven out of India, it swept through Burmah, Siam, China, Thibet, Manchuria, Corea, Siberia, and finally, after twelve centuries, entered Japan. By this time the bare and bald original doctrines of Shaka (Buddha) were glorious in the apparel with which Asiatic imagination and priestly necessity had clothed and adorned them. The ideas of Shaka had been expanded into a complete theological system, with all the appurtenances of a stock religion. It had a vast and complicated ecclesiastical and monastic machinery, a geographical and sensuous paradise, definitely located hells and purgatories, populated with a hierarchy of titled demons, and furnished after the most approved theological fashion. Of these the priests kept the keys, regulated the thermometers, and timed or graded the torture or bliss. The system had, even thus early, a minutely catalogued hagiology. Its eschatology was well outlined, and the hierarchs claimed to be as expert in questions of casuistry as they were at their commercial system of masses still in vogue. General councils had been held, decrees had been issued, dogmas defined or abolished; Buddhism had emerged from philosophy into religion. The Buddhist missionaries entered Japan having a mechanism perfectly fitted to play upon the fears and hopes of an ignorant people, and to bring them into obedience to the new and aggressive faith.

If there was one country in which the success of Buddhism as a popular religion seemed foreordained, that country was Japan. It was virgin soil for any thing that could be called a religion. Before Buddhism came, very little worthy of the name existed. Day by day, each new ray of the light of research that now falls upon that gray dawn of Japanese history shows that Shintô was a pale and shadowy cult, that consisted essentially of sacrificing to the spirits of departed heroes and ancestors, with ceremonies of bodily purification, and that the coming of Buddhism quickened it, by the force of opposition, into something approaching a religious system. Swarms of petty deities, who have human passions, and are but apotheosized historical heroes, fill the pantheon of Shintô. The end and aim of even its most sincere adherents and teachers is political. Strike out the dogma of the divinity of the mikado and the duty of all Japanese to obey him implicity, and almost nothing is left of modern Shintô but Chinese cosmogony, local myth, and Confucian morals.*

If the heart of the ancient Japanese longed after a solution of the questions whence? whither? why?—if it yearned for religious truth, as the hearts of all men doubtless do—it must have been ready to welcome something more certain, tangible, and dogmatic than the bland emptiness of Shintô. Buddhism came to touch the heart, to fire the imagination, to feed the intellect, to offer a code of lofty morals, to point out a pure life through self-denial, to awe the ignorant, and to terrify the doubting. A well fed and clothed Anglo-Saxon, to whom conscious existence seems the very rapture of joy, and whose soul yearns for an eternity of life, may not understand how a human soul could ever long for utter absorption of being and personality, even in God, much less for total annihilation.

---

* "I have long endeavored to find out what there is in Shintô, but have long given it up, unable to find any thing to reward my labor, excepting a small book of Shintô prayers, in which man was recognized as guilty of the commission of sin, and in need of cleansing."—J. C. HEPBURN, M.D., LL.D., American, seventeen years resident in Japan, author of the *Japanese-English and English-Japanese Dictionary.*

"Shintô is in no proper sense of the term a religion." "It is difficult to see how it could ever have been denominated a religion." "It has rather the look of an original Japanese invention."—Rev. S. R. BROWN, D.D., American, author of *A Grammar of Colloquial Japanese,* seventeen years resident in Japan.

My own impressions of Shintô, given in an article in *The Independent* in 1871, remain unaltered after five years' further study and comparison of opinions, pro and con: "In its higher forms. Shintô is simply a cultured and intellectual atheism. In its lower forms, it is blind obedience to governmental and priestly dictates." The united verdict given me by native scholars, and even Shintô officials, in Fukui and Tôkiô, was, "Shintô is not a religion: it is a system of government regulations, very good to keep alive patriotism among the people." The effectual, and quite justifiable, use made of this tremendous political engine will be seen in the last chapter of Book I., entitled "The Recent Revolutions in Japan."

But, among the Asiatic poor, where ceaseless drudgery is often the lot for life, where a vegetable diet keeps the vital force low, where the tax-gatherer is the chief representative of government, where the earth-quake and the typhoon are so frequent and dreadful, and where the forces of nature are feared as malignant intelligences, life does not wear such charms as to lead the human soul to long for an eternity of it. No normal Japanese would thrill when he heard the unexplained announcement, "The gift of God is eternal life," or, "Whosoever believeth on me, though he were dead, yet shall he live." Such words would be painful to him, announcing only a fateful fact. To him life is to be dreaded; not because death lies at the end of it, but because birth and life again follow death, and both are but links in an almost endless chain. Herein lies the power of Buddhist preaching: "Believe in the true doctrine, and live the true believer's life," says the bonze, "and you will be born again into higher states of existence, thence into higher and higher heavens, until from paradise you rise as a purified and saintly soul, to be absorbed in the bosom of holy Buddha. Reject the truth, or believe false doctrine (*e.g.*, Christianity), and you will be born again thousands of times, only to suffer sickness and pain and grief, to die or be killed a thousand times, and, finally, to sink into lower and lower hells, before you can regain the opportunity to rise higher." This is really the popular form of Shaka's doctrine of metempsychosis. The popular Buddhism of Japan, at least, is not the bare scheme of philosophy which foreign writers seem to think it is. It is a genuine religion in its hold on man. It is a vinculum that binds him to the gods of his fathers. This form of Buddhism commended itself to both the Japanese sage and the igno-rant boor, to whom thought is misery, by reason of its definiteness, its morals, its rewards, and its punishments.

Buddhism has a cosmogony and a theory of both the microcosm and the macrocosm. It has fully as much, if not more, "science" in it than our mediaeval theologians found in the Bible. Its high intellectuality made noble souls yearn to win its secrets, and to attain the conquests over their lusts and passions, by knowledge.

Among the various sects of Buddhism, however, the understanding of the doctrine of Nirvana varies greatly. Some believe in the total nonentity of the human soul, the utter annihilation of consciousness; while others, on the contrary, hold that, as part of the divine whole, the human soul enjoys a measure of conscious personality.

Persecution and opposition at first united together the adherents of the new faith, but success and prosperity gave rise to schisms. New sects were founded in Japan, while many priests traveled abroad to Corea and China, and came back as new lights and reformers, to found new schools of thought and worship. Of these the most illustrious was Kôbô, famed not only as a scholar in Pali, Sanskrit, and Chinese, but as an eminently holy bonze, and the compiler of the Japanese alphabet, or syllabary, *i, ro, ha, ni, ho, he, to,* etc., in all forty-seven characters, which, with diacritical points, may be increased to the number of seventy. The *katagana* is the square, the *hiragana* is the script form. Kôbô was born A.D. 774; and died A.D. 835. He founded a temple, and the sect called Shin Gon (True Words). Eight sects were in existence in his time, of which only two now survive.

The thirteenth of the Christian era is the golden century of Japanese Buddhism; for then were developed those phases of thought peculiar to it, and sects were founded, most of them in Kiôto, which are still the most flourishing in Japan. Among these were, in 1202, the Zen (Contemplation); in 1211, the Jôdo (Heavenly Road); in 1262, the Shin (New); in 1282, the Nichiren. In various decades of the same century several other important sects originated, and the number of brilliant intellects that adorned the priesthood at this period is remarkable. Of these, only two can be noticed, for lack of space.

In A.D. 1222, there was born, in a suburb of the town of Kominato, in Awa, a child who was destined to influence the faith of millions, and to leave the impress of his character and intellect indelibly upon the minds of his countrymen. He was to found a new sect of Buddhism, which should grow to be one of the largest, wealthiest, and most influential in Japan, and to excel them all in proselyting zeal, polemic bitterness, sectarian bigotry, and intolerant arrogance. The Nichiren sect of Buddhists, in its six centuries of history, has probably furnished a greater number of brilliant intellects, uncompromising zealots, unquailing martyrs, and relentless persecutors than any other in Japan. No other sect is so fond of controversy. The bonzes of none other can excel those of the Nichiren *shiu* (sect) in proselyting zeal, in the bitterness of their theological arguments, in the venom of their revilings, or the force with which they hurl their epithets at those who differ in opinion or practice from them. In their view, all other sects than theirs are useless. According to their vocabulary, the adherents of Shin Gon are "not patriots;" those of Ritsu are "thieves and rascals;" of Zen, are "furies;" while those of certain other sects are sure and without doubt to go to hell. Among the Nichirenites are to be found more prayer-books, drums, and other noisy accompaniments of revivals, than in any other sect. They excel in the number of pilgrims, and in the use of charms, spells, and amulets. Their priests are celibates, and must abstain from wine, fish, and all flesh. They are the Ranters of Buddhism. To this day, a revival-meeting in one of their temples is a scene that often beggars description, and may deafen weak ears. What with prayers incessantly repeated, drums beaten unceasingly, the shouting of devotees who work themselves into an excitement that often ends in insanity, and sometimes in death, and the frantic exhortation of the priests, the wildest excesses that seek the mantle of religion in other lands are by them equaled, if not excelled. To this sect belonged Katô Kiyomasa, the bloody persecutor of the Christians in the sixteenth century, the "vir ter execrandus" of the Jesuits, but who is now a holy saint in the calendar of canonized Buddhists.

Nichiren (sun-lotus) was so named by his mother, who at conception had dreamed that the sun (*nichi*) had entered her body. This story is also told of other mothers of Japanese great men, and seems to be a favorite stock-belief concerning the women who bear children that afterward become men of renown or exalted holiness. The boy grew up surrounded by the glorious scenery of mountain, wave, shore, and with the infinity of the Pacific Ocean before him. He was a dreamy, meditative child. He was early put under the care of a holy bonze, but when grown to manhood discarded many of the old doctrines, and, being dissatisfied with the other sects, resolved to found one, the followers of which should be the holders and exemplars of the pure truth.

Nichiren was a profound student of the Buddhist classics, or sutras, brought from India, and written in Sanskrit and Chinese, for the entire canon of Buddhist holy books has at various times been brought from India or China, and translated into Chinese in Japan. Heretofore, the common prayer of all the Japanese Buddhists had been *"Namu, Amida Butsu"* (Hail, Amida Buddha! or, Save us, Eternal Buddha!). Nichiren taught that the true invocation was *"Namu miô hô rén ge kiô"* (Glory to the salvation-bringing book of the law; or, literally, Hail, the true way of salvation, the blossom of doctrine). This is still the distinctive prayer of the Nichiren sect. It is inscribed on the temple curtains, on their tombstones and wayside shrines, and was emblazoned on the banners carried aloft by the great warriors on sea and land who belonged to the sect. The words are the Chinese translation of *Mamah Saddharma-pundarika-sutra*, one of the chief canonical books of the Buddhist Scriptures, and in use by all the sects. Nichiren professed to find in it the true and only way of salvation, which the other expounders of Shaka's doctrine had not properly taught. He declared that the way as taught by him was the true and only one.

Nichiren founded numerous temples, and was busy during the whole of his life, when not in exile, in teaching, preaching, and itinerating.

He published a book called *Ankoku Ron* ("An Argument to tranquilize the Country"). The bitterness with which he attacked other sects
roused up a host of enemies against him, who complained to Hôjô
Tokiyori, the *shikken*, or holder of the power, at Kamakura, and prayed
to have him silenced, as a destroyer of the public peace, as indeed the
holy man was. The title of his book was by no means an exponent of
its tone or style.

Nichiren was banished to Cape Ito, in Idzu, where he remained
three years. On his release, instead of holding his tongue, he allowed it
to run more violently than ever against other sects, especially decrying
the great and learned priests of previous generations. Hôjô Tokiyori
again arrested him, confined him in a dungeon below ground, and
condemned him to death.

The following story is told, and devoutly believed, by his followers:
On a certain day he was taken out to a village on the strand of the
bay beyond Kamakura, and in front of the lovely island of Enoshima.
This village is called Koshigoyé. At this time Nichiren was forty-
three years old. Kneeling down upon the strand, the saintly bonze
calmly uttered his prayers, and repeated *"Namu miô hô ren gé kiô"*
upon his rosary. The swordsman lifted his blade, and, with all his
might, made the downward stroke. Suddenly a flood of blinding light
burst from the sky, and smote upon the executioner and the official
inspector deputed to witness the severed head. The sword-blade was
broken in pieces, while the holy man was unharmed. At the same
moment, Hôjô, the Lord of Kamakura, was startled at his revels in
the palace by the sound of rattling thunder and the flash of lightning,
though there was not a cloud in the sky. Dazed by the awful signs of
Heaven's displeasure, Hôjô Tokiyori, divining that it was on account
of the holy victim, instantly dispatched a fleet messenger to stay the
executioner's hand and reprieve the victim. Simultaneously the official
inspector at the still unstained blood-pit sent a courier to beg reprieve

for the saint whom the sword could not touch. The two men, coming from opposite directions, met at the small stream which the tourist still crosses on the way from Kamakura to Enoshima, and it was thereafter called Yukiai (meeting on the way) River, a name which it retains to this day. Through the pitiful clemency and intercession of Hôjô Tokimuné, son of the Lord of Kamakura, Nichiren was sent to Sado Island. He was afterward released by his benefactor in a general amnesty. Nichiren founded his sect at Kiôto, and it greatly flourished under the care of his disciple, his reverence Nichizo. After a busy and holy life, the great saint died at Ikégami, a little to north-west of the Kawasaki railroad station, between Yokohama and Tôkiô, where the scream of the locomotive and the rumble of the railway car are but faintly heard in its solemn shades. There are to be seen gorgeous temples, pagodas, shrines, magnificent groves and cemeteries. The dying presence of Nichiren has lent this place peculiar sanctity; but his bones rest on Mount Minobu, in the province of Kai, where was one of his homes when in the flesh.

While in Japan, I made special visits to many of the places rendered most famous by Nichiren, of his birth, labors, triumph, and death, and there formed the impressions of his work and followers which I have in this chapter set forth. So far as I am able to judge, none of the native theologians has stamped his impress more deeply on the religious intellect of Japan than has Nichiren. It may be vain prophecy, but I believe that Christianity in Japan will find its most vigorous and persistent opposers among this sect, and that it will be the last to yield to the now triumphing faith that seems clasping the girdle of world-victory in Japan.

Their astonishing success and tremendous power, and their intolerance and bigotry, are to be ascribed to the same cause—the precision, distinctness, and exclusiveness of the teachings of their master. In their sacred books, and in the sermons of their bonzes, the Nichirenites are exhorted to reflect diligently upon the peculiar blessings vouchsafed to them as a chosen sect, and to understand that they are favored above all others in privilege, that their doctrines are the only true ones, and that perfect salvation is attainable by no other method or system. It is next to impossible for them to fraternize with other Buddhists, and they themselves declare that, though all the other sects may combine into one, yet they must remain apart, unless their tenets be adopted. The proscription of other sects, and the employment of reviling and abuse as a means of propagation introduced by Nichiren, was a comparatively new thing in Japan. It stirred up persecution against the new faith and its followers; and this, coupled with the invincible fortitude and zeal of the latter, were together as soil and seed.

The era and developments of Nichiren may be called the second revival of Buddhism in Japan, since it infused into that great religion, which had, at the opening of the thirteenth century, reached a stage of passive quiescence, the spirit of proselytism which was necessary to keep it from stagnant impurity and heartless formality.

Though the success of Nichiren inaugurated an era of zeal and bigotry, it also awoke fresh life into that power which is the best representative of the religious life of the nation. Whether we call Buddhism a false or a true religion, even the most shallow student of the Japanese people must acknowledge that the pure religious, as well as the superstitious, character of the masses of the Japanese people has been fostered and developed more by Buddhism than by any and all other influences.

Some of the superstitions of the Nichirenites are gross and revolting, but among their beliefs and customs is the *nagaré kanjô* (flowing invocation). I shall call it "the mother's memorial." It is practiced chiefly by the followers of Nichiren, though it is sometimes employed by other sects.

A sight not often met with in the cities, but in the suburbs and country places frequent as the cause of it requires, is the *nagaré kanjô* (flowing invocation). A piece of cotton cloth is suspended by its four corners to stakes set in the ground near a brook, rivulet, or, if in the city, at the side of the water-course which fronts the houses of the better classes. Behind it rises a higher, lath-like board, notched several times near the top, and inscribed with a brief legend. Resting on the cloth at the brookside, or, if in the city, in a pail of water, is a wooden dipper. Perhaps upon the four corners, in the upright bamboo, may be set bouquets of flowers. A careless stranger may not notice the odd thing, but a little study of its parts reveals the symbolism of death. The tall lath tablet is the same as that set behind graves and tombs. The ominous Sanskrit letters betoken death. Even the flowers in their bloom call to mind the tributes of affectionate remembrance which loving survivors set in the sockets of the monuments in the grave-yards. On the cloth is written a name such as is given to persons after death, and the prayer, *"Namu miô hô ren gé kiô"* (Glory to the salvation-bringing Scriptures). Waiting long enough, perchance but a few minutes, there may be seen a passer-by who pauses, and, devoutly offering a prayer with the aid of his rosary, reverently dips a ladleful of water, pours it upon the cloth, and waits patiently until it has strained through, before moving on.

All this, when the significance is understood, is very touching. It is the story of vicarious suffering, of sorrow from the brink of joy, of one dying that another may live. It tells of mother-love and mother-woe. It is a mute appeal to every passer-by, by the love of Heaven, to shorten the penalties of a soul in pain.

The Japanese (Buddhists) believe that all calamity is the result of sin either in this or a previous state of existence. The mother who dies in childbed suffers, by such a death, for some awful transgression, it may be in a cycle of existence long since passed. For it she must leave her new-born infant, in the full raptures of mother-joy, and sink into the darkness of Hades, to wallow in a lake of blood. There must she groan and suffer until the "flowing invocation" ceases, by the wearing-out of the symbolic cloth. When this is so utterly worn that the water no longer drains, but falls through at once, the freed spirit of the mother, purged of her sin, rises to resurrection among the exalted beings of a higher cycle of existence. Devout men, as they pass by, reverently pour a ladleful of water. Women, especially those who have felt mother-pains, and who rejoice in life and loving offspring, repeat the expiatory act with deeper feeling; but the depths of sympathy are fathomed only by those who, being mothers, are yet bereaved. Yet, as in presence of nature's awful glories the reverent gazer is shocked by the noisy importunity of the beggar, so before this sad and touching memorial the proofs of sordid priest-craft chill the warm sympathy which the sight even from the heart of an alien might evoke.

The cotton cloth inscribed with the prayer and the name of the deceased, to be efficacious, can be purchased only at the temples. I have been told, and it is no secret, that rich people are able to secure a napkin which, when stretched but a few days, will rupture, and let the water pass through at once. The poor man can get only the stoutest and most closely woven fabric. The limit of purgatorial penance is thus fixed by warp and woof, and warp and woof are gauged by money. The rich man's napkin is scraped thin in the middle. Nevertheless, the poor mother secures a richer tribute of sympathy from her humble people; for in Japan, as in other lands, poverty has many children, while wealth mourns for heirs; and in the lowly walks of life are more pitiful women who have felt the woe and the joy of motherhood than in the mansions of the rich.

In Echizen, especially in the country towns and villages, the custom is rigidly observed; but though I often looked for the *nagaré kanjô* in Tôkiô, I never saw one. I am told, however, that they may be seen in the outskirts of the city. The drawing of one seen near Takéfu, in Echizen, was made for me by my artist-friend Ôzawa, a number of whose sketches appear in this work.

The Protestants of Japanese Buddhism are the followers of Shin shiu, founded by his reverence Shinran, in 1262. Shinran was a pupil of Hônen, who founded the Jodo shiu, and was of noble descent. While in Kiôto, at thirty years of age, he married a lady of noble blood, named Tamayori himé, the daughter of the Kuambaku. He thus taught by example, as well as by precept, that marriage was honorable, and that celibacy was an invention of the priests, not warranted by pure Buddhism. Penance, fasting, prescribed diet, pilgrimages, isolation from society, whether as hermits or in the cloister, and generally amulets and charms, are all tabooed by this sect. Nunneries and monasteries are unknown within its pale. The family takes the place of monkish seclusion. Devout prayer, purity, and earnestness of life, and trust in Buddha himself as the only worker of perfect righteousness, are insisted upon. Other sects teach the doctrine of salvation by works. Shinran taught that it is faith in Buddha that accomplishes the salvation of the believer.

Buddhism seems to most foreigners who have studied it but Roman Catholicism without Christ, and in Asiatic form. The Shin sect hold a form of the Protestant doctrine of justification by faith, believing in Buddha instead of Jesus. Singleness of purpose characterizes this sect. Outsiders call it Ikkô, from the initial word of a text in their chief book, Muriôju Kiô ("Book of Constant Life"). By others it is spoken of as Monto (gate-followers), in reference to their unity of organization. The Scriptures of other sects are written in Sanskrit and Chinese, which only the learned are able to read.

Those of Monto are in the vernacular Japanese writing and idiom. Other sects build temples in sequestered places among the hills. The Shin-shiuists erect theirs in the heart of cities, on main streets, in the centres of population. They endeavor, by every means in their power, to induce the people to come to them. In Fukui their twin temples stood in the most frequented thoroughfares. In Tôkiô, Ôzaka, Kiôto, Nagasaki, and other cities, the same system of having twin temples in the heart of the city is pursued, and the largest and finest ecclesiastical structures are the duplicates of this sect. The altars are on a scale of imposing magnificence, and gorgeous in detail. A common saying is, "As handsome as a Monto altar." The priests marry, rear families, and their sons succeed them to the care of the temples. In default of male issue, the husband of the daughter of the priest, should he have one, takes the office of his father-in-law. Many members of the priesthood and their families are highly educated, perhaps more so than the bonzes of any other sect. Personal acquaintance with several of the Monto priests enables me to substantiate this fact asserted of them.

The followers of Shinran have ever held a high position, and have wielded vast influence in the religious development of the people. Both for good and evil they have been among the foremost of active workers in the cause of religion. In time of war the Monto bonzes put on armor, and, with their families and adherents, have in numerous instances formed themselves into military battalions. We shall hear more of their martial performances in succeeding chapters.

After the death of Shinran, Renniô, who died in 1500, became the revivalist of Monto, and wrote the *Ofumi*, or sacred writings, which are now daily read by the disciples of this denomination. With the characteristic object of reaching the masses, they are written in the common script *hiragana* writing, which all the people of both sexes can read. Though greatly persecuted by other sectaries, they have continually increased in numbers, wealth, and power, and now lead all in intelligence and influence. To the charges of uncleanness which others bring against them, because they marry wives, eat and drink and live so much like unclerical men, they calmly answer, the bright rays of the sun shine on all things alike, and that it is not for them to call things unclean which have evidently been created for man's use; that righteousness consists neither in eating nor drinking, nor in abstinence from the blessings vouchsafed to mortals in this vale of woe; and that the maxims and narrow-minded doctrines, with the neglect of which they are reproached, can only have proceeded from the folly or vanity of men. They claim that priests with families are purer men than celibates in monasteries, and that the purity of society is best maintained by a married priesthood. Within the last two decades they were the first to organize their theological schools on the model of foreign countries, that their young men might be trained to resist Shintô or Christianity, or to measure the truth in either. The last new charge urged against them by their rivals is that they are so much like Christians, that they might as well be such out and out. Liberty of thought and action, an incoercible desire to be free from governmental, traditional, ultra-ecclesiastical, or Shintô influence—in a word, Protestantism in its pure sense, is characteristic of the great sect founded by Shinran.

To treat of the doctrinal difference and various customs of the different denominations would require a volume. Japanese Buddhism richly deserves thorough study, and a scholarly treatise by itself.* The part played by the great Buddhist sects in the national drama of history in later centuries will be seen as we proceed in our narrative.

---

* It is a question worthy the deepest research and fullest inquiry, as to the time occupied in converting the Japanese people to the Buddhist faith. It is not probable, as some foreigners believe, that Wani (see page 86) brought the knowledge of the Indian religion to Japan. The *Nihongi* gives the year 552 as that in which Buddhist books, images, rosarios, altar furniture, vestments, etc., were bestowed as presents at the imperial palace, and deposited in the court of ceremony. The imported books were diligently studied by a few court nobles, and in 584 several of them openly professed the new faith. In 585, a frightful pestilence that broke out was ascribed by the patriotic opponents of the foreign

faith to the anger of the gods against the new religion. A long and bitter dispute followed, and some of the new temples and idols were destroyed. In spite of patriotism and conservative zeal, the worship and ritual were established in the palace, new missionaries were invited from Corea, and in 624 two bonzes were given official rank, as primate and vice-primate. Temples were erected, and, at the death of a bonze, in 700, his body was disposed of by cremation—a new thing in Japan. In 741, an imperial decree, ordering the erection of two temples and a seven-storied pagoda in each province, was promulgated. In 765, a priest became Dai Jô Dai Jin. In 827, a precious relic—one of Shaka's (Buddha's) bones—was deposited in the palace. The master stroke of theological dexterity was made early in the ninth century, when Kôbô, who had studied three years in China, achieved the reconciliation of the native belief and the foreign religion, made patriotism and piety one, and laid the foundation of the permanent and universal success of Buddhism in Japan. This Japanese Philo taught that the Shintô deities, or gods, of Japan were manifestations, or transmigrations, of Buddha in that country, and, by his scheme of dogmatic theology, secured the ascendency of Buddhism over Shintô and Confucianism. Until near the fourteenth century, however, Buddhism continued to be the religion of the official, military, and educated classes, but not of the people at large. Its adoption by all classes may be ascribed to the missionary labors of Shinran and Nichiren, whose banishment to the North and East made them itinerant apostles. Shinran traveled on foot through every one of the provinces north and east of Kiôto, glorying in his exile, everywhere preaching, teaching, and making new disciples. It may be safely said that it required nine hundred years to convert the Japanese people from fetichism and Shintô to Buddhism.

It is extremely difficult to get accurate statistics relating to Japanese Buddhism. The following table was compiled for me by a learned bonze of the Shin denomination, in the temple of Nishi Honguanji, in Tsukiji, Tôkiô. I have compared it with data furnished by an ex-priest in Fukui, and various laymen.

The ecclesiastical centre of Japan has always been at Kiôto. The chief temples and monasteries of each sect were located there.

### Tabular List of Buddhist Sects in Japan

| Chief Sects (Shiu) | Total Number of Temples |
|---|---|
| I. Tendai. Founded by Chisha, in China: 3 sub-sects | 6,391 |
| II. Shingon. Founded by Kôbô, in Japan, A.D. 813: 3 sub-sects | 15,503 |
| III. Zen. Founded by Darma, in Japan: 6 sub-sects | 21,547 |
| IV. Jodo. Founded by Hônen, in Japan, 1173: 2 sub-sects | 9,819 |
| V. Shin. Founded by Shinran, in Japan, 1213: 5 sub-sects | 13,718 |
| VI. Nichiren. Founded by Nichiren, in Japan, 1262: 2 sub-sects | ...... |
| VII. Ji. Founded by Ippen, in Japan, 1288 | 586 |

Besides the above, there are twenty-one "irregular," "local," or "independent" sects, which act apart from the others, and in some cases have no temples or monasteries. A number of other sects have originated in Japan, flourished for a time, decayed, and passed out of existence. According to the census of 1872, there were in Japan 211,846 Buddhist *religieux* of both sexes and all grades and orders. Of these, 75,925 were priests, abbots, or monks, 9 abbesses; 37,327 were reckoned as novices or students, and 98,585 were in monasteries or families (mostly of Shin sect); 151,677 were males, 60,159 were females, and 9,621 were nuns. By the census of 1875, the returns gave 207,669 Buddhist *religieux*, of whom 148,807 were males, and 58,862 females.

## XVII

# The Invasion of the Mongol Tartars

During the early centuries of the Christian era, friendly intercourse was regularly kept up between Japan and China. Embassies were dispatched to and fro on various missions, but chiefly with the mutual object of bearing the congratulations to an emperor upon his accession to the throne. It is mentioned in the "Gazetteer of Echizen" (*Echi-zen Koku Mei Seiki Kô*) that embassadors from China, with a retinue and crew of one hundred and seventy-eight persons, came to Japan A.D. 776, to bear congratulations to the mikado, Kônin Tennô. The vessel was wrecked in a typhoon off the coast of Echizen, and but forty-six of the company were saved. They were fed and sheltered in Echizen. In A.D. 779, the Japanese embassy, returning from China, landed at Mikuni, the sea-port of Fukui. In 883, orders were sent from Kiôto to the provinces north of the capital to repair the bridges and roads, bury the dead bodies, and remove all obstacles, because the envoys of China were coming that way. The civil disorders in both countries interrupted these friendly relations in the twelfth century, and communications ceased until they were renewed again in the time of the Hôjô, in the manner now to be described.

In China, the Mongol Tartars had overthrown the Sung dynasty, and had conquered the adjacent countries. Through the Coreans, the Mongol emperor, Kublai Khan, at whose court Marco Polo and his uncles were then residing, sent letters demanding tribute and homage from Japan. Chinese envoys came to Kamakura, but Hôjô Tokimuné, enraged at the insolent demands, dismissed them in disgrace. Six embassies were sent, and six times rejected.

An expedition from China, consisting of ten thousand men, was sent against Japan. They landed at Tsushima and Iki. They were bravely attacked, and their commander slain. All Kiushiu having roused to arms, the expedition returned, having accomplished nothing. The Chinese emperor now sent nine envoys, who announced their purpose to remain until a definite answer was returned to their master. They were called to Kamakura, and the Japanese reply was given by cutting off their heads at the village of Tatsu no kuchi (Mouth of the Dragon), near the city. The Japanese now girded themselves for the war they knew was imminent. Troops from the East were sent to guard Kiôto. Munitions of war were prepared, magazines stored, castles repaired, and new armies levied and drilled. Boats and junks were built to meet the enemy on the sea. Once more Chinese envoys came to demand tribute. Again the sword gave the answer, and their heads fell at Daizaifu, in Kiushiu, in 1279.

Meanwhile the armada was preparing. Great China was coming to crush the little strip of land that refused homage to the invincible conqueror. The army numbered one hundred thousand Chinese and Tartars, and seven thousand Coreans, in ships that whitened the sea as the snowy herons whiten the islands of Lake Biwa. They numbered thirty-five hundred in all. In the Seventh month of the year 1281, the tasseled prows and fluted sails of the Chinese junks greeted the straining eyes of watchers on the hills of Daizaifu. The armada sailed gallantly up, and ranged itself off the castled city. Many of the junks were of immense proportions, larger than the natives of Japan had ever seen, and armed with the engines of European war fare, which their Venetian guests had taught the Mongols to construct and work.

The Japanese had small chance of success on the water; as, although their boats, being swifter and lighter, were more easily managed, yet many of them were sunk by the darts and huge stones hurled by the catapults mounted on their enemy's decks. In personal prowess the natives of Nippon were superior. Swimming out to the fleet, a party of thirty boarded a junk, and cut off the heads of the crew; but another company attempting to do so, were all killed by the now wary Tartars. One captain, Kusanojiro, with a picked crew, in broad day-light, sculled rapidly out to an outlying junk, and, in spite of a shower of darts, one of which took off his left arm, ran his boat along-side a Chinese junk, and, letting down the masts, boarded the decks. A hand-to-hand fight ensued, and, before the enemy's fleet could assist, the daring assailants set the ship on fire and were off, carrying away twenty-one heads. The fleet now ranged itself in a cordon, linking each vessel to the other with an iron chain. They hoped thus to foil the cutting-out parties. Besides the catapults, immense bow-guns shooting heavy darts were mounted on their decks, so as to sink all attacking boats. By these means many of the latter were destroyed, and more than one company of Japanese who expected victory lost their lives. Still, the enemy could not effect a landing in force. Their small detachments were cut off or driven into the sea as soon as they reached the shore, and over two thousand heads were among the tro-phies of the defenders in the skirmishes. A line of fortifications many miles long, consisting of earth-works and heavy palisading of planks, was now erected along-shore. Behind these the defenders watched the invaders, and challenged them to land.

There was a Japanese captain, Michiari, who had long hoped for this invasion. He had prayed often to the gods that he might have opportunity to fight the Mongols. He had written his prayers on paper, and, learning them, had solemnly swallowed the ashes. He was now overjoyed at the prospect of a combat. Sallying out from behind the breastwork, he defied the enemy to fight. Shortly after, he filled two boats with brave fellows and pushed out, apparently unarmed, to the fleet. "He is mad," cried the spectators on shore. "How bold," said the men on the fleet, "for two little boats to attack thousands of great ships! Surely he is coming to surrender himself." Supposing this to be his object, they refrained from shooting. When within a few oars-lengths, the Japanese, flinging out ropes with grappling-hooks, leaped on the Tartar junk. The bows and spears of the latter were no match for the two-handed razor-like swords of the Japanese. The issue, though for a while doubtful, was a swift and complete victory for the men who were fighting for their native land. Burning the junk, the surviving victors left before the surrounding ships could cut them off. Among the captured was one of the highest officers in the Mongol fleet.

The whole nation was now roused. Re-enforcements poured in from all quarters to swell the host of defenders. From the monasteries and temples all over the country went up unceasing prayer to the gods to ruin their enemies and save the land of Japan. The emperor and ex-emperor went in solemn state to the chief priest of Shinto, and, writing out their petitions to the gods, sent him as a messenger to the shrines at Isé. It is recorded, as a miraculous fact, that at the hour of noon, as the sacred envoy arrived at the shrine and offered the prayer—the day being perfectly clear—a streak of cloud appeared in the sky, which soon overspread the heavens, until the dense masses portended a storm of awful violence.

One of those cyclones, called by the Japanese *tai-fu*, or ôkazé, of appalling velocity and resistless force, such as whirl along the coasts of Japan and China during late summer and early fall of every year, burst upon the Chinese fleet. Nothing can withstand these maelstroms of the air. We call them typhoons; the Japanese say *tai-fu*, or ôkazé (great wind). Iron steamships of thousands of horse-power are almost unmanageable in them. Junks are helpless: the Chinese ships were these only. They were butted together like mad bulls. They were impaled on the rocks, dashed against the cliffs, or tossed on land like corks from the spray. They were blown over till they careened and filled. Heavily freighted with human beings, they sunk by hundreds. The corpses were piled on the shore, or floating on the water so thickly that it seemed almost possible to walk thereon. Those driven out to sea may have reached the main-land, but were probably overwhelmed. The vessels of the survivors, in large numbers, drifted to or were wrecked upon Taka Island, where they established themselves, and, cutting down trees, began building boats to reach Corea. Here they were attacked by the Japanese, and, after a bloody struggle, all the fiercer for the despair on the one side and the exultation on the other, were all slain or driven into the sea to be drowned, except three, who were sent back to tell their emperor how the gods of Japan had destroyed their armada. The Japanese exult in the boast that their gods and their heaven prevailed over the gods and the heaven of the Chinese.

This was the last time that China ever attempted to conquer Japan, whose people boast that their land has never been defiled by an invading army. They have ever ascribed the glory of the destruction of the Tartar fleet to the interposition of the gods at Isé, who thereafter received special and grateful adoration as the guardian of the seas and winds. Great credit and praise were given to the lord of Kamakura, Hôjô Tokimuné, for his energy, ability, and valor. The author of the *Guai Shi* says, "The repulse of the Tartar barbarians by Tokimuné, and his preserving the dominions of our Son of Heaven, were sufficient to atone for the crimes of his ancestors.

Nearly six centuries afterward, when "the barbarian" Perry anchored his fleet in the Bay of Yedo, in the words of the native annalist, "Orders were sent by the imperial court to the Shintô priests at Isé to offer up prayers for the sweeping-away of the barbarians."

Millions of earnest hearts put up the same prayers as their fathers had offered, fully expecting the same result.

To this day the Japanese mother in Kiushiu hushes her fretful infant by the question, "Do you think the Mogu (Mongols) are coming?" This is the only serious attempt at invasion ever made by any nation upon the shores of Japan.

# XVIII

# *The Temporary Mikadoate*

The first step taken after the overthrow of the military usurpation at Kamakura was to recall the mikado Go-Daigo from exile. With the sovereign again in full power, it seemed as though the ancient and rightful government was to be permanently restored. The military or dual system had lasted about one hundred and fifty years, and patriots now hoped to see the country rightly governed, without intervention between the throne and the people. The rewarding of the victors who had fought for him was the first duty awaiting the restored exile. The methods and procedure of feudalism were now so fixed in the general policy of the Government, that Go-Daigo, falling into the ways of the Minamoto and Hôjô, apportioned military fiefs as guerdons to his vassals. Among them was Ashikaga Takauji, to whom was awarded the greatest prize, consisting of the rich provinces of Hitachi, Musashi, and Shimôsa. To Kusunoki Masashigé were given Settsu and Kawachi; and to Nitta, Kôdzuké and Harima, besides smaller fiefs to many others.

This unfair distribution of spoils astounded the patriots, who expected to see high rank and power conferred upon Nitta and Kusunoki, the chief leaders in the war for the restoration, and both very able men. It would have been well had the emperor seen the importance of disregarding the claims and privileges of caste, and

exalted to highest rank the faithful men who were desirous of maintaining the dignity of the throne, and whose chief fear was that the
duarchy would again arise. Such a fear was by no means groundless,
for Ashikaga, elated at such unexpected favor, became inflamed
with a still higher ambition, and already meditated refounding the
shôgunate at Kamakura, and placing his own family upon the military throne. Being of Minamoto stock, he knew that he had prestige
and popularity in his favor, should he attempt the re-erection of the
shôgunate. Most of the common soldiers had fought rather against
Hôjô than against duarchy. The emperor was warned against this
man by his ministers; but in this case a woman's smiles and caresses
and importunate words were more powerful than the advice of sages.
Ashikaga had bribed the mikado's concubine Kadoko, and had so won
her favor that she persuaded her imperial lord to bestow excessive and
undeserved honor on the traitor.

The distribution of spoils excited discontent among the soldiers,
who now began to lose all interest in the cause for which they had
fought, and to murmur privately among themselves. "Should such an
unjust government continue," said they, "then are we all servants of
concubines and dancing-girls and singing-boys. Rather than be the
puppets of the mikado's amusers, we would prefer a shôgun again, and
become his vassals." Many of the captains and smaller clan-leaders
were also in bad humor over their own small shares. Ashikaga Takauji
took advantage of this feeling to make himself popular among the
disaffected, especially those who clung to arms as a profession and
wished to remain soldiers, preferring war to peace. Of such inflammable material the latent traitor was not slow to avail himself when
it suited him to light the flames of war.

Had the mikado listened to his wise counselor, and also placed
Kusunoki in an office commensurate with his commanding abilities,

and rewarded Nitta as he deserved, the century of anarchy and bloodshed which followed might have been spared to Japan.

Go-Daigo, who in the early years of his former reign had been a man of indomitable courage and energy, seems to have lost the best traits of his character in his exile, retaining only his imperious will and susceptibility to flattery. To this degenerate Samson a Delilah was not wanting. He fell an easy victim to the wiles of one man, though the shears by which his strength was shorn were held by a woman. Ashikaga was a consummate master of the arts of adulation and political craft. He was now to further prove his skill, and to verify the warnings of Nitta and the ministers. The emperor made Moriyoshi, his own son, shôgun. Ashikaga, jealous of the appointment, and having too ready access to the infatuated father's ear, told him that his son was plotting to get possession of the throne. Moriyoshi, hating the flatterer, and stung to rage by the base slander, marched against him. Ashikaga now succeeded by means of his ally in the imperial bed in making himself, in the eyes of the mikado, the first victim to the conspiracies of the prince. So great was his power over the emperor that he obtained from the imperial hand a decree to punish his enemy Moriyoshi as a *chôtéki*, or rebel, against the mikado.

Here we have a striking instance of what, in the game of Japanese state-craft, may be called the checkmate move, or, in the native idiom, *Ôté*, "king's hand." It is difficult for a foreigner to fully appreciate the prestige attaching to the mikado's person—a prestige never diminishing. No matter how low his actual measure of power, the meanness of his character, or the insignificance of his personal abilities, he was the Son of Heaven, his word was law, his command omnipotent. He was the fountain of all rank and authority. No military leader, however great his resources or ability, could win the popular heart or hope for ultimate success unless appointed by the emperor. He who

held the Son of Heaven in his power was master. Hence it was the
constant aim of all the military leaders, even down to 1868, to obtain
control of the imperial person. However wicked or villainous the
keeper of the mikado, he was master of the situation. His enemies
were *chôtéki*, or rebels against the Son of Heaven; his own soldiers
were the *kuan-gun*, or loyal army. Even might could not make right.
Possession of the divine person was more than nine-tenths—it was
the whole—of the law.

Moriyoshi, then, being *chôtéki*, was doomed. Ashikaga, having
the imperial order, had the *kuan-gun*, and was destined to win. The
sad fate of the emperor's son awakens the saddest feelings, and brings
tears to the eyes of the Japanese reader even at the present day. He was
seized, deposed, sent to Kamakura, and murdered in a subterranean
dungeon in the Seventh month of the year 1335.

His child in exile, the heart of the emperor relented. The scales fell
from his eyes. He saw that he had wrongly suspected his son, and that
the real traitor was Ashikaga. The latter, noticing the change that had
come over his master, left Kiôto secretly, followed by thousands of
the disaffected soldiery, and fled to Kamakura, which he had rebuilt,
and began to consolidate his forces with a view of again erecting the
Eastern capital, and seizing the power formerly held by the Hôjô.
Nitta had also been accused by Ashikaga, but, having cleared himself
in a petition to the mikado, he received the imperial commission to
chastise his rival. In the campaign which followed, the imperial forces
were so hopelessly defeated that the quondam imperial exile now
became a fugitive. With his loyal followers he left Kiôto, carrying
with him the sacred emblems of authority.

Ashikaga, though a triumphant victor, occupied a critical position.
He was a *chôtéki*. As such he could never win final success. He had
power and resources, but, unlike others equally usurpers, was not
clothed with authority. He was, in popular estimation, a rebel of the

deepest dye. In such a predicament he could not safely remain a day. The people would take the side of the emperor. What should he do? His vigor, acuteness, and villainy were equal. The Hôjô had deposed and set up emperors. It was Ashikaga who divided the allegiance of the people, gave Japan a War of the Roses (or Chrysanthemums), tilled the soil for feudalism, and lighted the flames of war that made Kiôto a cock-pit, abandoned the land for nearly two centuries and a half to slaughter, ignorance, and paralysis of national progress. To clothe his acts with right, he made a new Son of Heaven. He declared Kogen, who was of the royal family, emperor. In 1336, this new Son of Heaven gave Ashikaga the title of Sei-i Tai Shôgun. Kamakura again became the military capital. The duarchy was restored, and the War of the Northern and the Southern Dynasties began, which lasted fifty-six years.

The period 1333–1336, though including little more than two years of time, is of great significance as marking the existence of a temporary mikadoate. The fact that it lasted so short a time, and that the duarchy was again set up on its ruins, has furnished both natives and foreigners with the absurd and specious, but strongly urged, argument that the Government of Japan, by a single ruler from a single centre, is an impossibility, and that the creation of a dual system with a "spiritual" or nominal sovereign in one part of the empire, and a military or "secular" ruler in another, is a necessity. During the agitation of the question concerning the abolition of the dual system, and the restoration of the mikado in 1860–1868, one of the chief arguments of the adherents of the shôgunate against the scheme of the agitators, was the assertion that the events of the period 1333–1336 proved that the mikado could not alone govern the country, and that it must have duarchy. Even after the overthrow of the "Tycoon" in 1868, foreigners, as well as natives, who had studied Japanese history, fully believed and expected that in a year or two the present mikado's Government would be overthrown, and the "Tycoon" return to power, basing their belief on the fact that the mikadoate of 1333–1336 did not last. Whatever force such an argument might have had when Japan had no foreign relations, and no aliens on her soil to disturb the balance between Kiôto and Kamakura, it is certain that it counts for naught when, under altered conditions, more than the united front of the whole empire* is now required to cope with the political pressure from without.

---

* Certain writers, and one as late as 1873, dispute the right of Japan to be called an "empire," and the mikados to be styled "emperor," "inasmuch as they [the mikados] sent tribute to the Emperor of China." As matter of fact, none of the mikados ever did this, though one shôgun (Ashikaga Yoshimitsu, page 212) did. Chinese books, and even the official gazettes of Peking, speak of all nations—even England, France, and the United States—as "paying tribute" to China, and their envoys as "tribute-bearers." Japan has always remained in total political independence of the Middle Kingdom and her Hwang Ti. That Japan is an "empire," the absolutism of the mikado, the diversity of her forms of governmental administration, differing in Liu Kiu (having its lord, or feudal vassal), Yezo (territory governed by a special department), and in the main body of the empire, besides its varied nationalities—Japanese, Liu Kiuans, and Ainôs. This expression of sovereignty is graphically conveyed in the two Chinese characters, pronounced, in Japanese, Ko-tei (page 44–45, note), and Hwang Ti in Chinese. The Japanese rulers, borrowing their notions of government and imperialism from China, as those of modern Europe have from Rome, adopted the title for the mikado, who has ever ruled, not only over his own subjects of like blood, but over ebisu, or barbarians, and tributary people. When the character Ko is joined to Koku (country), we get Kô Koku, or "The Mikado's Empire," the idea emphasized being personal, or that of the mikado as government personified. When Tei is joined to Koku (Tei Koku Nihon, the blazon, or distinctive tablet, inscribed with four Chinese characters over the Japanese section at the Centennial Exposition at Philadelphia), we have the idea of an empire ruled by deity, or divine government—theocracy. The fact that Japan, though so much smaller than China, has always claimed equal dignity, power, and glory with her mighty neighbor, and the fact that there can not be two suns in the same heaven, helps to explain the deep-seated rivalry, mutual jealousy, and even contempt, which "the decayed old gentleman" and "the conceited young upstart" feel toward each other.

# XIX

# *The War of the Chrysanthemums*

The dynasty of the imperial rulers of Japan is the oldest in the world. No other family line extends so far back into the remote ages as the nameless family of mikados. Disdaining to have a family name, claiming descent, not from mortals, but from the heavenly gods, the imperial house of the Kingdom of the Rising Sun occupies a throne which no plebeian has ever attempted to usurp. Throughout all the vicissitudes of the imperial line, in plenitude of power or abasement of poverty, its members deposed or set up at the pleasure of the upstart or the political robber, the throne itself has remained unshaken. Unclean hands have not been laid upon the ark itself. As in the procession of life on the globe the individual perishes, the species lives on, so, though individual mikados have been dethroned, insulted, or exiled, the prestige of the line has never suffered. The loyalty or allegiance of the people has never swerved. The soldier who would begin revolution, or who lusted for power, would make the mikado his tool; but, however transcendent his genius and abilities, he never attempted to write himself mikado. No Japanese Cæsar ever had his Brutus, nor Charles his Cromwell, nor George his Washington. Not even, as in China, did one dynasty of alien blood overthrow another, and reign in the stead of a destroyed family. Such events are unknown in Japanese annals. The student of this people and their unique history can never understand them or their national life unless he measures the mightiness of the force, and recognizes the place of the throne and the mikado in the minds and hearts of its people.

There are on record instances in which the true heirship was declared only after bitter intrigue, quarrels, or even bloodshed. In the tenth century, Taira no Masakado, disappointed in not being appointed Dai Jô Dai Jin, left Kiôto, went to Shimôsa in the Kuantô, and set himself up as Shinnô, or cadet of the imperial line, and temporarily ruled the eight provinces of the East as a pseudo-mikado.* In 1139, the military families of Taira and Minamoto came to blows in Kiôto over the question of succession between the rival heirs, Shutoku and Go-Shirakawa. The Taira being victors, their candidate became mikado. During the decay of the Taira, they fled from Kiôto, carrying with them, as true emperor, with his suite and the sacred insignia, Antoku, the child, five

---

* Taira no Masakado, or, as we should say, Masakado Taira, was a man of great energy and of unscrupulous character. He was at first governor of Shimôsa, but aspired to rule over all the East. He built a palace on the same model as that of the mikado, at Sajima, in Shimotsuké, and appointed officers similar to those at the imperial court. He killed his uncle, who stood in the way of his ambition. To revenge his father's death, Sadamori, cousin to Masakado, headed two thousand men, attacked the false mikado, and shot him to death with an arrow, carrying his head as trophy and evidence to Kiôto, where it was exposed on the pillory. Shortly after his decease, the people of Musashi, living on the site of modern Tôkiô, being greatly afflicted by the troubled and angry spirit of their late ruler, erected a temple on the site within the second castle enceinte near Kanda Bridge, and in that part of the city district of Kanda (God's Field) now occupied by the Imperial Treasury Department. This had the effect of soothing the unquiet ghost, and the land had rest; and later generations, mindful of the power of a spirit that in life ruled all the Kuantô, and in death could afflict or give peace to millions at will, worshiped Masakado under the posthumous name of Kanda Miô Jin (Illustrious Deity of Kanda), his history having been forgotten, or transfigured into the form of a narrative, which to doubt was sin. When Iyéyasu, in the latter end of the sixteenth century, made Yedo his capital, he removed the shrine to a more

years old, who was drowned in the sea when the Taira were destroyed. The Minamoto at the same time recognized Gotoba.

It may be more analogical to call the wars of the Gen and Hei, with their white and red flags, the Japanese Wars of the Roses. Theirs was the struggle of rival houses. Now, we are to speak of rival dynasties, each with the imperial chrysanthemum.

In the time of the early Ashikagas (1336–1390) there were two mikados ruling, or attempting to rule, in Japan. The Emperor Go-Daigo had chosen his son Kuniyoshi as his heir, but the latter died in 1326. Kôgen, son of the mikado Go-Fushimi (1299–1301), was then made heir. Go-Daigo's third son Moriyoshi, however, as he grew up, showed great talent, and his father regretted that he had consented to the choice of Kôgen, and wished his own son to succeed him. He referred the matter to Hôjô at Kamakura, who disapproved of the plan. Those who hated Hôjô called Kôgen the "false emperor," refusing to acknowledge him. When Nitta destroyed Kamakura, and Go-Daigo was restored, Kogen retired to obscurity. No one for a moment thought of or acknowledged any one but Go-Daigo as true and only mikado. When, however, Ashikaga by his treachery had alienated the emperor from him, and was without imperial favor, and liable to punishment as a rebel, he found out and set up Kogen as mikado, and proclaimed him sovereign. Civil war then broke out.

---

eligible location on the hill in the rear of the Kanda River and the Suido, where, later, the university stood, and erected an edifice of great splendor, surrounded by groves and grounds of surpassing loveliness. This was perhaps only policy, to gain the popular favor by honoring the local gods; but it stirred up some jealousy among the "mikado-reverencers" and students of history who knew the facts. Some accused him of treasonable designs like those of Masakado. In 1868, when the mikado's troops arrived in Yedo, they rushed to the temple of Kanda Miô Jin, and, pulling out the idol or image of the deified Masakado, hacked it to pieces with their swords, wishing the same fate to all traitors. Thus, after nine centuries, the traitor received a traitor's reward, a clear instance of historic justice in the eyes of native patriots.

Into the details of the war between the adherents of the Northern emperor, Ashikaga, with his followers, on the one side, and Go-Daigo, who held the insignia of authority, backed by a brilliant array of names famous among the Japanese, on the other, I do not propose to enter. It is a confused and sickening story of loyalty and treachery, battle, murder, pillage, fire, famine, poverty, and misery, such as make up the picture of civil wars in every country. Occasionally in this period a noble deed or typical character shines forth for the admiration or example of succeeding generations. Among these none have exhibited more nobly man's possible greatness in the hour of death than Nitta Yoshisada and Kusunoki Masashigé.

On one occasion the army of Nitta, who was fighting under the flag of Go-Daigo, the true emperor, was encamped before that of Ashikaga. To save further slaughter, Nitta sallied out alone, and, approaching his enemy's camp, cried out: "The war in the country continues long. Although this has arisen from the rivalry of two emperors, yet its issue depends solely upon you and me. Rather than millions of the people should be involved in distress, let us determine the question by single combat." The retainers of Ashikaga prevailed on their commander not to accept the challenge. In 1338, on the second day of the Seventh month, while marching with about fifty followers to assist in investing a fortress in Echizen, he was suddenly attacked in a narrow path in a rice-field near Fukui by about three thousand of the enemy, and exposed without shields to a shower of arrows. Some one begged Nitta, as he was mounted, to escape. "It is not my desire to survive my companions slain," was his response. Whipping up his horse, he rode forward to engage with his sword, making himself the target for a hundred archers. His horse, struck when at full speed by an arrow, fell. Nitta, on clearing himself and rising, was hit between the eyes with a white-feathered shaft, and mortally wounded. Drawing his sword, he cut off his own head—a feat which the warriors of that time were trained to perform—so that his enemies might not recognize him. He was thirty-eight years old. His brave little band were slain by arrows, or killed themselves with their own hand, that they might die with their master. The enemy could not recognize Nitta, until they found, beneath a pile of corpses of men who had committed *hara-kiri*, a body on which, inclosed in a damask bag, was a letter containing the imperial commission in Go-Daigo's hand-writing, "I invest you with all power to subjugate the rebels." Then they knew the corpse to be that of Nitta. His head was carried to Kiôto, then in possession of Ashikaga, and exposed in public on a pillory. The tomb of this brave man stands, carefully watched and tended, near Fukui, in Echizen, hard by the very spot where he fell. I often passed it in my walks, when living in Fukui in 1871, and noticed that fresh blooming flowers were almost daily laid upon it —the tribute of an admiring people. A shrine and monument *in memoriam* were erected in his native place during the year 1875.

The brave Kusunoki, after a lost battle at Minatogawa, near Hiôgo, having suffered continual defeat, his counsels having been set at naught, and his advice rejected, felt that life was no longer honorable, and solemnly resolved to die in unsullied reputation and with a soldier's honor. Sorrowfully bidding his wife and infant children goodbye, he calmly committed *hara-kiri*, an example which his comrades, numbering one hundred and fifty, bravely followed.

Kusunoki Masashigé was one of an honorable family who dwelt in Kawachi, and traced their descent to the great-grandson of the thirty-second mikado, Bidatsu (A.D. 572–585). The family name, Kusunoki ("Camphor"), was given his people from the fact that a grove of camphor-trees adorned the ancestral gardens of the mansion. The twelfth in descent was the Vice-governor of Iyo. The father of Masashigé held land assessed at two thousand *koku*. His mother, desiring a child, prayed to the god Bishamon for one hundred days, and Masashige was born after a pregnancy of fourteen months. The mother, in devout gratitude, named the boy Tamon (the Sanskrit name of Bishamon), after the god who had heard her prayers. The man-child was very strong, and at seven could throw boys of fifteen at wrestling. He received his education in the Chinese classics from the priests in the temple, and exercised himself in all manly and warlike arts. In his twelfth year he cut off the head of an enemy, and at fifteen studied the Chinese military art, and made it the solemn purpose of his life to overthrow the Kamakura usurpation, and restore the mikado to power. In 1330, he took up arms for Go-Daigo. He was several times besieged by the Hôjô armies, but was finally victorious with Nitta and Ashikaga. When the latter became a rebel, defeated Nitta, and entered Kiôto in force, Kusunoki joined Nitta, and thrice drove out the troops of Ashikaga from the capital. The latter then fled to the West, and Kusunoki advised the imperialist generals to follow them up and annihilate the rebellion. His superiors, with criminal levity, neglecting to do this, the rebels collected together, and again advanced, with increased strength by land and water, against Kiôto, having, it is said, two hundred thousand men. Kusunoki's plan of operations was rejected, and his advice ignored. With Nitta he was compelled to bear the brunt of battle against overwhelming forces at Minato gawa, near Hiôgo, and was there hopelessly defeated. Kusunoki, now feeling that he had done all that was possible to a subordinate, and that life was no longer honorable, retired to a farmer's house at the village of Sakurai, and there, giving him the sword bestowed on himself by the mikado, admonished his son Masatsura to follow the soldier's calling, cherish his father's memory, and avenge his father's death. Sixteen of his relatives, with unquailing courage, likewise followed their master in death.

Of all the characters in Japanese history, that of Kusunoki Masashigé stands pre-eminent for pureness of patriotism, unselfishness of devotion to duty, and calmness of courage. The people speak of him in tones of reverential tenderness, and, with an admiration that lacks fitting words, behold in him the mirror of stainless loyalty. I have more than once asked my Japanese students and friends whom they considered the noblest character in their history. Their unanimous answer was "Kusunoki Masashigé." Every relic of this brave man is treasured up with religious care; and fans inscribed with poems written by him, in facsimile of his handwriting, are sold in the shops and used by those who burn to imitate his exalted patriotism.* His son Masatsura lived to become a gallant soldier.

The war, which at first was waged with the clearly defined object of settling the question of the supremacy of the rival mikados, gradually lost its true character, and finally degenerated into a *mêlée* and free fight on a national scale. Before peace was finally declared, all the original leaders had died, and the prime object had been, in a great measure, forgotten in the lust for land and war. Even the rival emperors lost much of their interest, as they had no concern in brawls by which petty chieftains sought to exalt their own name, and increase their territory by robbing their neighbors. In 1392, an envoy from Ashikaga persuaded Go-Kaméyama to come to Kiôto and hand over the regalia to Go-Komatsu, the Northern emperor. The basis of peace was that Go-Kaméyama should receive the title of Dai Jô Tennô (ex-emperor), Go-Komatsu be declared emperor, and the throne be occupied alternately by the rival branches of the imperial family. The

---

* I make no attempt to conceal my own admiration of a man who acted according to his light, and faced his soldierly ideal of honor, when conscience and all his previous education told him that his hour had come, and that to flinch from the suicidal thrust was dishonor and sin. No enlightened Japanese of to-day would show himself brave by committing *hara-kiri*, as the most earnest writers, thinkers, and even soldiers admit. Fukuzawa, the learned reformer and pedagogue, and a chaste and eloquent writer, in one of his works condemns the act of Kusunoki, not mentioning him by name, however, as lacking

ceremony of abdication and surrender of regalia, on the one hand, and of investiture, on the other, were celebrated with due pomp and solemnity in one of the great temples in the capital, and the war of fifty-six years duration ceased. All this redounded to the glory and power of the Ashikaga.

The period 1336–1392 is of great interest in the eyes of all native students of Japanese history. In the *Dai Nihon Shi*, the Southern dynasty are defended as the legitimate sovereigns, and the true descendants of Ten Shô Dai Jin, the sun-goddess; and the Northern dynasty are condemned as mere usurpers. The same view was taken by Kitabataké Chikafusa, who was the author of the Japanese Red-book, who warned the emperor Go-Daigo against Ashikaga, and in 1339 wrote a book to prove that Go-Daigo was mikado, and the Ashikaga's nominee a usurper. This is the view now held in modern Japan, and only those historians of the period who award legitimacy to the Southern dynasty are considered authoritative. The Northern branch of the imperial family after a few generations became extinct.*

the element of true courage, according to the enlightened view. He explains and defends the Christian ideas on the subject of suicide. His book created great excitement and intense indignation in the minds of the samurai at first; but now he carries with him the approbation of the leading minds in Japan, especially of the students.

* The names of the "Northern," or "False," emperors are Kôgen, Kômiô, Shinko, Go-Kôgon, Go-Enyiu, and Go-Komatsu.

## XX

# *The Ashikaga Period*

The internal history of Japan during the period of time covered by the actual or nominal rule of the thirteen shôguns of the Ashikaga family, from 1336 until 1573, except that portion after the year 1542, is not very attractive to a foreign reader. It is a confused picture of intestine war.

Ashikaga Takauji, the founder of the line was a descendant of the Minamoto Yoshikuni, who had settled at Ashikaga, a village in Shimotsuké, in the eleventh century. He died in 1356. His grandson Yoshimitsu, called the Great Ashikaga, was made shôgun when ten years old, and became a famous warrior in the South and West. After the union of the two dynasties, he built a luxurious palace at Kiôto, and was made Dai Jô Dai Jin. He enjoyed his honors for one year. He then retired from the world to become a shaven monk in a Buddhist monastery.

Under the Hôjô, the office of shôgun was filled by appointment of the imperial court; but under the Ashikaga the office became hereditary in this family. As usual, the man with the title was, in nearly every case, but a mere figure-head, wielding little more personal power than that of the painted and gilded simulacrum of the admiral that formerly adorned the prow of our old seventy-four-gun ships. During this period the term Kubô sama, applied to the shôguns, and used so frequently by the Jesuit fathers, came into use. The actual work of government was done by able men of inferior rank. The most noted of these was Hosokawa Yoriyuki, who was a fine scholar as well as a warrior. It was through his ordering that the young shôgun Yoshimitsu was well trained, and had for his companions noble youths who excelled in literary and military skill. This was vastly different from Hôjô Tokimasa's treatment of the sons of Yoritomo. He attempted the reform of manners and administration. He issued five mottoes for the conduct of the military and civil officers. They were: 1. Thou shalt not be partial in amity or enmity. 2. Thou shalt return neither favor nor vengeance. 3. Thou shalt not deceive, either with a right or a wrong [motive]. 4. Thou shalt not hope dishonestly [for a bribe]. 5. Thou shalt not deceive thyself.

The pendulum of power during this period oscillated between Kiôto and Kamakura; a tai (or "great") shôgun ruling at the former, and a shôgun at the latter place. An officer called the *shikken* was the real ruler of the capital and the central provinces; and another called the *kuan-rei* (Governor of the Kuantô), of Kamakura and the East. War was the rule, peace the exception. Feudal fights; border brawls; the seizure of lands; the rise of great clans; the building, the siege, and the destruction of castles, were the staple events. Every monastery was now a stronghold, an arsenal, or a camp. The issue of a combat or a campaign was often decided by the support which the bonzes gave to one or the other party. The most horrible excesses were committed, the ground about Kiôto and Kamakura, both of which were captured and recaptured many times, became like the *chitama* (blood-pits) of the execution-ground. Villages, cities, temples, monasteries, and libraries were burned. The fertile fields lay waste, blackened by fire, or covered from sight, as with a cloth, by dense thickets of tall weeds, which, even in one summer's time, spring with astonishing fecundity from the plethoric soil of Japan. The people driven from their homes by war returned to find a new wilderness, resounding with the din of devouring insects. The people of gentle birth fled to mountain caves. Education was neglected. The common herd grew up in ignorance and misery. Reading and writing, except among the priests and nobles, were unknown arts which the warriors scorned. War was the only lucrative trade, except that of the armorers or sword-makers. Famine followed on the footsteps of war, and with pestilence slew her tens of thousands. Pirates on the seas ravaged not only the coasts of Japan, but those of China and Corea, adding pillage and rapine to the destruction of commerce. The Chinese mothers at Ningpo even now are heard to frighten their children by mentioning the names of the Japanese pirates. On land the peasantry were impressed in military service to build castles or intrenched camps; or, the most daring, becoming robbers, made their nests in the mountains and plundered the traveler, or descended upon the merchant's store-house. Japan was then the paradise of thieves. To all these local terrors were added those gendered in the mind of man by the convulsions of nature. Earthquakes, volcanic eruptions, floods, tidal waves, typhoons, and storms seem to have been abnormally frequent during this period. The public morals became frightfully corrupted, religion debased. All kinds of strange and uncouth doctrines came into vogue. Prostitution was never more rampant. It was the Golden Age of crime and anarchy.

The condition of the emperors was deplorable. With no revenues, and dwelling in a capital alternately in the possession of one or the other hostile army; in frequent danger from thieves, fire, or starvation; exposed to the weather or the dangers of war, the narrative of their sufferings excites pity in the mind of even a foreign reader, and from the native draws the tribute of tears. One was so poor that he depended upon the bounty of a noble for his food and clothing; another died in such poverty that his body lay unburied for several days, for lack of money to have him interred. The remembrance of

the wrongs and sufferings of these poor emperors fired the hearts
and nerved the arms of the men who in 1868 fought to sweep away
forever the hated system by which such treatment of their sovereign
became possible.

So utterly demoralized is the national, political, and social life
of this period believed to have been, that the Japanese people make
it the limbo of all vanities. Dramatists and romancers use it as the
convenient ground whereon to locate every novel or play, the plot of
which violates all present probability. The chosen time of the bulk of
Japanese dramas and novels written during the last century or two is
that of the late Ashikagas. The satirist or writer aiming at contemporary folly, or at blunders and oppression of the Government, yet
wishing to avoid punishment and elude the censor, clothes his characters in the garb and manners of this period. It is the potter's field
where all the outcasts and Judases of moralists are buried. By common
consent, it has become the limbo of playwright and romancer, and the
scape-goat of chronology.

The act by which, more than any other, the Ashikagas have earned
the curses of posterity was the sending of an embassy to China in
1401, bearing presents acknowledging, in a measure, the authority
of China, and accepting in return the title of Nippon Ô, or King of
Japan. This, which was done by Ashikaga Yoshimitsu, the third of
the line, was an insult to the national dignity for which he has never
been forgiven. It was a needless humiliation of Japan to her arrogant
neighbor, and done only to exalt the vanity and glory of the usurper
Ashikaga, who, not content with adopting the style and equipage of
the mikado, wished to be made or called a king, and yet dared not
usurp the imperial throne.* The punishment of Ashikaga is the curse
of posterity. In 1853, when the treaty with the United States was made,

---

* The Ashikaga line of shoguns comprised the following:

a similar insult to the sovereign and the nation, as well as a contemptible deception of the American envoy and foreigners, was practiced by the shôgun calling himself "Tycoon" (Great King, or Sovereign of Japan). In this latter instance, as we know, came not the distant anathema of future generations, but the swift vengeance of war, the permanent humiliation, the exile to obscurity, of the Tokugawa family, and the abolition of the shôgunate and the dual system forever.

It was during the first of the last three decades of the Ashikaga period that Japan became known to the nations of Europe; while firearms, gunpowder, and a new and mighty faith were made known to the Japanese nation.

| | | | |
|---|---|---|---|
| 1. Takauji | 1335–1357 | 9. Yoshihisa | 1472–1489 |
| 2. Yoshinori | 1358–1367 | 10. Yoshitané | 1490–1493 |
| 3. Yoshmitsu | 1368–1393 | 11. Yoshizumi | 1494–1507 |
| 4. Yoshimochi | 1394–1422 | 12. Yoshitané (same as the 10th) | 1508–1520 |
| 5. Yoshikadzu | 1423–1425 | 13. Yoshiharu | 1521–1545 |
| 6. Yoshinori | 1428–1440 | 14. Yoshiteru | 1546–1567 |
| 7. Yoshikatsu | 1441–1448 | 15. Yoshiaki | 1568–1573 |
| 8. Yoshimasa | 1449–1471 | | |

The term Kubô sama, so often used by the Jesuit and Dutch writers, was not an official title of the shôgun, but was applied to him by the common people. When at first anciently used, it referred to the mikado, or, rather, the mikado who had abdicated, or preceded the ruling sovereign; but later, when the people saw in the Kamakura court and its master so close an imitation of the imperial style and capital, they began gradually to speak of the shôgun as the Kubô, with, however, only the general meaning of "the governing power," or the nobleman who enjoyed the right of riding to the court in a car, and entering the imperial palace. The term was in use until 1868, but was never inherent in any office, being rather the exponent of certain forms of etiquette, privilege, and display, than of official duties. The Jesuit fathers nearly always speak of the mikado as the Dairi (see page 39), and at first erroneously termed the daimios "kings." Later on, they seemed to have gained a clear understanding of the various titles and official relations. In some works the Kuambaku (with *dono*, lord, attached) is spoken of as "emperor." Nobunaga, who became Nai Dai Jin, is also called "emperor." During the supremacy of the military rulers at Kamakura and Yedo, the offices and titles, though purely civil, once exclusively given to nobles at the mikado's court, were held by the officials of the shôgunate.

In later chapters, the writer of this work has fallen into the careless and erroneous practice of calling daimiôs "princes." The term "prince" should be employed only in speaking of the sons of the mikado, or members of the imperial family. "Collectively, the daimiôs were lords or barons, and all ranks of the peerage were represented among them, from the kokushi, or dukes, down to the hatamoto, or knights."

# XXI

# *Life in the Middle Ages*

History, as usually written, gives the impression that the normal condition of mankind is that of war. Japanese students who take up the history of England to read, lay it down convinced that the English people are a blood-loving race that are perpetually fighting. They contrast their own peaceful country with the countries of Europe, to the detriment of the latter. They turn most gladly from the monotonous story of battle, murder, and sieges, to Buckle, Guizot, or Lecky, that they may learn of the victories no less renowned than those of war which mark as mile-stones the progress of the race. I greatly fear that from lack of literary skill my readers will say that my story of Japan thus far is a story of bloody war; but such, indeed, it is as told in their own histories. Permanent, universal peace was unknown in Japan until, by the genius of Iyéyasu in the sixteenth century, two centuries and a half of this blessing were secured. Nevertheless, in the eight centuries included between the eighth and the sixteenth of our era were many, and often lengthened, intervals of peace. In many sequestered places the sandal of the warrior and the hoof of the war-horse never printed the soil. Peace in the palace, in the city, in the village, allowed the development of manners, arts, manufactures, and agriculture. In this period were developed the characteristic growths of the Japanese intellect, imagination, social economy, and manual skill that have made the hermit nation unique in the earth and Japanese art productions the wonder of the world.

In this chapter, I shall simply glance at some of the salient features of life in Japan during the Middle Ages.

The introduction of continental or Chinese civilization into Japan was not a simple act of adoption. It was rather a work of selection and assimilation. As in this nineteenth century, the Japanese is no blind copyist, he improves on what he borrows. Although the traveler from China entering Japan can see in a moment whence the Japanese have borrowed their civilization, and though he may believe the Japanese to be an inferior type to that of the Chinese, he will acknowledge that the Japanese have improved upon their borrowed elements fully as much as the French have improved upon those of Roman civilization. Many reflecting foreigners in Japan have asked the question why the Japanese are so unlike the Chinese, and why their art, literature, laws, customs, dress, workmanship, all bear a stamp peculiar to themselves, though they received so much from them? The reason is to be found in the strength and persistence of the primal Japanese type of character, as influenced by nature, enabling it to resist serious alteration and radical change. The greatest conquests made by any of the imparted elements of continental civilization was that of Buddhism, which became within ten centuries the universally popular religion. Yet even its conquests were but partial. Its triumph was secured only by its adulteration. Japanese Buddhism is a distinct product among the many forms of that Asiatic religion. Buddhism secured life and growth on Japanese soil only by being Japanized, by being grafted on the original stock of ideas in the Japanese mind. Thus, in order to popularize the Indian religion, the ancient native heroes and the local gods were all included within the Buddhist pantheon, and declared to be the incarnations of Buddha in his various forms. A class of deities exist in Japan who are worshiped by the Buddhists under the general name of *gongen*. They are all deified Japanese heroes, warriors, or famous men. Furthermore, many of the old rites and ceremonies of Shintô were altered and made use of by the bonzes. It may be doubted whether Buddhism could have ever been popular in Japan, had it not become thoroughly Japanized. Some of the first-fruits of the success of the new religion was the erection of temples, pagodas, idols, wayside shrines, monasteries, and nunneries; the adoption of the practice of cremation, until then unknown; and the cessation of the slaughter of animals for food. The largest and richest of the ecclesiastical structures were in or near Kiôto. The priests acted as teachers, advisers, counselors, and scribes, besides officiating at the altars, shriving the sick, and attending the sepulture of the dead.

Among the orders and sects which grew and multiplied were many similar to those in papal Europe—mendicants, sellers of indulgences, builders of shrines and images, and openers of mountain paths. The monasteries became asylums for the distressed, afflicted, and persecuted. In them the defeated soldier, the penniless and the dissatisfied, the refugee from the vendetta, could find inviolate shelter. To them the warrior after war, the prince and the minister leaving the palace, the honors and pomp of the world, could retire to spend the remnant of their days in prayer, worship, and the offices of piety. Often the murderer, struck with remorse, or the soldier before his bloody victim, would resolve to turn monk. Not rarely did men crossed in love, or the offspring of the concubine displaced by the birth of the legitimate son, or the grief-stricken father, devote himself to the priestly life. In general, however, the ranks of the bonzes were recruited from orphans or piously inclined youth, or from overstocked families. To the nunneries, the fertile soil of bereavement, remorse, unrequited love, widowhood furnished the greater number of sincere and devout nuns. In many cases, the deliberate choice of wealthy ladies, or the necessity of escaping an uncongenial marriage planned by relatives, undesirable attentions, or the lusts of rude men in unsettled times, gave many an inmate to the convents.

In general, however, natural indolence, a desire to avoid the round of drudgery at the well, the hoe, or in the kitchen, or as nurse, sent the majority of applicants to knock at the convent doors. Occasionally a noble lady was won to recluse life from the very apartments of the emperor, or his ministers, by the eloquence of a bonze who was more zealous than loyal. In a few of the convents, only ladies of wealth could enter. The monk and nun, in Japanese as in European history, romance, and drama, and art, are staple characters. The rules of these monastic institutions forbade the eating of fish or flesh, the drinking of saké, the wearing of the hair or of fine clothes, indulgence in certain sensuous pleasures, or the reading of certain books. Fastings, vigils, reflection, continual prayer by book, bell, candle, and beads, were enjoined. Pious pilgrimages were undertaken. The erection of a shrine, image, belfry, or lantern by begging contributions was a frequent and meritorious enterprise. There stand today thousands of these monuments of the piety, zeal, and industry of the mediæval monks and nuns. Those at Nara and Kamakura are the most famous. The Kamakura Dai Butsu (Great Buddha) has been frequently described before. It is a mass of copper 44 feet high, and a work of high art. The image at Nara was first erected in the eighth century, destroyed during the civil wars, and recast about seven hundred years ago. Its total height is 53 1/2 feet; its face is 16 feet long, and 9 1/2 feet wide.The width of its shoulders is 28 7/10 feet. Nine hundred and sixty-six curls adorn its head, around which is a halo 78 feet in diameter, on which are sixteen images, each 8 feet long. The casting of the idol is said to have been tried seven times before it was successfully accomplished, and 3,000 tons of charcoal were used in the operation. The metal, said to weigh 450 tons, is a bronze composed of gold (500 pounds), mercury (1,954 pounds), tin (16,827 pounds),  and copper (986,080 pounds). Many millions of tons of copper were mined and melted to make these idols. Equally renowned were the great temple-bells of Kiôto, and of Miidera, and various other monasteries. Some of these were ten feet high, and adorned with sacred texts from the Buddhist Scriptures, and images of heavenly beings, or Buddha on the sacred lotus in Nirvana, in high relief. As usual, the nimbus, or halo, surrounds his head. Two dragon-heads formed the summit, and ear, by which it was hung to its beam by an iron ink. The bell was struck on a raised round spot, by a hammer of wood—a small tree-trunk swung loosely on two ropes. After impact, the bellman held the beam on its rebound, until the quivering monotone began to die away. Few sounds are more solemnly sweet than the mellow music of a Japanese temple-bell. On a still night, a circumference of twenty miles was flooded by the melody of the great bell of Zôzôji. The people learned to love their temple-bell as a dear friend, as its note changed with the years and moods of life.

The casting of a bell was ever the occasion of rejoicing and public festival. When the chief priest of the city announced that one was to be made, the people brought contributions in money, or offerings of bronze gold, pure tin, or copper vessels. Ladies gave with their own hands the mirrors which had been the envy of lovers, young girls laid their silver hair-pins and *bijouterie* on the heap. When metal enough and in due proportion had been amassed, crucibles were made, earth-furnaces dug, the molds fashioned, and huge bellows, worked by standing men at each end, like a seesaw, were mounted; and, after due prayers and consultation, the auspicious day was appointed. The place selected was usually on a hill or commanding place. The people, in their gayest dress, assembled in picnic parties, and with song and dance and feast waited while the workmen, in festal uniform, toiled, and the priests, in canonical robes, watched. The fires were lighted, the bellows oscillated, the blast roared, and the crucibles were brought to the proper heat and the contents to fiery fluidity, the joy of the crowd increasing as each stage in the process was announced. When the molten flood was finally poured into the mold, the excitement of the spectators reached a height of uncontrollable enthusiasm. Another pecuniary harvest was reaped by the priests before the crowds dispersed, by the sale of stamped kerchiefs or paper containing a holy text, or certifying to the presence of the purchaser at the ceremony, and the blessing of the gods upon him therefor. Such a token became an heir-loom; and the child who ever afterward heard the solemn boom of the bell at matin or evening was constrained, by filial as well as holy motives, to obey and reverence its admonitory call. The belfry was usually a separate building apart from the temple, with elaborate cornices and roof.

In addition to the offices of religion, many of the priests were useful men, and real civilizers. They were not all lazy monks or idle bonzes. By the Buddhist priests many streams were spanned with bridges, paths and roads made, shade or fruit trees planted, ponds and ditches for purposes of irrigation dug, aqueducts built, unwholesome localities drained, and mountain passes discovered or explored. Many were the school-masters, and, as learned men, were consulted on subjects beyond the ken of their parishioners. Some of them, having a knowledge of medicine, acted as physicians. The sciences and arts in Japan all owe much to the bonzes who from Corea personally introduced many useful appliances or articles of food. Several edible vegetables are still named after the priests, who first taught their use. The exact sciences, astronomy and mathematics, as well as the humanities, owe much of their cultivation and development to clerical scholars. In the monasteries, the brethren exercised their varied gifts in preaching, study, calligraphy, carving, sculpture, or on objects of ecclesiastical art.

The monuments by which the memory of many a saintly bonze is still kept green exist to-day as treasures on the altars, or in the temple or its shady precincts, in winged words or material substance. A copy of the Buddhist Scriptures, a sacred classic, in roll or bound volume, might occupy a holy penman before his brush and ink-stone for years. The manuscript texts which I have often seen in the hall of worship on silky paper bound in damask, in Japanese monasteries, could not be improved in elegance and accuracy by the printer's art. The transcription of a sutra on silk, made to adorn the wall of a shrine, in many cases performed its mission for centuries.

Another monk excelled in improvisation of sacred stanzas, another painted the pictures and scrolls by which the multitude were taught by the priest, with his pointer in hand, the mysteries of theology, the symbols of worship, the terrors of the graded hells and purgatories, and the felicities of Nirvana. Another of the fraternity, with cunning hand, compelled the wonder of his brethren by his skill in carving. He could, from a log which to-day had its bark on, bring forth in time the serene countenance of Buddha, the ravishing beauty of Kuanon, the Goddess of Mercy, the scowling terrors of the God of War, the frightful visage of Fudo, or the hideous face of the Lord of Hell. Another was famous for molding the clay for the carver, the sculptor, or the bronze-smith. Many articles of altar furniture, even to the incense-sticks and flowers, were often made entirely by clerical hands.

During the Middle Ages, the arts of pottery, lacquering, gilding, bronze-casting, engraving and chasing, chisel and punch work, sword-making, goldsmith's work, were brought to a perfection never since excelled, if indeed it has been equaled. In enameled and inlaid metal work the hand of the Japanese artisan has undoubtedly lost its cunning. Native archaeologists assert that a good catalogue of "lost arts" may be made out, notably those of the composition and application of violet lacquer, and the ancient *cloisonné* enamel. The delicacy of tact, freedom of movement, and perfection of finish visible on Japanese work, are the result of long hereditary application and concentrated skill. Hidden away in sequestered villages, or occupying the same workshop in cities for centuries, generations of craftsmen wrought upon one class of objects, until from the workman's hand is born the offspring of a long pedigree of thought and dexterity. Japanese antiquarians fix the date of the discovery of lacquer-ware variously at A.D. 724 and 900. Echizen, from the first, has been noted for the abundance and luxuriant yield of lacquer-trees, and the skill of her workmen in extracting the milk-white virgin sap, which the action of the air turns to black, and which by pigments is changed to various colors. In the thirteenth century the art of gold-lacquering attained the zenith of perfection. Various schools of lacquer art were founded, one excelling in landscape, another in marine scenery, or the delineation, in gold and silver powder and varnish, of birds, insects, and flowers. The masters who flourished during the Hôjô period still rule the pencil of the modern artist.

Kiôto, as the civil and military as well as ecclesiastical capital of the empire, was the centre and standard of manners, language, and etiquette, of art, literature, religion, and government. No people are more courtly and polished in their manners than the Japanese, and my visit to Kiôto in 1873 impressed me with the fact that the citizens of this proud *miako* surpass all others in Japan in refined manners, and the graces of address and etiquette. The direct influences of court life have made themselves perceptibly felt on the inhabitants of the city.

From this centre radiated the multifarious influences which have molded the character of the nation. The country priest came as pilgrim to the capital as to the Holy City, to strengthen his faith and cheer his soul amidst its inspirations, to see the primate and magnates of his sect, to pray at the famous shrines, to study in the largest monasteries, under the greatest lights and holiest teachers. Returning to his parish, new sanctity was shed from his rustling robes. His brethren welcomed him with awe, and the people thronged to see and venerate the holy man who had drunk at the very fountains of the faith. The temple coffers grew heavy with the weight of offerings because of him. The sons of the noblemen in distant provinces were sent to Kiôto to be educated, to learn reading and writing from the priests, the perfection of the art of war in the army, the etiquette of palace life as pages to, or as guests of, the court nobles. The artisan or rich merchant from Ôshiu or Kadzusa, who had made the journey to Kiôto, astonished his wondering listeners at home with tales of the splendor of the processions of the mikado, the wealth of the temples, the number of the pagodas, the richness of the silk robes of the court nobles, and the wonders which the Kiôto potters and vase-makers, sword-forgers, goldsmiths, lacquerers, crystal-cutters, and bronze-molders, daily exposed in their shops in profusion.

In Kiôto also dwelt the poets, novelists, historians, grammarians, writers, and the purists, whose dicta were laws. By them were written the great bulk of the classic literature, embracing poetry, drama, fiction, history, philosophy, etiquette, and the numerous diaries and works on travel in China, Corea, and the remote provinces of the country, and the books called "mirrors" (*kagami*) of the times, now so interesting to the antiquarian student. Occasionally nobles or court ladies would leave the luxury of the city, and take up their abode in a castle, tower, pagoda, or temple room, or on some mountain overlooking Lake Biwa, the sea, or the Yodo River, or the plains of Yamato; and amidst its inspiring scenery, with tiny table, ink-stone and brush, pen some prose epic or romance, that has since become an immortal classic. Almost every mansion of the nobles had its "looking-room," or "Chamber of Inspiring View," whence to gaze upon the landscape or marine scenery. Rooms set apart for this aesthetic pleasure still form a feature of the house of nearly every modern native of means.

On many a coigne of vantage may be seen also the summer-houses or rustic booths, where gather pleasure parties on picnics.

In the civil administration of the empire, the chief work was to dispense justice, punish offenders, collect taxes, and settle disputes. After the rude surveys of those days, the boundaries of provinces and departments were marked by inscribed posts of wood or stone. Before the days of writing, the same end was secured by charcoal buried in the earth at certain points, the durability of which insured the mark against decay. The peasants, after the rice-harvest was over, brought their tribute, or taxes, with joyful ceremony, to the government granaries in straw bags, packed on horses gayly decorated with scarlet housings, and jingling with clusters of small bells. A relic of this custom is seen in the bunches of bells suspended by red cotton stuff from the rear of the pack-saddle, which dangle musically from the ungainly haunches of the native sumpters.

From earliest times there existed *séki* (guard gates or barriers) between the various provinces at mountain passes or strategic points. As feudalism developed, they grew more numerous. A fence of palisades, stretched across the road, guarded the path through which, according to time, or orders of the keepers, none could pass with arms, or without the pass-word or passport. Anciently they were erected at the Hakoné and other mountain passes, to keep up the distinction between the Ainos and the pure Japanese. The possession of these barriers was ever an important object of rival military commanders, and the shifts, devices, and extraordinary artifices resorted to by refugees, disguised worthies, and forbidden characters, furnish the historian, the novelist, and dramatist with some of their most thrilling episodes.

It is related of Yoshitsuné, after he had incurred the wrath of Yoritomo, that, with Benkei, his servant, he arrived at a guard gate kept by some Genji soldiers, who would have been sure to arrest him had they discovered his august personality. Disguised as wandering priests of the Buddhist sect Yama-bushi, they approached the gate, and were challenged by the sentinel, who, like most of his class at that time, was ignorant of writing. Benkei, with great dignity, drawing from his bosom a roll of blank paper, began, after touching it reverently to his forehead, to extemporize and read aloud in choicest and most pious language a commission from the high-priest at the temple of Hokoji, in Kiôto, in which stood the great image of Buddha, authorizing him to collect money to cast a colossal bell for the temple. At the first mention of the name of his reverence the renowned priest, so talismanic in all the empire, the soldier dropped down on his knees with face to the ground, and listened with reverent awe, unaware that the paper was as blank as the reader's tongue was glib. To further lull suspicion, Benkei apologized for the rude conduct of his servant-boy, who stood during the reading, because he was only a boor just out of the rice-fields; and, giving him a kick, bid him get down on his marrow-bones, and not stand up in the presence of a gentleman and a soldier. The ruse was complete. The illustrious youth and his servant passed on.

Medical science made considerable progress in the course of centuries. The *materia medica*, system, practice, and literature of the healing art were borrowed from China; but upon these, as upon most other matters, the Japanese improved. Acupuncture, or the introduction of needles into living tissues for remedial purposes, was much improved by the Japanese. The puncturing needles, as fine as a hair, were made of gold, silver, or tempered steel, by experts. The bones, large nerves, or blood-vessels were carefully avoided in the process, which enjoyed great repute in cases of a peculiar violent colic, to which the natives are subject, and which sometimes becomes endemic. On the theory that this malady was caused by wind, holes were made in the stomach or abdomen, to the mystic number of nine—corresponding to the nine apertures of the body. Moxa (Japanese, *mokusa*; *mo*, fire, from *moyeru*, to burn, and *kusa*, herb, grass), or the burning of a small cone of cottony fibres of the artemisia, on the back or feet, was practiced as early as the eleventh century, reference being made to it in a poem written at that time. A number of ancient stanzas and puns relating to Mount Ibuki, on the sides of which the mugwort grows luxuriantly, are still extant. To this day it is an exception to find the backs of the common people unscarred with the spots left by the moxa. The use of mercury in corrosive sublimate was very anciently known. The dô-sha powder, however, which was said to cure various diseases, and to relax the rigid limbs of a corpse, was manufactured and sold only by the bonzes (Japanese, *bôzu*) of the Shin Gon sect. It is, and always was, a pious fraud, being nothing but unefficacious quartz sand, mixed with grains of mica and pyrites.*

Of the mediæval sports and pastimes within and without of doors, the former were preferred by the weak and effeminate, the latter by the hale and strong. Banquets and carousals in the palace were frequent.

---

* See in Titsingh a long account of the wonderful virtues and effects claimed for the dô-sha ("dosia") powder, and in various other old writers on Japan, who have gravely described this humbug. I once tested this substance thoroughly by swallowing a tea-spoonful, without experiencing any effects. It might cause, but not cure, a headache. I also used up a packageful of the holy sand, purchased at an orthodox Shin Gon temple, upon a stiffened corpse that had but a short time previous become such, but no unlimbering of the rigid body took place. I also fused a quantity of the certified "drug" with some carbonate of soda, dissolved the resultant mass in distilled water, and upon adding a few drops of hydrochloric acid, a precipitate of gelatinous silica was the result. I also subjected the dô-sha to careful microscopic examination, finding it only quartz sand, with flakes of other minerals. That the "corpse" in my experiment was that of an old dog does not affect the validity of the test. It may be remembered also that gelatinous silica is the substance sometimes used to adulterate butter. The main objection to such butter is that one can buy sand in a cheaper form; and the same may be said of that nostrum in the ecclesiastical quackery and *materia theologica* of Japan called *dô-sha*.

The brewing of saké from rice was begun, according to record, in the third century, and the office of chief butler even earlier. The native sauce, *shô-yu*, made of fermented wheat and beans, with salt and vinegar, which the cunning purveyors of Europe use as the basis of their high-priced piquant sauces, was made and used as early as the twelfth century. The name of this saline oil (*shô*, salt; *yu*, oil) appears as "soy" in our dictionaries, it being one of the three words (soy, bonze, moxa) which we have borrowed from the Japanese. At the feasts, besides the wine and delicacies to please the palate, music, song, and dance made the feast of reason and the flow of soul, while witty and beautiful women lent grace and added pleasure to the festivities.

In long trailing robes of white, crimson, or highly figured silk, with hair flowing in luxuriance over the shoulders, and bound gracefully in one long tress which fell below the waist behind, maids and ladies of the palace rained glances and influence upon the favored ones. They fired the heart of admirers* by the bewitching beauty of a well-formed hand, foot, neck, face, or form decked with whatever added charms cosmetics could bestow upon them. Japanese ladies have ever been

---

* The following is the native ideal of a Japanese woman, given by a young Japanese gentleman at the International Congress of Orientalists held at Paris in 1873: "I will commence, gentlemen, with the head, which is neither too large nor too small. Figure to yourself large black eyes, surmounted by eyebrows of a strict arch, bordered by black lashes; a face oval, white, very slightly rose-colored on the cheeks, a straight high nose; a small, regular, fresh mouth, whose thin lips disclose, from time to time, white teeth ranged regularly; a narrow forehead, bordered by long, black hair, arched with perfect regularity. Join this head by a round neck to a body large, but not fat, with slender loins, hands and feet small, but not thin; a breast whose swell (*saillie*) is not exaggerated. Add to these the following attributes: a gentle manner, a voice like the nightingale, which makes one divine its artlessness; a look at once lively, sweet gracious, and always charming; witty words pronounced distinctly, accompanied by charming smiles; an air sometimes calm, gay, sometimes thoughtful, and always majestic; manners noble, simple, a little proud, but without ever incurring the accusation of presumption."

noted for neatness, good taste, and, on proper occasions, splendor and luxuriance of dress. With fan, and waving long sleeve, the language of secret but outwardly decorous passion found ample expression. Kisses, the pressure of the hand, and other symbols of love as expressed in other lands, were then, as now, unknown. In humble life also, in all their social pleasures the two sexes met together to participate in the same delights, with far greater freedom than is known in Asiatic countries. As, however, wives or concubines had not always the attractions of youth, beauty, wit, maidenly freshness, or skill at the *koto*, the *geisha*, or singing-girl, then as now, served the saké, danced, sung, and played, and was rewarded by the gold or gifts of the host, or perhaps became his Hagar. The statement that the empress was attended only by "vestals who had never beheld a man" is disproved by a short study of the volumes of poetry, amorous and otherwise, written by them, and still quoted as classic. As to the standard of virtue in those days, I believe it was certainly not below that of the later Roman empire, and I am inclined to believe it was far above it.

In the court at Kiôto, besides games of skill or chance in the house, were foot-ball, cock-fighting, falconry, horsemanship, and archery. The robust games of the military classes were hunting the boar, deer, bear, and smaller game. Hunting by falcons, which had been introduced by some Corean embassadors in the time of Jingu Kôgô, was almost as extensively practiced as in Europe, almost every feudal lord having his perch of falcons. Fishing by cormorants, though a useful branch of the fisherman's industry, was also indulged in for pleasure. The severe exercise of hunting for sport, however, never became as absorbing and popular in Japan as in Europe, being confined more to the professional huntsman, and the seeker for daily food.

The court ladies shaved off their eyebrows, and painted two sable bars or spots on the forehead resembling false eyebrows. In addition to the gentle tasks of needle-work and embroidery, they passed the time in games of chess, checkers, painted shells, and a diversion peculiar to the palace, in which the skill of the player depended on her sensitiveness in appreciating perfumes, the necessary articles being vials of fragrant extracts. Their pets were the peculiar little dogs called *chin*. They stained their teeth black, like the women of the lower classes; an example which the nobles of the sterner sex followed, as they grew more and more effeminate. One of the staple diversions of both sexes at the court was to write poetry, and recite it to each other. The emperor frequently honored a lady or noble by giving the chosen one a subject upon which to compose a poem. A happy thought, skillfully wrought stanza, a felicitous grace of pantomime, often made the poetess a maid of honor, a concubine, or even an empress, and the poet a minister or councilor.

Another favorite means of amusement was to write and read or tell stories—the Scheherezade of these being a beautiful lady, who often composed her own stories. The following instance is abbreviated from the *Onna Dai Gaku* ("Woman's Great Study"): Isé no Taiyu was a daughter of Sukéichika, the mikado's minister of festivals, and a highly accomplished lady. None among the ladies of the court could equal her. One day a branch of luxuriant cherry - blossoms was brought from Nara. The emperor gave it to her, and asked her to extemporize a verse. She did so, and the courtiers were all astonished at the beauty and delicate sentiment of the verse.

Here is another: Murasaki Shikibu was the daughter of the lord of Echizen. One day a lady of Kamo asked if there was any new entertaining literature or novels, as the empress-dowager wished to read something new. The lady invited Murasaki to write some stories. She, knowing that the great Chinese scholar Shomei completed his collection of the essays of ancient writers by building a high house and secluding himself in it, had a high tower erected at Ishiyama overlooking Lake Biwa, and affording a glorious view of the mountains, especially in the moonlight. There she retired, and one night when the full moon shone upon the waters she was so inspired that she wrote in one night two chapters of the *Genji Monogatari*,* a book containing fifty-four chapters in all, which she finished in a few weeks. She

---

* The various forms of inarticulate language, by pantomime, flowers, art, and symbolism, in Japan differ in many respects from those expressed by us. Among the gestures partly or wholly unknown to them are nictation, kissing, shaking hands, shrugging the shoulders, and the contemptuous gyratory motion of the thumb set against the nose, with the fingers upright. Flirtation is practiced not by the use of the fan or the handkerchief (which is of paper), but with a wave of the right hand, with palms downward, or by the fair charmer waving her long sleeve. Instead of winking, they convey the same meaning by twitching the left corner of the mouth, or rolling the eyeballs to the right or left. The girls simper by letting their eyelids fall, and the language of woman's eyes is in other respects the same as with us, as Japanese poetry shows. Jealousy is indicated by the erecting the two forefingers on the forehead, in allusion to the monster which in Japan has horns and black hide, but not green eyes. A jilt who wishes to give her lover "the mitten" sends him a branch of maple, the color (*iro*) of whose leaves has changed, like her love (*iro*).

Turning up the nose and curling the lip in scorn are achieved with masterly skill. In agony, the hands are not clasped, but put upright, palm to palm, at length. People shake their heads to mean "no," and nod them to mean "yes."

Among the peculiarities in their code of etiquette, eructation is permissible in company at all times, and after a hearty meal is rather a compliment to the host. On the other hand, to attend to the requirements of nasal etiquette, except with face apart from the company, is very bad manners. Toothpicks must not be used, but in a semi-secret way, and with the left hand covering the mouth. At banquets, the fragrant bark on these is carved ornamentally, and under a shaving loosened from the white wood is written in tiny script a pun, witticism, bon-mot, or sentimental proposal, like that on the "secret papers" on bonbons at our refreshments. At feasts or daily meals, all such matters as carving, slicing, etc., are looked upon as out of place, and properly belonging to servant's work and in the kitchen. In clothing, the idea that garments ought to be loose and flowing, so as to conceal the shape of the body and its parts, and give no striking indication of sex, as among us, was never so general as in China. In hair-dressing, besides marking age and sex, the female coiffure had a language of its own. Generally a keen observer could distinguish a maiden, a married wife, a widow who was willing to marry the second time, and the widow who intended never to wed again. As marks of beauty, besides the ideals

presented it to the empress-dowager, who gave it to the mikado. To this day it is a classic.

Sei Shonagon was the daughter of Kiyowara no Motosuké. She was one of the imperial concubines. She was well read in Japanese and Chinese literature, and composed poetry almost from infancy, having a wonderful facility of improvisation. One day, after a fall of snow, she looked out from the southern door of the palace. The emperor, having passed round the wine-cup to his lords and ladies at the usual morning assembly of the courtiers and maids of honor, said, "How is the snow of Kuroho?" No one else understood the meaning, but Sei Shonagon instantly stepped forward and drew up the curtains, revealing the mountains decked in fresh-fallen snow. The emperor was delighted, and bestowed upon her a prize. Sei Shonagon had understood his allusion to the line in an ancient poem which ran thus:

"The snow of Kuroho is seen by raising the curtains."

Once when a certain kugé was traveling in a province, he came, on a moonlight night, to a poor village in which the cottages had fallen into picturesque decay, the roofs of which gleamed like silver. The sight of the glorified huts inspired the noble with such a fine frenzy that he sat up all night gazing rapturously on the scene, anon composing stanzas. He was so delighted that he planned to remain in the place several days. The next morning, however, the villagers, hearing of the presence of so illustrious a guest among them, began

---

spoken of on page 37, large ears were thought desirable, especially those with long lobes. Fat people were much admired, and a rotund physique considered a good gift of nature. Many of the striking details of military and social etiquette, such as falling on hands and knees, with forehead on the floor or on the prone hand, and the simultaneous noisy sucking-in of the breath, which sounds and seems so ridiculous to the foreigner, are very ancient.

busily to repair the ruin, and to rethatch the roofs. The kugé, seeing all his poetic visions dispelled by this vandal industry, ordered his bullock-car, and was off, disgusted.

During the first centuries of writing in Japan, the spoken and the written language were identical. With the study of the Chinese literature, and the composition of works by the native literati almost exclusively in that language, grew up differences between the colloquial and literary idiom and terminology. The infusion of a large number of Chinese words into the common speech steadily increased; while the learned affected a pedantic style of conversation, so interlarded with Chinese words, names, and expressions, that to the vulgar their discourse was almost unintelligible. Buddhism also made Chinese the vehicle of its teachings, and the people everywhere became familiar, not only with its technical terms, but with its stock phrases and forms of thought. To this day the Buddhist, or sham-religious, way of talking is almost a complete tongue in itself, and a good dictionary always gives the Buddhistic meaning of a word separately. In reading or hearing Japanese, the English-speaking resident continually stumbles on his own religious cant and orthodox expressions, which he believes to be peculiar to his own atmosphere, that have a meaning entirely different from the natural sense: "this vale of tears," "this evil world," "gone to his reward," "dust and ashes," "worm of the dust," and many phrases which so many think are exclusively Christian or evangelical, are echoed in Japanese. So much is this true, that the missionaries, in translating religious books, are at first delighted to find exact equivalents for many expressions desirable in technical theology, or for what may fairly be termed pious slang, but will not use them, for fear of misleading the reader, or rather of failing to lead him out of his old notions into the new faith which it is desired to teach. So general have the use and affectation of Chinese become, that in many instances the pedantic Chinese name or word has been retained in the mouths of the people, while the more beautiful native term is almost lost. In general, however, only the men were devoted to Chinese, while the cultivation of the Japanese language was left to the women. This task the women nobly discharged, fully maintaining the credit of the native literature. Mr. W. G. Aston says, "I believe no parallel is to be found in the history of European letters, to the remarkable fact that a very large proportion of the best writings of the best age of Japanese literature was the work of women." The *Genji Monogatari* is the acknowledged standard of the language for the period to which it belongs, and the parent of the Japanese novel. This, with the classics *Isé Monogatari* and *Makura Zoshi*, and much of the poetry of the time, are the works of women.

It is to be noted that the borrowed Chinese words were taken entirely from the written, not the colloquial, language of China, the latter having never been spoken by the Japanese, except by a few interpreters at Nagasaki. The Japanese literary style is more concise, and retains archaic forms. The colloquial abounds in interjectional and onomato-poetic words and particles, uses a more simple inflection of the verb, and makes profuse use of honorific and polite terms. Though these particles defy translation, they add grace and force to the language. As in the English speech, the child of the wedded Saxon and Norman, the words which express the wants, feelings, and concerns of every-day life—all that is deepest in the human heart—are for the most part native; the technical, scientific, and abstract terms are foreign. Hence, if we would find the fountains of the musical and beautiful language of Japan, we must seek them in the hearts, and hear them flow from the lips, of the mothers of the Island Empire. Among the anomalies with which Japan has surprised or delighted the world may be claimed that of woman's achievements in the domain of letters. It was woman's genius, not man's, that made the Japanese a literary language. Moses established the Hebrew, Alfred the Saxon, and Luther the German tongue in permanent form; but in Japan, the mobile forms of speech crystallized into perennial beauty under the touch of woman's hand.

# XXII

# *The Growth and Customs of Feudalism*

Japan, of all the Asiatic nations, seems to have brought the feudal system to the highest state of perfection. Originating and developing at the same time as in Europe, it became the constitution of the nation and the condition of society in the seventeenth century. When in Europe the nations were engaged in throwing off the feudal yoke and inaugurating modern government, Japan was riveting the fetters of feudalism, which stood intact until 1871. From the beginning of the thirteenth century, it had come to pass that there were virtually two rulers in Japan, and as foreigners, misled by the Hollanders at Déshima, supposed, two emperors.

The growth of feudalism in Japan took shape and form from the early division of the officials into civil and military. As we have seen, the Fujiwara controlled all the civil offices, and at first, in time of emergency, put on armor, led their troops to battle, and braved the dangers of war and the discomforts of the camp. In time, however, this great family, yielding to that sloth and luxury which ever seem, like an insidious disease, to ruin greatness in Japan, ceased to take the field themselves, and delegated the uncongenial tasks of war to certain members of particular noble families. Those from which the greatest number of shôguns were appointed were the Taira and Minamoto, that for several centuries held the chief military appointments. As

luxury, corruption, intrigue, and effeminacy increased at the capital, the difficulty of keeping the remote parts of the empire in order
increased, especially in the North and East. The War Department
became disorganized, and the generals at Kiôto lost their ability to
enforce their orders.

Many of the peasants, on becoming soldiers, had, on account
of their personal valor or merit, been promoted to the permanent
garrison of household troops. Once in the gay capital, they learned
the details of intrigue and politics. Some were made court pages, or
attendants on men of high rank, and thus learned the routine of official duty. They caught the tone of life at court, where every man was
striving for rank and his own glory, and they were not slow to imitate
their august examples. Returning to their homes with the prestige of
having been in the capital, they intrigued for power in their native districts, and gradually obtained rule over them, neglecting to go when
duty called them to Kiôto, and ignoring the orders of their superiors
in the War Department. The civil governors of the provinces dared
not to molest, or attempt to bring these petty tyrants to obedience.
Having armor, horses, and weapons, they were able to train and equip
their dependents and servants, and thus provide themselves with an
armed following.

Thus was formed a class of men who called themselves warriors,
and were ever ready to serve a great leader for pay. The natural consequence of such a state of society was the frequent occurrence of village
squabbles, border brawls, and the levying of black-mail upon defense-
less people, culminating in the insurrection of a whole province. The
disorder often rose to such a pitch that it was necessary for the court
to interfere, and an expedition was sent from Kiôto, under the command of a Taira or Minamoto leader. The shogun, instead of waiting to
recruit his army in the regular manner —a process doubtful of results
in the disorganized state of the War Department and of the country in

general—had immediate recourse to others of these veteran "warriors," who were already equipped, and eager for a fray.

Frequent repetition of the experience of the relation of brothers in arms, of commander and commanded, of rewarder and rewarded, gradually grew into that of lord and retainers. Each general had his special favorites and followers, and the professional soldier looked upon his commander as the one to whom his allegiance was directly due. The distant court at Kiôto, being utterly unable to enforce its authority, put the whole power of quieting the disturbed districts, whenever the disorder increased beyond the ability of the civil magistrate to repress it, into the hands of the Minamoto and Taira. These families thus became military clans and acquired enormous influence, enjoyed the monopoly of military patronage, and finally became the virtual rulers of the land.

The power of the sword was, as early as the twelfth century, lost to the court, which then attempted, by every means in its power, to check the rising influence of the military families and classes. They began by denying them high rank, thus putting them under social ban. They next attempted to lay an interdict upon the warriors by forbidding them to ally themselves with either the Taira or the Minamoto. This availed nothing, for the warriors knew who rewarded them. They then endeavored, with poor success, to use one family as a check upon the other. Finally, when the Minamoto, Yoriyoshi, and Yoshiiyé conquered all the north of Hondo, and kept in tranquillity the whole of the Kuantô for fifteen years, even paying governmental expenses from their private funds, the court ignored their achievements. When they petitioned for rewards to be bestowed on their soldiers, the dilatory and reluctant, perhaps jealous, nobles composing the court not only neglected to do so, but left them without the imperial commission, and dishonored their achievements by speaking of them as "private feuds." Hence they took the responsibility, and conferred upon their soldiers grants of the conquered land in their own name. The Taira followed the same policy in the south and west.

When Yoritomo became Sei-i Tai Shôgun at Kamakura, erected the dual system, and appointed a military with a civil governor of each province in the interest of good order, feudalism assumed national proportions. Such a distribution soon ceased to be a balance, the military pan in the scale gained weight and the civil lost until it kicked the beam. At the end of the Hôjô domination, the court had lost the government of the provinces, and the kugé (court nobles) had been despoiled and impoverished by the buké (military). So thoroughly had feudalism become the national polity, that in the temporary mikadoate, 1534–1536, the Emperor Go-Daigo rewarded those who had restored him by grants of land for them to rule in their own names as his vassals.

Under the Ashikagas, the hold of even the central military authority, or chief daimiô, was lost, and the empire split up into fragments. Historians have in vain attempted to construct a series of historical maps of this period. The pastime was war—a game of patchwork in which land continually changed possessors. There was no one great leader of sufficient power to overawe all; hence might made right; and whoever had the ability, valor, or daring to make himself pre-eminent above his fellows, and seized more land, his power would last until he was overcome by a stronger, or his family decayed through the effeminacy of his descendants. During this period, the great clans with whose names the readers of the works of the Jesuits and Dutch writers are familiar, or which have been most prominent since the opening of the empire, took their rise. They were those of Hosokawa, Uyésugi, Sataké, Takéda, the "later Hôjô of Odawara," Môri, Ôtomo, Shimadzu, Riuzôji, Ota, and Tokugawa.

As the authority of the court grew weaker and weaker, the allegiance which all men owed to the mikado, and which they theoretically acknowledged, was changed into loyalty to the military chief. Every man who bore arms was thus attached to some "great name" (daimiô), and became a vassal (kérai). The agricultural, and gradually the other classes, also put themselves, or were forcibly included, under the protection of some castle lord or nobleman having an armed following. The taxes, instead of being collected for the central government, flowed into the treasury of the local rulers. This left the mikado and court without revenue. The kugé, or Kiôto nobles, were thus stripped of wealth, until their poverty became the theme for the caricaturist. Nevertheless, the eye of their pride never dimmed. In their veins, they knew, ran the blood of the gods, while the daimiôs were only "earth-thieves," and the parvenus of feudalism. They still cherished their empty titles; and to all students of history their poverty was more honorable than all the glitter of the shôgun's train, or the splendor of the richest daimiô's mansion.

The daimiôs spent their revenues on their retainers, their personal pleasures, and in building castles. In almost every feudal city, or place of strategic importance, the towers, walls, and moats of these characteristic specimens of Japanese architecture could be seen. The strictest vigilance was maintained at the castle-gates, and a retainer of another daimiô, however hospitably entertained elsewhere, was never allowed entrance into the citadel. A minute code of honor, a rude sort of chivalry, and an exalted sense of loyalty were the growth of the feudal system.

Many of the mediæval military customs were very interesting. During this period the habit originated of the men shaving the hair off their temples and from the middle of the scalp, and binding the long cue into a top-knot, which was turned forward and laid on the scalp. The object of this was to keep the hair out of the eyes during battle, and also to mark the wearer as a warrior. Gradually it became a universal custom, extending to all classes.

When, in 1873, the reformers persuaded the people to cut off their knots and let their hair grow, the latter refused to "imitate the foreigners," and supposed they were true conservatives, when, in reality, the ancient Japanese knew nothing of shaven faces and scalps, or of topknots. The ancient warriors wore mustaches, and even beards. The practice of keeping the face scrupulously bare, until recently so universally observed except by botanists and doctors, is comparatively modern.

The military tactics and strategic arts of the Japanese were anciently copied from the Chinese, but were afterward modified as the nature of the physical features of their country and the institutions of feudalism required. No less than seven distinct systems were at different times in vogue; but that perfected by Takéda and Uyésugi, in the Ashikaga period, finally bore off the palm. These tactics continued to command the esteem and practice of the Japanese until the revolution wrought by the adoption of the European systems in the present century. The surface of the country being so largely mountainous, uneven, and covered with rice-swamps, cavalry were but little employed. A volley of arrows usually opened the battle, followed by a general engagement along the whole line. Single combats between commanders of hostile armies were of frequent occurrence. When they met on the field, their retainers, according to the strict etiquette of war, gave no aid to either, but encouraged them by shouts, as they called out each other's names and rushed to the combat. The battle slackened while the leaders strove, the armies becoming spectators. The victor cut off the head of his antagonist, and, holding it up, shouted his name and claimed the victory. The triumph or defeat of their leaders often decided the fate of the army. Vengeance against the victor was not permitted to be taken at the time, but must be sought again, the two armies again joining battle. The fighting over, those who had slain distinguished personages must exhibit their heads before their chiefs, who bestowed rewards upon them. This practice still continues; and during the expedition in Formosa in 1874, the chief trophies were the heads of the Boutan cannibals; though the commander, General Saigô, attempted to abolish the custom. Whoever saved his chieftain's life on the field was honored with the place of highest rank in the clan. These customs had a tremendous influence in cultivating valor and a spirit of loyalty in the retainer toward the prince. The meanest soldier, if brave and faithful, might rise to the highest place of honor, rank, emolument, and influence. The bestowal of a reward, the investiture of a command, or military promotion, was ever an occasion of impressive ceremony.

Even in time of peace the samurai never appeared out-of-doors unarmed, invariably wearing their two swords in their girdle. The offensive weapons—spears long and short, the bows, arrows, and quiver, and battle-axes—were set on their butts on the porch or vestibule in front of the house. Within doors, in the *tokonoma*, or recess, were ranged in glittering state the cuirass, helmet, greaves, gauntlets, and chain-mail. Over the sliding partitions, on racks, were the long halberds, which the women of the house were trained to use in case of attack during the absence of the men.

The gate of a samurai, or noble's, house was permanently guarded by his armed retainers, who occupied the porter's lodge beside it. Standing upright and ready were three long instruments, designed to entangle, throw down, and pin to the earth a quarrelsome applicant. Familiar faces passed unchallenged, but armed strangers were held at bay till their business was known. A grappling-iron, with barbed tongues turned in every direction, making a ball of hooks like an iron hedgehog, mounted on a pike-staff ten feet long, thrust into the Japanese loose clothing, sufficed to keep at a wholesome length any swash-buckler whose sword left its sheath too easily. Another spiked weapon, like a double rake, could be thrust between his legs and bring him to the earth. A third, shaped like a pitchfork, could hold him helpless under its wicket arch. Three heavy quarter staves were also ready, to belabor the struggling wight who would not yield, while swords on the racks hung ready for the last resort, or when intruders came in numbers. On rows of pegs hung wooden tickets about three inches square, branded or inscribed with the names of the retainers and servants of the lord's house, which were handed to the keeper of the gate as they passed in or out.

The soldiers wore armor made of thin scales of iron, steel, hardened hide, lacquered paper, brass, or shark-skin, chain-mail, and shields. The helmet was of iron, very strong, and lined within by buckskin. Its flap of articulated iron rings drooped well around the shoulders. The visor was of thin lacquered iron, the nose and mouth pieces being removable. The eyes were partially protected by the projecting front piece. A false mustache was supposed to make the upper lip of the warrior dreadful to behold. On the frontlet were the distinguishing symbols of the man, a pair of horns, a fish, an eagle, dragon, buck-horns, or flashing brass plates of various designs. Some of the helmets were very tall. Katô Kiyomasa's was three feet high. On the top was a hole, in which a pennant was thrust, or an ornament shaped like a pear inserted. The "pear-splitter" was the fatal stroke in combat and the prize-cut in fencing. Behind the corslet on the back was another socket, in which the clan flag was inserted. The breastplate was heavy and tough; the arms, legs, abdomen, and thighs were protected by plates joined by woven chains. Shields were often used; and for forlorn-hopes or assaults, cavalrymen made use of a stuffed bag resembling a bolster, to receive a volley of arrows. Besides being missile-proof, it held the arrows as spoils. On the shoulders, hanging loosely, were unusually wide and heavy brassarts, designed to deaden the force of the two-handed sword-stroke. Greaves and sandals completed the suit, which was laced and bound with iron clamps, and cords of buckskin and silk, and decorated with crests, gilt tassels, and glittering insignia.

Suits of armor were of black, white, purple, crimson, violet, green, golden, or silver colors.

The rations of the soldiers were rice, fish, and vegetables. Instead of tents, huts of straw or boughs were easily erected to form a camp. The general's head-quarters were inclosed by canvas, stretched on posts six feet high, on which his armorial bearings were wrought. The weapons were bows and arrows, spear, sword, and, rarely, battle-axes and bow-guns; for sieges, fire-arrows. The general's scabbard was of tiger-skin. Supplies of this material were obtained from Corea, where the animal abounds. His baton was a small lacquered wand, with a cluster of strips of thick white paper dependent from the point. Flags, banners, and streamers were freely used; and a camp, castle, or moving army, in time of war, with its hundreds and thousands of flags, presented a gay and lively appearance. Drums, hard-wood clappers, and conch-shells sounded the reveille, the alarm, the onset, or the retreat.

Owing to the nature of the ground, consisting chiefly of mountains and valleys, or plains covered with rice-swamps intersected by narrow paths, infantry were usually depended upon. In besieging a castle, the intrenchments of the investing army consisted chiefly of a line of palisades or heavy planks, propped up from within by hinged supports, at an angle of forty-five degrees, behind which the besiegers fought or lived in camp life, while sentinels paced at the gates. Lookouts were posted on overlooking hills, in trees, or in towers erected for the purpose. Sometimes huge kites able to sustain a man were flown, and a bird's-eye view of the interior of the enemy's castle thus obtained. Fire, treachery, stratagem, starvation, or shooting at long range having failed to compel surrender, an assault took place, in which the gates were smashed in, or the walls scaled. Usually great loss resulted before the besiegers were driven off, or were victorious. Rough surgery awaited the wounded. An arrow-barb was usually pulled out by a jerk of the pincers. A sabre-cut was sewed or bound together with tough paper, of which every soldier carried a supply. The wonderfully adhesive, absorptive, and healing power of the soft, tough, quickly wet, easily hardening, or easily kept pliable, Japanese paper made excellent plasters, bandages, tourniquets, cords, and towels. In the dressing of wounds, the native doctors to this day, as I have often had occasion to witness, excel.

*Seppuku* (belly-cut) or *hara-kiri* also came into vogue about the time of the beginning of the domination of the military classes. At first, after a battle, the vanquished wounded fell on their swords, drove them through their mouth or breast, or cut their throats. Often a famous soldier, before dying, would flay and score his own face beyond recognition, so that his enemies might not glory over him. This grew into a principle of honor; and frequently the unscathed survivors, defeated, and feeling the cause hopeless, or retainers whose master was slain, committed suicide. Hence arose, in the Ashikaga period, the fashion of wearing two swords; one of which, the longer, was for enemies; the other, shorter, for the wearers own body. The practice of *hara-kiri* as a judicial sentence and punishment did not come into vogue until in the time of the Tokugawas.

Thrust into a tiny scabbard at the side of the dirk, or small sword, was a pair of chopsticks to eat with in camp. Anciently these were skewers, to thrust through the top-knot of a decapitated enemy, that the head might be easily carried. Besides, or in lieu of them, was a small miniature sword, *ko-katana* (little sword), or long, narrow knife. Although this was put to various trivial uses, such as those for which we employ a penknife, yet its primary purpose was that of the card of the owner. Each sword was adorned with some symbol or crest, which served to mark the clan, family, or person of the owner.

The Satsuma men wore swords with red-lacquered scabbards. Later, the Tokugawa vassals, who fought in the battle of Sékigahara, were called "white hilts," because they wore swords of extraordinary length, with white hilts. The bat, the falcon, the dragon, lion, tiger, owl, and hawk, were among the most common designs wrought in gold, lacquer, carving, or alloy on the hilts, handles, or scabbard; and on the *ko-katana* was engraved the name of the owner.

Feudalism was the mother of brawls innumerable, and feuds between families and clans continually existed. The wife whose husband was slain by the grudge-bearer brought up her sons religiously to avenge their father's death. The vendetta was unhindered by law and applauded by society. The moment of revenge selected was usually that of the victim's proudest triumph. After promotion to office, succession to patrimony, or at his marriage ceremony, the sword of the avenger did its bloody work. Many a bride found herself a widow on her wedding-night. Many a child became an orphan in the hour of the father's acme of honor. When the murder was secret, at night, or on the wayside, the head was cut off, and the avenger, plucking out his *ko-katana*, thrust it in the ear of the victim, and let it lie on the public highway, or sent it to be deposited before the gate of the house. The *ko-katana*, with the name engraved on it, told the whole story.

Whenever the lord of a clan wished his rival or enemy out of the way, he gave the order of Herodias to her daughter to his faithful retainers, and usually the head in due time was brought before him, as was John's, on a charger or ceremonial stand.

The most minutely detailed etiquette presided over the sword, the badge of the gentleman. The visitor whose means allowed him to be accompanied by a servant always left his long sword in his charge when entering a friend's house; the salutation being repeated bowing of the forehead to the floor while on the hands and knees, the breath being sucked in at the same time with an impressive sound. The degree of obeisance was accurately graded according to rank. If alone, the visitor laid his sword on the floor of the vestibule. The host's servants, if so instructed by their master, then, with a silk napkin in hand, removed it inside and placed it, with all honor, on the sword-rack. At meetings between those less familiar, the sheathed weapon was withdrawn from the girdle and laid on the floor to the right, an indication of friendship, since it could not be drawn easily. Under suspicious circumstances, it was laid to the left, so as to be at hand. On short visits, the dirk was retained in the girdle; on festal occasions, or prolonged visits, it was withdrawn. To clash the sheath of one's sword against that of another was a breach of etiquette that often resulted in instantaneous and bloody reprisal. The accompanying cut by Hokusai represents such a scene. The story is a true one, and well told by Mitford. Fuwa Banzaëmon—he of the robe marked with the *nurétsubami* (swallow in a shower)—and Nagoya Sanzaburô—he of the coat figured with the device of lightning—both enemies, and *rônin*, as their straw hats show, meet, and intentionally turn back to back and clash scabbards, holding their hands in tragic attitude. In a moment more, so the picture tells us, the insulted scabbards will be empty, and the blades crossed in deadly combat. In the story, which has been versified and dramatized, and which on the boards will hold an audience breathless, Nagoya finally kills Fuwa. The writing at the side of the sketch gives the clue to the incident: *saya-até* (scabbard-collision), equivalent to our "flinging down the gauntlet."

To turn the sheath in the belt as if about to draw was tantamount to a challenge. To lay one's weapon on the floor of a room, and kick the guard toward a person, was an insult that generally resulted in a combat to the death. Even to touch another's weapon in any way was a grave offense. No weapon was ever exhibited naked for any purpose, unless the wearer first profusely begged pardon of those present. A wish to see a sword was seldom made, unless the blade was a rare one. The owner then held the back of the sword to the spectator, with the edge toward himself, and the hilt, wrapped in the little silk napkin which gentlemen always carry in their pocket-books, or a piece of white paper, to the left. The blade was then withdrawn from the scabbard, and admired inch by inch, but never entirely withdrawn unless the owner pressed his guest to do so, when, with much apology, the sword was entirely withdrawn and held away from those present. Many gentlemen took a pride in making collections of swords, and the men of every samurai family wore weapons that were heir-looms, often centuries old. Women wore short swords when traveling, and the palace ladies in time of fires armed themselves.

In no country has the sword been made an object of such honor as in Japan. It is at once a divine symbol, a knightly weapon, and a certificate of noble birth. "The girded sword is the soul of the samurai." It is "the precious possession of lord and vassal from times older than the divine period." Japan is "the land of many blades." The gods wore and wielded two-edged swords. From the tail of the dragon was born the sword which the Sun-goddess gave to the first emperor of Japan. By the sword of the clustering clouds of heaven Yamato-Daké subdued the East. By the sword the mortal heroes of Japan won their fame.

"There's naught 'twixt heaven and earth that man need fear, who carries at his belt this single blade." "One's fate is in the hands of Heaven, but a skillful fighter does not meet with death." "In the last days, one's sword becomes the wealth of one's posterity." These are the mottoes graven on Japanese swords.

Names of famous swords belonging to the Taira, Minamoto and other families are, "Little Crow," "Beard-cutter," "Knee-divider." The two latter, when tried on sentenced criminals, after severing the heads from the body, cut the beard, and divided the knee respectively. The forging of these swords occupied the smith sixty days. No artisans were held in greater honor than the sword-makers, and some of them even rose to honorary rank. The forging of a blade was often a religious ceremony. The names of Munéchicka, Masamuné, Yoshimitsu, and Muramasa, a few out of many noted smiths, are familiar words in the mouths of even Japanese children. The names, or marks and dates, of famous makers were always attached to their blades, and from the ninth to the fifteenth century were sure to be genuine. In later times, the practice of counterfeiting the marks of well-known makers came into vogue. Certain swords considered of good omen in one family were deemed unlucky in others.

I had frequent opportunities of examining several of the masterpieces of renowned sword-makers while in Japan, the property of kugés, daimiôs, and old samurai families, the museum at Kamakura being especially rich in famous old blades. The ordinary length of a sword was a fraction over two feet for the long and one foot for the short sword. All lengths were, however, made use of, and some of the old warriors on horseback wore swords over six feet long.

The Japanese sword-blade averages about an inch in width, about seven-eighths of which is a backing of iron, to which a face of steel is forged along its entire length. The back, about one-fourth of an inch thick, bevels out very slightly to near the centre of the blade, which then narrows to a razor edge. The steel and the forging line are easily distinguished by a cloudiness on the mirror-like polish of the metal. An inch and a quarter from the point, the width of the blade having been decreased one-fourth, the edge is ground off to a semi-parabola, meeting the back, which is prolonged, untouched; the curve of the whole blade, from a straight line, being less than a quarter of an inch. The guard is often a piece of elaborate workmanship in metal, representing a landscape, water-scene, or various emblems. The hilt is formed by covering the prolonged iron handle by shark-skin and wrapping this with twisted silk. The ferule, washers, and cleets are usually inlaid, embossed, or chased in gold, silver, or alloy. The rivets in the centre of the handle are concealed by designs, often of solid gold, such as the lion, dragon, cock, etc.

In full dress, the color of the scabbard was black, with a tinge of green or red in it, and the bindings of the hilt of blue silk. The taste of the wearer was often displayed in the color, size, or method of wearing his sword, gay or proud fellows affecting startling colors or extravagant length. Riven through ornamental ferules at the side of the scabbards were long, flat cords of woven silk of various tints, which were used to tie up the flowing sleeves, preparatory to fighting. Every part of a sword was richly inlaid, or expensively finished. Daimiôs often spent extravagant sums on a single blade, and small fortunes on a collection. A samurai, however poor, would have a blade of sure temper and rich mountings, deeming it honorable to suffer for food, that he might have a worthy emblem of his social rank as a samurai. A description of the various styles of blade and scabbard, lacquer, ornaments, and the rich vocabulary of terms minutely detailing each piece entering into the construction of a Japanese sword, the etiquette to be observed, the names, mottoes, and legends relating to them, would fill a large volume closely printed. A considerable portion of native literature is devoted to this one subject.

The bow and arrows were the chief weapons for siege and long-range operations. A Japanese bow has a peculiar shape, as seen in the engraving. It was made of well-selected oak (kashi), incased on both sides with a semi-cylinder of split bamboo toughened by fire. The three pieces composing the bow were then bound firmly into one piece by thin withes of rattan, making an excellent combination of lightness, strength, and elasticity. The string was of hemp. Arrows were of various kinds and lengths, according to the arms of the archer. The average length of the war-arrow was three feet. The "turnip-head," "frog-crotch," "willow-leaf," "armor-piercer," "bowel-raker," were a few of the various names for arrows. The "turnip-top," so named from its shape, made a singing noise as it flew. The "frog-crotch," shaped like a pitchfork, or the hind legs of a leaping-frog, with edged blades, was used to cut down flags or sever helmet lacings. The "willow-leaf" was a two-edged, unbarbed head, shaped like the leaf of a willow. The "bowel-raker" was of a frightful shape, well worthy of the name; and the victim whose diaphragm it penetrated was not likely to stir about afterward. The "armor-piercer" was a plain bolt-head, with nearly blunt point, well calculated to punch through a breastplate. Barbs of steel were of various shape; sometimes very heavy, and often handsomely open-worked. The shaft was of cane bamboo, with string-piece of bone or horn, whipped on with silk. Quivers were of leather, waterproof paper, or thin lacquered wood, and often splendidly adorned. Gold-inlaid weapons were common among the rich soldiers, and the outfit of an officer often cost many hundreds of dollars. Not a few of these old tools of war have lost their significance, and have become household adornments, objects of art, or symbols of peace. Such especially are the emblems of the carpenter's guilds, which consist of the half-feathered "turnip-head" arrow, wreathed with leaves of the same succulent, and the "frog-crotch," inserted in the mouth of a dragon, crossed upon the ancient mallet of the craft. These adorn temples or houses, or are carried in the local parades and festivals.

As Buddhism had become the professed religion of the entire nation, the vast majority of the military men were Buddhists. Each had his patron or deity. The soldier went into battle with an image of Buddha sewed in his helmet, and after victory ascribed glory to his divine deliverer. Many temples in Japan are the standing monuments of triumph in battle, or vows performed. Many of the noted captains, notably Kato, inscribed their banners with texts from the classics or the prayers, "Namu Amida Butsu," or "Namu miô hô," etc., according to their sect. Amulets and charms were worn almost without exception, and many a tale is told of arrows turned aside, or swords broken, that struck on a sacred image, picture, or text. Before entering a battle, or performing a special feat of skill or valor, the hero uttered the warrior's prayer, "Namu Hachiman Dai-bosatsu" (Glory to Hachiman, the incarnation of Great Buddha). Though brave heroes must, like ordinary men, pass through purgatory, yet death on the battle-field was reckoned highly meritorious, and the happiness of the warrior's soul in the next world was secured by the prayers of his wife and children.

[*Note on the Development of Feudalism.*—A thoroughly competent critic in *The Japan Mail* of November 25th, 1876, in a review of this work, criticising the author's treatment of Japanese feudalism, says: "In Japan, as in other Asiatic countries, the two main functions of government were the collection of the land revenue and the repression of rapine. In the palmy days of the mikado's power, both these functions were united in the hands of the prefects, who were appointed from Kiôto, with a tenure of office restricted to four years. What Yoritomo ostensibly did was to procure a division of these two departments of governmental activity, leaving one (the collection of revenue) to the mikado's functionaries, and obtaining the control of the other (the repression of crime) for himself. This control he acquired not.....in virtue of his military office of Sei-i-Tai Shôgun, but by cloaking his military power under the guise of his civil title, So Tsui-ho Shi, which might well be rendered Chief Commissioner of Police, or High Constable of the Realm. The extension of the system of appointing military magistrates, which was found to work so well in the Kuantô, to the central and western provinces, was effected some years before he received his rank of Barbarian-quelling Generalissimo. The second step in the direction of feudalism.....was the system, initiated by the Ashikaga shô-guns, of making the military magistracies hereditary in the families of their own nominees. The third was when Hidéyoshi parceled out the fiefs without reference to the sovereign, by titles granted in his own names. This was the precedent that Iyéyasu followed when he based the power of his dynasty on the tie of personal fealty of the Fudai daimiôs and hatamotos to himself and his successors as lords-paramount of their lands."]

# XXIII

# Nobunaga, the Persecutor of the Buddhists

In the province of Echizen, a few miles from Fukui, on the sea-coast, stands the mountain of Ochi, adorned with many a shrine and sacred portal, and at its foot lies the village of Ota. Tradition states that nearly a thousand years ago the pious bonze, Tai Chô, ascended and explored this mountain, which is now held sacred and resorted to by many a pilgrim. Here, in uninterrupted harmony, dwelt for centuries priests of both the native Shintô and Buddhist *cultus*, until 1868, when, in the purification, all Shintô shrines were purged of Buddhist symbolism and influences, as of a thing unclean. The priests were wont to make occasional journeys to Kiôto, the ecclesiastical centre of the country. Centuries before the troublous times of Ashikaga, and during the period of the Taira and Minamoto, one of the Shintô priests, while on his way through Ômi, stopped at Tsuda, and lodged with the *nanushi*, or head-man of the village, and asked him for one of his sons for the priesthood. The host gave him his step-son, whom the priest named Ota Chikazané.

That boy was of Taira blood, the great-grandson of Kiyomori. His father, Sukémori, had been killed by the Minamoto, but his mother had fled to Ômi, and the head-man of the village of Tsuda had married her.

The mother, though grieving for the loss of her son, doubtless, as a pious woman, rejoiced to see him in such excellent hands. The lad was returned to Ota, and lived in the village. He grew up, married as became a *kannushi* (custodian of a Shintô shrine), and founded a family of Shinto priests. He was the common ancestor of the famous hero of Echizen, Shibata Katsuiyé, and of the renowned Nobunaga, who deposed the Ashikaga, persecuted the Buddhists, encouraged the Jesuits, and restored, to a great extent, the supremacy of the mikado. In the "History of the Church," a portrait is given of Nobunaga, which is thus translated by Dr. Walter Dixon. He is described as "a prince of large stature, but of a weak and delicate complexion, with a heart and soul that supplied all other wants; ambitious above all mankind; brave, generous, and bold, and not without many excellent moral virtues; inclined to justice, and an enemy to treason. With a quick and penetrating wit, he seemed cut out for business. Excelling in military discipline, he was esteemed the fittest to command an army, manage a siege, fortify a town, or mark out a camp, of any general in Japan, never using any heads but his own. If he asked advice, it was more to know their hearts than to profit by their advice. He sought to see into others, and to conceal his own counsel, being very secret in his designs. He laughed at the worship of the gods, convinced that the bonzes were impostors abusing the simplicity of the people, and screening their own debauches under the name of religion."

Nobunaga had four generals, whom the people in those days were wont to nickname, respectively, "Cotton," " Rice," "Attack," "Retreat." The one was so fertile of resources that he was like cotton, that can be put to a multitude of uses; the second was as absolutely necessary as rice, which, if the people be without for a day, they die; the third excelled in onset; the fourth, in skillful retreat. They were Hidéyoshi, Goroza, Shibata, and Ikéda. A firth afterward joined him, whose name was Tokugawa Iyéyasu. These three names, Nobunaga, Hidéyoshi, and Iyéyasu, are the most renowned in Japan.

Nobunaga first appears on the scene in 1542. His father, after the fashion of the times, was a warrior, who, in the general scramble for land, was bent on securing a fair slice of territory. He died in 1549, leaving to his son his arms, his land, and his feuds. Nobunaga gained Suruga, Mino, Ômi and Mikawa, Isé and Echizen, in succession. Having possession of Kiôto, he built the fine castle of Nijô, and took the side of Ashikaga Yoshiaki, who by his influence was made shôgun in 1558. Six years later, the two quarreled. Nobunaga arrested and deposed him, and the power of this family, which had lasted two hundred and thirty-eight years, came to an end. From this time there was no Sei-i Tai Shôgun, until Iyéyasu obtained the office, in 1604. By the aid of his commanders, Hidéyoshi and Iyéyasu, he brought large portions of the empire under his authority, and nominally that of the mikado, in whose name he governed. He became Naidaijin (inner great minister), but never shôgun. The reason of this, doubtless, was that the office of shôgun was by custom monopolized by the Minamoto family and descendants, whereas Nobunaga was of Taira descent. Like Yoritomo, he was a skillful and determined soldier, but was never able to subdue the great clans. Unlike him, he lacked administrative power, and was never able to follow up in peace the victories gained in war.

He met his death in Kiôto, when in the fullness of his power and fame, in the following manner. Among his captains was Akéchi, a brave, proud man, who had taken mortal offense at his leader. One day, while in his palace, being in an unusually merry and familiar mood, Nobunaga put Akéchi's head under his arm, saying he would make a drum of it struck it with his fan, like a drumstick, playing a tune. Akéchi did not relish the joke, and silently waited for revenge. His passion was doubtless nursed and kept warm by a previous desire to seize the place and power and riches of his chief.

In those days treachery was a common and trivial occurrence, and the adherent of to-day was the deserter of to-morrow. The opportunity did not delay. Nobunaga had sent so large a re-enforcement into the west, to Hidéyoshi, who was fighting with Môri, that the garrison at the capital was reduced to a minimum. Akéchi was ordered to the Chiugoku, and pretended to march thither. Outside the city he disclosed his plan of killing Nobunaga, whom he denounced to his officers, and promised them rich booty. They returned to Kiôto, and surrounded the temple of Honnôji, where their victim was then residing. Hearing of the unexpected presence of so many soldiers in armor around his dwelling, he drew aside the window of his room to ascertain the cause. He was struck by an arrow, and instantly divined the situation, and that escape was impossible. He then set the temple on fire, and committed suicide. In a few minutes the body of the great hero was a charred crisp.

An uninscribed tomb of polygonal masonry, built in his honor, stands in the *ten-shiu*, or keep, of his most famous castle, Azuchi yama, on a high hill looking out upon the white walls of the fortress of Hikoné, the blue lake of Biwa, and the towering grandeur of Ibuki yama. He died at the age of forty-nine.

The position of Ota Nobunaga in Japanese history would be illy understood were the reader to regard him merely as a leader in clan fights, who by genius and vigor rose above the crowd of petty military adventurers, or even as one who wished to tranquilize and unify all Japan for the mikado. We must inquire why it is that no man has won more execration and anathemas from the Buddhists in Japan than he. They look upon him as an incarnate demon sent to destroy their faith.

The period of the Ashikaga was that in which the Buddhist priests reached the acme of power. Their monasteries were often enormous stone-walled and moated fortresses. The bonzes kept armor and arsenals full of weapons to don and use themselves, or to equip the armies in their pay when it suited their pleasure to cope with or assist either of the changing sides, or to take spoil of both. Many bloody battles took place between rival sects, in which temples were burned down, villages fired, and hundreds on both sides killed. Part of what is now the immense castle of Ôzaka belonged to the Ikko or Shin sect.

At Hiyeizan, on Lake Biwa, was the most extensive monastery in Japan. The grounds, adorned and beautified with the rarest art of the native landscape gardener, inclosed thirteen valleys and over five hundred temples, shrines, and priestly dwellings. Here thousands of monks were congregated. They chanted before gorgeous altars, celebrated their splendid ritual, reveled in luxury and licentiousness, drank their saké, eat the forbidden viands, and dallied with their concubines, or hatched plots to light or fan the flames of feudal war, so as to make the quarrels of the clans and chiefs redound to their aggrandizement. They trusted profoundly to their professedly sacred character to shield them from all danger.

For these bonzes Nobunaga had no respect. His early life among the priests had doubtless destroyed whatever reverence he might have had for their sanctity. His education as a Shintôist made him hate the Buddhists as enemies. The bonzes continually foiled his schemes, and he saw that, even if war between the clans ceased, the existence of these monasteries would jeopard the national peace. He resolved to destroy them.

In the Ninth month, 1571, says the *Nihon Guai Shi*, he encamped at Séta, and ordered his generals to set Hiyeizan on fire. The generals, surprised at the order, lost countenance, and exhorted him not to do it, saying, "Since Kuammu Tennô [782–806] built this monastery, nearly a thousand years ago, it has been esteemed the most vigilant against the devil. No one has yet dared to injure these temples; but now, do you intend to do so? How can it be possible?" To this Nobunaga answered: "I have put down the thieves against the emperor [*koku-zoku*, robbers of country]; why do you hinder me thus? I intend to tranquilize the whole land, and revive the declining power of the imperial Government. I continually make light of my life for the mikado's sake, and hence I have no rest for a single day. Last year I subdued Settsu, and both castles were about to be surrendered, when Yoshikagé [Daimiô of Echizen] and Nagamasa [Daimiô of Ômi] attacked my rear, and I was obliged to raise the siege and retrace my steps. My allowing the priests to remain on this mountain was in order that I might destroy them. I once dispatched a messenger to the priests, and set before them happiness and misery. The bonzes never obeyed my word, but stoutly assisted the wicked fellows, and so resisted the imperial army [*ôshi*, or *kuangun*]. Does this act not make them [*kokuzoku*] country-thieves? If I do not now take them away, this great trouble will continue forever. Moreover, I have heard that the priests violate their own rules; they eat fish and stinking vegetables [the five odorous plants prohibited by Buddhism—common and wild leek, garlic, onions, scallions], keep concubines, and roll up the sacred books [never untie them to read them or pray]. How can they be vigilant against evil, or preserve justice? Then surround their dwellings, burn them down, suffer no one to live."

The generals, incited by the speech of their commander, agreed. On the next day an awful scene of butchery and conflagration ensued. The soldiers set fire to the great shrines and temples; and while the stately edifices were in flames, plied sword, lance, and arrow. None were permitted to escape. Without discrimination of age or sex, the toothless dotard, abbot, and bonze, maid-servant and concubine and children, were speared or cut down without mercy. This was the first great blow at Buddhism.

In 1579, the two great sects of Nichiren and Jôdo held a great discussion upon religious subjects, which reached such a point of acrimony that the attention of the Government was called to it, and it was continued and finished before Nobunaga, at his castle at Azuchi yama, on the lands of which he had already allowed the Jesuits to build churches. A book called *Azuchi Ron*, still extant, contains the substance of the argument on both sides. One result of the wordy contest was the suppression of a sub-sect of Jôdo, whose doctrines were thought to be dangerous to the State.

The immense fortified temple and monastery called Honguanji, in Ôzaka, was the property of the Monto, or Shin sect of Buddhists, and the retreat and hiding-place of Nobunaga's enemies. The bonzes themselves were his most bitter haters, because he had so encouraged the Jesuits. They had taken the side of his enemies for over twelve years. At last, when some of his best captains had been killed by "grass-rebels," or ambuscaders, who fled into the monastery, he laid siege to it in earnest, with the intention of serving the inmates as he did those of Hiyeizan. Within the enceinte, crowded in five connecting fortresses, were thousands of women and children, besides the warriors and priests. Another frightful massacre seemed imminent. The place was so surrounded that every attempt of the garrison to escape was cut off. On an intensely dark night, under cover of a storm then raging, several thousands of the people, of all sexes and ages, attempted to escape from one of the forts. They were overtaken and slaughtered. The main garrison shortly afterward learned the fate of their late comrades by seeing a junk, dispatched by the victors, laden with human ears and noses, approach the castle with its hideous cargo. Another outpost of the castle was surrendered. In the second month of the siege, a sortie in force was repelled by showers of arrows and matchlock balls; but, in the fighting, Nobunaga's best officers were slain. The besieging army finally occupied three of the five in the net-work of fortresses. Thousands ("twenty thousand") of the garrison had been killed by arrow and ball, or had perished in the flames, and the horrible stench of burning flesh filled the air for miles. The fate of the main body within the walls was soon to be decided.

The mikado, grieving over the shedding of so much blood, sent three court nobles and a priest of another sect to persuade the garrison to yield. A conference of the abbot and elders was called, and a surrender decided upon. The castle was turned over to Nobunaga, and from that day until the present has remained in the hands of the Government. Pardon was granted to the survivors, and the bonzes scattered to the other large monasteries of their sect. To this day, the great sects in Japan have never fully recovered from the blows dealt by Nobunaga. Subsequently, rulers were obliged to lay violent hands upon the strongholds of ecclesiastical power that threatened so frequently to disturb the peace of the country; but they were able to do it with comparative ease, because Nobunaga had begun the work with such unscrupulous vigor and thoroughness.

# XXIV

# *Hidéyoshi's Enterprises—The Invasion of Corea*

There are hundreds of mura, or villages, in Japan, called Nakamura (*naka*, middle; *mura*, village), for the same reason that there are many Middletowns in English-speaking countries, but none of them claim to be the birthplace of Hidéyoshi except that in the district of Aichi, in Owari. There, in 1536, lived a peasant called Yasuké, whose wife bore a wizen-faced, pithecoid baby, who grew up to be a cunning and reckless boy. Instead of going out to the hill-sides, grass-hook in hand and basket on back, to cut green fodder for horses, or standing knee-deep in the mud-pulp of the rice-fields weeding the young plants, returning at night, with hoe on shoulder, he lived on the streets, and sharpened his wits, afraid of no one. While a mere boy, he became a *bettô*, or groom, to Nobunaga, who noticed the boy's monkey face and restless eyes, and encouraged him to become a soldier, which he did.

The number and variety of names possessed by him in his life-time illustrate well the confusing custom in vogue among the Japanese of frequently changing their names. The reader of the native literature or of foreign works of Japan is perplexed, among the multitude of names and titles, to distinguish the personage to whom they belong. When there are many actors in the scene, and each is known by a half-dozen aliases, confusion becomes confounded, and the patience is sorely taxed.

In this work I designate one person by one name, although apparent anachronisms must thereby be committed, and the eyes of the scholar be often annoyed. It has, until recently, in Japan been the custom for every samurai to be named differently in babyhood, boyhood, manhood, or promotion, change of life or residence, in commemoration of certain events, or on account of a vow, or from mere whim. Thus, at his birth, Hidéyoshi's mother having, as it is said, dreamed that she had conceived by the sun, called him Hiyoshi marô (good sun). Others dubbed him Ko chiku (small boy), and afterward Saru matsu (monkey-pine). As a soldier, he enlisted as Kinoshita Tokichiro, the first being an assumed name. As he grew famous, he was nicknamed Momen Tokichi ("Cotton" Tokichi). When a general, from a mere whim, he made himself a name by uniting two syllables, *ha* and *shiba*, making Hashiba, from the names of two of his generals, Ni-wa or ha, and Shibata, which the Jesuits wrote, as the Portuguese orthography required, Faxiba.

When, in 1586, he attained the rank of Kuambaku (Cambaku dono of the Jesuits), or premier, his enemies, who were jealous of the parvenu, spoke of him as Saru Kuan ja, or crowned monkey. How he obtained this high office, even with all the limitless store of cunning impudence and egotism, is not known, for no one except nobles of Fujiwara blood had ever filled that office, it being reserved exclusively for members of that family. He obtained from the emperor the patent of a family name, and he and his successors are known in history as the Toyotomi family, he being Toyotomi Hidéyoshi. In 1591 he resigned his high office, and was succeeded by his son. Hence he took the title of taikô, and the people referred to him as Taikô sama, just as they put the term *sama* (Mr., or Sir, Honorable, etc.) after the titles of emperor, shôgun, other titled officials, or after the name of any person. Japanese address foreigners as "Smith sama," or "Smith san," or an infant as "baby san," instead of "Mr. Smith," "the baby," etc. The term *sama* fulfills, in a measure, the function of the definite article or demonstrative pronoun, or serves as a social handle. Hence, in foreign works, Hidéyoshi, the taikô; or that one of the many taikô, called Hidéyoshi, is referred to as Taikô sama.

Hidéyoshi was a man of war from his youth up. His abilities and soldierly qualities made him a favorite commander. His banner consisted of a cluster of gourds. At first it was a single gourd. After each battle another was added, until at last it became an imposing sheaf. The standard-bearer carried aloft at the head of the columns a golden representation of the original model, and wherever Hidéyoshi's banner moved there was the centre of victory.

At the death of Nobunaga, the situation was as follows: His third son, Nobutaka, was ruler over Shikoku; Shimadzu (Satsuma) was fighting with Ôtomo, and seizing his land in Kiushiu. Hidéyoshi and Nobuwo, second son of Nobunaga, with the imperial army, were fighting with Môri, Prince of Chôshiu, who held ten provinces in the West. Iyeyasu, ruler of eight provinces in the Kuantô, was in the field against Hôjô of Odawara. Shibata held Echizen. Hidéyoshi and Iyéyasu were the rising men, but the former attained first to highest power. Immediately on hearing of Nobunaga's death, Hidéyoshi made terms with Môri, hastened to Kiôto, and defeated and slew Akéchi. The fate of this assassin has given rise to the native proverb, "Akéchi ruled three days." His name and power were now paramount. The prizes of rank were before him, for the mikado and court could not oppose his wishes. Of his master's sons, one had died, leaving an infant; the second son was assisted by Iyéyasu, with whom Hidéyoshi had made a compromise; the third, Nobutaka, was weak, and endeavored, seconded by his chief captain, Shibata, who had married the sister of Nobunaga, to maintain his rights. Hidéyoshi marched into Mino, defeated him, pursued Shibata into Echizen, and, after several skirmishes, burned his castle. The account of this, as given by the Jesuits, is as follows: "Among the confederates of Nobutaka was one Shibata dono, brother-in-law to Nobunaga. He was besieged in the fortress of Shibata [in what is now Fukui]; and seeing no way of escape, he, having dined with his friend's wife and children and retainers, set fire to his castle, first killing his wife, his children, and the female servants; and his friends, following his example, afterward committed suicide, and lay there wallowing in their blood, till the fire kindled, and burned them to ashes."

My residence in Fukui, during the year 1871, was immediately on the site of part of Shibata's old castle. His tomb stands under some venerable old pine-trees some distance from the city. When I visited it, the old priest who keeps the temple, since erected, brought out several old boxes carefully labeled, and reverently opened them. One contained the rusty breastplate and other portions of Shibata's armor, picked up after the fire. Other relics saved from the ashes were shown me. The story, as it fell from the old bonze's lips, and was translated by my interpreter, is substantially that given by the native historians.

Having fled, after many defeats, he reached the place now called Fukui. Hidéyoshi, in hot pursuit, fixed his camp on Atagoyama, a mountain which overlooks the city, and began the siege, which he daily pressed closer and closer. Being hopelessly surrounded, and succor hopeless, Shibata, like a true Epicurean, gave a grand feast to all his captains and retainers, in anticipation of the morrow of death. All within the doomed walls eat, drank, sung, danced and made merry, for the morrow was not to see them in this world. At the height of the banquet, Shibata, quaffing the parting cup before death, addressed his wife thus: "You may go out of the castle and save your life. You are a woman; but we are men, and will die. You are at liberty to marry another." His wife, the sister of Nobunaga, with a spirit equal to his, was moved to tears, thanked her lord for his love and kindness, and declared she would never marry another, but would die with her husband. She then composed a farewell stanza of poetry, and, with a soul no less brave because it was a woman's, received her husband's dirk into her heart.

Like true Stoics, Shibata and his companions put all the women and children to the death they welcomed, and for which they gave thanks; and then, with due decorum and ceremony, opening their own bodies by *hara-kiri*, they died as brave Japanese ever love to die, by their own hands, and not by those of an enemy.

Hidéyoshi, on his return to Kiôto, began a career of usefulness, developing the resources of the empire and strengthening the power of the emperor. Knowing it was necessary to keep his captains and soldiers busy in time of inaction, and having a genius for the works of peace as well as war, he built splendid palaces at Kiôto, improved the city, and paved the bed of the river Kamo with broad, flat stones. He laid the foundations of the future commercial greatness of Ôzaka by enlarging the site of the monastery destroyed by Nobunaga, building the immense fortress, only part of which still remains, the pride of the city, enlarged and deepened the river, and dug many of the hundreds of canals which give this city whatever right it may have to be called the Venice of Japan. It had, when I saw it in 1871, over eleven hundred bridges, one of them of iron. He fortified Fushimi, the strategic key of Kiôto, with a triple-moated castle, erected colossal towers and pagodas in many places. He sequestrated the flourishing commercial port of Nagasaki from the Daimiô of Ômura, and made it the property of the crown. Neither Déshima nor Pappenberg was then historic; but the lovely scenery was as much the subject of admiration as it is now. His policy was to forgive those who had fought against him, and not to put them to death, as Nobunaga had done, who, in the course of his life, had killed his brother, father-in-law, and many of his enemies. He reformed the revenues. His rule was highly popular, for, in his execution of justice, he cared little for rank, name, or family line, or services done to himself. He was successful in inducing Iyéyasu, after the latter had secured the taikô's mother as hostage, to come to Kiôto and pay homage to the emperor; and the two rivals becoming friends, Iyéyasu married the taikô's sister. Môri, lord of the Western provinces, also came to the capital, and acknowledged him as his superior.

Among his other works, Hidéyoshi followed out the policy of Nobunaga, destroyed the great monastery at Kumano, the bonzes of which claimed the province of Kii. He was never made shôgun, not being of Minamoto blood; but having become Kuambaku, and being surrounded by nobles of high birth and the lofty etiquette of the court, he felt the need of a pedigree. No one at court knew who his grand-father was, if, indeed, he was aware himself. He made out that his  mother was the daughter of a kugé, who, in the disturbed times of Ashikaga, had fled from Kiôto, and, while in poverty and great distress, had married his father, but had conceived him before her marriage.

In his youth he had wedded a peasant girl; but as he rose step by step to eminence, he kept on marrying until he had a number equal to that of the polygamous English king, Henry VIII; but, unlike that monarch, he enjoyed them all at once, and caused none of them to lose her head. The last two of his spouses were, respectively, a daughter of the house of Maëda, of the rich province of Kaga, and the Princess Azai, from Ômi, daughter of the wife of Shibata Katsuiyé, whom the Jesuits, under the name of Kita Mandocoro, say was the first wife of the taikô, "sweetest and best beloved." He had no son until in old age.

The immoderate ambition of Hidéyoshi's life was to conquer Corea, and even China. It had been his dream when a boy, and his plan when a man. When under Nobunaga, he had begged of him the revenue of Kiushiu for one year and weapons, while he himself would provide the ships and provisions, offering to subdue Corea, and with an army of Coreans to conquer China, and thus make the three countries one. His master laughed, but he kept thinking of it. When in the Kuantô, he visited Kamakura, and saw an image of Yoritomo, such as one may still see in the temple of Tsurugaöka. Rubbing and patting its back, the parvenu thus addressed the illustrious effigy: "You are my friend. You took all the power under Heaven (in Japan). You and I, only, have been able to do this; but you were of a famous family, and not like me, sprung from peasants. I intend, at last, to conquer all the earth, and even China. What think you of that?" Hidéyoshi used to say, "The earth is the earth's earth"—a doctrine which led him to respect very slightly the claim of any one to land which he coveted, and had won by his own efforts.

Under the declining power of Ashikaga, all tribute from Corea had ceased and the pirates who ranged the coasts scarcely allowed a precarious trade to exist. The Sô family, who held Tsushima, however, had a small settlement in Corea. Some Chinese, emigrating to Japan, told Hidéyoshi of the military disorganization and anarchy in China, which increased his desire to "peep into China." He then sent two embassies in succession to Corea to demand tribute. The second was successful. He also sent word to the Emperor of China by some Liu Kiu tribute-bearers that if he (the Emperor of China) would not hear him, he would invade his territory with an army. To the Corean envoy he recounted his exploits, and announced his intentions definitely.

Several embassies crossed and recrossed the sea between Corea and Japan, Hidéyoshi meanwhile awaiting his best opportunity, as the dispatch of the expedition depended almost entirely on his own will. His wife, Azai, had borne him a child, whom he loved dearly, but it died, and he mourned for it many months. One day he went out to a temple, Kiyomidzu, in Kiôto, to beguile the sad hours. Lost in thought, in looking over the western sky beyond the mountains, he suddenly exclaimed to his attendant, "A great man ought to employ his army beyond ten thousand miles, and not give way to sorrow." Returning to his house, he assembled his generals, and fired their enthusiasm by recounting their exploits mutually achieved. He then promised to march to Peking, and divide the soil of China in fiefs among them. They unanimously agreed, and departed to the various provinces to prepare troops and material. Hideyoshi himself went to Kiushiu.

On his way, some one suggested that scholars versed in Chinese should accompany the expedition. Hideyoshi laughed, and said, "This expedition will make the Chinese use our literature." After worshiping at a shrine, he threw up a handful of one hundred "cash" in front of the shrine, and said, "If I am to conquer China, let the heads show it." The Japanese copper and iron *zeni*, or *kas*, have Chinese characters representing the chronological period of coinage on one side, and waves representing their circulation as money on the reverse. The lettered side is "head," the reverse is "tail." All the coins which the taikô flung up came down heads. The soldiers were delighted with the omen. Maps of Corea were distributed among the commanders of the eight divisions, and the plan of the expedition and their co-operation explained.

Kato Kiyomasa, who hated the Christians, and who afterward became their bitterest persecutor, was commander of the first; and Konishi Yukinaga, the Christian leader, and a great favorite of the Jesuits, of the second. These divisions were alternately to lead the van. The naval and military force that embarked is set down in the *Guai Shi* at five hundred thousand men. A reserve of sixty thousand was kept ready in Japan as re-enforcements. Many of the generals, captains, and private soldiers were of the Christian faith. Kato despised Konishi, and they were not friends. The latter was the son of a druggist, and persisted, to the disgust of the high-born Kato, in carrying a banner representing a paper medicine-bag, such as can be seen swinging in front of a native drug-shop to-day. He probably took his cue from the august parvenu, the taikô.

Hidéyoshi expected to lead the army himself; but being sixty years old, and infirm, and his aged mother sorrowing so that she could not eat on account of it, he remained behind. He gave Kato flag, saying, "This was given me by Ota [Nobunaga] when I marched against Môri [Chôshiu]." To Konishi he presented a fine horse, saying, "With this gallop over the bearded savages [Coreans]." All being ready, the fleet set sail amidst the shouts of the army and the thunder of cannon on the shore. Hidéyoshi had attempted to buy or charter two Portuguese ships, but was unsuccessful, and the fleet consisted of large junks. They were detained off Iki Island by stormy weather. As soon as it was calm, Konishi, well acquainted with the route, sailed away with his division, arrived at Fusan, in Southern Corea, first, and seized the castle. Without allowing his troops to rest, he urged them on to other triumphs, that the glory might be theirs alone, and not be shared by the other troops, who would soon arrive. Another large castle was stormed, several towns captured, and brilliant victories won. Three days later, Kato arrived, and heard, to his chagrin, of his rival's advance into the interior. He exclaimed, "The boy has taken my route; I shall not follow in his tracks." He then burned the town, which Konishi had spared, and advanced into the country by another way.

Corea was divided into eight circuits, and the taikô's plan had been for each corps of the army to conquer a circuit. The Corean king appointed a commander-in-chief, and endeavored to defend his country, but the Japanese armies were everywhere victorious. After many battles fought, and fortresses stormed, nearly all the provinces of the eight circuits were subdued, and the capital, Kenkitai, was taken. The king and his son fled. At one great battle, ten thousand Coreans are said to have been killed, and their ears cut off and preserved in salt or saké. The forts were garrisoned by Japanese troops. The Coreans asked the aid of China, and a Chinese army of assistance was sent forward, and after several severe battles the Japanese were compelled to fall back. Reserves from Japan were dispatched to Corea, and the Japanese were on the point of invading China, when, in 1598, the death of the taikô was announced, and orders were received from their Government to return home. A truce was concluded, and Corean envoys accompanied Konishi to Japan.

The conquest of Corea, thus ingloriously terminated, reflects no honor on Japan, and perhaps the responsibility of the outrage upon a peaceful nation rests wholly upon Hidéyoshi. The Coreans were a mild and peaceable people, wholly unprepared for war. There was scarcely a shadow of provocation for the invasion which was nothing less than a huge filibustering scheme. It was not popular with the people or the rulers, and was only carried through by the will of the taiko. While Japan was impoverished by the great drain on its resources, the soldiers abroad ruthlessly desolated the homes and needlessly ravaged the land of the Coreans. While the Japanese were destroying the liberties of the Coreans, the poor natives at home often pawned or sold themselves as slaves to the Spaniards and Portuguese slave-traders. The sacrifice of life on either side must have been great, and all for the ambition of one man. Nevertheless, a party in Japan has long held that Corea was, by the conquests of the third and sixteenth centuries, a part of the Japanese empire, and the reader will see how in 1872, and again in 1875, the cry of "On to Corea!" shook the nation like an earthquake.

The taikô died on the 15th of September, 1598. Before his death, he settled the form of government, and married his son Hidéyori, then six years old, to the granddaughter of Iyéyasu, and appointed five *tairô*, or ministers, who were to be guardians of the boy, and to acknowledge him as his father's successor. As Iyéyasu was the rising man, the taikô hoped thus to gain his influence, so that the power might descend in his own family. The last thoughts of the hero were of strengthening the citadel at Ôzaka. The old hero was buried in the grounds of Kodaiji, in Kiôto.

The victorious army, returning from Corea, brought much spoil, and fine timber to build a memorial temple to the memory of the dead hero. Among other trophies were several thousands of ears, which, instead of heads, the Japanese carried back to raise a barrow in Kiôto. The temple was erected on a hill on the west side of Kiôto by his wife, who, after the death of her husband, became a nun. This splendid edifice was afterward burned, and the site of the taikô's remains is uncertain.

In the city still stands the Mimidzuka (ear-tomb), a monument of characteristic appearance. It consists of a cube, sphere, and pagoda-curve, surmounted by two spheroids, the top-stone rising to a point. The mound is seven hundred and twenty feet in circumference, and ninety feet in height; the pedestal at the top being twelve feet square, and the monument twelve feet high. As usual on Buddhist tombs or ecclesiastical edifices, a Sanskrit letter is carved on each side of the four faces of the cube. Beneath this tomb is a barrow, covering the dissevered ears of thousands of Coreans; but the most enduring monuments of the great taikô were the political institutions, and the works of peace reared by his genius and labor.

It is not difficult to account for the tone of admiration and pride with which a modern Japanese speaks of "the age of Taikô." There are many who hold that he was the real unifier of the empire, and that Iyéyasu merely followed in his footsteps, perfecting the work which Hidéyoshi began. Certain it is that in many of the most striking forms of national administration, and notably in bestowing upon his vassals grants of land, and making the conditions of tenure loyalty to himself and family, Iyéyasu was but the copyist of the taikô. In his time, the arts and sciences were not only in a very flourishing condition, but gave promise of rich development. The spirit of military enterprise and internal national improvement was at its height. Contact with the foreigners of many nations awoke a spirit of inquiry and intellectual activity; but it was on the seas that genius and restless activity found their most congenial field.

This era is marked by the highest perfection in marine architecture, and the extent and variety of commercial enterprises. The ships built in this century were twice or thrice the size, and vastly the superior in model, of the junks that now hug the Japanese shores, or ply between China and Japan. The pictures of them preserved to the present day show that they were superior in size to the vessels of Columbus, and nearly equal in sailing qualities to the contemporary Dutch and Portuguese galleons. They were provided with ordnance, and a model of a Japanese breech-loading cannon is still preserved in Kiôto. Ever a brave and adventurous people, the Japanese then roamed the seas with a freedom that one who knows only of the modern shore-bound people would scarcely credit. Voyages of trade, discovery, or piracy had been made to India, Siam, Burmah, the Philippines, Southern China, the Malay Archipelago, and the Kuriles, on the north, even in the fifteenth century, but were most numerous in the sixteenth. The Japanese gave the name to the island of Roson (Luzon), and the descendants of Japanese pirates or traders are still to be found in numbers in this archipelago. In the city of Ayuthaya, on the Menam, in Siam, a flourishing sea-port, the people call one part of the place the "Japanese quarter." The Japanese literature contains many references to these adventurous sailors; and when the records of the Far East are thoroughly investigated, and this subject fully studied, very interesting results will be obtained, showing the wide-spread influence of Japan at a time when she was scarcely known by the European world to have existence.

# XXV

## *Christianity and Foreigners**

It seems now nearly certain that when Columbus set sail from Spain to discover a new continent, it was not America he was seeking; for of that he knew nothing. His quest was the land of Japan. Marco Polo, the Venetian traveler, had spent seventeen years (1275–1292) at the court of the Tartar emperor, Kublai Khan, and while in Peking had heard of a land lying to the eastward called, in the language of the Chinese capital, Jipangu, from which our modern name, Japan, has been corrupted. Columbus was an ardent student of Polo's book, which had been published in 1298. He sailed westward across the Atlantic to find this kingdom of the sun-source. He discovered, not Japan, but an archipelago in America, on whose shores he eagerly inquired concerning Jipangu. The torch of modern discovery thus kindled by him was handed on by Vasco da Gama, and a host of brave Portuguese navigators, who drove their keels into the once unknown seas of the Orient, and came back to tell of densely populated empires

---

* In compiling this chapter, I have made use of Hildreth's *Japan as it Was and Is*; Léon Pagés' *Histoire de la Religion Chrétienne au Japon*; Charlevoix's *Histoire du Christianismeau Japon*; Dixon's *Japan*; *Shimabara: A Japanese Account of the Christian Insurrection in 1637*; the Japanese Encyclopædia, *San Sai Dzu Yé*; and the able paper of Herr Von Brandt (Minister of the North German Confederation in Japan) read before the German Asiatic Society of Japan.

enriched with the wealth that makes civilization possible, and of which Europe had scarcely heard. Their accounts fired the hearts of the zealous who longed to convert the heathen, aroused the cupidity of traders who thirsted for gold, and kindled the desire of monarchs to found empires in Asia.

As the Spaniards had founded an empire in America, Portugal was then nearing the zenith of her maritime glory. Mendez Pinto, a Portuguese adventurer, seems to have been the first European who landed on Japanese soil. On his return to Europe, he told so many wonderful stories that he was dubbed, by a pun on his Christian name, "the mendacious." His narrative was, however, as we now know, substantially correct. Pinto, while in China, had got on board a Chinese junk, commanded by a pirate. They were attacked by another corsair, their pilot was killed, and the vessel was driven off the coast by a storm. They made for the Liu Kiu Islands; but, unable to find a harbor, put to sea, and after twenty-three days beating about, sighted the island of Tané (*Tanégashima*, island of the seed), off the south of Kiushiu, and landed. The name of the island was significant. The arrival of those foreigners was the seed of troubles innumerable. The crop was priestcraft of the worst type, political intrigue, religious persecution, the Inquisition, the slave-trade, the propagation of Christianity by the sword, sedition, rebellion, and civil war. Its harvest was garnered in the blood of sixty thousand Japanese.

The native histories recount the first arrival of Europeans on Tanégashima in 1542, and note that year as the one in which fire-arms were first introduced. Pinto and his two companions were armed with arquebuses, which delighted this people, ever ready to accept whatever will tend to their advantage. They were even more impressed with the novel weapons than by the strangers. Pinto was invited by the Daimiô of Bungo to visit him, which he did. The natives began immediately to make guns and powder, the secret of which was taught them by their visitors. In a few years, as we know from Japanese history, fire-arms came into general use. To this day many country people call them "Tanégashima." Thus, in the beginning, hand-in-hand came foreigners, Christianity, and fire-arms. To many a native they are still each and equal members of a trinity of terrors, and one is a synonym of the other. Christianity to most of "the heathen" still means big guns and powder.

In those days commerce and piracy, war and religion, were closely united; and the sword and the cross were twin weapons, like the cimeter and the Koran of the Turks, by which the pious robbers of the most Christian empires of Spain and Portugal went forth to conquer weak nations.

The pirate-trader who brought Pinto to Japan cleared twelve hundred percent on his cargo, and the three Portuguese returned, loaded with presents, to China. This new market attracted hundreds of Portuguese adventurers to Japan, who found a ready welcome at the hands of the impressible people. The daimiôs vied with each other in attracting the foreigners to their shores, their object being to obtain the weapons, and get the wealth which would increase their power, as the authority of the Ashikaga shôguns had before this time been cast off, and each chief was striving for local supremacy.

The missionary followed the merchant. Already the Portuguese priests and Franciscan friars were numerous in India and the straits. A native of Satsuma named Anjirô, who, having killed a man, had fled to Pinto's boat, and was carried off by him, after the long suf-ferings of remorse reached Goa, becoming a convert to Christianity. Learning to read and write Portuguese, and having mastered the whole Christian doctrine, he became Xavier's interpreter. To the question whether the Japanese would be likely to accept Christianity, Anjirô answered—in words that seem fresh, pertinent, and to have been uttered but yesterday, so true are they still—that "his people would not immediately assent to what might be said to them, but they would investigate what I might affirm respecting religion by a multitude of questions, and, above all, by observing whether my conduct agreed with my words. This done, the king (daimiô), the nobility, and adult population would flock to Christ, being a nation which always follows reason as a guide." The words are recorded by Xavier himself.

In 1549, the party of two Jesuits and two Japanese landed at Kagoshima, in Satsuma. Xavier, after studying the rudiments of the language, beyond which he never advanced, and making diligent use of the pictures of the Virgin and Child, soon left the capital of this war-like clan, for the city had not been favored with the commerce of the Portuguese; and, as the missionaries had not come to improve the material resources of the province, they were not warmly welcomed. He then went to Bungo and Nagato. Besides having an interpreter, though unable to preach, he used to read the Gospel of Matthew translated by Anjirô into Japanese, and Romanized. Though unable to understand much of it, he read it in public with great effect. There trade was flourishing and enriching the daimiôs, and he was warmly received by them. His next step was a journey to Kiôto. There, instead of the extraordinary richness of the sovereign's palace, which he had expected to see plated with gold on the roofs and ceilings, with tables of the same metal, and all the other wonders as related by Marco Polo, he found it but a city which wars and fires had rendered desolate, and almost uninhabitable, except as a camp. Here he employed the policy of austerity and poverty, his appearance being that of a beggar, though later he used wealth and great display in his ministrations, with marked effect. The mikado's (dairi) authority, he found, was merely nominal; the shogun, Ashikaga Yoshitéru, ruled only over a few provinces around the capital. Every one's thoughts were of war, and battle was imminent. The very idea of an interview with the mikado was an absurdity, and one with the Kubô sama (shô-gun) an impossibility, his temporary poverty not permitting him to make a present effectively large enough for the latter, and rendering him contemptible in the eyes of the people. He attempted to preach several times in the streets, but, not being master of the language, failed to secure attention, and after two weeks left the city disgusted. Not long after, having turned his attention to the furtherance of trade and diplomacy, he departed from Japan, disheartened by the realities of missionary work. He had, however, inspired others, who followed him, and their success was amazingly great. Within five years after Xavier visited Kiôto, seven churches were established in the vicinity of the city itself, while scores of Christian communities had sprung up in the south-west. In 1581, there were two hundred churches, and one hundred and fifty thousand native Christians. In Bungo, where Xavier won his way by costly gifts, as he did in Suwo by diplomacy; in Harima and Ômura, the daimiôs themselves had professed the new faith, while Nobunaga, the hater of the Buddhists, openly favored the Christians, and gave them eligible sites upon which to build dwellings and churches. Ready to use any weapons against the bonzes, Nobunaga hoped to use the foreigners as a counterpoise to their arrogance.

In 1583, an embassy of four young noblemen was dispatched by the Christian daimiôs of Kiushiu to the pope, to declare themselves vassals of the Holy See. Eight years afterward, having had audience of Philip II of Spain, and kissed the feet of the pope at Rome, they returned, bringing with them seventeen Jesuit missionaries—an important addition to the many Portuguese religious of that order already in Japan. Spanish mendicant friars from the Philippine Islands, with Dominicans and Augustans, also flocked into the country, preaching and zealously proselyting. The number of "Christians" at the time of the highest success of the missionaries in Japan was, according to their own figures, six hundred thousand—a number which I believe is no exaggeration, the quantity, not quality, being considered. The Japanese, less accurately, set down a total of two million nominal adherents to the Christian sects, large numerical statements in Japanese books being untrustworthy, and often worthless. Among their converts were several princes, and large numbers of lords and gentlemen in high official position, generals and captains in the army, and the admiral and officers of the Japanese fleets. Several of the ladies of the households of Hidéyoshi, Hidéyori, and Iyéyasu, besides influential women of noble blood in many provinces whose rulers were not Christians, added to their power, while at the seat of government the chief interpreter was a Jesuit father. Churches, chapels, and residences of the fathers were numbered by thousands, and in some provinces crosses and Christian shrines were as numerous as the kindred evidences of Buddhism had been before. The fathers and friars had traveled or preached from one end of the western half of Hondo to the other; northward in Echizen, Kaga, Echigo, and Ôshiu, and in the provinces of the Tôkaidô. They had also one church in Yedo.

The causes of this astonishingly rapid success of the Jesuits are to be sought in the mental soil which the missionaries found ready prepared for their seed. It was in the later days of the Ashikaga, when Xavier arrived in Japan. Centuries of misrule and anarchy had reduced the people, on whom the burdens of war fell, to the lowest depths of poverty and misery. The native religions then afforded little comfort or consolation to their adherents. Shintô had sunk to a myth almost utterly unknown to the people, and so overshadowed by Buddhism that only a few scholars knew its origin. Buddhism, having lost its vitalizing power, had degenerated into a commercial system of prayers and masses, in which salvation could be purchased only by the merit, of the deeds and prayers of the priests. Nevertheless, its material and outward splendor were never greater. Gorgeous vestments, blazing lights, imposing processions, altars of dazzling magnificence, and a sensuous worship captivated the minds of the people, while indulgences were sold, and saints' days and holidays and festivals were multiplied.

The Japanese are an intensely imaginative people; and whatever appeals to the æsthetics of sense, or fires the imagination, leads the masses captive at the will of their religious leaders. The priests of Rome came with crucifixes in their hands, eloquence on their lips, and with rich dresses, impressive ceremonies, processions, and mysteries outdazzled the scenic display of the Buddhists. They brought pictures, gilt crosses, and images, and erected gorgeous altars, which they used as illuminated texts for their sermons. They preached the doctrine of an immediate entrance into paradise after death to all believers, a doctrine which thrilled their hearers to an uncontrollable pitch of enthusiasm. Buddhism promises rest in heaven only after many transformations, births, and the repeated miseries of life and death, the very thought of which wearies the soul. The story of the Cross, made vivid by fervid eloquence, tears and harrowing pictures and colored images, which bridged the gulf of remoteness, and made the act of Calvary near and intensely real, melted the hearts of the impressible natives. Furthermore, the transition from the religion of India to that of Rome was extremely easy. The very idols of Buddha served, after a little alteration with the chisel, for images of Christ. The Buddhist saints were easily transformed into the Twelve Apostles. The Cross took the place of the *torii*. It was emblazoned on the helmets and banners of the warriors, and embroidered on their breasts. The Japanese soldiers went forth to battle like Christian crusaders. In the roadside shrine Kuanon, the Goddess of Mercy, made way for the Virgin, the mother of God. Buddhism was beaten with its own weapons. Its own artillery was turned against it. Nearly all the Christian churches were native temples, sprinkled and purified. The same bell, whose boom had so often quivered the air announcing the orisons and matins of paganism, was again blessed and sprinkled, and called the same hearers to mass and confession; the same lavatory that fronted the temple served for holy-water or baptismal font; the same censer that swung before Amida could be refilled to waft Christian incense; the new convert could use unchanged his old beads, bells, candles, incense, and all the paraphernalia of his old faith in celebration of the new.

Almost every thing that is distinctive in the Roman form of Christianity is to be found in Buddhism: images, pictures, lights, altars, incense, vestments, masses, beads, wayside shrines, monasteries, nunneries, celibacy, fastings, vigils, retreats, pilgrimages, mendicant vows, shorn heads, orders, habits, uniforms, nuns, convents, purgatory, saintly and priestly intercession, indulgences, works of supererogation, pope, archbishops, abbots, abbesses, monks, neophytes, relics and relic-worship, exclusive burial-ground, etc., etc., etc.

The methods which the foreign priests employed to propagate the new faith were not such as commend themselves to a candid mind. The first act of propagation was an act of Mariolatry. They brought with them the spirit of the Inquisition, then in full blast in Spain and Portugal, which they had used there for the reclamation of native and Dutch heretics. In Japan they began to attack most violently the character of the native bonzes, and to incite their converts to insult the gods, destroy the idols, and burn or desecrate the old shrines. They made plentiful use of the gold furnished liberally by the kings of Portugal and Spain, under the name of "alms." In two years and a half Xavier received one thousand doubloons (fifteen thousand dollars) for the support of his mission. This abundance of the foreign precious metal was noticed especially by the native rulers. In Kiushiu the daimiôs themselves became Christians, and they compelled their subjects to embrace their religion. The people of whole districts of country were ordered to become Christians, or to leave their land

and the homes of their fathers, and go into banishment. The bonzes were exiled or killed; and fire and sword, as well as preaching, were employed as instruments of conversion. Furthermore, fictitious miracles were frequently got up to utilize the credulity of the superstitious in furthering the spread of the faith, glowing accounts of which may be found in Léon Pagés' *Histoire de la R. C.* Not only do the native Japanese writers record these things as simple matter of fact, but the letters of the Jesuits themselves, and the books written by them, teem with instances of ferocious cruelty and pious fraud wrought in their behalf, or at their instigation. The following passages from the Jesuit Charlevoix's *Histoire du Christianisme au Japon* are translated by Dr. Walter Dixon in his *Japan*: "Sumitanda, King of Ômura, who had become a Christian in 1562, declared open war against the devils [bonzes]. He dispatched some squadrons through his kingdom to ruin all the idols and temples without any regard to the bonzes' rage.... In 1577, the lord of the island of Amacusa [Amakusa] issued his proclamation, by which his subjects—whether bonzes or gentlemen, merchants or tradesmen—were required either to turn Christians, or to leave the country the very next day. They almost all submitted, and received baptism, so that in a short time there were more than twenty churches in the kingdom. God wrought miracles to confirm the faithful in their belief." The Daimiô of Takatsuki, Settsu, "labored with a zeal truly apostolic to extirpate the idolaters out of his states. He sent word that they should either receive the faith, or be gone immediately out of his country, for he would acknowledge none for his subjects but such as acknowledged the true God. The declaration obliged them all to accept instruction, which cut out work enough for all the fathers and missionaries at Meaco [Miako]."

The Daimiô of Bungo at one time, during war, destroyed a most prodigious and magnificent temple, with a colossal statue, burning three thousand monasteries to ashes, and razing the temples to the ground. The comment of the Jesuit writer on this is, "This ardent zeal of the prince is an evident instance of his faith and charity." This does not, however, sound like an echo of the song once heard above the Bethlehem hills, few echoes of which the Japanese have as yet heard.

As the different orders, Jesuits, Franciscans, and Augustinians, increased, they began to trench upon each other's parishes. This gave rise to quarrels, indecent squabbles, and mutual vituperation, at which the pagans sneered and the bonzes rejoiced. While the friars of these orders were rigorously excommunicating each other, thinking heathen were not favorably impressed with the new religion. Christianity received her sorest wound in the house of her friends.

At this time, also, political and religious war was almost universal in Europe, and the quarrels of the various nationalities followed the buccaneers, pirates, traders, and missionaries to the distant seas of Japan. The Protestant, Dutch, and English stirred up the hatred and fear of the Japanese against the papists, and finally against each other. Spaniards and Portuguese blackened the character of the heretics, and as vigorously abused each other when it served their interest. All of which impelled the shrewd Japanese to contrive how to use them one against the other, an art which they still understand. All foreigners, but especially Portuguese, then were slave-traders, and thousands of Japanese were bought and sold and shipped to Macao, in China, and to the Philippines. The long civil wars, and the misery caused by them, and the expedition to Corea, had so impoverished the people that slaves became so cheap that even the Malay and negro servants of the Portuguese, speculated in the bodies of Japanese slaves who were bought and sold and transported. Hidéyoshi repeatedly issued decrees threatening with death these slave-traders, and even the purchasers. The sea-ports of Hirado and Nagasaki were the resort of the lowest class of adventurers from all European nations, and the result was a continual series of uproars, broils, and murders among the foreigners, requiring ever and anon the intervention of the native authorities to keep the peace. To the everlasting honor of some of the Jesuit bishops and priests be it said, they endeavored to do all they could to prevent the traffic in the bodies of men.

Such a picture of foreign influence and of Christianity, which is here drawn in mild colors, as the Japanese saw it, was not calculated to make a permanently favorable impression on the Japanese mind.

While Nobunaga lived, and the Jesuits basked in his favor, all was progress and victory. Hidéyoshi, though at first favorable to the new religion, issued, in 1587, a decree of banishment against the foreign missionaries. The Jesuits closed their churches and chapels, ceased to preach in public, but carried on their proselyting work in private as vigorously as ever, averaging ten thousand converts a year, until 1590. The Spanish mendicant friars, pouring in from the Philippines, openly defied the Japanese laws, preaching in their usual garb in public, and in their intemperate language. This aroused Hidéyoshi's attention, and his decree of expulsion was renewed. Some of the churches were burned. In 1596, six Franciscan, three Jesuit, and seventeen Japanese converts were taken to Nagasaki, and there crucified. Still the Jesuits resided in the country, giving out to the people that the Spaniards nourished the political designs against Japan, and that the decrees of expulsion had been directed against the priests of that nation, and that the late outburst of persecution was an explosion of zeal on the part of a few subordinate officials. Several of the generals of the army in Corea still openly professed the Christian faith.

When the taikô died, affairs seemed to take a more favorable turn, but only for a few years. The Christians looked to Hidéyori for their friend and quasi-leader. The battle of Sékigahara, and the defeat of Hidéyori's following, blew their hopes to the winds; and the ignominious death of Ishida, Konishi, and Ôtani, the Christian generals who had witnessed a good confession both as warriors and as upholders of the faith in Corea and at home, drove their adherents to the verge of despair. Iyéyasu re-adjusted the feudal relations of his vassals in Kiushiu; and as the taikô had also re-arranged the fiefs, the political status of the Christians was profoundly altered. The new daimios, carrying the policy of their predecessors as taught them by the Jesuits, but reversing its direction, began to persecute their Christian subjects, and to compel them to renounce their faith. The native converts resisted even to blood and the taking-up of arms. This was an entirely new thing under the Japanese sun. Hitherto the attitude of the peasantry to the Government had been one of passive obedience and slavish submission. The idea of armed rebellion among the farmers was something so wholly new that Iyéyasu suspected foreign instigation. Color was given to this idea by the fact that the foreigners still secretly or openly paid court to Hidéyori, and at the same time freely dispersed gold and gifts, in addition to religious comfort, to the persecuted. Iyéyasu became more vigilant as his suspicions increased, and, resolving to crush this spirit of independence and intimidate the foreign emissaries, met every outbreak with bloody reprisals. In 1606, an edict from Yedo forbade the exercise of the Christian religion, but an outward show of obedience warded off active persecution. In 1610, the Spanish friars again aroused the wrath of the Government by defying its commands, and exhorting the native converts to do likewise. In 1611, Iyéyasu obtained documentary proof of what he had long suspected, viz., the existence of a plot on the part of the native converts and the foreign emissaries to reduce Japan to the position of a subject state. The chief conspirator, Ôkubo, then Governor of Sado, to which place thousands of Christian exiles had been sent to work the mines, was to be made hereditary ruler by the foreigners. The names of the chief native and foreign conspirators were written down, with the usual seal of blood from the end of the middle finger of the ringleader. With this paper was found concealed, in an iron box in an old well, a vast hoard of gold and silver.

Iyéyasu now put forth strenuous measures to root out utterly what he believed to be a pestilent breeder of sedition and war. Fresh edicts were issued, and in 1614 twenty-two Franciscan, Dominican, and Augustinian friars, one hundred and seventeen Jesuits, and hundreds of native priests and catechists, were embarked by force on board junks, and sent out of the country.

In 1615, Iyéyasu pushed matters to an extreme with Hidéyori, who was then entertaining some Jesuit priests; and, calling out the troops of Kiushiu and the Kuantô, laid siege to the castle of Ôzaka. A battle of unusual ferocity and bloody slaughter raged, on the 9th of June, 1615, ending in the burning of the citadel, and the total defeat and death of Hidéyori and thousands of his followers. The Jesuit fathers say that one hundred thousand men perished in this brief war, of which vivid details are given in the *Histoire de la Religion Chrétienne.* The Christian cause was now politically and irretrievably ruined. Hildredth remarks that Catholicism in Japan "received its death-blow in that same year in which a few Puritan pilgrims landed at Plymouth to plant the obscure seeds of a new and still growing Protestant empire."

The exiled foreign friars, however, kept secretly returning, apparently desirous of the crown of martyrdom. Hidétada, the shôgun, now pronounced sentence of death against any foreign priest found in the country. Iyémitsu, his successor, restricted all foreign commerce to Nagasaki and Hirado; all Japanese were forbidden to leave the country on pain of death; and in 1624 all foreigners, except Dutch and Chinese, were banished from Japan, and an edict was issued commanding the destruction of all vessels beyond a certain diminutive size, and restricting the universal model in ship-building to that of the coasting junk. Fresh persecutions followed, many apostate lords and gentry now favoring the Government. Fire and sword were used to extirpate Christianity, and to paganize the same people who in their youth were Christianized by the same means. Thousands of the native converts fled to China, Formosa, and the Philippines. All over the empire, but especially at Ôzaka and in Kiushiu, the people were compelled to trample on the cross, or on a copper plate engraved with the representation of "the Christian criminal God." The Christians suffered all sorts of persecutions. They were wrapped in straw sacks, piled in heaps of living fuel, and set on fire. All the tortures that barbaric hatred or refined cruelty could invent were used to turn thousands of their fellow-men into carcasses and ashes. Yet few of the natives quailed, or renounced their faith. They calmly let the fire of wood cleft from the crosses before which they once prayed consume them, or walked cheerfully to the blood-pit, or were flung alive into the open grave about to be filled up. Mothers carried their babes at their bosoms, or their children in their arms to the fire, the sword, or the precipice's edge, rather than leave them behind to be educated in the pagan faith. If any one doubt the sincerity and fervor of the Christian converts of to-day, or the ability of the Japanese to accept a higher form of faith, or their willingness to suffer for what they believe, they have but to read the accounts preserved in English, Dutch, French, Latin, and Japanese, of various witnesses to the fortitude of the Japanese Christians of the seventeenth century. The annals of the primitive Church furnish no instances of sacrifice or heroic constancy, in the Coliseum or the Roman arenas, that were not paralleled on the dry river-beds and execution-grounds of Japan.

Finally, in 1637, at Shimabara, the Christians rose by tens of thousands in arms, seized an old castle, repaired and fortified it, and raised the flag of rebellion. Armies from Kiushiu and the Kuantô, composed mainly of veterans of Corea and Ôzaka, were sent by the shôgun to besiege it. Their commanders expected an easy victory, and sneered at the idea of having any difficulty in subduing these farmers and peasants. A siege of two months, by land and water, was, however, necessary to reduce the fortress.\* Thousands of the rebels, were hurled from the rock of Pappenburg, or were banished to various provinces, or put to death by torture. Others escaped, and fled to the island of Formosa, joining their brethren already there. The edicts prohibiting the "evil sect" were now promulgated and published permanently all over the empire, and new ones commanded that, as long as the sun should shine, no foreigners should enter Japan, or natives leave it. The Dutch gained the privilege of a paltry trade and residence on the little fan-shaped island of Déshima (outer island), in front of Nagasaki. Here, under degrading restrictions and constant surveillance, lived a little company of less than twenty Hollanders, who were allowed one ship per annum to come from the Dutch East Indies and exchange commodities of Japan for those of Holland.

After nearly a hundred years of Christianity and foreign intercourse, the only apparent results of this contact with another religion and civilization were the adoption of gunpowder, and fire-arms as weapons, the use of tobacco, and the habit of smoking, the making of sponge-cake (still called Castira—the Japanese form of Castile), the naturalization into the language of a few foreign words, the introduction of new and strange forms of disease, among which the Japanese count the scourge of the venereal virus, and the permanent addition to that catalogue of terrors which priest and magistrate in Asiatic countries ever hold as weapons to overawe the herd. For centuries the mention of that name would bate the breath, blanch the cheek, and smite with fear as with an earthquake shock. It was the synonym of sorcery, sedition, and all that was hostile to the purity of the home and the peace of society. All over the empire, in every city, town, village, and hamlet; by the roadside,

---

\* Dr. Geerts, in the *Chrysanthemum*, Jan., 1883, and in the *Transactions of the Asiatic Society of Japan*, vol. xi., with original documents, vindicates the Dutch from the aspersions cast upon them by Tavernier and Kaempfer.

ferry, or mountain pass; at every entrance to the capital, stood the public notice-boards, on which, with prohibitions against the great crimes that disturb the relations of society and government, was one tablet, written with a deeper brand of guilt, with a more hideous memory of blood, with a more awful terror of torture, than when the like superscription was affixed at the top of a cross that stood between two thieves on a little hill outside Jerusalem. Its daily and familiar sight startled ever and anon the peasant to clasp hands and utter a fresh prayer, the bonze to add new venom to his maledictions, the magistrate to shake his head, and to the mother a ready word to hush the crying of her fretful babe. That name was Christ. So thoroughly was Christianity, or the *"Jashiu mon"* (corrupt sect), supposed to be eradicated before the end of the seventeenth century, that its existence was historical, remembered only as an awful scar on the national memory. No vestiges were supposed to be left of it, and no knowledge of its tenets was held, save by a very few scholars in Yedo, trained experts, who were kept, as a sort of spiritual blood-hounds, to scent out the adherents of the accursed creed.

So perfect was the work done, that the Government believed fully, as Europeans, and among them Mr. Lecky, who uses the example to strengthen his argument, that "persecution had extirpated Christianity in Japan." It was left to our day, since the recent opening of Japan, for them to discover that a mighty fire had been smolder-ing for over two centuries beneath the ashes of persecutions. As late as 1829, seven persons, six men and an old woman, were crucified in Ôzaka, on suspicion of being Christians and communicating with foreigners. When the French brethren of the Mission Apostolique, of Paris, came to Nagasaki in 1860, they found in the villages around them over ten thousand people who held the faith of their fathers of the seventeenth century.

A few interesting traces and relics of the century of Christianity and foreigners still exist in Japan. In the language the names of God

(*Deus*), Holy Spirit (*Espiritu Santo*), Jesus (*Yesu*), and Christ (*Kirishito*) have remained. Castira is still the name of sponge-cake, so universally used, and the making of which was first taught by the men of Castile; and the Japanese having no *l*, change that letter into *r*. The Japanese have no word for bread; they use the Latin *pan*. The words *taffel* (table), *Dontaku* (Sunday), *cuppu* (cup), *rauda* (laudanum), *yerikter* (electricity), *bouton* (button), *briki* (tin), and many of the names of drugs and medicines, and rare metals and substances, terms in science, etc., and even some in common use, are but the Japanized forms of the Dutch words. I have seen "Weird Specifica" and "Voum Von Mitter" in large Roman letters, or in *katagana*, advertised on the hanging signs of the drug-shops in every part of the country I have been in, from Kobé to near Niigata, and other travelers have noticed it nearly everywhere in Japan. It is the old or incorrect spelling of the name of some Dutch nostrum.

The natives speak of Christianity as the religion of the "Lord of Heaven." The destruction of the Christian churches, crosses, images, etc., was so thorough that the discovery of relics by modern seekers has been very rare. A few years ago, shortly after Perry's arrival, there was in Suruga a cave, to which the country people resorted in large numbers, on account of the great efficacy believed to reside in an image of the mother of Shaka (Buddha), with her infant in her arms. The idol was reputed to have healed many diseases. An educated samurai, who hated all foreigners and their ways and works, especially the "Jesus doctrine," happening to enter the cave, perceived in a moment that the image was a relic of the old Christian worship. It was nothing else than an image of the Virgin Mary and the infant Jesus. The samurai dashed it to pieces.

The attempts of the English and French to open a permanent trade with Japan are described in Hildredth's "Japan as It Was and Is." Captain John Saris, with the ships *Clove*, *Thomas*, and *Hector*, left

England in April, 1611, with letters from the king, James I of England, to the "emperor" (shôgun) of Japan. Landing at Hirado, he was well received, and established a factory in charge of Mr. Richard Cocks. With Will Adams and seventeen of his company, Saris set out to see Iyéyasu, who was then living at the modern Shidzuoka. He touched at Hakata, traversed the Inland Sea, past Shimonoséki, to Ôzaka; thence by boat to Fushimi, thence by horse and palanquin to Sumpu (Shidzuoka). In the interview accorded the English captain, Iyéyasu invited him to visit his son, Hidétada, the ruling shôgun at Yedo. Saris went to Yedo, visiting, on his way, Kamakura and the great copper image of Dai Butsu, some of the Englishmen going inside of it and shouting in it for the fun of the thing. They also wrote their own names inside of it, as foreign tourists, visitors, and even personal friends of republican rulers do to this day, and as the natives have always done, to immortalize themselves. After a stay in Yedo, they touched at Uraga; thence returned to Sumpu, where a treaty, or privileges of trade, in eight articles, was signed and given to Saris. It bore the signature of Minamoto Iyéyasu.

After a tour of three months, Saris arrived at Hirado again, having visited Kiôto, where he saw the splendid Christian churches and Jesuit colleges, on his way. After discouraging attempts to open a trade with Siam, Corea, and China, and hostilities having broken out between them and the Dutch, the English abandoned the project of permanent trade with Japan; and all subsequent attempts to reopen it failed.

Will Adams, who was an English pilot, and the first of his nation in Japan, is spoken of frequently, and in no flattering terms, by the Jesuit fathers. He arrived in Japan in 1607, and lived in or near Yedo till he died, in 1620. By the sheer force of a manly, honest character, this sturdy Briton, "who may have seen Shakespeare and Ben Jonson" and Queen Elizabeth, rose into favor with Iyéyasu, and gained the regard of the people. His knowledge of ship-building, mathematics, and foreign affairs made him a very useful man. Although treated with honor and kindness, he was not allowed to leave Japan. He had a wife and daughter in England. He was made an officer, and given the revenues of the village of Hémi, in Sagami, near the modern Yokosuka, where are situated the dry-docks, machine-shops, and ship-building houses in which the modern war-vessels of the imperial navy are built and launched—a fitting location, so near the ground made classic by this exile from the greatest marine nation in the world. Will Adams had a son and daughter born to him in Japan, and there are still living Japanese who claim descent from him. One of the streets of Yedo was named after him, Anjin Chô (Pilot Street), and the people of that street still hold an annual celebration on the 15th of June in his honor, one of which I attended in 1873. When Adams died, he, and afterward his Japanese wife, were buried on the summit of one of the lovely hills overlooking the Bay of Yedo, Goldsborough Inlet, and the surrounding beautiful and classic landscape. Adams chose the spot himself. The people of Yedo erected memorial-stone lanterns at his tomb. Perry's fleet, in 1854, anchored within the very shadow of the Englishman's sepulchre. In May, 1872, Mr. Walters, of Yokohama, after a study of Hildreth and some search, discovered the tomb, which others had sought for in vain. Two neat stone shafts, in the characteristic style of native monumental architecture, set on a stone pediment, mark the spot. I visited it, in company of the bonze in charge of the Shin shiu temple of the village, in July, 1873.

In Charlevoix's *Histoire du Christianisme au Japon*, it is related that the Abbé Sidotti, an Italian priest, came to Manila, with the intention of landing in Japan, and once more attempting to regain Japan to Christianity. After several years' waiting, he persuaded the captain of a vessel to take him to Satsuma and set him ashore. This was done in 1709. He was arrested and sent to Yedo. There he was confined in a house in the city district, called Koishikawa, on the slope of a hill ever since called Kirishitan zaka (Christian slope), as the valley at the foot is called Kirishitan dani (Christian valley), and the place Kirishitan gumi (Christian neighborhood). Here the censors, judges, scholars, and interpreters assembled, and for many days examined him, asking many questions and gaining much information concerning foreign countries. In another building near by, an old man and woman who had professed Christianity, and had been compelled to recant, were confined. After the Abbé's arrival, exhorted by him, they again embraced their old faith. The Abbé gave his name as Jean Baptiste. He made a cross of red paper, which he pasted on the wall of his room. He was kept prisoner, living for several years after his arrival, in Yedo, and probably died a natural death.

About ten years ago, the Rev. S. R. Brown, D.D., discovered a book called *Sei Yô Ki Bun* (Annals of Western Nations), in three volumes, written by the Japanese scholar who examined the Abbé. The books contain a summary of the history and judicial proceedings in the case, and the information gained from the Italian. The whole narrative is of intensest interest. While in Tôkiô, in 1874, I endeavored to find the site of the Inquisition, and the martyr's tomb.

Tradition says that the Abbé was buried on the opposite slope of the valley corresponding to that on which he lived, under an old pine-tree, near a spring. Pushing my way through scrub bamboo along a narrow path scarcely perceptible for the undergrowth, I saw a nameless stone near a hollow, evidently left by a tree that had long since fallen and rotted away. A little run of water issued from a spring hard by. At the foot was a rude block of stone, with a hollow for water. Both were roughly hewn, and scarcely dressed with the chisel. Such stones in Japan mark the graves of those who die in disgrace, or unknown, or uncared for. This was all that was visible to remind the visitor of one whose heroic life deserved a nobler monument.

The influence of a century of Papal Christianity in Japan on the national ethics and character was *nil*. A careful examination has not revealed any trace of new principles of morals adopted by the Japanese from foreigners in the sixteenth, as has been gained in the nineteenth century, though the literary, scientific, and material gains were great. The Japanese mental constitution and moral character have been profoundly modified in turn by Buddhism and Confucianism, but the successive waves of Christianism that passed over Japan left no sediment teeming with fertility, rather a barren waste like that which the river-floods leave in autumn. I should be glad to see these statements disproved. Let us hope that the Christianity of the present, whether Catholic, Protestant, or Russo-Greek, may work a profounder and more beneficent revolution in faith and moral practice, and that only that kingdom may be established which is not of this world.

## XXVI

# *Iyéyasu, the Founder of Yedo*

The last of struggles of rival military factions for the possession of power is now to be narrated, and the weary record of war and strife closed. Since 1159, when the Taira and Minamoto came to blows in the capital, and the imperial palace fell into the hands of armed men, and the domination of the military families began, until the opening of the seventeenth century the history of Japan is but that of civil war and slaughter. The history of two centuries and a half that followed the triumphs of Iyéyasu is that of profound peace. Few nations in the world have enjoyed peace so long.

The man who now stood foremost among men, who was a legislator as well as warrior, who could win a victory and garner the fruits of it, was Tokugawa Iyéyasu, the hero of Sékigahara, the most decisive battle in Japanese history, the creator of the perfected dual system and of feudalism, and the founder of Yedo.

Yedo is not an ancient city. Its site becomes historic when Yamato Daké, in the second century of our era, marched to conquer the Eastern tribes. In later times, the Minamoto chieftains subdued the plains of the Kuantô. Until the twelfth century, the region around the Bay of Yedo was wild, uncivilized, and sparsely populated, and the inhabitants were called by the polished Kiôto people "Adzuma Ebisu," or Eastern boors.

In the fifteenth century, a small castle was built on the rising ground within the western circuit of the present stronghold, and near Kôji machi (Yeast Street), where now stands the British Legation. East of the castle was a small relay village, Ô Temma Chô, near the modern site of the prison, at which officials or travelers, on their way to Kamakura or Kiôto, *viâ* the Tôkaidô, might stop for rest and refreshment, or to obtain fresh *kagos* (palanquins), bearers, and baggage-carriers. The name of the commander of the castle, Ôta Dokuan, a retainer of the shôgun at Kamakura, and a doughty warrior, is still preserved in the memories of the people, and in poetry, song, art, and local lore. A hill in the north of the city, a delightful picnic resort, bears his name, and the neighborhood of Shiba was his favorite drill-ground and rendezvous before setting out on forays or campaigns.

One romantic incident, in which a maiden of equal wit and beauty bore chief part, has made him immortal, though the name of the fair one has been forgotten. One day, while out hawking near Yedo, a heavy shower of rain fell. Dismounting from his horse, he, with his attendant, approached a house, and in very polite terms begged the loan of a grass rain-coat (*mino*). A pretty girl, daughter of the man of the house, came out, listened, blushing, to the request, but, answering not a word, ran to the garden, plucked a flower, handed it, with mischief in her eyes, to the hero, and then coquettishly ran away. Ôta, chagrined and vexed at such apparently frivolous manners and boorish inhospitality, and the seeming slight put upon his rank, returned in wrath, and through the rain, to his castle, inwardly cursing the "Adzuma Ebisu," who did not know how to treat a gentleman. It happened that, shortly after, some court nobles from Kiôto were present, sharing the hospitalities of the castle at Yedo, to whom he related the incident. To his own astonishment, the guests were delighted. "Here," said they, "in the wilderness, and among the 'Adzuma Ebisu,' is a gentle girl, who is not only versed in classic poetry, but had the wit and maidenly grace to apply it in felicitous style." Ôta had asked for a rain-coat (*mino*); the little coquette was too polite to acknowledge she had none. How could she say "no" to such a gallant? Rather, to disguise her negative, she had handed him a mountain camellia; and of this flower the poet of Yamato had, centuries ago, sung: "Although the mountain camellia has seven or eight petals, yet I grieve to say it has no seed" (*mino*).

After the death of Ota, no name of any great note is attached to the unimportant village or fortress; but in 1590, at the siege of Odawara, Hidéyoshi suggested to his general, Iyéyasu, Yedo as the best site for the capital of the Kuantô. After the overthrow of the "later Hôjô" clan, and the capture of their castle at Odawara, Iyéyasu went to Yedo and began to found a city. He set up his court, and watched his chances.

Iyéyasu was born at Okasaki, in Mikawa, in 1542; he served with Nobunaga and with Hidéyoshi; again fought with the latter, and again made terms with him. His first possessions were Mikawa and Suruga. In the latter province he built a fine castle at Sumpu (now called Shidzuoka), and made it his residence for many years. He seems to have had little to do with the Corean expedition. While busy in building Yedo in 1598, he received news of the taikô's sickness, attended his death-bed, and was urged to swear to protect the interests of Hidéyori, then six years old. He evasively declined.

The prospects of the boy were not very fine. In the first place, few people believed him to be the son of the taikô. In the second place, the high-spirited lords and nobles, who prided themselves on their blood and lineage, detested Hidéyoshi as an upstart, and had been kept in curb only by his indomitable will and genius. They were still more incensed at the idea of his son Hidéyori, even if a true son, succeeding. Again: Hidénobu, the nephew of Nobunaga, was living, and put in a claim for power. His professed conversion to Christianity gave him a show of support among the Christian malcontents. As for Iyéyasu, he was suspected of wishing to seize the military power of the whole empire. The strong hand of the taikô was no longer felt. The abandonment of the Corean invasion brought back a host of men and leaders, flushed with victory and ambition. Differences sprung up among the five governors. With such elements at work—thousands of men, idle, to whom war was pastime and delight, princes eager for a fray in which land was the spoil, more than one man aspiring to fill the dead master's place—only a spark was needed to kindle the blaze of war.

The governors suspected Iyéyasu. They began to raise an army. Iyéyasu was not to be surprised. He followed the example of his rivals, and watched. I shall not tax the patience of the reader to follow through the mazes of the intricate quarrels which preceded the final appeal to arms. Suffice to say, that after the seizure and reseizure of the citadel of Ôzaka and the burning of the taikô's splendid palace in Fushimi, the army of the league and the army of Iyéyasu met at Sékigahara (plain of the barrier), in Ômi, near Lake Biwa.

By this battle were decided the condition of Japan for over two centuries, the extinction of the claims of the line of Nobunaga and Hidéyoshi, the settlement of the Tokugawa family in hereditary succession to the shôgunate, the fate of Christianity, the isolation of Japan from the world, the fixing into permanency of the dual system and of feudalism, the glory and greatness of Yedo, and peace in Japan for two hundred and sixty-eight years.

In the army of the league were the five governors appointed by the taikô, and the lords and vassals of Hidéyoshi, and most of the generals and soldiers who had served in the Corean campaigns. Among them were the clans of Satsuma, Chôshiu, Uyésugi, and Ukita, with the famous Christian generals, Konishi and Ishida. This army, one hundred and eighty thousand strong, was a heterogeneous mass of veterans, acting under various leaders, and animated by various interests. As the leaders lacked unity of purpose, so the army was made the victim of discordant counsels and orders. On the other hand, the army of one man, Iyéyasu, had one soul, one discipline, and one purpose. The Castle of Gifu, in Mino, was captured by one of his captains. On the 1st of October, 1600, Iyéyasu marched from Yedo over the Tôkaidô with a re-enforcement of thirty thousand troops. His standard was a golden fan and a white flag embroidered with hollyhocks. The diviners had declared "the road to the West was shut." Iyéyasu answered, "Then I shall open it by knocking." On the thirteenth day he arrived at Gifu, where he effected a junction with his main body. Some one offered him a persimmon (ôgaki). He said, as it fell in his hand, "Ôgaki waga te ni otsuru" ("Ôgaki has fallen into my hand "). He threw it down, and allowed his attendants to eat the good-omened and luscious pieces.

The battle-field at Sékigahara is an open, rolling space of ground, lying just inside the eastern slope of hills on the west wall of Lake Biwa, and part of the populous plain drained by the Kiso gawa, a branch of which crosses the field and winds round the hill, on which, at that time, stood a residence of the Portuguese missionaries. The Nakasendô,* one of the main roads between Yedo and Kiôto, enters

---

* The Nakasendô (Central Mountain Road) is three hundred and eighty-one miles long. It begins at the Bridge of Sanjô, over the river at Kiôto, and ends at Nihon Bridge in Tôkiô. It was used, in part, as early as the second century, but was more fully opened in the early part of the eighth century. It passes through Ômi, Mino, Shinano, Kôdzuké, terminating in Musashi. It can be easily traversed in fourteen days; but the tourist who can understand and appreciate all he sees would be reluctant to perform the tour, if for pleasure, in less than a month. There are on the route nine *togé* (mountain passes). It carries the traveler through the splendid scenery of Shinano, which averages twenty-five hundred feet above the sea-level, along Lake Biwa, and nearly its whole length is classic ground. The Nakasendô is sometimes called the Kisokaidô. An excellent guide-book, in seven volumes, full of good engravings, published in 1805, called *Kisoji Meishô Dzuyé* ("Collection of

from Ômi, and bisects the field from west to east, while from the north-west, near the village of Sékigahara, the road enters from Echizen. By this road the writer, in 1872, came to reach the classic site and study the spot around which cluster so many stirring memories. The leaders of the army of the league, having arranged their plans, marched out from the Castle of Ôgaki at early morn on the fifteenth day of the Ninth month. They built a fire on a hill overlooking the narrow path, to guide them as they walked without keeping step. It was raining, and the armor and clothes of the soldiers were very wet. At five o'clock they reached the field, the Satsuma clan taking up their position at the foot of a hill facing east. Konishi, the Christian hero of Corea, commanded the left centre, Ishida the extreme left. Four famous commanders formed, with their corps, the right wing. Reserves were stationed on and about the hills facing north. The cavalry and infantry, according to the *Guai Shi* figures, numbered one hundred and twenty-eight thousand.

At early morn of the same day one of the pickets of Iyéyasu's out-posts hastened to the tent of his general and reported that all the enemy had left the Castle of Ôgaki. Other pickets, from other points, announced the same reports simultaneously. Iyéyasu, in high glee, exclaimed, "The enemy has indeed fallen into my hand." He ordered his generals to advance and take positions on the field, himself leading the centre. His force numbered seventy-five thousand.

This was the supreme moment of Iyéyasu's life. The picture as given us by native artist and tradition is that of a medium-sized and rotund man, of full, round, and merry face, who loved mirth at the right time and place, and even when others could not relish or see

Pictures of Famous Places on the Nakasendô"), furnishes the information that makes a sight of the famous places very enjoyable. The heights of the *togé* are as follows: 620, 2150, 3060, 4340, 3680, 5590, 3240, and 4130 feet, respectively.

its appropriateness. Of indomitable will and energy, and having a genius for understanding men's natures, he astonished his enemies by celerity of movement and the promptitude with which he followed up his advantages. Nevertheless, he was fond of whims. One of these was to take a hot bath before beginning a battle; another was to issue ambiguous orders purposely when he wished to leave a subordinate to act according to his own judgment. On the present occasion, his whim was to go into battle with armor donned, but with no helmet on, knotting his handkerchief over his bare forehead. A dense fog hung like a pall over the battle-field, so that one could not see farther than a few feet.

The two armies, invisible, stood facing each other. However, Iyéyasu sent an officer with a body of men with white flags, who advanced six hundred feet in front of the main army, to prevent surprise. At eight o'clock the fog lifted and rolled away, and the two hosts de-scried each other. After a few moments' waiting, the drums and conchs of the centre of each army sounded, and a sharp fire of matchlocks and a shower of arrows opened the battle. The easterners at first wavered, and till noon the issue was doubtful. Cannon were used during the battle, but the bloodiest work was done with the sword and spear. One of the corps in the army of the league deserted and joined the side of Iyéyasu. At noon, the discipline and unity of the eastern army and the prowess and skill of Iyéyasu triumphed. Ordering his conch-blowers and drummers to beat a final charge, and the reserves having joined the main body, a charge was made along the whole line. The enemy, routed, broke and fled. Nearly all the wounded, and hundreds of unscathed on the battle-field, committed *hara-kiri* in order not to survive the disgrace. The pursuers cut off the heads of all overtaken, and the butchery was frightful. The grass was dyed red, and the moor became literally, not only an Aceldama, but a Golgotha. According to the *Guai Shi's* exaggerated figures, forty thousand heads were cut off. Of the Eastern army four thousand were slain, but no general was killed. The soldiers assembled, according to custom, after the battle in the centre of the field, to show their captives and heads. On this spot now stands a memorial mound of granite masonry within a raised earthen embankment, surrounded and approached from the road by rows of pine-trees. On the Kiôto side of the village, near the shrine of Hachiman, may be seen a *kubidzuka* (barrow, or pile of heads), the monument of this awful slaughter, and one of the many such evidences of former wars which careful travelers in Japan so often notice.

Iyéyasu went into the fight bare-headed. After the battle he sat down upon his camp-stool, and ordered his helmet to be brought. All wondered at this. Donning it with a smile, and fastening it securely, he said, quoting the old proverb, "After victory, knot the cords of your helmet." The hint was taken and acted upon. Neither rest nor negligence was allowed.

The Castle of Hikoné, on Lake Biwa, was immediately invested and captured. Ôzaka was entered in great triumph. Fushimi and Kiôto were held; Chôshiu and Satsuma yielded. Konishi and Mitsuda were executed on the execution-ground in Kiôto. The final and speedy result was that all Japan submitted to the hero who, after victory, had knotted the cords of his helmet.

# XXVII

# *The Perfection of Duarchy and Feudalism*

We have traced the rise and fall of no fewer than six families that held governing power in their persons or in reality. These were in succession the Sugawara, Fujiwara, Taira, Minamoto, Hôjô, and Ashikaga. The last half of the sixteenth century witnessed the rise, not of great families, but of individuals, the mark of whose genius and energy is stamped upon Japanese history. These three individuals were Nobunaga, Hidéyoshi, and Iyéyasu. Who and what were they?

Nobunaga was one of many clan-leaders who, by genius and daring, rose above the crowd, and planned to bring all the others in subjection to himself, that he might rule them in the mikado's name. From having been called *Baka Dono* (Lord Fool) by his enemies, he rose to be Nai Dai Jin, and swayed power equal to a shôgun, but he never received that name or honor; for not being a Minamoto, he was ineligible. But for this inviolable precedent, Nobunaga might have become Sei-i Tai Shôgun, and founded a family line as proud and powerful as that of the Tokugawas of later time.

Who was Hidéyoshi? This question was often asked, in his own time, by men who felt only too keenly *what* he was. This man, who manufactured his own ancestry on paper, was a parvenu from the peasant class, who, from grooming his master's horses in the stable, continued his

313

master's work, as shogun, in the field, and, trampling on all precedent, amazed the Fujiwara peers by getting the office of kuambaku.

Who was Iyéyasu? Neither of his two predecessors had Minamoto blood. Iyéyasu, though at first an obscure captain under Nobunaga, was of true Genji stock. The blood of mikados, and of the great conquerors of Eastern Japan, was in his veins. He was destined to eclipse even the splendor of his forefathers. He was eligible, by right of descent, to become Sei-i Tai Shôgun, or chief of all the daimiôs.

The family of Tokugawa took its name from a place and river in Shimotsuké, near Ashikaga and Nitta—which are geographical as well as personal names—claimed descent from the mikado Seiwa through the Minamoto Yoshiiyé, thence through that of Nitta Yoshisada. Tokugawa Shiro, the father of Iyéyasu, lived in the village of Matsudaira, in Mikawa. Iyéyasu always signed the documents sent to foreigners, Minamoto no Iyéyasu.

As it is the custom in Japan, as in Europe, to name families after places, the name of this obscure village, Matsudaira, was also taken as a family name by nearly all vassals, who held their lands by direct grant from Iyéyasu. In 1867, no fewer than fifty-four daimiôs were holding the name Matsudaira. The title of the daimiô in whose capital the writer lived in 1871, was Matsudaira Echizen no Kami.

The Tokugawa crest was a circle inclosing three leaves of the *awoi* (a species of mallow, found in Central Japan) joined at the tips, the stalks touching the circle. This gilded trefoil gleamed on the Government buildings and property of the shôgun, and on the official documents, boats, robes, flags, and tombs. On Kaempfer's and Hildreth's books there is printed under it the misleading legend, "Insignia *Imperatoris* Japonici." The trefoil flag fluttered in the breeze when Commodore Perry made his treaty under its shadow. To this day many foreigners suppose it to be the national flag of Japan. It was simply the family crest of the chief daimio in Japan.

*Crest of Tokugawa Family*

The imperial court, yearning for peace, and finding in Iyéyasu the person to keep the empire in order, command universal obedience, and satisfy the blood requirements of precedent to the office, created him Sei-i Tai Shôgun, and it was left to Minamoto Tokugawa Iyéyasu to achieve the perfection of duarchy and Japanese feudalism.

Let us see how he arranged the chess-board of the empire. There were his twelve children, a number of powerful princes of large landed possessions whom he had not conquered, but conciliated; the lesser daimiôs, who had joined him in his career; his own retainers of every grade; and a vast and miscellaneous array of petty feudal superiors, having grants of land and retinues of from three to one hundred followers. The long hereditary occupation of certain lands had given the holders a right which even Iyeyasu could not dispute. Out of such complexity and chaos, how was such a motley array of proud and turbulent men to be reduced to discipline and obedience? Upon such a palimpsest, how was an accurate map to be drawn, or a durable legible record to be written? Iyéyasu had force, resources, and patience. He was master of the arts of conciliation and of letting alone. He could wait for time to do its work. He would give men the opportunity of being conquered by their own good sense.

Of Iyéyasu's twelve children, three daughters married the daimiôs of Mimasaka, Sagami, and Hida. Of his nine sons, Nobuyasu died before his father became shôgun. Hidéyasu, his second son, had been adopted by the taikô, but a son was born to the latter. Iyéyasu then gave his son the province of Echizen. Hence the Echizen clansmen, as relatives of the shôgunal family, were ever their stanchest supporters, even until the cannon fired at Fushimi in 1868. Their crest was the same trefoil as that of their suzerain. When Hideyasu was enfeoffed with Echizen, many prominent men and heads of old families, supposing that he would, of course, succeed his father in office, followed him to his domain, and lived there. Hence in Fukui, the capital of Echizen, in which I lived during the year 1871, I became acquainted with the descendants of many proud families, whose ancestors had nursed a profound disappointment for over two centuries; for Iyéyasu chose his third son, Hidétada, who had married a daughter of the taiko, to succeed him in the shogunate.

Tadayashi, fifth son of Iyéyasu, whose title was Matsudaira Satsuma no Kami, died young. At his death five of his retainers disemboweled themselves, that they might follow their young master into the happy land. This is said to be the last instance of the ancient custom of *jun-shi* (dying with the master), such as we have noticed in a former chapter. During the early and mediaeval centuries occur authentic instances of such immolation, or the more horrible test of loyalty in the burial of living retainers to their necks in the earth, with only the head above ground, who were left to starve slowly to death. Burying a man alive under the foundations of a castle about to be built or in the pier of a new bridge, was a similar instance of lingering superstitions.

In the *Bu Kan* ("Mirror of the Military Families of Japan"), a complete list of the "Yedo nobility," or clans, no record is given of

Iyéyasu's sixth and ninth male children. On his three last sons were bestowed the richest fiefs in the empire, excepting those of Satsuma, Kaga, Mutsu, Higo, and a few others—all-powerful daimios, whose lands Iyéyasu could not touch, and whose allegiance was only secured by a policy of conciliation. These three sons were invested with the principalities of Owari, Kii, and Mito. They founded three families, who were called Gosanké (the three illustrious families), and from these, in case of failure of heirs in the direct line, the shôgun was to be chosen. The assessed revenue of these families were 610,500, 555,000, and 350,000 koku of rice, respectively. They were held in great respect, and wielded immense influence. Their yashikis in Yedo were among the largest, and placed in the most conspicuous and commanding sites of the city. At the tombs of the shôguns at Shiba and Uyéno, the bronze memorial lanterns presented in honor of the deceased ruler are pre-eminent above all others for their size and beauty.

In the course of history down to 1868, it resulted that the first seven shôguns were descendants of Iyéyasu in the line of direct heirs.* From

---

\* Shôguns of the Tokugawa Family

| | | | |
|---|---|---|---|
| 1. Iyéyasu | 1603–1604 | 9. Iyéshige | 1745–1762 |
| 2. Hidétada | 1605–1622 | 10. Iyéharu | 1762–1786 |
| 3. Iyémitsu | 1623–1649 | 11. Iyénori | 1787–1837 |
| 4. Iyétsuna | 1650–1680 | 12. Iyéyoshi | 1838–1852 |
| 5. Tsunayoshi | 1681–1708 | 13. Iyésada\* | 1853–1858 |
| 6. Iyénobu | 1709–1712 | 14. Iyémochi | 1858–1866 |
| 7. Iyétsugu | 1713–1716 | 15. Yoshinobu† | 1866–1868 |
| 8. Yoshimuné | 1717–1744 | | |

\* First shôgun ever styled Tai-kun ("Tycoon") in a treaty document. The last three shôguns were styled Tai-kun by themselves and foreigners.

† Keiki, or Hitotsubashi, the last Sei-i Tai Shôgun, still living (1876) at Shidzuoka, in Suraga.

the eighth, and thence downward to the sixteenth, or next to the last, the shôguns were all really of the blood of Kii. The Owari family was never represented on the seat of Iyéyasu. It was generally believed, and is popularly stated, that as the first Prince of Mito had married the daughter of an enemy of Iyéyasu, the Mito family could not furnish an heir to the shôgunate. In 1867, however, as we shall see, Keiki, a son of Mito, but adopted into the Hitotsubashi family, became the thirty-ninth and last Sei-i Tai Shôgun of Japan, the fifteenth and last of Tokugawa, and the fourth and last "Tycoon" of Japan.

Next to the Gosanké ranked the Kokushiu (*koku*, province; *shiu*, ruler) daimiôs, the powerful leaders whom Iyéyasu defeated, or won over to obedience, but never tamed or conquered. He treated them rather as equals less fortunate in the game of war than himself. Some of them were direct descendants of the Kokushiu appointed by Yoritomo, but mess were merely successful military adventurers like Iyéyasu himself. Of these, Kaga was the wealthiest. He ruled over Kaga, Noto, and Etchiu, his chief city and castle being at Kanézawa. His income was 1,027,000 koku. The family name was Maëda. There were three cadet families ranking as Tozama, two with incomes of 100,000, the other of 10,000 koku. The Maëda crest consisted of five circles, around ten short rays representing sword-punctures. The Shimadzu family of Satsuma ruled over Satsuma, Ôzumi, Hiuga, and the Liu Kiu Islands—revenue, 710,000 koku; chief city, Kagoshima. There was one cadet of the house of Shimadzu, with a revenue of 27,000 koku. The crest was a white cross* within a circle.

---

* This cruciform figure of the Greek pattern puzzled Xavier, who suspected theology in it. It has been a perpetual mare's-nest to the many would-be anti-quarians, who burn to immortalize themselves by unearthing Christian relics in Japan. It is a standard subject of dissertation by new-comers, who help to give a show of truth to the platitude of the ports, that "the longer one lives in Japan, the less he knows about it." It is simply a horse's bit-ring.

The Datté family ruled over the old northern division of Hondo, called Mutsu; capital, Sendai; revenue, 325,000 koku. There were three cadet families, two having 30,000 koku; and one, Uwajima, in Iyo, 100,000. Their crest was two sparrows within a circle of bamboo and leaves.

The Hosokawa family ruled Higo; income 540,000: the chief city is Kumamoto, in which is one of the finest castles in Japan, built by Kato Kiyomasa. Of three cadets whose united incomes were 81,300 koku, two had cities in Higo, and one in Hitachi; crest, eight disks around a central smaller disk.

The Kuroda family ruled Chikuzen; revenue, 520,000; chief city Fukuöka; crest, a black disk. One cadet in Kadzusa had 30,000 koku; crest, a slice of cucumber. Another in Chikuzen; revenue, 50,000; crest, Wistaria flowers.

The Asano family ruled Aki; chief city, Hiroshima; revenue, 426,000; one cadet.

The Môri family ruled Chôshiu; chief city, Hagi; revenue, 369,000. Of three cadet families, two were in Nagato, one was in Suwo. Their united incomes, 100,000 koku; crest, a kind of water-plant.

The above are a few specimens from the thirty-six families outside of the Tokugawa, and the subject (*fudai*) clans, who, though not of the shôgunal family, took the name of Matsudaira. There were, in 1862, two hundred and sixty-seven feudal families, and as many daimiôs of various rank, income, and landed possessions. Japan was thus divided into petty fragments, without real nationality, and utterly unprepared to bear the shock of contact with foreigners.

The Tozama [outside (of the shôgunal family) nobility] were cadet families of the Kokushiu, or the smaller landed lords, who held hered-itary possessions, and who sided with Iyéyasu in his rise to power. There were, in 1862, ninety whose assessed revenue ranged from ten to one hundred thousand koku each.

The Fudai (literally, successive generations) were the generals, captains, and retainers, both civil and military, on whom Iyéyasu bestowed land as rewards. They were the direct vassals of the Tokugawa family. The shôgun could order any of them to exchange their fiefs, or could increase or curtail their revenues at will. They were to the shôgun as the old "Six Guards" of Kiôto, or household troops of the mediæval mikadoate. There were, in 1862, one hundred and fifteen of this class, with lands assessed at from ten to one hundred thousand koku. It was only the fudai, or lower-grade daimiôs, who could hold office under the Yedo bakufu, and one became regent, as we shall see.

When once firmly seated on the throne, Iyéyasu found himself master of almost all Japan. His greatest care was to make such a disposal of his lands as to strike a balance of power, and to insure harmony among the host of territorial nobility, who already held or were about to be given lands. It must not be forgotten that Iyéyasu and his successors were, both in theory and reality, vassals of the emperor, though they assumed the protection of the imperial person. Neither the shôgun nor the daimiôs were acknowledged at Kiôto as nobles of the empire. The lowest kugé was above the shôgun in rank. The shôgun could obtain his appointment only from the mikado. He was simply the most powerful among the daimiôs, who had won that preeminence by the sword, and who, by wealth and power, and a skillfully wrought plan of division of land among the other daimiôs, was able to rule for over two and a half centuries. Theoretically, he was *primus inter pares*; in actuality, he was supreme over inferiors. The mikado was left with merely nominal power, dependent upon the Yedo treasury for revenue and protection, but he was still the fountain of honor and preferment, and, with his court formed what was the lawful, and, in the last analysis, the only true power. There was formed at Yedo the *de facto*, actual administrative government of the empire. With the imperial family, court, and nobles, Iyéyasu had nothing to do except as vassal and guardian. He simply undertook to settle the position and grade the power of the territorial nobles, and rule them by the strong hand of military force. Nevertheless, real titles were bestowed only by the emperor; and an honor granted, however empty of actual power, from the Son of Heaven in Kioto was considered immeasurably superior to any gift which the awe-compelling chief daimiô in Yedo could bestow. The possession of rank and official title is the ruling passion of a Japanese. The richest daimiôs, not content with their power and revenue, spent vast sums of money, and used every influence at the Kiôto court, to win titles, once, indeed, the exponent of a reality that existed, but, since the creation of the duarchy and the decay of the mikado's actual power, as absurdly empty as those of the mediatized princes of Germany, and having no more connection with the duties implied than the title of Pontifex Maximus has with those of Chief Bridge-builder in Rome.

The head of the proud Shimadzu family, with his vast provinces of Satsuma, Hiuga, Ôzumi, and the Liu Kiu Islands, cared as much for the pompous vacuity of Shuri no daibu ("Chief of the Office of Ecclesiastical Carpenters") as to be styled Lord of Satsuma.

It is in the geographical distribution of his feudal vassals that the genius of Iyéyasu is seen. Wherever two powerful clans that still bore a grudge against the Tokugawa name were neighbors, he put between them one of his own relatives or direct vassals, which served to prevent the two daimiôs from combining or intriguing. Besides disposing of his enemies so as to make them harmless, his object was to guard the capital, Kiôto, so that aspiring leaders could never again seize the person of the mikado, as had been repeatedly done in times past. He thus removed a chronic element of disorder.

Echizen commands Kiôto from the north; it was given to his eldest son. Ômi guards it from the east; it was divided among his direct vassals, while Owari and Kii were assigned to his sons. His fudai vassals, or "household troops," were also ranged on the west, while to the south-west was Ôzaka, a city in the government domain, ruled by his own officials. Thus the capital was completely walled in by friends of Tokugawa, and isolated from their enemies.

Môri, once the lord of ten provinces, and the enemy of Tokugawa, was put away into the extreme south-west of Hondo, all his territories except Nagato and Suwo being taken from him, and given to Tokugawa's direct vassals. Opposite to Nagato were Kokura and Chikuzen, enemies of Nagato. We shall see the significance of this when we treat of events leading to the Restoration (1853–1868). Shikoku was properly divided, so as to secure a preponderance of Tokugawa's most loyal vassals. Kiushiu was the weakest part of the system; yet even here Satsuma was last and farthest away, and Higo, his feudal rival and enemy, was put next, and the most skillful disposition possible made of the vassals and friends of Tokugawa.

In the daimiôates succession to their lands was hereditary, but not always to the oldest son, since the custom of adoption was very prevalent, and all the rights of a son were conferred on the adopted one. Often the adopted child was no relation of the ruler. Sickly infants were often made to adopt a son, to succeed to the inheritance and keep up the succession. One of the most curious sights on occasions of important gatherings of samurai, was to see babies and little boys dressed in men's clothes, as "heads of families," sustaining the dignity of representing the family in the clan. I saw such a sight in 1871.

One great difference between the Japanese system and that of entails in Europe lay in this, that the estate granted to each daimio could not be added to, or diminished, either by marriage, or by purchase, or by might, except by express permission and grant from the shôgun, the superior of all.

Next to the daimiôs ranked the *hatamoto*, or flag-supporters (*hata*, flag; *moto*, root, under), who were vassals of the shôgun—his special dependence in war time—having less than ten thousand koku revenue. Each had from three to thirty retainers in his train. They were, in most cases, of good family, descendants of noted warriors. They numbered eighty thousand in various parts of the empire, but the majority lived in Yedo. They formed the great body of military and civil officials. The *gokenin*, many of the descendants of Iyéyasu's private soldiers, were inferior in wealth and rank to the hatamoto, but with them formed the hereditary personal following of the shôgun, and constituted the Tokugawa clan proper, whose united revenues amounted to nearly nine million koku. The shôgun, or chief daimiô of the empire, has thus unapproachable military resources, following, and revenue, and could overawe court and emperor above, princes and vassals beneath.

All included within the above classes and their military retainers were samurai, receiving hereditary incomes of rice from the Government. They were privileged to wear two swords, to be exempt from taxes. They may be styled the military-literati of the country. To the great bulk of these samurai were given simply their daily portion of rice; to others, rations of rice for from two to five persons. Some of them received small offices or positions, to which land or other sources of income were attached. The samurai's ideas of honor forbade him to do any work or engage in any business. His only duty was to keep perfunctory watch at the castle or his lord's house, walk in his lord's retinue, or on stated occasions appear in ceremonial dress. His life was one of idleness and ease; and, as may be imagined, the long centuries of peace served only to develop the dangerous character of this large class of armed idlers. Some, indeed, were studious, or engaged with zeal in martial exercises, or became teachers; but the majority spent their life in eating, smoking, and lounging in brothels and tea-houses, or led a wild life of crime in one of the great cities. When too deeply in debt, or having committed a crime, they left their homes and the service of their masters, and roamed at large. Such men were called *rônins*, or "wave-men." Usually they were villains, ready for any deed of blood, the reserve mercenaries from which every conspirator could recruit a squad. Occasionally, the rônin was a virtuous citizen, who had left the service of his lord for an honorable purpose.

Ill fared it with the merchants. They were considered so low in the social scale that they had no right in any way to oppose or to remonstrate with the samurai. Among the latter were many noble examples of chivalry, men who were ever ready to assist the oppressed and redress their wrongs, often becoming knights-errant for the benefit of the wronged orphan and the widow, made so by a murderer's hand. But among the hatamoto and gokenin, especially among the victors of Sékigahara, cruelties and acts of violence were not only frequent and outrageous, but winked at by the Government officials. These blackmailers, in need of funds for a spree, would extort money under various pretexts, or none at all, from helpless tradesmen; or their servants would sally out to a tea-house, and, having eaten or drunk their fill, would leave without paying, swaggering, drunk, and singing between their tipsy hiccoughs. Remonstrances from the landlord would be met with threats of violence, and it was no rare thing for them, in their drunken fury, to slash off his head. Yet these same non-producers and genteel loafers were intensely sensitive on many points of honor, and would be ready at any moment to die for their master. The possession of swords, and the arrogance bred of their superiority as a privileged class, acted continually as a temptation to brawls and murder.

Edinburgh, in the old days of the clans, is perhaps the best illustration of Yedo during the Tokugawa times. Certain localities in Yedo at night would not suffer by a comparison with the mining regions of California during the first opening of the diggings, when to "eat" a man, or to kill an Indian before breakfast, was a feather in the cap of men who lived with revolvers constantly in their belts. As there were always men in the gulches of whom it was a standing prophecy that they would "die with their boots on," so there was many a man in every city of Japan of whom it would be a nine days' wonder should he die with his head on. Of such men it was said that their death would be *inujini* (in a dog's place).

Yet the merchant and farmer were not left utterly helpless. The Otokodaté were gallant and noble fellows, not of the samurai class, but their bitter enemies. The swash-bucklers often met their match in these men, who took upon themselves to redress the grievances of the unarmed classes. The Otokodaté were bound together into a sort of guild to help each other in sickness, to succor each other in peril, to scrupulously tell the truth and keep their promises, and never to be guilty of meanness or cowardice. They lived in various parts of Japan, though the most famous dwelt in Yedo. They were the champions of the people, who loved and applauded them. Many a bitter conflict took place between them and the overbearing samurai, especially the "white-hilts." The story of their gallant deeds forms the staple of many a popular story, read with delight by the common people.

Below the samurai, or gentry, the three great classes were the farmers, artisans, and merchants. These were the common people. Beneath them were the *etas*, who were skinners, tanners, leather-dressers, grave-diggers, or those who in any way handled raw-hide or buried animals. They were the pariahs, or social outcasts, of Japan. They were not allowed to enter a house, or to eat or drink, sit or cook at the same fire with other persons. These people were said by some to be descendants of Corean prisoners; by others, to have been originally the people who killed animals for feeding the imperial falcons. As Buddhism prohibited the eating of animals as food, the eta were left out of the pale of society. The *hinin* (not human) were the lowest class of beggars, the squatters on waste lands, who built huts along the road, and existed by soliciting alms. They also attended to the execution of criminals and the disposal of their corpses. In general, they were filthy and disgusting, in their rags and dirt.

There were thus, according to one division, eight classes of society: 1st, the kugé, Kiôto or court nobility; 2d, the daimiôs, Yedo or territorial nobles; 3d, the buké, or hatamoto, or samurai of lower rank than that of daimiô and priest; 4th, landed proprietors without title, and farmers, called *hiyakushô*; 5th, artisans, carpenters, etc., called *shokunin*; 6th, merchants, shop-keepers, and traders, called *akindo*; 7th, actors, prostitutes, genteel beggars, etc.; 8th, tanners, skinners, hinin, and eta.

Another division is that into four classes: 1st, military and official—samurai; 2d, agricultural—farmer; 3d, laboring—artisan; 4th, trading—merchant. Below the level of humanity were the eta and hinin.

This was the constitution of society in Japan during the rule of the Tokugawa until 1868.

Iyéyasu, in 1600 and the years following, employed an army of 300,000 laborers in Yedo, in enlarging the castle, digging moats and canals, grading streets, filling marshes, and erecting buildings. His fleets of junks brought granite from Hiôgo for the citadel and gate buttresses, and the river-boats the dark stone for the walls of the enceinte. His faith in the future of the city was shown in his ordering an immense outer ditch to be dug, which far more than completely encircled both castle and city, and gates and towers to be built, when as yet there was no wall connecting, or dwelling-houses within them, and city people sauntered out into the country to see and laugh at them. According to tradition, the great founder declared that walls would be built, and the city extend far beyond them. The prediction was verified; for it is probable that within fifty years, as we know from old maps of Yedo, the land east of the river was built upon, and the city had spread to within two-thirds of its present proportions, and before the year 1700 had a population of over 500,000 souls. Yedo never did have, as the Hollanders guessed, and as our old text-books, in stereotyped phrase, told us, 2,500,000 souls. It is probable that, in

1857, when Mr. Townsend Harris, the American envoy, first entered it, it had as many as 1,000,000. In 1872, by official census, the population of Tôkiô, including that of the villages around it and under the municipal jurisdiction, was 925,000; of the city proper, 790,000 permanent residents, to which should be added nearly 100,000 floating population.

Outside of Yedo, the strength of the great unifier was spent on the public roads and highways, especially the Tôkaidô, or road skirting the Eastern Sea, which begins at Kiôto and ends at Tôkiô. He arranged fifty-three stations (*shiku*, relays, or post-stations), at which were hotels, pack-horses, baggage-coolies, and palanquin-bearers. A regular code of regulations to govern the movements of the daimiôs and nobles when traveling—the etiquette to be observed, the scale of prices to be charged—was duly arranged, and continued in force until 1868. The roads, especially the mountain-passes, bridges, and ferries, were improved, and one *ri* (measure of two and two-fifth miles) hillocks to mark the distances set up. The regulations required that the main roads should be thirty-six feet wide, and be planted with pine-trees along their length. Cross-roads should have a width of eighteen feet; foot-paths, six; and of by-paths through the fields, three feet. At the ferry-landing on either bank of a river there was to be an open space of about three hundred and sixty feet. Various other regulations, pertaining to minute details of life, sumptuary laws, and feudal regulations, were promulgated, and gradually came into force throughout the empire.

To defend the Kuantô, and strengthen his position as military ruler of the empire, he built or improved the nine castles of Mito, Utsunomiya, Takasaki, Odawara, and five others in the Kuantô. At Sumpu, Ôzaka, and Nijô, in Kiôto, were also fine castles, and to their command officers were assigned. All these, and many other enterprises, required a vast outlay of money. The revenue of the empire amounted to nearly 30,000,000 koku (165,000,000 bushels) of rice. Of this, nearly 9,000,000 koku were retained as the revenue of the Tokugawas. The mines were government property; and at this time the gold of Sado was discovered, which furnished Iyéyasu with the sinews of war and peace. This island may be said to be a mass of auriferous quartz, and has ever since been the natural treasure-house of Japan.

Iyéyasu had now the opportunity to prove himself a legislator, as well as a warrior. He began by granting amnesty to all who would accept it. He wished the past forgotten. He regretted that so much blood had been spilled. He entered upon a policy of conciliation that rapidly won to his side all the neutral and nearly all the hostile clans. There were some who were still too proud or sullen to submit or accept pardon. These were left quietly alone, the great unifier waiting for the healing hand of time. He felt sure of his present power, and set himself diligently to work during the remainder of his life to consolidate and strengthen that power so that it would last for centuries.

Iyéyasu was created Sei-i Tai Shôgun in 1603. Only twice during his life-time was peace interrupted. The persecution of the Christians was one instance, and the brief campaign against Hidéyori, the son of the taikô, was the second. Around this young man had gathered most of the malcontents of the empire. Iyéyasu found or sought a ground of quarrel against him, and on the 3d of June, 1615, attacked the Castle of Ôzaka, which was set on fire. A bloody battle, the last fought on the soil for two hundred and fifty-three years, resulted in the triumph of Iyéyasu, and the disappearance of Hidéyori and his mother, who were probably consumed in the flames. His tomb, however, is said to be in Kagoshima. It is most probably a cenotaph.

The greatest of the Tokugawas spent the last years of his life at Sumpu (Shidzuoka), engaged in erasing the scars of war, securing the triumphs of peace, perfecting his plans for fixing in stability his system of government, and in collecting books and manuscripts. He bequeathed his "Legacy," or code of laws (see Appendix), to his chief retainers, and advised his sons to govern in the spirit of kindness. He died on the 8th of March, 1616. His remains were deposited temporarily at Kuno Zan, a few miles from Sumpu, on the side of a lovely mountain overlooking the sea, where the solemnity of the forest monarchs and the grandeur of sea and sky are blended together. Acting upon the dying wish of his father, Hidétada had caused to be erected at Nikkô Zan, one hundred miles north of Yedo, a gorgeous shrine and mausoleum. The spot chosen was on the slope of a hill, on which, eight centuries before, the saintly bonze Shôdô, following Kôbô Daishi's theology, had declared the ancient Shintô deity of the mountain to be a manifestation of Buddha to Japan, and named him the Gongen of Nikkô. Here Nature has glorified herself in snow-ranges of mighty mountains, of which glorious Nantaizan reigns king, his feet laved by the blue splendors of the Lake Chiuzenji, on which his mighty form is mirrored. Nikkô means *sunny splendor*; and through Japanese poetry and impassioned rhetoric ever sparkle the glories of the morning's mirror in Chiuzenji, and the golden floods of light that bathe Nantaizan. The water-fall of Kiri Furi (falling mist); and of Kégon, the lake's outlet, over seven hundred feet high; the foaming river, grassy green in its velocity; the colossal forests and inspiring scenery, made it the fit resting-place of the greatest character in Japanese history.

In 1617, his remains were removed from Kuno, and in solemn pageantry moved to Nikkô, where the imperial envoy, vicar of the mikado, court nobles from Kiôto, many of his old lords and captains, daimiôs, and the shôgun Hidétada, awaited the arrival of the august ashes. The corpse was laid in its gorgeous tomb, before which the vicar of majesty presented the gohei, significant of the apotheosis of the mighty warrior, deified by the mikado as the divine vice-regent of the gods of heaven and earth, under the title Sho ichi i Tô Shô Dai Gongen, or "Noble of the first Degree of the first Rank, Great Light of the East, Great Incarnation of Buddha." During three days, a choir of Buddhist priests, in their full canonical robes, intoned the *Hokké* sacred classic ten thousand times. It was ordained that ever afterward the chief priest of Nikkô should be a prince of the imperial blood, under the title of Rinnôji no miya.

Of Hidétada, the successor of Iyéyasu, there is little to record. The chief business of his life seems to have been to follow out the policy of his father, execute his plans, consolidate the central power, establish good government throughout the empire, and beautify, strengthen, and adorn Yedo.

Iyémitsu, the grandson of Iyéyasu, is acknowledged to have been the ablest ruler of all the Tokugawas after the founder, whose system he brought to perfection. In 1623, he went to Kiôto to do homage to the mikado, who invested him with the title of Sei-i Tai Shôgun. By this time many of the leaders and captains who had fought under Iyéyasu, or those who most respected him for his prowess, were dead or superannuated, and had been succeeded by their sons, who, as though fated to follow historical precedent, failed to possess the vigor of their fathers, their associations being those of peace, luxury, and the effeminacy which follows war.

Iyémitsu was a martinet as well as a statesman. He proposed that all the daimiôs should visit and reside in Yedo during half the year. Being at first treated as guests, the shôgun coming out to meet them in the suburbs, they swore allegiance to his rules, sealing their signatures, according to custom, with blood drawn from the third finger of the right hand. Gradually, however, these rules became more and more restrictive, until the honorable position degenerated into a condition tantamount to mere vassalage. Their wives and children were kept as hostages in Yedo, and the rendition of certain tokens of respect, almost equivalent to homage to the shôgun, became imperative. During his rule the Christian insurrection and massacre at Shimabara took place. The Dutch were confined to Déshima. Yedo was vastly improved. Aqueducts, still in excellent use, were laid, to supply the city with water. To guard against the ever-threatening enemy, fire, watch-towers, or lookouts, such as are to be seen in every city, were erected in great numbers. Bells are hung at the top and a code of signals, and a prescribed number of taps give the locality and progress of the conflagration. Mints were established, coins struck, weights and measures fixed; the system of official espionage, checks, and counter-checks established; a general survey of the empire executed; maps of the various provinces and plans of the daimiôs' castles were made, and their pedigrees made out and published; the councils called Hiôjô-sho (Discussion and Decision), and Wakadoshiyori (Assembly of Elders), established, and Corean envoys received.

The height of pride and ambition which Iyémitsu had already reached is seen in the fact that, in a letter of reply from the bakufu to Corea, the shôgun is referred to as Tai Kun ("Tycoon"), a title never conferred by the mikado on any one, nor had Iyémitsu any legal right to it. It was assumed in a sense honorary or meaningless to any Japanese, unless highly jealous of the mikado's sovereignty, and was intended to overawe the "barbarian" Coreans. It is best explainable in the light of the Virgilian phrase, *magna pars fui*, or the less dignified "Big Indian I."

The building of the fine temples of Toyeizan, at Uyéno, in Yedo, and at Nikkô, were completed in Iyémitsu's time, he making five journeys thither. He died in 1649, after a prosperous rule of twenty-six years, and was buried with his grandfather at Nikkô.

The successors of Iyéyasu, the shôguns of the Tokugawa dynasty, fourteen in all, were, with one exception, buried alternately in the cemeteries of Zôzôji and Tôyeizan, in the city districts of Shiba and Uyéno. These twin necropolises of the illustrious departed were the  chief glories of Yedo, which was emphatically the city of the Tokugawas. The remains of six of them lie in Uyéno, and six in Shiba, while two are at Nikkô.

During the summer of 1872, in company with an American friend and three of my brightest students, I made a journey to Nikkô, and for nearly a week reveled in its inspiring scenery and solemn associations. During my three years' residence in Tôkiô, I visited these twin sacred places many times, spending a half-day at a visit. No one has described these places better than Mr. Mitford, in his *Tales of Old Japan*. He says: "It is very difficult to do justice to their beauty in words. I have the memory before me of a place green in winter, pleasant and cool in the hottest summer, of peaceful cloisters, of the fragrance of incense, of the subdued chant of richly robed priests, and the music of bells of exquisite designs, harmonious coloring, and rich gilding. The hum of the vast city outside is unheard here. Iyéyasu himself, in the mountains of Nikkô, has no quieter resting-place than his descendants in the heart of the city over which he ruled."

Passing through an immense red portal on the north side of Shiba, we enter the precincts of the sacred place through a long, wide avenue, lined by overarching firs, and rendered solemnly beautiful by their shade. A runner is usually on hand to conduct visitors to the gate, inside of which a priest is waiting. We enter a pebbled court-yard, in which are ranged over two hundred large stone lanterns. These are the gifts of the fudai daimios. Each lantern is inscribed with the name of the donor, the posthumous title of the deceased shôgun, the name of the temple at Shiba, and the province in which it is situated, the date of the offering, and a legend, which states that it is reverently offered. On the following page is the reading on one, and will serve as a specimen:

TO THE
## ILLUSTRIOUS TEMPLE OF LEARNING*

[Posthumous title of the sixth Shôgun Iyénobu]

## THIS STONE LANTERN,

SET UP BEFORE TEE TOMB AT THE TEMPLE OF ZÔZÔJI,

## IN MUSASHI,

IS REVERENTLY OFFERED
BY THE
RULING DAIMIÔ,
NOBLE OF THE FIFTH RANK,

## MASUYAMA FUJIWARA MASATO,

LORD OF TSUSHIMA,

IN THE SECOND YEAR OF THE PERIOD OF STRICT VIRTUE,
IN THE CYCLE OF THE WATER DRAGON

[1711].

Passing through a handsomely gilt and carved gate-way, we enter another court-yard, the sides of which are gorgeously adorned. Within

---

* The *hômiô*, or posthumous titles of thirteen Tokugawa shôguns, are: 1, Great Light of the East; 2, Chief Virtue; 3. Illustrious Enterprise; 4, Strict Holding; 5, Constant System; 6, Literary Brightness; 7, Upholder of the Plan; 8, Upholder of Virtue; 9, Profound Faith; 10, Steady Brightness; 11, Learned Reverence; 12, Learned Carefulness; 13, Rigid Virtue.

the area are bronze lanterns, the gift of the Kokushiu daimiôs. The six very large gilded lanterns standing by themselves are from the Go San Ké, the three princely families, in which the succession to the office of shôgun was vested. To the left is a monolith lavatory; and to the right is a splendid building, used as a depository of sacred utensils, such as bells, gongs, lanterns, etc., used only on *matsuri*, or festival days. Passing through another handsome gate which eclipses the last in richness of design, we enter a roofed gallery somewhat like a series of cloisters. In front is the shrine, a magnificent specimen of native architecture.

Sitting down upon the lacquered steps, we remove our shoes, while the shaven bonze swings open the gilt doors, and reveals a transept and nave, laid with finest white matting, and ceiled in squares wrought with elaborate art. The walls of the transept are arabesqued, and the panels carved with birds and flowers—the fauna of Japan, both real and mythical—and the various objects in Japanese sacred and legendary art. In each panel the subjects are different, and richly repay study. The glory of motion, the passionate life of the corolla, and the perfection of nature's colors have been here reproduced in inanimate wood by the artist. At the extremity of the nave is a short flight of steps. Two massive gilt doors swing asunder at the touch of priestly hands, and across the threshold we behold an apocalypse of splendor. Behind the sacred offertories, on carved and lacquered tables, are three reliquaries rising to the ceiling, and by their outer covering simulating masses of solid gold. Inside are treasured the tablets and posthumous titles of the august deceased. Descending from this sanctum into the transept again, we examine the canonical rolls, bell, book, and candles, drums and musical instruments, with which the Buddhist rites are celebrated and the liturgies read. Donning our shoes, we pass up a stone court fragrant with blossoming flowers, and shaded with rare and costly trees of every variety, form, and height, but overshadowed by the towering firs. We ascend a flight of steps, and are in another pebbled and stone-laid court, in which stands a smaller building, called a *haiden*, formerly used by the living shôgun as a place of meditation and prayer when making his annual visit to the tombs of his forefathers. Beyond it is still another flight of stone steps, and in the inclosure is a plain monumental urn, "This is the simple ending to so much magnificence"—the solemn application of the gorgeous sermon.

The visitor, on entering the cemetery by the small gate to the right of the temple, and a few feet distant from the great belfry, will see three tombs side by side. The first to the left is that of Iyénobu, the sixth of the line, who ruled in 1709–1713. The urn and gates of the tomb are of bronze. The tomb in the centre is that of Iyéyoshi, the twelfth, who ruled 1838–1854. The third, to the right, is that of Iyémochi, the fourteenth shogun, who ruled 1858–1866, and was the last of his line who died in power.

From the tomb of Iyémochi, facing the east and looking to the left, we may see the tombs of Iyétsugu (1713–1716), the seventh, and of Iyéshige (1745–1762), the ninth, shôgun. Descending the steps and reaching the next stone platform, we may, by looking down to the left, see the tombs of a shôgun's wife and two of his children. The court-yards and shrines leading to the tombs of Iyétsugu and Iyéshige are fully as handsome as the others. Hidétada (1606–1623), the second prince of the line, is buried a few hundred yards south of the other tombs. The place is easily found. Passing down the main avenue, and turning to the right, we have a walk of a furlong or two up a hill, on the top of which, surrounded by camellia-trees, and within a heavy stone palisade, is a handsome octagon edifice of the same material. A mausoleum of gold lacquer rests upright on a pedestal. The tomb, a very costly one, is in a state of perfect preservation. On one side of the path is a curiously carved stone, representing Buddha on his death-bed. The

great temple of Zôzôji belonged to the Jôdo sect, within whose pale the
Tokugawas lived and died.*

---

* This splendid temple and belfry was reduced to ashes on the night of
December 31st, 1874, by a fanatic incendiary. It had been sequestrated by
the Imperial Government, and converted into a Shintô *miya*. On a perfectly
calm midnight, during a heavy fall of snow, the sparks and the flakes mingled
together with indescribable effect. The new year was ushered in by a perpen-
dicular flood of dazzling green flame poured up to an immense height. The
background of tall *cryptomeria* trees heightened the grandeur of the fiery
picture. As the volatilized gases of the various metals in the impure copper sheathing of the roof and sides glowed and sparkled, and streaked the
iridescent mass of flame, it afforded a spectacle only to be likened to a near
observation of the sun, or a view through a colossal spectroscope. The great
bell, whose casting had been superintended by Iyémitsu, and by him presented
to the temple, had for two hundred years been the solemn monitor, inviting the
people to their devotions. Its liquid notes could be heard, it is said, at Odawara.
On the night of the fire the old bell-ringer leaped to his post, and, in place of
the usual solemn monotone, gave the double stroke of alarm, until the heat
had changed one side of the bell to white, the note deepening in tone, until,
in red heat, the ponderous link softened and bent, dropping its burden to the
earth. It is to be greatly regretted that the once sacred grounds of Shiba groves
are now desecrated and common. *"Sic transit gloria Tokugawarum."*

The family of Tokugawa, the city of Yedo, and the institutions of peaceful
feudalism took their rise and had their fall together. When the last shôgun
resigned in 1868, Yedo became the Tôkiô, or national capital, and with Old
Yedo, feudalism and Old Japan passed away. The desperate efforts afterward
made in 1874 at Saga, in Hizen, in 1876 at Kumamoto, in Higo, and in Satsuma
in 1877, to overthrow the mikado's government, were but the expiring throes
of feudalism. Old Japan has forever passed away, to live only in art, drama,
and literature. The student will find the following monographs valuable and
interesting: "The Streets and Street Names of Yedo," in *Transactions of the
Asiatic Society of Japan*," 1873. *The Tôkiô Guide*, and *Map of Tôkiô, with Notes
Historical and Explanatory*; Yokohama, 1872. "The Castle of Yedo," by T. R.
H. M'Clatchie, a valuable paper read before the Asiatic Society, Dec. 22d,
1877, and printed in the *Japan Mail* for Jan. 12th, 1878, and in the society's
*Transactions* for 1878. Mitford's *Tales of Old Japan. Chiushingura; or, The Loyal
League*, a Japanese Romance (of the 47 Ronins), enriched with native illustra-
tions, notes, and appendix; New York, 1876. *Japanese Heraldry*, by T. R. H.

M'Clatchie, in Asiatic Society's *Transactions* for 1877. The best glimpse into everyday humble life is afforded in *Our Neighborhood; or, Sketches in the Suburbs of Yedo*, by T. A. P. (T. A. Purcell, M.D.); Yokohama, 1874. In Alcock's *Three Years in Japan* (New York, Harper & Brothers) and Hildredth's *Japan* are also some good pictures as seen by foreign eyes.

## XXVIII

# *The Recent Revolutions in Japan**

It is the popular impression in the United States and in Europe that the immediate cause of the fall of the shôgun's Government, the restoration of the mikado to supreme power, and the abolition of the dual and feudal systems was the presence of foreigners on the soil of Japan. No one who has lived in Dai Nippon, and made himself familiar with the currents of thought among the natives, or who has studied the history of the country, can share this opinion. The foreigners and their ideas were the occasion, not the cause, of the destruction of the dual system of government, which would certainly have resulted from the operation of causes already at work before the foreigners arrived. Their presence served merely to hasten what was already inevitable.

I purpose in this chapter to expose the true causes of the recent marvelous changes in Japan. These comprise a three-fold political revolution within, a profound alteration in the national policy toward foreigners, and the inauguration of social reforms which lead us to hope that Japan has rejected the Asiatic, and adopted the European, ideal of civilization. I shall attempt to prove that these causes operated mainly *from within*, not from without; from impulse, not from impact; and that they were largely intellectual.

---

* Reprinted and enlarged from the *North American Review* of April, 1875.

The history of Japan, as manifested in the current of events since the advent of Commodore Perry, has its sources in a number of distinct movements, some logically connected, others totally distinct from the rest. These were intended to effect: 1. The overthrow of the shôgun, and his reduction to his proper level as a vassal; 2. The restoration of the true emperor to supreme power; 3. The abolition of the feudal system and a return to the ancient imperial régime; 4. The abolition of Buddhism, and the establishment of pure Shintô as the national faith and the engine of government. These four movements were historically and logically connected. The fifth was the expulsion of the foreign "barbarians," and the dictatorial isolation of Japan from the rest of the world; the sixth, the abandonment of this design, the adoption of Western civilization, and the entrance of Japan into the comity of nations. The origin of the first and second movements must be referred to a time distant from the present by a century and a half; the third and fourth, to a period within the past century; the fifth and sixth, to an impulse developed mainly within the memory of young men now living.

There existed, long before the advent of Perry, definite conceptions of the objects to be accomplished. These lay in the minds of earnest thinkers, to whom life under the dual system was a perpetual winter of discontent, like snow upon the hills. In due season the spring would have come that was to make the flood. The presence of Perry in the Bay of Yedo was like an untimely thaw, or a hot south-wind in February. The snow melted, the streams gathered. Like houses built upon the sand, the shôgunate and the feudal system were swept away. They were already too rotten and worm-eaten to have the great fall which the simile might suggest. The mikado and the ancient ark of state floated into power. Buddhism stood as upon a rock, damaged, but firm. The foreigner, moored to the pile-driven foundations of his treaties, held his own more firmly than before. The flood in full momentum was swollen by a new stream and deflected into a new channel. Abandoning the attempt to defy the gravitation of events, to run up the hill of a past forever sloping backward into the impossible, the flood found surcease with the rivers of nations that make the ocean of human solidarity.

The chief motors of these movements were intellectual. Neither the impact of foreign cannon-balls at Kagoshima or Shimonoséki, nor the heavy and unjust indemnities demanded from the Japanese, wrought of themselves the events of the last ten years, as foreigners so complacently believe. An English writer resident in Japan concludes his translation of the "Legacy of Iyéyasu" by referring to it as the "constitution under which this country [Japan] was governed until the time within the recollection of all, when it gave way to the irresistible momentum of a higher civilization." The translator evidently means that the fall of the dual form of government and the feudal system was the direct result of contact with the higher civilization of Europe and America. English writers on Japan seem to imply that the bombardment of Kagoshima was the paramount cause that impelled Japan to adopt the foreign civilization.

Much, also, has been said and written in praise of Japan for her abolition of the feudal system by a "stroke of the pen," and thus "achieving in one day what it required Europe centuries to accomplish." An outsider, whose knowledge of Dai Nippon is derived from our old text-books and cyclopedias, or from non-resident book-makers, may be so far dazed as to imagine the Japanese demi-gods in state-craft, even as the American newspapers make them all princes. To the writer, who has lived in a daimiô's capital before, during, and after the abolition of feudalism, the comparison suggests the reason why the Irish recruit cut off the leg instead of the head of his enemy. Long before its abolition, Japanese feudalism was ready for its grave. The overthrow of the shôgun left it a headless trunk. To cut off its legs and bury it was easy, and in reality this was what the mikado's Government did, as I shall show.

As it would be vain to attempt to comprehend our own late civil war by beginning at Sumter, or even with the Compromise measures of 1851; so one will be misled who, in attempting to understand the Japan of to-day, looks only at events since Perry's time. The roots of the momentous growth of 1868 are to be found within the past centuries.

Yoritomo's acts were in reality the culmination of a long series of usurpations, begun by the Taira. Under the plea of military necessity, he had become an arch-usurper. In the period 1184–1199 A.D. began that dual system of government which has been the political puzzle of the world; which neither Kaempfer, nor the Déshima Hollanders, nor the Portuguese Jesuits seem ever to have fully understood; which has filled our cyclopedias and school-books with the misleading non-sense about "two emperors," one "spiritual" and the other "secular;" which led the astute Perry and his successors to make treaties with an underling; which gave rise to a vast mass of what is now very amus-ing reading, embracing much prophecy, fiction, and lamentations, in the Diplomatic Correspondence from Japan; and which keeps alive that venerable solecism heard among a few Rip Van Winkles in Japan, who talk, both in Japanese and English, about the "return of the tycoon to power." There never was but one emperor in Japan; the shogun was a military usurper, and the bombastic title "tycoon" a diplomatic fraud.

We have seen how the policy of Yoritomo was continued by the Hôjô, the Ashikaga, and the Tokugawas, who consummated the per-manent separation of the throne and the camp. The custom of the shoguns going to Kiôto to do the mikado homage fell into desuetude after the visit of Iyémitsu. The iron-handed rule of the great com-mander at Yedo was felt all over the empire, and after centuries of war it had perfect peace. Learning flourished, the arts prospered. So perfect was the political machinery of the bakufu that the power of the mikado seemed but a shadow, though in reality it was vastly greater than foreigners ever imagined.

The dwellings of the two rulers at Yedo and Kiôto, of the domineering general and the overawed emperor, were typical of their positions. The mikado dwelt, unguarded, in a mansion surrounded by gardens inclosed within a plaster wall, in a city which was the chosen centre of nobles of simple life, highest rank, and purest blood, men of letters, students, and priests, and noted for its classic history and sacred associations, monasteries, gardens, and people of courtly manners and gentle life. The shôgun lived in a fortified and garrisoned castle, overlooking an upstart city full of arsenals, vassal princes, and military retainers. The feelings of the people found truest expression in the maxim, "The shôgun all men fear; the mikado all men love."

The successors of Iyéyasu, carrying out his policy, having exterminated the "corrupt sect" (Christianity), swept all foreigners out of the empire, and bolting its sea-barred gates, proceeded to devise and execute measures to eliminate all disturbing causes, and fix in eternal stability the peaceful conditions which were the fruit of the toils of his arduous life. They deliberately attempted to prevent Chronos from devouring his children.

According to their scheme, the intellect of the nation was to be bounded by the Great Wall of the Chinese classics, while to the hierarchy of Buddhism—one of the most potent engines ever devised for crushing and keeping crushed the intellect of the Asiatic masses—was given the ample encouragement of government example and patronage. An embargo was laid upon all foreign ideas. Edicts commanded the destruction of all boats built upon a foreign model, and forbade the building of vessels of any size or shape superior to that of a junk, Death was the penalty of believing in Christianity, of traveling abroad, of studying foreign languages, of introducing foreign customs. Before the august train of the shôgun men must seal their upper windows, and bow their faces to the earth. Even to his tea-jars and cooking-pots the populace must do obeisance with face in the dust. To study ancient history, which might expose the origin of the shôgunate, was forbidden to the vulgar, and discouraged among the higher. A rigid censorship dried the life-blood of many a master spirit, while the manufacture and concoction of false and garbled histories which extolled the reigning dynasty, or glorified the dual system of government as the best and only one for Japan, were encouraged. There were not wanting poets, fawning flatterers, and even historians, who in their effusions styled the august usurper the Ô-gimi (Chinese, *tai-kun*, or "tycoon"), a term meaning great prince, or exalted ruler, and properly applied only to the mikado. The blunders, cruelties, and oppressions of the Tokugawa rulers were, in popular fiction and drama, removed from the present, and depicted in plots laid in the time of the Ashikagas, and the true names changed. One of the most perfect systems of espionage and repression ever devised was elaborated to fetter all men in helpless subjection to the great usurper. An incredibly large army of spies was kept in the pay of the Government. Within such a hedge, the Government itself being a colossal fraud, rapidly grew and flourished public and private habits of lying, and deceit in all its forms, until the love of a lie apparently for its own sake became a national habit. When foreigners arrived in the Land of the Gods during the decade following Perry's arrival, they concluded that the lying which was everywhere persistently carried on in the Government and by private persons with such marvelous facility and unique originality was a primal characteristic of Japanese human nature. The necessity of hoodwinking the prying eyes of the foreigners, lest they should discover the fountain of authority, and the true relation of the shôgun, gave rise to the use of official deception that seemed as variegated as a kaleidoscope and as regular as the laws of nature. The majority of the daimiôs who had received lands and titles from the shôgun believed their allegiance to be forever due to him, instead of to the mikado, a belief stigmatized as rank treason by the students of history. As for the common people, the great mass of them forgot, or never knew, that the emperor had ever held power or governed his people; and being officially taught to believe him to be a divine personage, supposed he had lived thus from time immemorial. Knowing only of the troubled war times before the "great and good" Tokugawas, they believed devoutly in the infallibility, paternal benevolence, and divine right of the Yedo rulers.

The line of shôguns, founded by Iyéyasu, was the last that held, or ever will hold, the military power in Japan. To them the Japanese people owe the blessing of nearly two hundred and seventy years of peace. Under their firm rule the dual form of government seemed fixed on a basis unchangeable, and the feudal system in eternal stability. There did not exist, nor was it possible there should arise, causes such as undermined the feudalism of Europe. The Church, the Empire, free cities, industrialism—these were all absent. The eight classes of the people were kept contented and happy. A fertile soil and genial clime gave food in unstinted profusion, and thus was removed a cause which is a chronic source of insurrection in portions of China. As there was no commerce, there was no vast wealth to be accumulated, nor could the mind of the merchant expand to a limit dangerous to despotism by fertilizing contact with foreigners. All learning and education, properly so called, were confined to the samurai, to whom also belonged the sword and privilege. The perfection of the governmental machinery at Yedo kept, as was the design, the daimiôs poor and at jealous variance with each other, and rendered it impossible for them to combine their power. No two of them ever were allowed to meet in private or to visit each other without spies. The vast army of eighty thousand retainers of the Tokugawas, backed by the following of some of the richest clans, such as Owari, Kii, Mito, and Echizen, who were near relatives of the shogunal family, together with the vast resources in income and accumulation, made it appear, as many believed, that the overthrow of the Tokugawas, or the bakufu, or the feudal system, was a moral impossibility.

Yet all these fell to ruin in the space of a few months! The bakufu is now a shadow of the past. The Tokugawas, once princes and the gentry of the land, whose hands never touched other tools than pen and sword, now live in obscurity or poverty, and by thousands keep soul and body together by picking tea, making paper, or digging the mud of rice-fields they once owned, like the laborers they once despised. Their ancestral tombs at Kuno, Shiba, Uyéno, and Nikkô, once the most sacred and magnificently adorned of Japanese places of honor, are now dilapidating in unarrested neglect, dishonor, and decay. The feudal system, at the touch of a few daring parvenus, crumbled to dust like the long undisturbed tenants of catacombs when suddenly moved or exposed to the light of day. Two hundred and fifty princes, resigning lands, retainers, and incomes, retired to private life in Tôkiô at the bidding of their former servants, acting in the name of the mikado. They are now quietly waiting to die. They are the "dead facts stranded on the shores of the oblivious years."

What were the causes of these three distinct results? When began the first gathering of the waters which burst into flood in 1868, sweeping away the landmarks of centuries, floating the old ship of state into power, impelling it, manned with new men and new machinery, into the stream of modern thought, as though Noah's ark had been equipped with engines, steam, and propellers? To understand the movement, we must know the currents of thought, and the men who produced the ideas.

There were formerly many classes of people in Japan, but only three of these were students and thinkers. The first comprised the court nobles, the literati of Kiôto; the second, the priests, who brought into existence that mass of Japanese Buddhistic literature, and originated and developed those phases of the India cultus which have made Japanese Buddhism a distinct product of thought and life among the manifold developments of the once most widely professed religion in the world. This intellectual activity and ecclesiastical growth culminated in the sixteenth century. Since that time Japanese thought has been led by the samurai, among whom we may include the priests of Shintô. The modern secular intellectual activity of Japan attained its highest point during the latter part of the last and the first quarter of the present century. Even as far back as the seventeenth century, the students of ancient history began to understand clearly the true nature of the duarchy, and to see that the shôgunate could exist only while the people were kept in ignorance. From that time Buddhism began to lose its hold on the intellect of the samurai and lay educated classes. The revival of Chinese learning, especially the Confucian and Mencian politico-ethics, followed. Buddhism was almost completely supplanted as a moral force. The invasion of Corea was one of the causes tributary to this result, which was greatly stimulated by the presence of a number of refugee scholars, who had fled from China on the overthrow of the Ming dynasty. The secondary influence of the fall of Peking and the accession of the Tartars became a parallel to the fall of Constantinople and the dispersion of the Greek scholars through Europe in the thirteenth century. The relation between the sovereign (mikado) and vassal (shôgun) had become so nearly mythical, that most Japanese fathers could not satisfy the innocent and eager questions of their children as to who was sovereign of Japan. The study of the Confucian moral scheme of "The Five Relations" (*i.e.*, sovereign and minister, parent and child, husband and wife, elder and younger brother, and between friends), in which the first and great requirement is the obedience of the vassal to his lord, aroused an incoercible desire among the samurai to restore and define that relation so long obscured. This spirit increased with every blunder of the bakufu; and when the revolution opened, "the war-cry that led the imperial party to victory was *Daigi meibun*, or the 'King and the subject;' whereby it was understood that the distinction between them must be restored, and the shôgun should be reduced to the proper relation of subject or servant to his sovereign."*

The province of Mito was especially noted for the number, ability, and activity of its scholars. In it dwelt the learned Chinese refugees as guests of the daimiô. The classic, which has had so powerful an influence in forming the public opinion which now upholds the mikado's throne, is the product of the native scholars, who submitted their text for correction to the Chinese scholars. The second Prince of Mito, who was born 1622, and died 1700, is to be considered, as was first pointed out by Mr. Ernest Satow, as "the real author of the movement which culminated in the revolution of 1868." Assembling around him a host of scholars from all parts of Japan, he began the composition of the *Dai Nihon Shi*, or "History of Japan." It is written in the purest Chinese, which is to Japan what Latin is to learning in Europe, and fills two hundred and forty-three volumes, or matter about equal to Mr. Bancroft's "History of the United States." It was finished in 1715, and immediately became a classic. Though diligently studied, it remained in manuscript, copied from hand to hand by eager students, until 1851, when the wide demand for it induced its publication in print. The tendency of this book, as of most of the many publications of Mito,† was to direct the minds of the people to the mikado as the true and only source of authority, and to point out the historical fact that the shôgun was a military usurper. Mito, being a

---

* Arinori Mori: Introduction to *Education in Japan*, p. 26.
† See article "Japan, Literature of," in the *American Cyclopædia*.

near relative of the house of Tokugawa, was allowed greater liberty in stating his views than could have been granted to any other person. The work begun by Mito was followed up by the famous scholar, Rai Sanyo, who in 1827, after twenty years of continuous labor, completed his *Nihon Guai Shi* ("External History of Japan"), in which he gives the history of each of the military families, Taira, Minamoto, Hôjô, Ashikaga, etc., who held the governing power from the period of the decadence of the mikados. This work had to pass the ordeal of the censorate at Yedo, and some of the volumes were repeatedly purged by the censors before they were allowed to be published. The unmistakable animus of this great book is to show that the mikado is the only true ruler, in whom is the fountain of power, and to whom the allegiance of every Japanese is due, and that even the Tokugawas were not free from the guilt of usurpation.

The long peace of two centuries gave earnest patriots time to think. Though the great body of the people, both the governing and the governed classes, enervated by prolonged prosperity and absence of danger, cared for none of these things, the serious students burned to see the mikado again restored to his ancient authority. *This motive alone would have caused revolution in due time.* They felt that Japan had retrograded, that the military arts had sunk into neglect, that the war spirit slumbered. Yet on all sides the "greedy foreigners" were eying the Holy Country. Already the ocean, once a wall, was a highway for wheeled vessels. The settlement of California and the Pacific coast made the restless Americans their neighbors on the east, with only a wide steam ferry between. American whalers cruised in Japanese waters, and hunted whales in sight of the native coasters. American ships repeatedly visited their harbors to restore a very few of the human waifs which for centuries in unintermitted stream had drifted up the Kuro Shiwo and across the Pacific, giving to America wrecks and spoils, her tribes men, her tongues words, and perhaps the civilization which in Peru and Mexico awoke the wonder and tempted the cupidity of the Spanish marauders. Defying all precedent, and trampling on Japanese pride and isolation, the American captains refused to do as the Hollanders, and go to Nagasaki, and appeared even in the Bay of Yedo. The long scarfs of coal-smoke were becoming daily matters of familiar ugliness and prognostics of doom. The steam-whistle heard by the junk sailors—as potent as the rams' horns of old—had already thrown down their walls of exclusion. The "black ships" of the "barbarians" passing Matsumaë in one year numbered eighty-six. Russia, on the north, was descending upon Saghalin; the English, French, Dutch, and Americans were pressing their claims for trade and commerce. The bakufu was idle, making few or no preparations to resist the fierce barbarians. Far-sighted men saw that, in presence of foreigners, a collision between the two centres of government, Yedo and Kiôto, would be immediate as it was inevitable. When it should come, in the nature of the case, the shôgunate must fall. The samurai would adhere to the mikado's side, and the destruction of the feudal system would follow as a logical necessity. It was the time of luxury, carousal, and the stupor of licentious carnival with most of the daimiôs, but with others of gloomy forebodings.

Another current of thought was flowing in the direction of a restored mikadoate. It may be called the revival of the study of pure Shintô, and, in examining the causes of the recent revolution, can not be overlooked. The introduction of Buddhism and Chinese philosophy greatly modified or "corrupted" the ancient faith. A school of modern writers has attempted to purge modern Shinto, and present it in its original form.

According to this religion, Japan is pre-eminently the Land of the Gods, and the mikado is their divine representative and vicegerent. Hence the duty of all Japanese implicitly to obey him. During the long reign of the shoguns, and of Buddhism, which they favored and professed, few, indeed, knew what pure Shintô was. Its Bible is the *Kojiki*, compiled A.D. 712. Several other works, such as the *Nihongi*, *Manyoshiu*, are nearly as old and as valuable in the eyes of Shintô scholars as the *Kojiki*. They are written in ancient Japanese, and can be read only by special students of the archaic form of the language. The developments of a taste for the study of ancient native literature and for that of history were nearly synchronous. The neglect of pure Japanese learning for that of Chinese had been almost universal, until Keichiu, Kada, and other scholars revived its critical study. The bakufu discouraged all such investigation, while the mikado and court at Kiôto lent it all their aid, both moral and, as it is said, pecuniary. Mabuchi (1697–1769), Motoöri (1730–1801), and Hirata (1776–1843), each successively the pupil of the other, are the greatest lights of pure Shintô; and their writings, which are devoted to cosmogony, ancient history, and language, the true position of the mikado and the Shintô cultus, exerted a lively influence at Kiôto, in Mito, in Echizen, Satsuma, and in many other provinces, where a political party was already forming, with the intention of accomplishing the abolition of the bakufu and a return to the Ôsei era. The necessary result of the study of Shintô was an increase of reverence for the mikado. Buddhism, Chinese influence, Confucianism, despotism, usurpation, and the bakufu were, in the eyes of a Shintôist, all one and the same. Shintô, the ancient true religion, all which a patriot could desire, good government, national purity, the Golden Age, and a life best explained by the conception of the "millennium" among Christians, were synonymous with the mikado and his return to power. The arguments of the Shintôists helped to swell the tide that came to its flood at Fushimi. Throughout and after the war of 1868–1870, there were no more bitter partisans who urged to the last extremes of logic and severity the issues of the war and the "reformation." It was the study of the literature produced by the Shintô scholars and the historical writers that formed the public opinion that finally overthrew the shôgunate, the bakufu, and feudalism.

Long before foreigners arrived, the seeds of revolution were above the soil. The old Prince of Mito, a worthy descendant of his illustrious ancestor, tired of preaching Shintô and of persuading the shôgun to hand over his authority to the mikado, resolved, in 1840, to take up arms and to try the wager of battle. To provide the sinews of war, he seized the Buddhist monasteries, and melted down their enormous bronze bells and cast them into cannon. By prompt measures the bakufu suppressed his preparations for war, and imprisoned him for twelve years, releasing him only in the excitement consequent upon the arrival of Perry.

Meanwhile Satsuma, Chôshiu, and other Southern clans were making extensive military preparations, not merely to be in readiness to drive out the possible foreign invaders, but, as we now know, and as events proved, to reduce the shôgun to his proper level as one of many of the mikado's vassals. The ancestors of these most powerful clans had of old held equal rank and power with Iyéyasu, until the fortunes of war turned against them. They had been overcome by force, or had sullenly surrendered in face of overwhelming odds. Their adhesion to the Tokugawas was but nominal, and only the strong pressure of superior power was able to wring from them a haughty semblance of obedience. They chafed perpetually under the rule of one who was in reality a vassal like themselves. On more than one occasion they openly defied and ignored the bakufu's orders; and the purpose, scarcely kept secret, of the Satsuma and Chôshiu clans was to destroy the shogunate, and acknowledge no authority but that of the mikado.

From the Southern clans rose, finally, the voice in council, the secret plot, the *coup d'etat*, and the arms in the field that wrought the purpose for which Mito labored. Yet they would never have been successful, had not a public sentiment existed to support them, which the historical writers had already created by their writings. The scholars could never have gratified their heart's wish, had not the sword and pen, brain and hand—both equally mighty—helped each other.

Notably pre-eminent among the Southern daimiôs, in personal characteristics, abilities, energy, and far-sightedness, was the Prince of Satsuma. Next to Kaga, he was the wealthiest of all the daimiôs. Had he lived, he would doubtless have led the revolutionary movement of 1868. Besides giving encouragement to all students of the ancient literature and history, he was most active in developing the material resources of his province, and in perfecting the military organization, so that, when the time should be ripe for the onslaught on the bakufu, he might have ready for the mikado the military provision to make his government a complete success. To carry out his plans, he encouraged the study of the Dutch and English languages, and thus learned the modern art of war and scientific improvement. He established cannon-foundries and mills on foreign principles. He saw that something more was needed. Young men must visit foreign countries, and there acquire the theory and practice of the arts of war and peace. The laws of the country forbade any subject to leave it, and the bakufu was ever on the alert to catch runaways. Later on, however, by a clever artifice, a number of the brightest young men, about twenty-seven in number, got away in one vessel to Europe, and, despite the surveillance of the Yedo officials, others followed to England and the United States. Among these young men were some who are now high officials of the Japanese Government.

The renown of this prince extended all over the empire, and numbers of young men from all parts of the country flocked to be his pupils or students. Kagoshima, his capital, became a centre of busy manual industry and intellectual activity. Keeping pace with the intense energy of mind and hand was the growing sentiment that the days of the bakufu were numbered, that its fall was certain, and that the only fountain of authority was the mikado. The Satsuma samurai and students all looked to the prince as the man for the coming crisis, when, to the inexpressible grief of all, he sickened and died, in 1858. He was succeeded in actual power by Shimadzu Saburo, his younger brother. No master ever left more worthy pupils; and those most trusted and trusting, among many others, were Saigô, Ôkubo, and Katsu. The mention of these names calls up to a native the most stirring memories of the war. Saigô became the leader of the imperial army. Ôkubo, the implacable enemy of the bakufu, was the master-spirit in council, and the power behind the throne which urged the movement to its logical consequences. At this moment, the annihilator of the Saga rebellion, crowned with diplomatic laurels, and the conqueror of a peace at Peking, he stands leader of the Cabinet, and the foremost man in Japan. Katsu advised the bakufu not to fight Chôshiu, and his master to resign his position, thus saving Yedo from destruction. The lesser men of note, pupils of Satsuma, who now hold positions of trust, or who have become disinterested Cincinnati, to show their patriotism, are too many to mention.

Familiarity with the facts above exposed will enable one to understand the rush of events that followed the arrival of the American envoy. The bakufu was apparently at the acme of power. The shôgun Iyéyoshi at Yedo was *fainéant*. The mikado at Kiôto, Koméi Tennô, father of the present emperor, was a man who understood well his true position, hated the bakufu as a nest of robbers, and all foreigners as unclean beasts. Within the empire, all was ripe for revolution. Beneath the portentous calm, those who would listen could hear the rumble of the political earthquake. From without came puffs of news, like atmospheric pulses portending a cyclone. On that 8th day of July, 1853, the natural sea and sky wearing perfect calm, the magnificent fleet of the "barbarian" ships sailed up the Bay of Yedo. It was the outer edge of the typhoon. The *Susquehanna* was leading the squadrons of seventeen nations.

There was one spectator upon the bluffs at Yokohama who was persuaded in his own mind that the men who could build such ships as those; who were so gentle, kind, patient, firm; having force, yet using it not; demanding to be treated as equals, and in return dealing with Japanese as with equals, could not be barbarians. If they were, it were better for the Japanese to become barbarous. That man was Katsu, now the Secretary of the Japanese Navy.

The barbarian envoy was a strange creature. He was told to leave the Bay of Yedo and go to Nagasaki. He impolitely refused, and staid and surveyed, and was dignified. This was anomalous. Other barbarians had not acted so; they had quietly obeyed orders. Furthermore, he brought letters and presents, all directed "To the Emperor of Japan." The shôgun was not emperor, but he must make believe to be so. It would not do to call himself the mikado's general only. This title awed sufficiently at home; but would the strangers respect it? A pedantic professor ("not the Prince of Dai Gaku") in the Chinese college (Dai Gaku Kô) at Yedo was sent to treat with the barbarian Perry. A chopper of Chinese logic, and a stickler for exact terms, the pedant must, as in duty bound, exalt his master. He inserted, or at least allowed to be used in the treaties the title *tai-kun*, a purely Chinese word, which in those official documents signified that he was the supreme ruler of all Japan. This title had never been bestowed upon the shôgun by the mikado, nor had it ever been used in the imperial official documents. The bakufu and the pedantic professor, Hayashi, did not mean to lie to the true sovereign in Kiôto. The bakufu, like a frog, whose front is white, whose back is black, could look both ways, and present two fronts. Seen from Kiôto, the lie was white; that is, "meant nothing." Looked at by those unsuspecting dupes, the barbarians, it was black;

that is, "The august Sovereign of Japan," as the preamble of the Perry treaty says. Yet to the jealous emperor and court this white lie was, as ever white lies are, the blackest of lies. It created the greatest uneasiness and alarm. The shôgun had no shadow of right to this bombastic figment of authority.

It was a new illustration in diplomacy of Æsop's Fable No. 26. The great Yedo frog puffed itself to its utmost to equal the Kiôto ox, and it burst in the attempt. The last carcass of these batrachians in diplomacy was buried in Shidzuoka, a city ninety-five miles south-west of Tôkiô, in 1868. The writer visited this ancient home of the Tokugawas in 1872, and in a building within a mile of the actual presence of the last and still living "tycoon," and within shouting distance of thousands of his ex-retainers, saw scores of the presents brought by Commodore Perry lying, many of them, in mildew, rust, or neglect. They were all labeled "Presented by the——— ————of the United States to the Emperor of Japan." Yet the mikado never saw them. The Japanese excel at a jibe, but when did they perpetrate sarcasm so huge? The mikado's government, with Pilate's irony, had allowed the tycoon to keep the presents, with the labels on them!

We may fairly infer that so consummate a diplomatist as Perry, had he understood the true state of affairs, would have gone with his fleet to Ôzaka, and opened negotiations with the mikado at Kiôto, instead of with his lieutenant at Yedo. Perhaps he never knew that he had treated with an underling.

The immediate results of the opening of the ports to foreign commerce in 1859 were the disarrangement of the prices of the necessaries of life, and almost universal distress consequent thereon, much sickness and mortality from the importation of foreign diseases, to which was added an exceptional succession of destructive earthquakes, typhoons, floods, fires, and storms. In the midst of these calamities the shôgun, Iyésada, died.

An heir must be chosen. His selection devolved upon the tairô, or regent, Ii, a man of great ability, daring, and, as his enemies say, of unscrupulous villainy. Ii,* though socially of low rank, possessed almost supreme power. Ignoring the popular choice of Keiki (the seventh son of the Daimiô of Mito), who had been adopted by the house of Hitotsubashi, he chose the Prince of Kii, a boy twelve years of age. In answer to the indignant protests of the princes of Mito,† Echizen, and Owari, he shut them up in prison, and thus alienated from his support the near relatives of the house of Tokugawa. It was his deliberate intention, say his enemies, to depose the mikado, as the Hôjô did, and set up a boy emperor again. At the same time, all who opposed him or the bakufu, or who, in either Kiôto, Yedo, or elsewhere, agitated the restoration of the mikado, he impoverished, imprisoned, exiled, or

---

* The premier, Ii, was the Daimiô of Hikoné, a castled town and fief on Lake Biwa, in Mino; revenue, three hundred and fifty thousand koku. He was at the head of the *fudai*. His personal name was Nawosuké; his title at the emperor's court was *kamon no kami*—head of the bureau of the Ku Nai Shô (imperial household)—having in charge the hangings, curtains, carpets, mats, and the sweeping of the palace on state occasions. His rank at Kiôto was Chiujô, or "general of the second class." In the bakufu, he was prime minister, or "tairo." He had a son, who was afterward educated in Brooklyn, New York.

† It would be impossible in brief space to narrate the plots and counterplots at Yedo and Kiôto during the period 1860–1868. As a friendly critic (in *The Hiôgo News*, June 9th, 1875) has pointed out, I allow that the Prince of Mito, while wishing to overthrow the shôgunate, evidently wished to see the restoration accomplished with his son, Keiki, in a post of high honor and glory. While in banishment, secret instructions were sent from Kiôto, which ran thus: "The bakufu has shown great disregard of public opinion in concluding treaties without waiting for the opinion of the court, and in disgracing princes so

beheaded. Among his victims were many noble scholars and patriots, whose fate excited universal pity.*

---

closely allied by blood to the shôgun. The mikado's rest is disturbed by the spectacle of such misgovernment, when the fierce barbarian is at our very door. Do you, therefore, assist the bakufu with your advice; expel the barbarians; content the mind of the people; and restore tranquillity to his majesty's bosom."—*Kinsé Shiriaku*, p. 11, Satow's translation. This letter was afterward delivered up to the bakufu, shortly after which (September, 1861) the old prince died. The Mito clan was for many years afterward divided into two factions, the "Righteous" and the "Wicked." There is no proof that the Prince of Mito poisoned Iyésada, except the baseless guess of Sir Rutherford Alcock, which has a value at par with most of that writer's statements concerning Japanese history.

* Among others was Yoshida Shoin, a samurai of Chôshiu, and a student of European learning. He was the man who tried to get on board Commodore Perry's ship at Shimoda (Perry's "Narrative," p. 485–488). He had been kept in prison in his clan since 1854. He wrote a pamphlet against the project of taking up arms against the bakufu, for which he was rewarded by the Yedo rulers with his liberty. After Ii's arbitrary actions, Yoshida declared that the shôgunate could not be saved, and must fall. When the shôgun's ministers were arresting patriots in Kiôto, Yoshida resolved to take his life. For this plot, after detection, he was sent to Yedo in a cage, and beheaded. This ardent patriot, whose memory is revered by all parties, was one of the first far-sighted men to see that Japan must adopt foreign civilization, or fall before foreign progress, like India. The national enterprises now in operation were urged by him in an able pamphlet written before his death.

Another victim, a student of European literature, and a fine scholar in Dutch and Chinese, named Hashimoto Sanai, of Fukui, brother of my friend Dr. Hashimoto, surgeon in the Japanese army, fell a martyr to his loyalty and patriotism. This gentleman was the instrument of arousing an enthusiasm for foreign science in Fukui, which ultimately resulted in the writer's appointment to Fukui. Hashimoto saw the need of opening peaceful relations with foreigners, but believed that it could safely be done only under the restored and unified government. Under a system of divided authority, he held that the ruin of Japan would result. Had Perry treated with the mikado, foreign war might possibly have resulted, though very probably not. By treating with the counterfeit emperor in Yedo, civil war, foreign hostilities, impoverishment of the country, and national misery, prolonged for years, were inevitable.

The mikado being by right the supreme ruler, and the shôgun merely a vassal, no treaty with foreigners could be binding unless signed by the mikado.

The shôgun or his ministers had no right whatever to sign the treaties. Here was a dilemma. The foreigners were pressing the ratification of the treaties on the bakufu, while the mikado and court as vigorously refused their consent. Ii was not a man to hesitate. As the native chronicler writes: "He began to think that if, in the presence of these constant arrivals of foreigners of different nations, he were to wait for the Kiôto people to make up their minds, some unlucky accident might bring the same disasters upon Japan as China had already experienced. He, therefore, concluded a treaty at Kanagawa, and affixed his seal to it, after which he reported the transaction to Kiôto."

This signature to the treaties without the mikado's consent stirred up intense indignation at Kiôto and throughout the country, which from one end to the other now resounded with the cry, "Honor the mikado, and expel the barbarian." In the eyes of patriots, the regent was a traitor. His act gave the enemies of the bakufu a legal pretext of enmity, and was the signal of the regent's doom. All over the country thousands of patriots left their homes, declaring their intention not to return to them until the mikado, restored to power, should sweep away the barbarians. Boiling over with patriotism, bands of assassins, mostly rônins, roamed the country, ready to slay foreigners, or the regent, and to die for the mikado. On the 23d of March, Ii was assassinated in Yedo, outside the Sakurada gate of the castle, near the spot where now stand the offices of the departments of War and Foreign Affairs, and the Gothic brick buildings of the Imperial College of Engineering. Then followed the slaughter of insolent foreigners, and in some cases of innocent ones, and the burning of their legations, the chief object in nearly every case being to embroil the bakufu with foreign powers, and thus hasten its fall. Some of these amateurs, who in foreign eyes were incendiaries and assassins, and in the native view noble patriots, are now high officials in the mikado's Government.

The prestige of the bakufu declined daily, and the tide of influence and power set in steadily toward the true capital. The custom of the shogun's visiting Kiôto, and doing homage to the mikado, after an interval of two hundred and thirty years, was revived, which caused his true relation to be clearly understood even by the common people, who then learned for the first time the fact that the rule existed, and had been so long-insolently ignored. The Prince of Echizen, by a special and unprecedented act of the bakufu, and in obedience to orders from the Kiôto court, was made premier. By his own act, as many believe, though he was most probably only the willing cat's-paw of the Southern daimiôs, he abolished the custom of the daimiôs' forced residence in Yedo. Like wild birds from an opened cage, they, with all their retainers, fled from the city in less than a week. Yedo's glory faded like a dream, and the power and greatness of the Tokugawas came to naught. Few of the clans obeyed any longer the command of the bakufu, and gradually the hearts of the people fell away. "And so," says the native chronicler, "the prestige of the Tokugawa family, which had endured for three hundred years; which had been really more brilliant than Kamakura in the age of Yoritomo on a moonlight night when the stars are shining; which for more than two hundred and seventy years had forced the daimiôs to come breathlessly to take their turn of duty in Yedo; and which had, day and night, eighty thousand vassals at its beck and call, fell to ruin in the space of one morning."

The clans now gathered at the true *miako*, Kiôto, which became a scene of gayety and bustle unknown since the days of the Taira Ending their allegiance to the bakufu, they began to act either according to their own will, or only at the bidding of the court. They filled the imperial treasury with gold, and strengthened the hands of the Son of Heaven with their loyal devotion. Hatred of the foreigner, and a desire to fill their empty coffers with the proceeds of commerce, swayed the minds of many of them like the wind among reeds. Others wished to open the ports in their fiefs, so as to pocket the profits of foreign commerce, which the bakufu enjoyed as its monopoly. A war of pamphlets ensued, some writers attempting to show that the clans owed allegiance to the bakufu; others condemning the idea as treasonable, and, having the historic facts on their side, proved the mikado to be the sole sovereign. The bakufu, acting upon the pressure of public opinion in Kiôto, and in hopes of restoring its prestige, bent all its efforts to close the ports and persuade the foreigners to leave Japan. For this purpose they sent an embassy to Europe. To hasten their steps, the ronins now began the systematic assassination of all who opposed their plans, pillorying their heads in the dry bed of the river in front of the city. As a hint to the Tokugawa "usurpers," they cut off the heads of wooden images of the first three Ashikaga shoguns, and stuck them on poles in public. The rônins were arrested; Chôshiu espoused their side, while Aidzu, who was governor of the city, threw them into prison. The mikado, urged by the clamorous braves, and by kugé who had never seen one of the "hairy foreigners," nor dreamed of their power, issued an order for their expulsion from Japan. The Chôshiu men, the first to act, erected batteries at Shimonoséki. The bakufu, which was responsible to foreigners, commanded the clan to disarm. They refused, and in July, 1863, fired on foreign vessels. They obeyed the mikado, and disobeyed the shôgun. During the next month, Kagoshima was bombarded by a British squadron.

On the 4th of September, the Chôshiu cannoneers fired on a bakufu steamer, containing some men of the Kokura clan who were enemies of Chôshiu, and who had given certain aid and comfort to foreign vessels, and refused to fire on the latter. The Chôshiu men in Kiôto besought the mikado to make a progress to Yamato, to show to the empire his intention of taking the field in person against the barbarians. The proposal was accepted, and the preliminaries arranged, when suddenly all preparations were stopped, Chôshiu became an object of blackest suspicion, the palace gates were doubly guarded, the city was thrown into violent commotion; while the deliberations of the palace ended in the expulsion of Sanjô Sanéyoshi (now Dai Jô Dai Jin), Sawa (Minister of Foreign Affairs, 1870–'71), and five other court nobles, who were deprived of their rank and titles, while eighteen others were punished, and all retainers or members of the family of Môri (Chôshiu) were peremptorily "forbidden to enter the capital"—a phrase that made them outlaws. An army was levied, and the city put in a state of defense.

The reason of this was, that the Chôshiu men were accused of plotting to get possession of the mikado's person, in order to dictate the policy of the empire. The eighteen kugé and the six ringleaders were suspected of abetting the plot. This, and the firing on the steamer containing their envoys, roused the indignation of the bakufu, and the clans loyal to it, especially Aidzu, to the highest pitch. The men of Chôshiu, accompanied by the seven kugé, fled, September 30th, 1863, to their province.

Chôshiu now became the rendezvous of deserters and rônins from all parts of Japan. In July of the following year, 1864, a body of many hundred of irresponsible men of various clans, calling themselves "Irregulars," arrived in Kiôto from the South, to petition the mikado to restore Môri and the seven nobles to honor, and to drive out the barbarians. Aidzu and the shôgun's vassals were for attacking these men with arms at once. The mikado, not adopting the views of the petitioners, returned them no answer. On July 30th, the "Irregulars" were increased by many hitherto calm, but now exasperated, Chôshiu men, and encamped in battle array in the suburbs, where they were joined, August 15th, by two karôs, and two hundred men from Chôshiu, sent by Prince Môri to restrain his followers from violence.

While thus patiently waiting, a notification that they were to be punished was issued, August 19th, to them by the court, then under the influence of Aidzu, and Keiki was put in command of the army of chastisement.

With tears and letters of sorrowful regret to their friends at court, the Chôshiu men and the rônins, in a written manifesto vindicated the justness of their cause, swore vengeance against Aidzu, whose troops were encamped in the imperial flower-garden, and then asking pardon of the Son of Heaven "for making a disturbance so near the base of the chariot" (the throne), they accepted the wager of battle, and rushed to the attack. "The crisis had arrived," says the native chronicler, "and the spirit of murder filled and overflowed heaven and earth. The term *chôtéki*, which for centuries had been obsolete, now again came into being. Many myriads of habitations were destroyed, and millions of people were plunged into a fiery pit." On the 20th of August, 1864, at day-dawn, the battle began, the Chôshiu men advancing in three divisions, numbering in all thirteen hundred men, their design being to attack the nine gates of the imperial palace and surround the flower-garden. The Tokugawa and Aidzu troops were backed by those of Echizen, Hikoné, Kuwana and others. The battle raged furiously for two days, involving the city in a conflagration, which, fanned by a gale, reduced large quarters of it to a level of ashes. The fighting was by men in armor, equipped mostly with sword, arrow, cannon, and musket: 811 streets, 27,400 houses, 18 palaces, 44 large and 630 small yashikis, 60 Shintôshrines, 115 Buddhist temples, 40 bridges, 400 beggar's huts, and one eta village were destroyed by the flames; 1,216 fire-proof store-houses were knocked to pieces by the cannonading kept up after the battle to prevent the Chôshiu men from hiding in them. "The capital, surrounded by a nine-fold circle of flowers, entirely disappeared in one morning in the smoke of the flames of a war fire." The homeless city populace fled to the suburbs,

dwelling on roofless earth, pestered by the heat and clouds of mos-
quitoes, while men in soldiers' dress played the robber without fear or
shame. "The Blossom Capital became a scorched desert." The Choshiu
were utterly defeated, and driven out of the city. Thirty-seven of them
were decapitated in prison.

The next month the bakufu begged the imperial court to deprive
the Môri family and all its branches of their titles. Elated with success, an order was issued to all the clans to march to the chastisement
of the two provinces of Nagato and Suwo. The Tokugawa intended
thus to set an example to the wavering clans, and give proof of the
power it still possessed. During the same month, September 5th and
6th, 1864, Shimonoséki was bombarded by an allied fleet bearing the
flags of four foreign nations. After great destruction of life and property, the generous victors demanded an "indemnity" of three million
Mexican dollars. The brave clan, having defied the bakufu at Kiôto,
dared the prowess of the "civilized world," and stood to their guns at
Shimonoséki till driven away by overwhelming numbers of balls and
men, now prepared to face the combined armies of the shôgunate.

Then was revealed the result of the long previous preparation in the
South for war. The Chôshiu clansmen, united and alert, were lightly
dressed, armed with English and American rifles, drilled in European
tactics, and abundantly provided with artillery, which they fired rapidly and with precision. They had cast away armor, sword, and spear.
Chôshiu had long been the seat of Dutch learning, and translations
of Dutch military works were numerously made and used there. Their
disciplined battalions were recruited from the common people, not
from the samurai alone, were well paid, and full of enthusiasm. The
bakufu had but a motley, half-hearted army, many of whom, when the
order was given to march, straightway fell ill, having no stomach for the
fight. Some of the most influential clans declined or refused outright to

join the expedition, whose purpose was condemned by almost all the wisest leaders, notably by Katsu, the shôgun's adviser.

A campaign of three months, in the summer of 1866, ended in the utter and disgraceful defeat of the bakufu, and the triumph of Chôshiu. The clans not yet in the field refused to go to the front. The prestige of the shôgunate was now irretrievably ruined.

The young shôgun, worn out with ceaseless anxiety, died at Ôzaka, September 19th, 1866. He had secured the mikado's consent to the treaties, on the condition that they should be revised, and that Hiôgo should never be opened as a port of foreign commerce. He was succeeded by Keiki, his former rival, who was appointed head of the Tokugawa family by the court October, 1866. On the 6th of January, 1867, he was made shogun. He had repeatedly declined the position. He brought to it numerous private virtues, but only the firmness of a feather for the crisis at hand. The average Japanese lacks the stolidity and obstinacy of the Chinaman, and fickleness is supposed to be his chief characteristic. Keiki, as some of his once best friends say, was fickleness personified. If, with the help of counselors, he could make up his mind to one course of action, the keenest observers could never forecast the change liable to ensue when new advisers appeared. It is evident that the appointment of such a man at this crisis served only to precipitate the issue. His popularity at the court most probably arose from the fact that he was opposed to the opening of Hiôgo and Ôzaka to the foreigners.

In October, 1867, the Prince of Tosa openly urged the new shogun to resign; while many able samurai, Saigô, Ôkubo, Gotô, Kido, Hirozawa, Komatsu, backed by such men of rank as Shimadzu Saburô, and the ex-princes of Echizen, Uwajima, Hizen, and Tosa, urged the formation of the Government on the basis of the ante-shôgun era prior to 1200 A.D. They formed so powerful a combination that on the

9th of November, 1867, the vacillating Keiki, yielding to the force of public opinion, tendered his resignation as Sei-i Tai Shôgun.

This was a long step toward the ancient régime. Yet, as in Japan, whichever party or leader has possession of the mikado is master of the situation; and as the Aidzu clan, the most stanchly loyal to the Tokugawa family, kept guard at the gates of the imperial palace, it was still uncertain where the actual power would reside—whether in the Tokugawa clan, in the council of daimiôs, or, where it rightfully belonged, with the imperial court. The influential samurai of Satsuma, and Chôshiu, and the princes of Tosa, Echizen, and Uwajima were determined not to let the question hang in suspense. Gradually, small parties of the soldiers of the combination assembled in the capital. Saigô and Ôkubo, Kido, Gotô, and Iwakura, were too much in earnest to let the supreme opportunity slip. They began to stir up the court to take advantage of the critical moment, the mikado Koméi being dead, and, by a bold *coup d'etat*, abolish the office of shôgun and the bakufu, and re-establish the Government on the ancient basis, with the young emperor at the head.

On the 3d of January, 1868, the troops of the combination (Satsuma, Tosa, Echizen, Aki, and Owari) suddenly took possession of the palace gates. The court nobles hitherto surrounding the boy emperor were dismissed, and only those favoring the views of the combination were admitted to the palace. The court, thus purged, issued an edict in the name of the mikado, which stated that the government of the country was now solely in the hands of the imperial court. The bakufu and office of shôgun were abolished. A provisional government, with three grades of office, was formed, and the positions were at once filled by men loyal to the new rulers. The family of Môri was rehabilitated, and the seven banished nobles were recalled. Sanjô and Iwakura were made assistants to the supreme administrator, Arisugawa Miya, a prince of the blood.

The indignation of the retainers of Tokugawa knew no bounds. The vacillating shôgun now regretted his resignation, and wished himself back in power. He left Kiôto with the clans still loyal to him, with the professed intention of calming the passions of his followers, but in reality of seizing Ôzaka, and blocking up the communications of the Southerners. Shortly after, in Yedo, on the 19th of January, the yashikis of the Satsuma clan were stormed and burned by the bakufu troops. The Princes of Owari and Echizen were sent by the court to invite Keiki to join the new Government, and receive an appointment to office even higher than he had held before. He promised to do so, but no sooner were they gone than he yielded to Aidzu's warlike counsel to re-enter Kiôto in force, drive out the "bad counselors of the young emperor," and "try the issue with the sword." He was forbidden by the court to approach the city with a military following. Barriers were erected across the two roads leading to the capital, and the Southern clansmen, numbering about two thousand, posted themselves behind them, with artillery. Keiki set out from Ôzaka on the evening of the 27th of January, with the Aidzu and Kuwana clans in the front of his following, amounting to over ten, or, as some say, thirty thousand men. At Fushimi his messengers were refused passage through the barriers. The *kuan-gun* (loyal army, Kiôto forces) fired their cannon, and the war was opened. The shôgun's followers, by their last move on the political chess-board, had made themselves chôtéki. Their prestige had flown.

The battle lasted three days. In the presence of overwhelming forces, the Southern samurai showed not only undaunted valor, but the result of previous years of military training. The battle was not to the strong. It was to the side of intelligence, energy, coolness, and valor. The shôgun's army was beaten, and in wild disorder fled to Ôzaka, the historic castle of which was burned by the loyal army. The chief, unrecognized, found refuge upon an American vessel, and, reaching Yedo on one of his own ships, sought the seclusion of his castle. His own family retainers and most of the subject clans (fudai), and the daimiôs of Aidzu, Sendai, and others of the North and East, urged him to renew the fight and restore his prestige. One of his ministers earnestly begged him to commit *hara-kiri*, urging its necessity to preserve the honor of the Tokugawa clan. His exhortation being unsuccessful, the proposer solemnly opened his own bowels. With a large army, arsenals, munitions of war, and fleet of ships vastly exceeding those of the mikado, his chances of success were very fair. But this time the vassal was loyal, the waverer wavered no more. Refusing to listen to those who advised war, abhorring the very idea of being a chôtéki, he hearkened to the counsel of his two highest ministers, Katsu and Ôkubo Ichizô, and declaring that he would never take up arms against his lord, the mikado, he retired to private life. The comparison of this man with Washington because he refused to head an army, and thus save the country from a long civil war, does not seem to be very happy, though I have heard it made. Personally, Keiki is a highly accomplished gentleman, though ambitious and weak. Politically, he simply did his duty, and made discretion the better part of valor. It is difficult to see in him any exalted traits of character or evidences of genius; to Katsu and Ôkubo is due the last and best decision of his life. Katsu, the old pupil of Satsuma and comrade of Saigô, had long foreseen that the governing power must and ought of right to revert to the mikado, and, braving odium and assassination, he advised his master to resign. The victorious Southerners, led by Saigô, were in the southern suburb of Yedo, waiting to attack the city. To reduce a Japanese city needs but a torch, and the impatient victors would have left of Yedo little but ashes had there been resistance. Katsu, meeting Saigô, assured him of the submissive temper of the shôgun, and begged him to spare the city. It was done. The fanatical retainers of Keiki made the temple grounds of Uyéno their stronghold. On the 4th of July they were attacked and routed, and the magnificent temple, the pride of the city, laid in ashes. The theatre of war was then transferred to the highlands of Aidzu at Wakamatsu, and thence to Matsumaë and Hakodaté in Yezo. Victory everywhere perched upon the mikado's brocade banner. By July 1st, 1869, all vestiges of the rebellion had ceased, and "the empire was grateful for universal peace."

The mikado's party was composed of the heterogeneous elements which a revolution usually brings forth. Side by side with high-souled patriots were disreputable vagrants and scalawags of every description, rônins, or low, two-sworded men, *jo-i*, or "foreigner-haters," "port-closers," and Shintô priests and students. There were a few earnest men whose darling hope was to see a representative government established, while fewer yet eagerly wished Japan to adopt the civilization of the West, and join the brotherhood of nations. These men had utilized every current and eddy of opinion to forward their own views and achieve their own purpose. The object common to all was the exaltation of the mikado. The bond of union which held the majority together was a determination to expel the foreigners or to revise the treaties so as to expunge the odious extra-territoriality clause—the thorn that still rankles in the side of every Japanese patriot. For eighteen months the energies of the *jo-i*, or "foreigner-haters," were utilized in the camp in fighting the rebellious Tokugawa retainers. The war over, the trials of the new Government began. The low, two-sworded men clamored for the fulfillment of the promise that the foreigners should be expelled from Japan and the ports closed. The Shintô officials induced the Government to persecute the native "Christians," demanded the abolition of Buddhism, the establishment of Shintô by edict, and the restoration of the Government on a purely theocratic basis, and echoed the cry of "Expel the barbarian." Even with the majority of the high officials there was no abandonment of the purpose to expel foreigners.

They intended to do it, but the wisest of them knew that in their present condition they were not able. Hence they simply wished to bide their time, and gain strength. It was a matter of difficulty to keep patient thousands of swaggering braves whose only tools for earning bread were their swords. The first attention was given to reorganizing a national army, and to developing the military resources of the empire. All this was done with the cherished end in view of driving out the aliens, closing the ports of commerce, and bringing back the days of dictatorial isolation. The desire for foreign civilization existed rather among the adherents of Tokugawa, among whom were many enlightened gentlemen, besides students and travelers, who had been to Europe and America, and who wished their country to take advantage of the inventions of the foreigners. Yet many of the very men who once wished the foreigners expelled, the ports closed, the treaties repudiated, who were *jo-i*, or "foreigner-haters," and who considered all aliens as only a few degrees above the level of beasts, are now members of the mikado's Government, the exponents of advanced ideas, the defenders and executors of philo-Europeanism, or Western civilization.

What caused the change that came over the spirit of their dreams? Why do they now preach the faith they once destroyed? "It was the lessons taught them at Kagoshima and Shimonoséki," say some. "It was the benefits they saw would arise from commerce," say others. "The child of the revolution was changed at nurse, and the Government now in power was put into its cradle by mistake or design," say others.

Cannon-balls, commerce, and actual contact with foreigners doubtless helped the scales to fall from their eyes, but these were helps only. All such means had failed in China, though tried for half a century. They would have failed in Japan also. It was *an impulse from within* that urged the Japanese to join the comity of nations. The noblest trait in the character of a Japanese is his willingness to change for the better when he discovers his wrong or inferiority. This led the leaders to preach the faith they once destroyed, to destroy the faith they once preached.

The great work of enlightening the mikado's followers was begun by the Japanese leaders, Ôkubo, Kido, Gotô, all of them students, both of the ancient native literature and of foreign ideas. It was finished by Japanese writers. The kugé, or court nobles, wished to ignore the existence of foreigners, drive them out of the country, or worry them by appointing officers of low rank in the Foreign Office, then an inferior sub-bureau. Ôkubo, Gotô, and Kido promptly opposed this plan, and sent a noble of the imperial court, Higashi Kuzé, to Hiôgo with Datté, Prince of Uwajima, to give the mikado's consent to the treaties, and to invite the foreign ministers to an audience with the emperor in Kiôto. The British and Dutch ministers accepted the invitation; the others declined. The train of the British envoy was assaulted by fanatic assassins, one resisting bullet, lance, and sabre of the English dragoons, only to lose his head by the sweep of the sword of Goto, who rode by the side of the foreigners, determined to secure their audience of the mikado. At first sight of the strangers, the conversion of the kugé was thorough and instantaneous. They made friends with the men they once thought were beasts.

In a memorial to the mikado, Ôkubo further gave expression to his ideas in a memorial that astounded the court and the wavering daimiôs, as follows: "Since the Middle Ages, our emperor has lived behind a screen, and has never trodden the earth. Nothing of what went on outside his screen ever penetrated his sacred ear; the imperial residence was profoundly secluded, and, naturally, unlike the outer world. Not more than a few court nobles were allowed to approach the throne, a practice most opposed to the principles of heaven. Although it is the first duty of man to respect his superior, if he reveres that superior too highly he neglects his duty, while a breach is created between the sovereign and his subjects, who are unable to convey their wants to him. This vicious practice has been common in all ages. But now let pompous etiquette be done away with, and simplicity become our first object. Kiôto is in an out-of-the-way position, and is unfit to be the seat of government. Let his majesty take up his abode temporarily at Ôzaka, removing his capital hither, and thus cure one of the hundred abuses which we inherit from past ages."

The memorial produced an immediate and lively effect upon the court. The young mikado, Mutsuhito, came in person to the meetings of the council of state, and before the court nobles and daimios took an oath, as an actual ruler, promising that "a deliberative assembly should be formed; all measures be decided by public opinion; the uncivilized customs of former times should be broken through; and the impartiality and justice displayed in the workings of nature be adopted as a basis of action; and that intellect and learning should be sought for throughout the world, in order to establish the foundations of the empire." This oath is the basis of the new Government.

These promises are either the pompous bombast of a puppet or the pregnant utterances of a sovereign, who in magnanimity and wisdom aspires to lead a nation into a higher life. That such words should in that sublime moment fall from the lips of the chief of an Oriental despotism excites our sympathetic admiration. They seem a sublime echo of affirmation to the prophetic question of the Hebrew seer, "Can a nation be born at once?" They sound like a glad harbinger of a new and higher national development, such as only those with the strongest faith in humanity believe possible to an Asiatic nation. As matter of fact, the words were uttered by a boy of sixteen years, who scarcely dreamed of the tremendous significance of the language put into his mouth by the high-souled parvenus who had made him emperor *de facto*, and who were resolved to have their ideas made the foundations of the new Government. The result of the memorial, and the ceaseless activity of Ôkubo and his colleagues, was the ultimate removal of the Government to Yedo. It is not easy for a foreigner to comprehend the profound sensation produced throughout the empire when the mikado left Kiôto to make his abode in another city. During a millennium, Kiôto had been the capital of Dai Nippon, and for twenty-five centuries, according to popular belief, the mikados had ruled from some spot near the site of the sacred city. A band of fanatics, fired with the Yamato damashi, religiously opposed, but in vain, his journey eastward. To familiarize his people with the fact that Yedo was now the capital, its name was changed to Tôkiô, or Eastern Capital.

Then was further developed the impulse to enter the path of modern civilization. While Ôkubo, Kido, Gotô, Iwakura, Sanjô, Itagaki, Ôki, and the rising officials sought to purge and strengthen the political system, the work of enlightening the people and the upstarts raised suddenly to power was done by Japanese writers, who for the first time dared, without suffering death, to tell their thoughts. A large measure of freedom of the press was guaranteed; newspapers sprung up in the capital. Kido, one of the prime movers and leaders, himself established one of the most vigorous, still in existence—the *Shimbun Zasshi*. The new Government acted with clemency equal to the standard in Christian nations, and most generously to the literary and scientific men among the retainers of the Tokugawas, and invited them to fill posts of honor under the Government. They sent none of the political leaders to the blood-pit, but by the gracious favor of the mikado these were pardoned, and the conciliation of all sections of the empire wisely attempted. Many of those who fought the loyal forces at Fushimi, Wakamatsu, and Hakodaté are now the earnest advocates of the restoration and its logical issues. Even Enomoto is envoy of the court of Tôkiô to that of St. Petersburg. All of the defeated daimios were restored to rank and income. A complete and happy reunion of the empire was the result. Some of the scholars declined office until the time when even greater freedom of speech and pen was permitted.

There were men who in the old days, braving odium, and even death, at the hands of the bakufu, had begun the study of the English and Dutch languages, and to feed their minds at the Occidental fountains. They were obliged to copy their books in manuscript, so rare were printed copies. Later on, the bakufu, forced by necessity to have interpreters and men skilled in foreign arts and sciences, chose these students, and sent them abroad to study. When the civil war broke out, they were recalled, reaching Japan shortly after the fighting began. They returned, says one of their number, "with their faces flushed with enthusiastic sympathy with the modern civilization of Christendom." Then they began the preparation of those original works and translations, which were eagerly read by the new men in power. Edition after edition was issued, bought, read, lent, and circulated. In these books the history of the Western nations was faithfully told; their manners and customs and beliefs were explained and defended; their resources, methods of thought and education, morals, laws, systems of governments, etc., were described and elucidated. Notably pre-eminent among these writers was the school-master, Fukuzawa. Western ideas were texts: he clothed them in Japanese words. He further pointed out the weaknesses, defects, and errors of his countrymen, and showed how Japan, by isolation and the false pride that scorned all knowledge derived from foreigners, had failed to advance like Europe or America, and that nothing could save his country from conquest or decay but the assimilation of the ideas which have made the foreigners what they are. There is scarcely a prominent or rising man in Japan but has read Fukuzawa's works, and gratefully acknowledges the stimulus and lasting benefit derived from them. Many of the leaders of the movement toward restoration, who joined it with the cry, "Expel the foreigners," found themselves, after perusal of these works, "unconsciously involved in the advance, without wish or invitation," and utterly unable to explain why they were in the movement. Fukuzawa has declined every one of the many flattering offers of office and power under the Government, and still devotes himself to his school and the work of teaching and translation, consuming his life in noble drudgery. He has been the interpreter of Western ideas and life, caring little about the merely external garnish and glitter of civilization. His books on "Western Manners and Customs," and his volumes of tracts and essays, have had an enormous circulation.

Nakamura, also a school-master, has, besides writing original tracts, translated a considerable body of English literature, John Stuart Mill's "Essay on Liberty," Smiles's "Self-help," and a few smaller works on morals and religion, which have been widely read. His memorial on the subject of Christianity and religious liberty made a very profound impression upon the emperor and court, and gave a powerful check to the ultra Shintoists. Mori, Mitsukuri, Kato, Nishi, Uchida, Uriu, have also done noble service as authors and translators. It is the writer's firm belief, after nearly four years of life in Japan, mingling among the progressive men of the empire, that the reading and study of books printed in the Japanese language have done more to transform the Japanese mind, and to develop an impulse in the direction of modern civilization, than any other cause or series of causes.

During the past decade the production of purely Japanese literature has almost entirely ceased. A few histories of recent events, a few war-poems and pamphlets urging the expulsion of the barbarians, were issued previous to the civil war; but since then almost the entire literary activity has been exhibited in translations, political documents, memoirs of "mikado-reverencers" who had been martyrs to their faith, and largely in the expression of Western ideas adapted to the understanding of the Japanese.

The war was ended by July, 1870. Rewards were distributed; and the Government was still further consolidated by creating definite offices, and making all titles, which had been for nearly six centuries empty names, to have reality and power. There was still, however, much dead wood in the ship of state, a condition of chronic strain, a dangerous amount of friction in the machinery, wrangling among the crew, and a vast freight of bad cargo that the purest patriots saw the good ship must "unload," if she was to be saved. This unloading was accomplished in the usual way, by dismissing hundreds of officials one day, and re-appointing on the next only those favorable to the desired policy of the mikado.

Furthermore, it became daily more certain that national development and peace could never be secured while the feudal system existed. The clan spirit which it fostered was fatal to national unity. So long as a Japanese meant by "my country" merely his own clan, loyalty might exist, but patriotism could not. The time seemed ripe for action. The press was busy in issuing pamphlets advocating the abolition of feudalism. Several of the great daimiôs, long before ready for it, now openly advocated the change. The lesser ones knew better than to oppose it. The four great clans, Satsuma, Chôshiu, Tosa, and Hizen, were the pioneers of the movement. They addressed a memorial to the throne, in which it was argued that the daimiôs' fiefs ought not to be looked on as private property, but as the mikado's own. They offered to restore the registers of their clans to the sovereign. These were the external signs of the times. Back of these, there were at least three men who were determined to sweep feudalism away utterly. They were Kido, Ôkubo, Iwakura. The first step was to abolish the appellation of court noble (kugé) and territorial prince (daimiô), and to designate both as *kuazoku*, or noble families. The former heads of clans were temporarily appointed chiji (governors of their clans). This smoothed the way. In September, 1871, the edict went forth calling the daimiôs to Tôkiô to retire to private life. With scarcely an exception, the order was quietly obeyed. The men behind the throne in Tôkiô were ready and even willing to shed blood, should their (the mikado's) commands be resisted, and they expected to do it. The daimiôs who were hostile to the measure knew too well the character of the men who framed the edict to resist it. The writer counts among the most impressive of all his life's experiences that scene in the immense castle hall of Fukui, when the Daimiô of Echizen bid farewell to his three thousand two-sworded retainers, and, amidst the tears and smiles and loving farewells of the city's populace, left behind him lands, revenue, and obedient followers, and retired to live as a private gentleman in Tôkiô.

Japan's feudalism began nearly eight centuries ago, and existed until within the year 1871. It was not a tower of strength in its last days. Long before its fall, it was an empty shell and a colossal sham. Feudalism is only alive and vigorous when the leaders are men of brain and action. Of all the daimiôs, there were not ten of any personal importance. They were amiable nobodies, great only in stomach or silk robes. Many were sensualists, drunkards, or titled fools. The real power in each clan lay in the hands of able men of inferior rank, who ruled their masters. *These are now the men who compose the present Government of Japan.* They rose against the shôgun, overthrew him, sent him to private life, and then compelled their masters, the daimiôs, to do likewise. They hold the emperor, and carry on the government in his name. The mikado, however, is much more of a ruler than his *fainéant* ancestors. Still, the source of government is the same. In 1872, by actual count, four-fifths of the men in the higher offices were of the four great clans of Chôshiu, Satsuma, Hizen, and Tosa. A like census in 1876 would show a larger proportion of officials from the northern and central provinces. Nevertheless, this is not sectionalism. The ablest men rise to office and power in spite of the locality of their birth. Natural ability asserts its power, and in the Cabinet and departments are now many of the old bakufu adherents, even Katsu, Ôkubo Ichizô, Enomoto, and several scions of the house of Tokugawa. The power has been shifted, not changed, and is displayed by moving new machinery and doing new work.

Who are now, and who have been, the actual leaders in Japan since 1868? They are Ôkubo, Kido, Iwakura, Sanjô, Gotô, Katsu, Soyéjima, Ôkuma, Ôki, Ito, and many others, of whom but two or three are kugé, while none is a daimiô. Almost all were simple samurai, or retainers of the territorial nobles.

The objects of the revolution of 1868 have been accomplished. The shôgunate and the feudal system are forever no more. The mikado is now the restored and beloved emperor. The present personage, a young man of twenty-four years of age, has already shown great independence and firmness of character, and may in future become as much the real ruler of his people as the Czar is of his. The enterprise of establishing Shintô as the national faith has failed vastly and ignominiously, though the old Shintô temples have been purged and many new ones erected, while official patronage and influence give the ancient cult a fair outward show. Buddhism is still the religion of the Japanese people, though doubtless on the wane.

To summarize this chapter: the shôgun was simply one of the many vassals of the mikado of comparatively inferior grade, and historically a usurper; the term "tycoon" was a diplomatic fraud, a title to which the shôgun had, officially, not the shadow of right; the foreign diplomatists made treaties with one who had no right whatever to make them; the bakufu was an organized usurpation; the stereotyped statements concerning a "spiritual" and a "secular" emperor are literary fictions of foreign book-makers; feudalism arose upon the decadence of the mikado's power; it was the chief hinderance to national unity, and was ready for its fall before the shock came; in all Japanese history the reverence for the mikado's person and the throne has been the strongest national trait and the mightiest political force; the bakufu exaggerated the mikado's sacredness for its own purposes; the Japanese are impressible and ever ready to avail themselves of whatever foreign aids or appliances will tend to their own aggrandizement: nevertheless, there exists a strong tendency to conserve the national type, pride, feelings, religion, and equality with, if not superiority to, all the nations of the world; the true explanation of the events of the last eight years in Japan is to be sought in these tendencies and the internal history of the nation; the shôgun, bakufu, and perhaps even feudalism would have fallen, had foreigners never landed in Japan; the movement toward modern civilization originated from within, and was not simply the result of foreign impact or pressure; the work of enlightenment and education, which alone could assure success to the movement, was begun and carried on by native students, statesmen, and simple patriots.

A mighty task awaited the new Government after the revolution of 1868. It was to heal the disease of ages; to uproot feudalism and sectionalism, with all their abuses; to give Japan a new nationality; to change her social system; to infuse new blood into her veins; to make a hermit nation, half blinded by a sudden influx of light, competitor with the wealthy, powerful, and aggressive nations of Christendom. It was a problem of national regeneration or ruin. It seemed like entering into history a second time, to be born again.

What transcendent abilities needed for such a task! What national union, harmony in council, unselfish patriotism required! What chief, towering above his fellows, would arise, who by mighty intellect and matchless tact could achieve what Yoritomo, or the Taikô, or Iyéyasu himself, or all, would be helpless to perform? At home were the stolidly conservative peasantry, backed by ignorance, superstition, priestcraft, and political hostility. On their own soil they were fronted by aggressive foreigners, who studied all Japanese questions through the spectacles of dollars and cents and trade, and whose diplomatists too often made the principles of Shylock their system. Outside, the Asiatic nations beheld with contempt, jealousy, and alarm the departure of one of their number from Turanian ideas, principles, and civilization. China, with ill-concealed anger, Corea with open defiance, taunted Japan with servile submission to the "foreign devils."

For the first time, the nation was represented to the world by an embassy at once august and plenipotentiary. It was not a squad of petty officials or local nobles going forth to kiss a toe, to play the part of figure-heads or stool-pigeons, to beg the aliens to get out of Japan, to keep the scales on foreign eyes, to buy gun-boats, or to hire employés. A noble of highest rank and blood of immemorial antiquity, vicar of majesty and national government, with four cabinet ministers, set out to visit the courts of the fifteen nations having treaties with Dai Nippon. These were Iwakura Tomomi, Ôkubo Toshimiti, Kido Takayoshi, Ito Hirobumi, and Yamaguchi Masaka. They were accompanied by commissioners representing every Government department, sent to study and report upon the methods and resources of foreign civilizations. They arrived in Washington, February 29th, 1872, and, for the first time in history, a letter signed by the mikado was seen outside of Asia. It was presented by the embassadors, robed in their ancient Yamato costume, to the President of the United States, on the 4th of March, Mr. Arinori Mori acting as interpreter. "The first president of the free republic" and the men who had elevated the eta to citizenship stood face to face in fraternal accord. The one hundred and twenty-third sovereign of an empire in its twenty-sixth centennial saluted the citizen-ruler of a nation whose century aloe had not yet bloomed. On the 6th of March they were welcomed on the floor of Congress. This day marked the formal entrance of Japan upon the theatre of universal history.

# *Japan in 1883*

O ur record of events in the last chapter closed with a notice of the treaty made with Corea, February 27th, 1876, a diplomatic triumph which so silenced the disaffected, and so strengthened the power of the Government, that immediate advantage was taken of it to disarm the samurai. In response to a public sentiment already grown strong, and especially to the memorial of December 7th, 1875, from Yamagata, the Minister of War, the Premier Sanjô, on the 28th of March, 1876, issued a proclamation abolishing the custom of wearing two swords: "No individual will henceforth be permitted to wear a sword unless he be in court dress, a member of the military or naval forces, or a police officer." This measure, first advocated by Arinori Mori, in 1870, now became law throughout the land—even in Satsuma.

The Coreans responded promptly to their treaty obligations. A Japanese steamer was sent to Fusan; and the embassy from Séoul, numbering eighty persons in all, landed at Yokohama May 29th, the ambassador receiving audience of the mikado June 1st. These Coreans were the first accredited to Japan since 1835, and none had come as far east as Yedo since the last century. Then they were the guests of the shôgun; but now direct official relations with the mikado were resumed, after a lapse of nearly a millennium. These men, in huge hats, and white, blue, and pink cotton or silk robes, were profusely entertained in Tôkiô. They visited the public buildings, schools, founderies, and arsenals, inspecting the curious things of the nineteenth century, but avoiding all white foreigners as though they were reptiles, and embarked for home June 18th.

Meanwhile the mikado, accompanied by several members of his cabinet, set out on a tour overland to Yezo. No emperor of Japan had ever visited the northern provinces, and the delight of the people at seeing their sovereign was intense. Visiting Nikkô and the castled towns along the route, the emperor made himself everywhere visible, allowing no check to be placed upon the business or behavior of the people, except that which their own sense of respect imposed. Among the excellent fruits of this tour were: the erection of a monument to the patriot Rin Shihei;* the making public of the documents and relics of Father Louis Sotelo;† and the gracious reception of an address to his majesty from the Greek Church Christians of Sendai, which augured the near future of complete religious toleration. The

---

* Rin Shihei, a native of Sendai—whose work *San Koku Tsuran Dzu-setsu* (*General View of the Three Kingdoms [tributary to Japan]*, i.e., *Corea, Yezo, and Riu Kiu*), was printed in 1785, and translated by Klaproth in 1832—was born in 1737. A far-seeing patriot, he studied military strategy while making pedestrian excursions over the whole of Japan, especially along the coast, and by learning from the Dutch at Nagasaki and the Russians in Yezo. He was keenly alive to the subject of national progress and defense. His maps and books fell under the eye of the censors (p. 323) of the shôgun, who ordered the plates of his publications to be destroyed, and had him thrown into prison, from which he never came out alive.

† Father Louis Sotelo was a Spanish Franciscan friar, who, with Hashikura Rokuyémon, a retainer of the daimiô of Sendai, sailed across the Pacific in a Japanese ship (p. 266) to Mexico in 1613, and thence reached Seville and Rome. They had audience of Pope Paul V., and Hashikura was made a Roman senator. They returned by way of Mexico to Japan; but Hashikura was compelled to renounce his faith, and Sotelo was martyred at Nagasaki. (See Hildreth's *Japan*, pp. 158,199.)

imperial journey, begun June 2d, was continued until the middle of July. His return to the capital amid many demonstrations of popular joy was soon after signalized by another bold stroke of power. On the 5th of August the measure, long before conceived, of extinguishing the hereditary pensions and life-incomes of the samurai, was proclaimed. Commutation in Government bonds, at from five to fourteen years' purchase, was made obligatory upon all. The scheme provided that the largest incomes should be extinguished first, and, when completed, will relieve the national Treasury of an annual burden of about $20,000,000. This act of the Government, which lightened the enforced poverty of thirty millions of people, and compelled the privileged classes to begin to earn their bread, was warmly welcomed by the masses.

On the 21st of August another measure in the interest of public economy and of centralization was carried out: the empire was redivided, and the sixty-eight *ken* or prefectures were reduced in number to thirty-five.

These radical measures enforced by the mikado's advisers—an irresponsible ministry, possessing slight facilities for adequately gauging public opinion—were not executed without protest within and without the cabinet. In the south-west, especially, were many earnest men, narrow and unprogressive, perhaps, who grieved deeply over the decay of old customs, the secularization of the Divine Country, the arbitrary policy and personal extravagance of "the bad councillors of the emperor," and his "imprisonment" by them, the influence of foreigners, the toleration of Christianity, and the loss of their swords and pensions. Among the leaders of these conservatives were Mayébara and Uyéno—the one a discharged office-holder, and the other a man of seventy—whose followers organized clubs named Jimpû (Divine Breath, or Wind) and Sonnô-Jôi (Reverence to the Mikado, and Expulsion of the Barbarian).

On the 24th of October a party of nearly two hundred of these fanatics, dressed in beetle-headed iron helmets and old armor made of steel and paper laced with silk, and armed with spears and swords, attacked the imperial garrison at Kumamoto, in Higo. They succeeded in injuring about three hundred of the troops before they were dispersed, taken prisoners, or had disemboweled themselves. Other uprisings, more easily quelled, took place in Kiushiu; while in Chôshiu, Mayébara led five hundred armed men vainly against the new order of things, in which rifles, cannon, telegraphs, and steamers played their part. As by some new Jove, with hands full of thunderbolts, these Titans of a later day were transfixed by the lightnings hurled from Tôkiô in the form of steamers and rifled artillery. Quiet was entirely restored by December. A few heads were struck off, hundreds of the *chôtéki* were exiled or degraded, and another of the throes of expiring feudalism was over.

The next insurrections were by men equipped in calico, with rush hats and straw sandals, gathered under banners of matting inscribed with mottoes daubed on in ink, and armed with spears made by pointing and fire-hardening staves of bamboos. These embattled farmers were enraged because the taxes had been changed from kind to money, and, instead of being assessed on the produce, were laid on the soil. Assaulting the local magistrates' offices, they had to be dispersed by the military, in some cases only after bloodshed. Time, good roads, banking facilities, clearer understanding of the purpose of the Government, have already changed temporary distress, caused by innovations, into satisfied prosperity.

These violent expressions of the real grievances of the agricultural class, on whom the burdens of taxation mainly fall—three-fourths, or $50,000,000, of the total revenue of the empire ($69,000,000), being drawn from the tax on land—hastened another beneficial reform. On the 4th of January, 1877, the national land-tax was reduced from three to two and a half per cent.—a loss to the Treasury of about $8,000,000. The local tax, formerly amounting to one-third of the land-tax, was reduced to one-fifth, or nearly one-half. About the same time two other sweeping measures of economy, intended as an offset, were carried out. Besides thus directly relieving the people, the salaries of nearly all the Government officers and the expenses of the departments were reduced, several thousand office-holders were discharged, the Department of Religion (Kiô Bu Shô) and the Prefecture of Police were abolished, and their functions transferred to the Home Department, and a saving of about $8,000,000 annually effected, to balance the loss to the Treasury from reform in the tax on land. Such a movement in official circles, popularly called a *jishin* (earthquake), met with the keen satisfaction of the majority, the joy of the citizens and peasantry being "beyond imagination." The Government now began to be less afraid of Satsuma; less careful, also, perhaps, to keep informed of the state of public opinion, since the press laws were excessively stringent, and there was no safety-valve for discontent.

The year 1876 will ever remain memorable as the critical year in Japanese journalism, when the severity of the press laws and Government prosecutions was more than equaled by the courage, firmness, and patience of a noble army of editors and writers, who crowded the jails of Japan, and joyfully suffered fines and imprisonment in order to secure a measure of "the freedom of the press"—a phrase which is the watch-word of liberty, not only in Europe and America, but among the Japanese also, in whose language it has become domesticated in common speech, like the new words which science, religion, and advancing political knowledge require for their expression.

Closely connected with all measures of genuine reform is the name of Kido, "the finest intellect" and "the brain and pen" of the revolution. While other leaders were eager and able to break down, Kido was pre-eminently the builder-up, and his genius essentially constructive.

Himself the purest representative of the mind of Japan, he had applied the logic of the cardinal doctrines of Japanese politics—the divine right of the mikado to govern his people—and feudalism fell. He believed in discussion, in the wisdom of the majority, and so he established newspapers and pleaded for representative assemblies. He incarnated the soul of peaceful progress. He opposed alike the Corean and Formosan war projects, and the too rapid capitalization of the samurai's pensions. He applied himself to master the details of local administration, and carefully studied the problems of taxation and municipal procedure, both at home and in Europe and America. To rare political ability he joined an unselfish patriotism and a stainless record. Amidst all the clash of opposing interests which the destruction of the old and the creation of new institutions called out the voice of Kido was ever authoritative. While Ôkubo represented the foreign side of the revolution, and Saigô the military genius of Old Nippon, Kido embodied in himself the best elements of New Japan. He had been especially earnest and influential in bringing about the reforms in taxation and governmental economy, and in the calling together of a deliberative body of the *ken* and *fu* magistrates, which, meeting in Tôkiô in 1875, was opened by the mikado in person, and presided over by himself. He was now hoping to conciliate the disaffected samurai of Kiushiu and the one man whom they trusted, after having been, as they believed, betrayed by Ôkubo and the irresponsible ministers in Tôkiô. Had Kido lived, the sad and costly civil war might not have broken out. In the moment of his country's greatest need this noble patriot, over-wearied and wounded in spirit, was seized with a disease which soon made him understand that his work was nearly over. He died at Kiôto, May 27th, 1877.

Ever since 1868 Satsuma had remained the one portion of the empire unassimilated to the life of progressive Japan. The old clan which of old had awed the Yedo shôguns now terrified the rest of the country. Goaded by hatred and long-cherished revenge, the Satsuma men, without any sympathy with the nation at large, had led in the overthrow of their enemies, the Tokugawas. The political education of most of the clansmen was purely feudal. Their compass of duty, vibrating between reverence to the mikado and hatred to barbarians, pointed to personal loyalty as their lodestar. Anything broader in scope than the old elements of Japanese politics—loyalty to their chief, clan-fights, struggles between rival factions for the person of the mikado, the reign of the sword held by the idle and privileged classes, the grinding of the peasantry, and the expulsion or subordination of foreigners—in a word, the virtues and the vices of feudalism—was not within their horizon. As for Saigô, their leader, with all the qualities in his character so attractive to a japanese, he lacked genuine patriotism, and probably aspired to be simply another "man on horseback," furnishing to history one more illustration of the Japanese variety of Cæsarism. Had not this ninth decade of the nineteenth century been one of steam and electricity, instead of armor and arrows, the Tôkiô ministers might have kneeled at the blood-pit as *chôtéki* while Saigô dictated to Dai Nippon as Sei-i Tai Shôgun. Providence meant it otherwise. The old style of Japanese Cæsarism was over.

After the revolution large numbers of Satsuma men had been appointed to posts of honor in the army, navy, and police force, while Saigô and Shimadzu Saburô were offered seats in the Cabinet; but one after another the liberal political measures were carried out against the sentiments of men steeped in the vices of feudalism. Peace with Corea, commutation of pensions, the abolition of swords, and the contempt cast upon the wearing of the top-knot—as significant of the feudal spirit to a Japanese of the old school as a Pawnee's war-lock is to the red rider of the prairie—were too much for both Saigô and Shimadzu. The former, retiring to Kagoshima, founded a military school, which was soon attended by the flower of Satsuma's youth, while nearly twenty thousand men in Satsuma and Ôzumi, living with their faces to the past, looked to Saigô as their master. The writer cherishes very vivid remembrances of walking unarmed in Tôkiô, and meeting face to face in narrow streets these fiery men of the old swashbuckler spirit. With their hair shorn off their temples, a general wildness of expression in their faces, a scowl of mingled defiance and contempt in their eyes, with their protruding swords and long red-lacquered scabbards, they seemed the incarnation of fanatical patriotism and diabolical pride. Their favorite proverb was, "Though the eagle be starving, he will not eat grain," and rather than earn their living by vulgar trade, and accept the new order of things, they would gratify their thirst for blood. So great was the influence and prestige of Satsuma, that the impression became general throughout the country that the Government was afraid of this one sullen clan. What lent additional danger to the situation was, that a large arsenal, equipped with steam machinery and full of military stores, together with two powder-mills, capable of turning out thirty thousand pounds of powder daily, stood near the city of Kagoshima.

Hitherto all revolts against the imperial authority had been minor and sporadic, and led by men of no special fitness for their task. That which we shall now describe was organized by the ablest military mind, backed by the best fighting blood in the empire. Had the Government remained inert much longer, the plans of Saigô would have been matured, and with ampler resources the issue might have been different, or the struggle prolonged to the ruin of the nation.

Wisely the rulers in Tôkiô resolved to precipitate the crisis, or at least unmask Saigô's designs, and a vessel was sent to Kagoshima, in January, 1877, under Admiral Kawamura, to remove the gunpowder. An attack threatened upon it by boats full of armed men was avoided by the admiral, but the arsenals and powder-mills were seized February 1st, 1877, by a body of two thousand five hundred samurai. At this time the mikado and most of his Cabinet were in Kiôto, whence they had come to inaugurate the opening of the railway between

Kôbé, Ôzaka, and Kiôto, which was celebrated on the 5th of February. At once recognizing the gravity of the situation, they dispatched the flower of the army and police to Kiushiu in steamers. All doubts as to Saigô's personal participation in the uprising were set at rest by his appearing before Kumamoto castle, to which he laid siege.

The Island of the Nine Provinces was ordered to be placed under martial law, and Saigô, now named Saigô Takamori, was degraded from his rank as Marshal of the Empire, and Prince Arisugawa no Miya was appointed to the supreme command. Saigô and his generals, Kirino, Beppu, and Shinohara, were branded as *chôtéki*, but Shimadzu Saburô remained loyal. The insurgent ports were blockaded, and fresh levies of troops were made and hurried forward. After a siege of fifty-five days, during which Kumamoto castle was nobly defended by Colonel Tani and his little band, Saigô was compelled to retreat.

The war soon became scattered. The imperial army, under Yamagata and Kawaji, marched in two large divisions from Kumamoto and Kagoshima, intending to inclose the rebels in a cordon. After many bloody skirmishes and a great battle, the two divisions effected a junction. Saigô Tsukumichi, a brother of the rebel leader, took the field in July, during which month, owing to the hard fighting, six thousand of the mikado's troops were killed or wounded. While the imperialists were largely raw levies from the peasantry and middle classes, the rebels were in the main the veteran samurai of 1868. Even their women fought under the rebel banner. Defending themselves in some instances by making a shield of the light, thick floor-mats, or *tatami*, the rebel swordsmen, by a sudden charge, drew the fire of the troops harmlessly, and rushing on them with their swords butchered them easily.

On the 16th of August, Saigô Takamori's forces, reduced to less than ten thousand men, were attacked at Nobéoka, an old natural stronghold, and the bloody conflict resulted in a complete victory for the imperialists. With a few hundred followers the rebel leaders escaped into Hiuga, whence, on the 2d of September, they made a dash on Kagoshima, and held it two weeks. Thence they were driven out to Shiroyama, a few miles from the city. There, on the 24th of September, Saigô, Kirino, and Murata, having less than four hundred followers, were attacked by fifteen thousand troops of the imperial army, with mortars, cannon, and rifles. Armed only with swords, the little band fought, scorning quarter. Many of them committed *hara-kiri*, and Saigô was beheaded by one of his friends, who as a favor performed this act of kindness. Not one of the imperial soldiers was killed. The three leaders and nearly three hundred of the band gladly met their death with unquailing courage, proud to die in blood by their own or at their comrades' hands, knowing no greater glory than to imitate Kusunoki and the ancient models of that ferocious military virtue of Old Japan— *Yamato damashii*.

This was the mightiest rebellion, inspired by the spirit of the past, against which the mikado's Government has had to cope. It was the supreme effort of defiance of the forces of feudalism and misrule against order and united government. The Old met the New— mediævalism was pitted against the nineteenth century, and failed. "What Saigô could not achieve, no imitator will presume to attempt." The rebellion cost Japan fifty millions of dollars. The rebel troops of Satsuma, Ôzumi, and Hiuga numbered 39,760, of whom 3,533 men were killed, 4,344 wounded, and 3,123 missing. Of the imperial army, probably an equal number or more suffered the fate of war, a very large proportion of wounds being cuts from the old two-handed sword-blades. In the cities and villages of Japan, once quite free from the sight of legless and armless men and the results of gunshot wounds, the spectacle of empty sleeves, of men hobbling on crutches, and of bullet-scarred victims of gunpowder wars, is no longer a rarity. In the treatment of the rebels the Government displayed a spirit of leniency unknown to Asia, and worthy of the Christian name. Of the 38,163 persons tried in Kiushiu, there were 295 acquitted, 35,918 pardoned, 20 fined, 117 degraded from the class of samurai, 1,793 condemned to imprisonment, with hard labor, for terms varying from thirty days to ten years. Twenty persons were decapitated.

Notwithstanding the war in the south, the enterprises of peace went on. The National Industrial Exhibition at Uyéno, on the site of the battle-ground of 1868 (p. 345), which was closely modeled upon the Centennial Exposition at Philadelphia, was opened August 21st, and closed November 30th, and was in every respect successful. During this time the cholera broke out in Japan, but by the stringent enforcement of sanitary measures its ravages were slight. Out of 11,675 cases, there were but 6,297 deaths—a victory of science no less renowned than that of the army at Nobéoka.

The year 1878 marked the first decade of the mikado's government by means of an irresponsible ministry. The oath made by His Majesty in Kiôto in 1868 to form a deliberative assembly had never been fully carried out. The earnest men in office were perhaps too busy to remind the mikado of his promise; but the equally earnest men outside, continually advancing in political knowledge, and seeing one cause of the troubles that afflicted the nation in the official ignorance of public sentiment, had lost no opportunity to make their convictions known. By agitation in the newspapers, by memorials to the Government, by public lectures, the subject was pressed. One or two steps had been taken. In 1875 a Senate (Genrô-in, or House of Eders) had been established, and an assembly of the ken governors—the creation of Kido—held one session in the capital, but only one. Under the pretext of the mikado's journey north in 1876, and of the war in Kiushiu in 1877, the meetings of this body had been adjourned, greatly to the irritation of those who clamored for it as a national right, and complained both of the excess of personal government, and of the flagrant defiance of popular rights as based on the mikado's oath.

Yet, more rapidly than the petitioners dreamed, the era of personal government was drawing to a close; and, as usual in Japanese politics, the new era was to be ushered in by assassination. Ôkubo was murdered in the public highway in broad daylight May 14th, 1878.

Within one year Japan lost her three ablest men—Kido, Saigô, and Ôkubo. Of all these, Ôkubo, by temperament, training, and character, was best fitted to be the interpreter of foreign ideas to his colleagues. Resolute, daring, ambitious, his will was iron and his action lightning. His burning desire, to raise his country from the low level of semi-civilized states to the height of equality with the proudest nations of the earth, created in him a ceaseless energy, that showed itself in a long list of reforms with which his name is inseparably associated. He expected almost to see his country regenerated in a life-time. His chief idea was the thorough unification of Japan, and the extirpation of all vestiges of the feudal spirit and of sectionalism. He believed that a railway built from Yezo to Kiushiu, even if it paid no dividend for a thousand years, would be of incalculable advantage to the country in unifying the people. In order to hasten the growth of a century in a decade, he considered, perhaps too blindly, a strongly centralized Government to be of the first necessity, and in this opinion he was seconded by his colleagues of like mind.*

Hence the error of these able men in not estimating at its proper value the equally eager desire of men outside the Government to take

---

* I remember, while present at a dinner given by the junior Prime Minister, Iwakura, at his house in Tôkiô (July 16th, 1874), an American lady asked him what had impressed him most while in America, and especially at Washington. He answered at once, "The strength of the central Government, which for a republic seemed incredible to me."

part in the tasks of civilization. Kido had warned them not to cling too closely to the traditions of paternal government, and the charge began to be made that Ôkubo was an enemy to public discussion and popular rights. Again the assassin's sword cast its shadow.

On the evening of May 13th, 1878, having been warned of the impending danger, Ôkubo expressed before a party of friends his belief in the decree of Heaven, that would protect him if his work were not yet done, but which otherwise would permit his death, even though he were surrounded by soldiers. His words were prophetic. He spoke better than he knew. His work—the work of personal government—was over; the era of representative government had begun. The next morning, while on his way to the mikado's palace, unarmed, he was murdered by six assassins, who were said to have been runaways from the Satsuma rebellion. The mikado immediately conferred upon his dead servant the highest rank, and elevated his sons to the nobility. The funeral cortege, in which princes, nobles, and the foreign diplomatic corps joined, was the most imposing ever seen in Tôkiô.*

The long step forward toward representative institutions was taken July 22d, by the proclamation for the calling of Provincial Parliaments, or Local Assemblies, composed of one delegate from each district

---

* Ôkubo's tall, arrowy form, luxuriant side-whiskers, large, expressive eyes, and eager, expectant bearing, gave him the appearance of a European rather than an Asiatic. When in Tôkiô I enjoyed frequent conversations with this distinguished statesman, the last of which was on the eve of leaving Japan for America (July 16th, 1874), during which Ôkuko asked many questions about American politics. When about to leave I informed him of my intention to write a work on Japan, explaining as best I could the recent revolutions, that Americans might understand their true nature. Ôkubo's piercing black eyes shone with pleasure for a moment, but immediately a shadow passed over his handsome face, and he said, "Your purpose is an excellent one. I am glad, and even grateful, that you intend to explain our affairs to your countrymen, but I wish that some one would write an instantly popular book explaining to our own people the intentions of the Government. Too many of them refuse to understand."

(*kori*), which were to sit once a year in each ken. Under the supervision of the Minister of the Interior, these bodies are empowered to discuss questions of local taxation, and to petition the central government on other matters of local interest. The qualifications for members and electors are limited by ability to read and write, and the payment of an annual land-tax of at least five dollars. Each registered voter, who must be twenty years of age, must himself write his own name and the name of the candidate voted for on a ballot. In this one respect the Japanese excels the American method. The foundations for further improvements were now broadly based.

To anticipate, and pass over details, except to notice the constant agitation kept up by new engines in Japanese politics—the press, the lecture platform, and the debating club—the mikado, yielding to the irresistible pressure of public opinion, expanded and confirmed his oath of 1868, in the famous proclamation of October 12th. 1881: "We therefore hereby declare, that We shall in the 23d year of Meiji (1890) establish a Parliament, in order to carry into full effect the determination We have announced ["gradually to establish a constitutional form of government"], and We charge our faithful subjects bearing our commissions to make, in the mean time, all necessary preparations to that end. With regard to the limitations upon the Imperial Prerogative, and the constitution of the Parliament, We shall decide hereafter, and shall make proclamation in due time."

Three political parties in Japan are now distinctly organized, each with its newspapers, clubs, mass meetings, and peripatetic lecturers, or "stump-speakers." They are the Constitutional Monarchists, Liberals, and Constitutional Reformers, with minor cliques representing various phases of radicalism or conservatism. Local societies cherishing socialistic, communistic, and even nihilist principles add to the variety of opinions now distinguishable in a once hermit nation, whose entire stock of political knowledge, a generation ago, consisted of the two ideas of personal loyalty and hatred of foreigners. As a Japanese writer remarked in the *Jiyu Shimbun*—the organ of the liberals—"The impulse of progress and innovation has invaded the nation with the strength of a rushing torrent. A totally new Japanese empire is in process of establishment."

Let us now glance at Japan's foreign policy and state-craft. With the Restoration of 1868 was born the desire to thoroughly consolidate the empire, and bring its outlying portions into closer relations to the throne. Some students of history will also say that the long-slumbering lust of conquest awoke to new vigor. A school of Japanese thinkers claimed that the fullest expression of nationality would include not only Riu Kiu, Yezo, Saghalin, and the Bonin Islands, as constituent portions, but also Corea and Eastern Formosa, as tributary dependencies—the last claim being based on Japanese settlement, as well as lack of Chinese jurisdiction. The solution of the Formosan and Corean problems was, as we have seen, soon reached. The Bonin Islands, first held in fief by Ogasawara, a daimiô, in 1593, and visited by a party of explorers from Nagasaki in 1675, who gave the name Munin, or Bonin (no man's), had been neglected by the Japanese for centuries, though long a noted resort of whalers. In 1823 the American Captain Coffin, and in 1827 Captain Beechy, an Englishman, visited the islands; and Commodore M. C. Perry, in 1854, stocked them with sheep, goats, and cattle. In 1877 there were on the islands a motley company of seventy persons, chiefly sailors from whaling-ships, Americans, Englishmen, and Hawaiians. In 1878 the islands were formally taken possession of in the name of the mikado, and a local government established by Japanese officers. Coffin Island will probably be the terminus of the proposed trans-Pacific submarine cable from San Francisco to Yokohama.

Saghalin and the Kurile Islands had been the debatable ground between the Japanese and Russians since 1790, the subject of conferences and mutual remonstrances, and the scene of some border-ruffianism and bloodshed. In 1875 Admiral Enomoto, at St. Petersburg, concluded a convention by which Japan received all the Kurile Islands, or Chi-shima, and Russia the whole of Saghalin. The Kuriles are rich sealing and fishing grounds, and Saghalin is now a flourishing penal settlement. The empire of Japan, as seen on the map of the world, now swings, by a long chain of islands at either end, between Kamschatka and Formosa.

The island of Yezo was placed under the care of a special ministry —the Kai Taku Shi, or Department for the Development of Yezo—and so administered until the year 1882. Its mineral and agricultural wealth, as exploited by American scientific men, is noted in the Appendix to this work. Many millions of dollars were spent in developing Yezo, under the oversight of Kuroda Kiyotaka—the negotiator of the Corean treaty, and a military leader of no mean abilities, as shown in the civil wars of 1868 and 1877. On January 11th, 1882 General Kuroda was appointed Cabinet Adviser, and the property and industrial undertakings of the department were sold—a proceeding which provoked a furious controversy among the political societies. On the 8th of February, Yezo was divided into the three ken, or prefectures, of Hakodaté, Némuro, and Sapporo, and governed like the rest of the empire.

Before examining into the matter of Riu Kiu let us glance at Corea, with which a more vigorous policy was determined upon immediately after the Satsuma rebellion. A legation was established in Séoul, and Hanabusa, one of the ablest of Japan's rising young men, appointed minister. In the Coreans the Japanese saw themselves as they had been—hermits in the market-place—and many of the foreigners' experiences with them before the opening of their ports were repeated in Corea, the Japanese in this case being the aliens and reputed aggressors. A fresh treaty opened Gensan (Corean, Wönsan), on the north-east coast, May 1st, 1880, and three months later a second embassy of portly

Corean men, in red, pink, green, violet, and azure visited Tôkiô, to pray that the opening of the port of In-chiun, near Séoul, be postponed. The Japanese refused their request. The Coreans were now divided into conservatives and radicals, or progressives and reactionists. Even among the liberals some favored friendship with and imitation of Japan, while others looked to China as ally and model. One view of the Japanese which gained ground in Corea, especially in 1881, was, that the Japanese were arbitrary and high-handed in their dealing, and an Exclusion-of-the-Japanese Party began to form. Evidently the same state of feeling characteristic of Old Japan existed in Corea, in which all the elements of a political explosion lay ready. To blind hatred of all foreigners there was added a conservative bigotry willing to fan popular passions and superstition into a flame, while of two great feudal houses in bitter hostility to each other, one was in, and the other out of power.

A third party, or embassy, composed of Corean liberals anxious to study civilization and progress in the neighbor-country, came to Japan in 1881. At this time it was uncertain whether the reactionists or progressives would sway the policy of the Séoul government. The young king, who had come to the throne in 1873, was backed in his enlightened policy by his consort and her relatives, the king's ministers; but arrayed against them were the Tai-wen Kun, the late regent, and father of the king, with his feudal retainers, and the conservative and reactionary literati who looked to him as their exponent and guide. As this old man had persecuted the Christians and driven off the French in 1866, and the Americans in 1871, and was still full of physical and mental vigor, he was a hopeful leader. The jealousy and bitterness between his family (Ni) and that of the queen's (Min) kept increasing daily. (See "Corea, the Hermit Nation.")

The treaty with the United States was made May 9th, 1882, at In-chiun, and soon after conventions were signed with Great Britain and other European nations. Drought prevailed throughout the country, and the bigoted conservatives wrought upon the superstitions of the masses by ascribing the lack of rain to the anger of the spirits, because treaties had been made with foreigners. The soldiery of the capital, led chiefly by officers of the house of Ni, were on the verge of mutiny because of arrears of pay. They were further exasperated because, while their rations of rice were stopped, or at least curtailed, the foreigners (Japanese) had plenty. These apparently trifling causes, acting at a time when the relations of the two noble houses of Min and Ni (the queen's and the ex-regent's, respectively) were so strained, provoked a bloody riot at Séoul, July 23d, 1882. The populace and soldiery attacked the rice-granaries, the Japanese legation, the royal palace, and the barracks, at which a picked force of native military were being drilled by a Japanese lieutenant. Four of the court ministers and a number of minor Corean officers were slain. The Japanese, after holding the mob at bay for over seven hours, rushed out of their burning quarters, charged the crowd, and made a dash for the royal palace. Finding no help there, they crossed the river and marched to In-chiun. While asleep in the governor's house they were again attacked, and started for the sea-shore. After some hours spent on the water they were rescued by the British survey-ship *Flying Fish*. There were but twenty-six survivors out of about forty persons. Séoul and the Corean Government were now under the control of the Tai-wen Kun and his mob.

Immediate and thorough preparations for war were made in Japan, and Hanabusa, after audience with the mikado in Tôkiô, was sent back to Séoul, which he entered August 16th, with an escort of five hundred men. After delays and a menace of war ample apologies were made, and the demands of Japan were acceded to. Corea agreed to pay $50,000 to the families of the slain and $500,000 to the Japanese government, to dispatch an embassy to Tôkiô to offer apologies, to allow an armed escort in Séoul, and to extend farther privileges to

Japanese officers and residents in Corea. Hanabusa was soon after promoted to be minister to Russia. A large deputation of Coreans visited Tôkiô in October, making a long stay, and receiving much attention from foreigners as well as natives.

China's action after the Corean riot and usurpation of Tai-wen Kun was remarkable and unjustifiable. Dispatching a large fleet, with several thousand soldiers, to the peninsula, the capital was occupied, and the king restored to power. Tai-wen Kun, entrapped on board a Chinese gun-boat, was kidnapped and taken to China, to live imprisoned as an exile. This object of high-handed assumption of power in a really independent state, and only nominally tributary, was evidently to checkmate the suspected designs of Japan, to assert Chinese supremacy, and to warn her ambitious neighbor that a third affair, like those of Formosa and Riu Kiu, was no longer possible.

This warlike policy of China is but an indication of the state of feeling between the rival nations, which must at some future day eventuate in war. Ever since Japan's full assumption of sovereignty over Riu Kiu, the relations between China and Japan have been strained. At this little island-kingdom, noted alike for its sugar and its peaceful character, let us now glance.

On a Mercator map of the Western Pacific, looked at from the east, the mikado's empire (cutting off Yezo) resembles a silk-worm erect, and spinning from its head (Kiushiu) a thread of islands which are strung along southwardly to Formosa. To this lengthened cord the name Okinawa (long rope) was very anciently given. The name—which the Japanese pronounce Riu Kiu, the Chinese Liu Kiu, and the islanders Loo Choo, which means sleeping dragon—well describes this land of perpetual afternoon. The people, numbering one hundred and twenty thousand—of whom as many as one-tenth lived on the public treasury—are true Japanese in origin, language, and dynasty, their first historical rulers having been descendants of the renowned

Tamétomo. As, however, the Riu Kiuans—calling China their father, and Japan their mother—sent tribute in junks to both countries, cultivated religious, literary, and friendly relations with either, both rival empires claimed the little kingdom. So long as neither nation asserted supreme right all was well. The Ming dynasty had given the Riu Kiu king a silver seal, and to his kingdom a name signifying "hanging-balls," intimating that the thirty-six islands of his petty domain were a fringe of tassels upon the skirts of China's robe. Hidéyoshi once demanded that the islanders should pay tribute only to Japan; but the Corean war coming on, he had never enforced his demand. In 1609 Iyéhisa, the daimiô of Satsuma, conquered the islands, and secured their tributary allegiance to his house and to the shôgun. China, however, knew nothing of this act of Japan until after it was over; nor, on the other hand, does any restriction seem to have been laid on the Riu Kiuans sending an annual tribute junk to Ningpo, China. Fifteen embassies from Riu Kiu visited Yedo, for investiture of the island-king, or to congratulate the shôguns upon their accession to power, between 1611 and 1850; but the same policy was pursued toward China also. Both Corea and Riu Kiu were political Issachars bowing down between two burdens  and two masters. After the revolution of 1868 Riu Kiu was made a *han* of the Japanese empire, and the king acknowledged the mikado as his suzerain. When, for the sake of the Riu Kiuans wrecked and murdered on Formosa, the Japanese sent an expedition to chastise the Botan savages, they took a step forward, and reducing the king to the status of a retired daimiô, erected Riu Kiu into a *ken*, or prefecture, like the other parts of the empire. To this the Riu Kiuans did not all agree, and continuing to send a junk to Ningpo, acted as suppliants for China's mercy; while the Peking government considered that Japan was feloniously cutting off the fringes of China's robe.

Under Japan's rule the sleepy dragon is waking up. Trade with Corea has begun, and with the other ports of Japan increased; and old customs are giving way to more enlightened methods of life. Yet still the irritation between Japan and China continues. China having already a large naval force and a numerous soldiery, the questions of increasing the number of costly iron-clad war vessels, of building new forts, of enlarging the army, and of levying taxes in order to provide the sinews of war, have engaged the attention of the Cabinet in Tôkiô during the past year. A hundred vessels of war and a standing army of one hundred thousand men are not considered too many in case of war with China; but to provide and maintain such a force would require vastly augmented resources, such as Japan, in this century at least, will never possess, her estimated total revenue for 1883 being but $66,814,122, of which every dollar is required. Forty ships and forty thousand soldiers are thought to be the minimum for safety in defense. Such enlargement of war material means, unfortunately, curtailment in the amount devoted to education. A national debt of $349,771,176 (May 31st, 1882) acts as a wholesome check upon too rapid expenditure. A revision of the treaties with foreign nations which will secure to Japan the rights of a sovereign state, especially the power, now wrongfully denied her, of regulating her own tariff, may enable her to swell her revenue, and thus in some measure provide for that collision with her giant neighbor which seems inevitable.

Christianity in three forms, Greek, Roman, and Reformed, is now a potent factor in the development of the nation. At the opening of the ports, in 1859, the Roman Catholics, with the advantage of historic continuity, began their labors at Yokohama and Nagasaki. The Holy Synod of Russia, five Protestant missionary societies—four American and one English—sent their agents to Japan. For ten years they were unable to make many disciples, and none openly, on account of the jealous hostility of the Japanese Government. The old anti-Christian edicts were enforced, and a native became a disciple of Jesus at the risk of his life. Some of the first teachers of the foreigners were thrown into prison, and several thousand villagers from Urakami, near Nagasaki, were deported to northern provinces, away from the influence of their French teachers. Meanwhile the language was being mastered, and the work of healing, teaching, and translation engaged in. The first Protestant church in Japan was organized in Japan by the Rev. J. H. Ballagh, of the Reformed Church in America, March 10th, 1872; the edifice, costing $6000, standing on part of the Perry treaty ground. Other churches were soon organized the first in Tôkiô, and the fourth in Japan, being on the 3d of September, 1873. During this year the anti-Christian edicts were removed, and Christian churches established in the interior, since which time the Christians have worshiped unmolested. Most of the important evangelical societies in Great Britain and the United States are now represented in the missionary work in Japan, and Sunday-schools, theological seminaries, native Christian associations, the press, Christian literature, Bible and tract distribution, public discussions, and open-air meetings are among the varied means used for the diffusion of Gospel truths.

To Protestant missionaries belongs the honor of having translated the Bible into Japanese. Eighty years of Roman Christianity in the sixteenth and seventeenth centuries failed to give the people of Japan the Scriptures in their own tongue. Gutzlaff, in 1838, and S. Wells Williams, in 1839, at Singapore, made the first attempts, which, after several tentative translations by Brown, Verbeck, Hepburn, Green, and others, ripened in the fruit of a complete Japanese New Testament in the high middle style of the language. This event of national importance was celebrated by a public meeting of the missionaries and native pastors in Tôkiô, April 19th, 1880. Many thousands of copies have been sold throughout the empire, and the Bible has now millions of readers. There are now probably forty thousand nominal Christians among the mikado's subjects. Shintô does not seem to flourish in the air of the nineteenth century, though Buddhism, especially the "Reformed" or Shin-shiu sect, which claims ten millions of adherents, is vigorously contesting with Christianity the possession of Japan.

The wondrous assimilation of the salient features of modern civilization by the Japanese has smoothed the path for success in Christian missionary labor which is marvelous. The literary hostility to Christianity was not at first great, nor is it yet of a character to inspire respect for the Japanese intellect. Nearly all the ammunition of the priests, pagans, and opponents of the new faith is furnished by translation from Occidental sources. The literary, medical, and pedagogic work of the missionaries has borne a mighty harvest of good to the nation at large, while the friendly rivalry between the common schools and the missionary educational institutions is most wholesome. The influences of the religion of Jesus are penetrating deeply into the social life of the people, and rooting themselves into heart and intellect alike. Licentiousness, intemperance, and lying are the moral cancers of the national character; but the ideals of Jesus are seen by an increasing number of the people to be the best inspiration to individual and national progress.

# *Japan in 1886*

The year of our Lord eighteen hundred and eighty-six, the nineteenth of the Restoration, and of the reign of Mutsuhito, the one hundred and twenty-third mikado of Japan, finds the empire at peace, and in full career of progress. The emperor, now thirty-three years of age, is surrounded with a new generation of advisers. The old heroes and counsellors of '68 have mostly passed away. The old nobilities—of court and of land—have shrunk to a status almost wholly non-political. With new men and times come new measures and problems.

Notable among those of national fame who have "changed their world" have been the junior premier Iwakura Tomomi, a noble of highest rank, and the elder prince Arisugawa. At an age still counted as mid-life by European statesmen, Iwakura sank in the plenitude of his influence, dying of an hereditary disease July 20, 1883. Born in Kiôto in 1825, of most illustrious ancestry, whose blood flowed from imperial and Minamoto stock, Iwakura was made personal attendant upon the Mikado Koméi at the age of twenty. Educated in traditions of antagonism to the Yedo system, he was, in 1861, on account of his opposition to the marriage of an imperial princess to a Tokugawa, forced into exile. Living in retirement and with shorn head during several years, he was yet in active communication with the leaders of the impending crisis; and in 1868, to the surprise of the Yedo authorities, he emerged at the head and front of the new movement. Until the age of forty-three he had never seen foreigners, but on his first interview with Sir Harry Parkes was converted to belief in their equality, humanity, and abilities. Heartily accepting the principles of western civilization, he sent his three sons to study under Guido F. Verbeck, at Nagasaki, and thence to the United States. For fifteen years he was the close counsellor of the young mikado, who in 1871 personally visited his subject, and said, "It is to you, under the favor of the gods, that we owe the flourishing condition of the empire." It was Iwakura who, when opportunity like a flame softened the national heart as wax, bade the mikado with his divine prestige stamp it, and give to the fusing mass the express image of a nation by the abolition of feudalism. Utterly fearless of all personal consequences, this foremost man among the nobility pressed to their conclusion the results of the revolution during his twelve years of incessant toil. Emerging scathless from repeated attempts upon his life, he died quietly in his bed. Buried with all possible funereal pomp, he received from the mikado the posthumous title of Dai Jô Dai Jin. Like Moses, having led a nation from narrow horizons to a higher outlook, he died at the right time. His death, as we shall see, paved the way for a closer union of the throne and the people. No successor to Iwakura—well named "Rock-throne"—could be found, while from below the new man for the new work was at hand.

Arisugawa Takahito no Miya, a prince of the blood and of the highest rank, father of the military leader who bore the imperial brocade banner in 1868, died January 24, 1886. Among others who have bowed to the harvest of death were many of the old daimiôs, the illustrious merchant Godai, of Ôzaka, several female children of the mikado, and so many promising young men who had entered or were anticipating public life, as to suggest painfully the weakness of the Japanese physique. The percentage of deaths among the students abroad and at home is a constant source of sorrow and disappointment. Of one hundred youths who begin their preparatory studies in the foreign language schools, not over five win their degrees at the Tôkiô University, over forty dropping out on account of disease or weakness.*

Other causes than the knock of Pallida Mors have operated in the retirement from public view of men once prominent. The tendency of Japanese politics, in its evolution towards the goal of 1890, has been to eliminate entirely the old nobility, and to advance to power men for the time bred in the lower social ranks. The composite government which rose on the ruins of the dual system in 1868 was founded on the theory of a union of the throne with the people, the only intermediary being the kugé, or court nobles. This took the form of a triple premiership of Dai-jins; Sanjô and Iwakura filling two of the three highest offices, while the details of administration were carried on by the ministers, who were men of the samurai class. Gradually the forces of intellect, of natural ability, and of education manifested themselves, driving out inferior men, unable to cope with the new problems of statecraft or to resist the pressure from below, and elevating to influential position the able men of low rank. These demanded not only office and hearing, but tangible recognition, in the form of social advancement, from the throne itself. In response to public opinion the mikado issued an edict dated June 6, 1884, which readjusted the system of nobility. In the newly-created orders of princes, marquises, counts, viscounts, and barons, were found many men once in the class of gentry only, who had performed distinguished services on behalf of their country. Nearly three hundred persons in the aristocracy of intellect were thus ennobled on the basis of merit. Orders and decorations have also

---

* Kéiki, "the last tycoon," was reported to have died in 1884. This was a mistake. In 1890 we read of his visiting the hot springs of Itami. On the 14th of April, 1889, a monument to his retainers slain in the civil war of 1868-70 was unveiled at Uyéno, Tôkiô.

been distributed with lavish hand to both natives and foreigners. It is expected that the nobles will furnish the personnel of the Upper House of Lords or Notables for the Parliament of 1890.

To this goal the forces of Japanese politics have kept steadily moving, though with many fluctuations and vicissitudes, among which have been the rise and fall of parties, plottings, riots, dynamite, suspicion, imprisonments, trials, release or executions. For various reasons the Liberal party was dissolved in October, 1884.

Within the Government circles there had been occasional shiftings of office without radical change: but a movement of almost revolutionary import took place at the end of 1885. The death of Iwakura, and the apparently approaching senility of Sanjô, gave the opportunity; while necessity, in view of the strides of time that wait for no man, forced the issue. With the unexpected suddenness of an earthquake shock, every member of the old court party was retired from active office, while young men educated abroad—Itô, Inouyé, Mori, Enomoto— stepped into the highest offices.

By recommendation (on paper at least) of Sanjô, and by decree of the mikado, December 22, 1885, the triple premiership, the privy council, and the ministries as then constituted were abolished. In their place a cabinet was established, at the head of which was a minister-president of state. The old boards of government, with a new one of communications (railways, telegraphs, mails), were reorganized in such a way as to discharge from public employ about eight thousand office-holders. The new crystallization of political forces is in the interest of democracy and economy, as well as of executive uniformity and vigor. All in the new cabinet are men of modern ideas, culture, and conviction, while the Asiatic features of the Government have retired into shadow. The Mikado Mutsuhito now meets his ministers in council, deliberates with them, and must share personal responsibility. The throne, by having several courses of intermediaries quietly and safely removed, is more nearly "broad-based upon the people's will." It may be that the future parliament will check any undue tendency in the ministry to bureaucracy. As yet it is uncertain whether the form of representative government in Japan will most closely approach the British or the Prussian model. It will be a bitter disappointment to the liberal patriots if the ministry is to be made responsible to the sovereign and not to the parliament.

The temptations which beset Asiatic nations in adopting the salient features of modern civilization to embark upon costly schemes of reform and equipment are great, and the possible dangers are greater. The Japanese Government seems wisely anxious to study economy and avoid undue expenditure. Besides reducing the once abnormal force of office-holders, western methods of book-keeping have been introduced into the public service, and the financial estimates for each year are reduced to the lowest point. The total national revenue for the nineteenth fiscal year of Meiji was $74,695,415, and the expenditure was $74,689,014. About $20,000,000 is applied yearly to the extinguishing of the national debt, which in 1885 was $245,427,329.

The customs returns of trade since 1868, published in July, 1886, shows that the foreign commerce of Japan is healthfully developing. In 1869 the exports were less than $13,000,000, but during each of the last five years they have not fallen below $30,000,000. The imports in 1868 were valued at ten and a half, in 1880 at thirty-six, and in 1885 at twenty-eight millions of dollars. The excess of imports over exports during eighteen years of foreign trade amounts to fifty-one millions. Great Britain has been the largest importer, but her imports have fallen from nineteen millions in 1880 to twelve millions in 1885. The United States takes most of the silk and tea of Japan, and returns machinery and oil, two-thirds of the exports to Japan being in petroleum. Japan's silk crop, in all its products, is valued at eighteen and a half millions of dollars, and her tea crop at over thirty-five millions of pounds. While the yield of tea has increased threefold since 1868, the price has fallen one-half. In the manufacture and export of art-products there has been a marked increase. This is manifested not only in the customs returns, but in the houses, gardens, and museums of Europe and America. Japan is already recognized as "the land of dainty decoration," and her art has added new elements of delight and surprise to the world's store.

The social revolution which has affected all classes in the mikado's empire has given rise to new industries and handicrafts. The concentration of capital, the improvement of labor, and the elevation of the working-classes through the influence of schools and the cheapening of justice, have changed the entire industrial system. The pitiful tales of the laborer's wrongs, as told in Mitford's "Tales of Old Japan," seem now mythical. The introduction of machinery and the establishment of large arsenals, founderies, mills, steamship and railway companies, seem to prove that Japan is not only providing for her own needs, but is developing her resources in order to enter as a competitor for the manufacturing supremacy among Asiatic nations. Fully equipped railroads, men-of-war, steam and sailing vessels, houses in European style, the product of native brain and muscle, are no longer curiosities. Patents are issued, inventions are encouraged, and museums are established in most of the large cities. In exhibitions of industry held in the provinces and capital, art, mechanical ingenuity, trades, and business are stimulated to higher excellence. In the expositions held in Europe, America, Australia, and India, the artistic ability, manual dexterity, and inventive genius of the Japanese have won abundant recognition. An exhibition of Asiatic products is to be held at Uyéno, in Tôkiô, in 1890.

It is a noteworthy fact that the opening of Japan to the world was coincident with the age of iron, steel, steam, and electricity. The telegraph, introduced in 1869, has become a net-work of fifteen thousand miles of wire. Four cables connect the island empire to the Asian main-land, two making landfall at Vladivostok, one at Fusan in Corea, and one at Shanghai in China. The telephone and the electric light are seen in the large cities. Of railways there were, in the summer of 1885, 265 miles open, 271 miles in course of construction, and 543 miles in contemplation. Except the railway from Sapporo to Poronai in Yezo, these roads are constructed and equipped on the British model. Most of the survey, engineering, and constructive work, and all of the mechanical labor on the new roads, are done by natives. The trains, engines, and offices are worked by Japanese, and the wood and lighter metal portions are made at home, the heavy castings, engines, and rails being brought from Great Britain. The Japan Mail Shipping Company employs a large fleet of steamships and sailing-vessels in their coasting trade and passenger lines to China, Corea, and the island portions of the empire. In 1885 the postal department forwarded nearly one hundred million letters and packages.

The return, in 1884, of the principal of the Shimonoséki Indemnity, so long unjustly withheld by the United States from Japan, has been of some assistance in carrying out her schemes of national improvement. Besides postal and money-order arrangement with the United States, a treaty of extradition was ratified by the Senate June 21, 1886. This important diplomatic action places Japan, so far as the American Government is concerned, upon the same footing as that of the most enlightened nations in Europe. In these two acts the United States leads the way in encouragement and recognition of Japan's purpose to assimilate her civilization to that of Christendom.

Ever since the American flag was first carried round the world by Major Shaw, of the United States First Artillery, the part played by our country towards Asiatic nations has been in the main kindly, honorable, and unselfish. In the renovation of Japan this disposition to assist and not to retard her progress has been manifest. In 1878, in Tôkiô, the Japanese themselves, in their own language and way, celebrated, with congratulations and rejoicing, the quarter-century of the arrival of Commodore M. C. Perry in Yedo bay.* Our American teachers, missionaries, and scientific men in active labors on the soil; our ministers in their diplomacy; our hospitable schools, homes, and friends in need welcoming the students;† our Government in treaties, have all shown a desire to assist Japan which is as sincere as it is morally beautiful. The standard political literature of the United States, translated and widely read, has done much to educate Japanese opinion, and to show how liberty may exist under law. Science, religion, the press, and public-schools are now training the Japanese people for their coming responsibilities. Nearly six hundred young men have, since the first exodus in 1865, been educated abroad at the public expense, most of them in the United States. An equal or greater number have attended foreign schools at their own charges, while the number of travellers and those who have intelligently studied western

* See the *Life of Matthew Calbraith Perry, a Typical American Naval Officer*, by the author of this work.

† The subject of the Japanese students abroad, how they came first to New Brunswick, N. J., with personal notes, statistics, etc., has been treated by the author in a pamphlet published in 1886 by the Rutgers College Alumni Association. During the civil war in Japan the Japanese students were unable to receive any remittances. A company of gentlemen and ladies in the Reformed [Dutch] Church was formed to loan them money without regard to future repayment. This generous behavior was warmly appreciated by the mikado's government. On the eve of their departure from the United States, in 1872, the ambassadors Iwakura and Ôkubo, in a letter to the Rev. John Mason Ferris, D.D., wrote: "The generous conduct exhibited by yourself and other gentlemen in this instance, as well as in all matters of educational interest pertaining to the Japanese youth, will do more to correct this impression [that "foreign nations did not entertain kindly feelings toward our people"], and will do more to cement the friendly relations of the two countries, than all other influences combined."

civilization cannot fall short of three thousand. The Japanese have now their legation, consulates, bank, clubs, and a Christian church in the United States. At least three thousand in various industrial capacities are living in Europe, China, Hawaii, and other countries. No year passes without seeing delegations of public inspectors or private students abroad, all restlessly eager to know the secrets of power possessed by the western nations.

Though the Japanese long ago accepted the axiom that "education is the basis of all progress," yet their efforts in intellectual advancement have been impeded by their long use of the Chinese graphic system. The best years of a student's life must be devoted to learning thousands of arbitrary characters in order to know how to read. To be a learned man in the Japan of today one must know, besides his own language, the cumbrous Chinese system of writing, with much of its body of learning, and, in addition, the English or some other modern European language. No youth are more burdened in obtaining an education than are the Japanese. Hence the vast sacrifice of health and life among them, and their early intellectual decay.

Fully realizing these indisputable facts, the thinking men of this generation have resolved to break the yoke, to cast off the incubus, and to free the intellect of the future. In 1884 the Rômaji Kai, or Roman-letter Association, was formed in Tôkiô, and has now six thousand members, native and foreign, among whom are all the missionaries. Their purpose is to supplant the Chinese character and native syllabary by the Roman alphabet as the vehicle of Japanese thought. They have demonstrated that all possible sounds and vocal combinations can be expressed by using twenty-two letters. They print a newspaper, edit text-books, and will transliterate popular and classic texts in the chosen letters of the alphabet now most widely used over all the earth. It has been proved that a child can learn to read the colloquial and book language in one-tenth of the time formerly required. The reform is making rapid progress; and if, as seems very probable the natives universally adopt the system, the gain to mind and body will be like that of adding youth and years to a nation's life.

By an imperial decree, issued November 29, 1884, the English language was made part of the order of studies in the common-schools. Over three million children and youth now attend daily the public institutions of learning. Education is both compulsory and free. English seems destined to become the speech of the educated and the vehicle of knowledge for all the mikado's subjects.

The progress of Christianity shows no sign of check or halt. To all three forms of the faith converts are flocking, but indications seem to show at present (1886) a greater relative gain to the churches of Reformed Christianity. The majority of the two hundred Protestant missionaries now working in the white harvest-field of Japan are Americans. The writer saw the organization of the first Protestant Christian church in Japan in 1872. There are now nearly two hundred organized churches (about half of which are self-supporting), with a membership of over thirteen thousand. In 1885 the adult converts baptized numbered 3,115. Native Christian helpers, assisting the foreign teachers, number about two hundred and fifty, of whom seventy are ordained ministers. The native Christians contributed in 1885 over twenty thousand dollars. The systems of heathenism are waning, and the chief supporters of Buddhism are now old men and women. The shaven-pated priests no longer hold the monopoly of fees for the performance of burial rites. Both belief and burial are now free. Religious liberty has become a fact. The attitude of the intelligent people is that of friendliness towards what they believe to be the best religion and the one which Japan ought to have.

Japan's opportunity seems unique in history. Under Divine Providence she began renascence at a time coincident with the highest development of the forces—spiritual, mental, and material—that

control human society. Christianity, the press, and steam are trans-
forming the nation. Under such continuing auspices people and rulers
confront the twentieth year of Meiji (Enlightened Peace), the twenty-
five hundred and forty-seventh "from the foundation of the empire,"
and the eighteen hundred and eighty-seventh of the Christian era.

# Japan in 1890

Taking our survey of Japan in 1890, and writing in mid-August with the election returns before us, it seems that the one event which dwarfs all others since the year 1886, if not indeed since the Japanese became a nation, is the proclamation of the Constitution of February 11, 1889. In accordance with this instrument, the emperor shares with his people the work and responsibilities of government.

The possibility of an Asiatic nation's becoming constitutional and representative in government excites surprise and even incredulity in the minds of Western people. Since the solidity and permanence of any form of political organization must depend upon how far it is rooted in the past, and is in accord with the genius and necessities of a people, let us examine the process by which the present status of Japan has been attained. Is the Constitution of 1889 a manufacture or a growth?

A rapid view shows us that in all Japanese history the central force has been the reverence of the people for the throne, while the actual administration has always been in the hands of some one family, clan, or clan combination. Passing over the "ages eternal" of mythology, and reckoning that the traditions of the house or tribe of Yamato are trustworthy from the fourth century, then the imperial line of Japan has been in existence, by blood and adoption, nearly sixteen hundred years. Yet, excepting the individuals Nobunaga and Hidéyoshi, the actual rulers of the empire have been men of the Fujiwara, Taira, Minamoto, Hôjô, Ashikaga, and Tokugawa families; and, since 1868, of the "Sa-cho-to," or the Satsuma, Chôshiu, and Tosa clan combination. For the first time in Japanese history the intermediary of family or clan control of the throne is now to be abolished. The meaning of the Constitution of 1889—the expansion of the oath of 1868—is that the emperor invites his PEOPLE to share with him the duties of government. This time it is not a family, a clan, or a combination, but the nobles, gentry, and people; but who are the people?

As there has been no true history of Japan yet written—that is, one which sifts utterly the truth from early and late fable and mythology—so there exists no accurate history of the Japanese people. What passes for history in the bald and dry native annals is the story of their conquerors, masters, and tax-collectors. We see clearly outlined, however, the separation of classes. At first there were only tribes and chiefs, the subjugators and the subjugated, agriculturists and nomads. Then, in a long course of war, the soldiers, finding nearly permanent employment, keep sword, spear, and armor, while the farmers clinging to hoe and hook, two classes are formed out of the mass of inhabitants beyond the court and beneath the nobles. Those men, whose business it was to *samurai* the mikado—that is, to serve or attend upon the orders of the emperor, made up the military class; the farmers, as being next below, forming the most ancient and honorable of the lower classes. Among the social grades, formed by gradual evolution and isolation during the intervals of peace, may be named the merchant, artisan, and people of other occupations, even to the outcast *eta* and *hinin*. Since 1868 all the grades below the samurai, or gentry, have been fused into one class, the *hei-min*, or people.

The chief feature in the old Japanese political system was its tendency to dualism. The division of the people into soldiers and farmers, and of officers into civil and military, or *kugé* and *buké*, was a process which, in the absence of foreign pressure or enemies, ended in a division of the functions of government into those of the throne and the camp, with two rulers and two capitals. Gradually this process of dualism became one of disintegration. Authority slipped from the centres, and was held locally by province lords, or daimiôs, each striving for himself; until, duarchy having degenerated into feudalism, Japan had no unity, but was a mass of warring factions. Politically or socially, the comminution could no further go. Even when "the man on horseback" by military force was able to clamp together some sort of a political edifice, the order thus kept was only of the sort possible when there was no pressure from the outside, and when no foreign enemy threatened. For over two centuries the military despotism of Tokugawa held in peace by a most elaborate and complicated system an empire which consisted of about three hundred petty kingdoms, within each of which was a social conglomeration of a dozen or more different classes.

Old Japan was a museum of political curiosities, while on the graded shelves of the social classification was catalogued every specimen, from a god to the creatures labelled "not human." Under outward splendor and picturesqueness, only a few far-seeing men saw that, first of all, Japan needed unity; fewer discerned that the country must have government by men and not by custom; fewest yet that to be a great nation Japan must have a people.

Heretofore "public opinion" has been the exclusive property of the samurai. "The people," in the modern, not to say the American, sense, have not yet grown to consciousness, though the 11th of February, 1889, was the day of birth. Nineteen-twentieths of the inhabitants of Japan have been simply burden-bearers and tax-payers; now they are becoming "the people." Japan, having cast off dualism, feudalism, and other divisive elements, has entered upon a higher process of unity. The people are now learning who and what they are.

Glancing now at the various forms of government, we discern in the early ages a rudimentary feudalism, probably brought by the Yamato conquerors from the Amoor or Sungari valleys. After this follow in order centralized monarchy, duarchy, elaborate feudalism, and then, in 1868, a composite government formed on the theory of a union of the throne and "the people"—that is, the samurai. In this government, the chief intermediaries being the triple premiership and other various minor and temporary political expedients, the actual administration was carried on by able samurai, formerly men of low social rank, but well fitted for the work in hand. In a survey of the twenty-one years of the government of Meiji several facts stand out prominently; the first is that the former ruling class of daimios and other nobles, and the people, have had very little, if any, political power; second, that the Meiji statesmen have shown in their actions a curious, perhaps admirable, combination of opportunism and far-sighted statecraft; third, that natural force, ability, and education have driven out incompetency; fourth, that despite all obstacles, they have led the nation steadily forward to the goal set before them at the Restoration, and far beyond it; fifth, that Japan is to-day vastly less the land of lies and sham than in the old days of seclusion, and is more and more the country of reality and truth.

In brief, Old Japan was the result of certain conditions, chief of which was isolation from the rest of the world. So long as no leaven from without was dropped into the mass, the old constitution of society and government could remain stable. When, however, in addition to the movements in the minds of scholars and thinkers previous to A.D. 1853, which of themselves would have precipitated revolution and compelled reconstruction, there was poured into Japan the ferment of Christian civilization, the entire structure was doomed. A new society, as well as a new government, must arise. Despotism, division, and sectionalism had to give way in order that national unity should

emerge. The old society, split up by feudalism, priestcraft, and ignorance, must be first simplified, and by education, enlightenment, and
freedom the nation be strengthened and uplifted. Public opinion, as
the basis of national action, must be the real, though regulated, feeling
of all, from emperor to *eta*. In the attainable ideal system the humblest
member of the body politic is a man, and the highest nothing more.

That there were men who before 1853, the year of Perry's arrival
at Uraga, thus thought and felt, and to this end devoted their lives,
is manifest from tradition, history, and the writings of such men
as Takéno Choyé, Watanabé Kwazan, Hashimoto Sanai, Fujita
Séinoshin, Sakama Shuri, Yoshida Torajirô, Yokoi Héishiro,
Matsudaira Yoshinaga, daimiô of Echizen, and many other noble
morning-stars of reformation. Under various pretexts, whether of
opposition to foreigners or to the Bakufu, these far-sighted patriots
"veiled their larger purpose." Highest in rank and influence, and
most eager for national unity and representative government, the
pupil of Yokoi Héishiro, and probably the ablest of all the daimiôs,
was Matsudaira, lord of Echizen, who had already begun to form,
in his own dominions, before Perry's arrival, a miniature of the New
Japan of the Meiji era. He was one of the first to propose to the Yedo
Government the calling of a council of daimiôs to deliberate upon
the American proposal to enter into treaty relations. In thus seeking
the "public opinion" of the country as represented by the feudal clans,
and in the holding, during many days and nights in 1854, of the great
council of both active and retired daimios, in Yedo, we see the first
step towards the national parliament of 1890.

Yet this very step revealed the weakness of the despotism of Yedo
thus called to confront a new problem. To behold the Yedo autocrats,
who had hitherto by force required only instant obedience of their vassals, humbly inviting them to conference was a startling revelation to
men who watched every movement of the Bakufu. The samurai were

aroused at once, but finding few or no leaders among their masters, the daimiôs, who, with the noteworthy exceptions of Echizen, Mito, Hizen, Tosa, and Uwajima, formed a Sahara of mediocrity, the thinking men turned for leadership to the court nobles in Kiôto, and then strove to win their feudal masters to their side.

When confronted by Townsend Harris, and by the envoys of Europe who followed after, who demanded residence and trade, there was a choice, to the bakufu, between two methods of policy. One was represented by Ii Kamon no Kami, who, with probably a noble motive, chose the method of the autocrat, increasing despotism under the plea of necessity. The other method was represented in the person of Matsudaira, daimiô of Echizen,* who had national modern and Western ideas, and believed that all acts of government should be upon the basis of public opinion. The one was destined to illustrate the truth that government in Old Japan was "despotism tempered by assassination." The other lived to see grandly illustrated the capacity of the nation for representative and constitutional government, dying

---

* The Marquis Matsudaira Yoshinaga, or Shungaku, was born in Yedo, A.D. 1827, and died in Tôkiô, June 2, 1890. In 1838 he was adopted as a son by the daimiô of Echizen, and in 1843 became active ruler in Fukui. He introduced various reforms in the arts of development and defence. He built a gun factory, cannon foundery, and powder-mill; introduced vaccination, Dutch medical practice and military tactics, the study of Dutch, and the translation of Dutch books; organized a hospital, a medical school, a college of literature, invited Yokoi Heishiro, the renowned Higo teacher, to be his counsellor, and made Fukui a hospitable place for scholars and far-sighted patriots. All this was done before 1854. At first opposed to foreign intercourse on account of the weakness of Japan, and the opponent of Ii Kamon no Kami, he became, in 1862, one of the most progressive men in Japan. After holding many offices of high honor under the government of Meiji, including the presidency of the university and head of the revenue department, he received from the mikado the highest honors possible to a living subject, rising to the second degree of the first rank.

in 1890. Heartily trusting the wisdom and abilities of the enlightened men of the southern and western clans, he, when Supreme Director of Affairs, in 1862, released them and the daimiôs from Yedo, made Kiôto the real capital, and there opened the then possible avenues for the expression of opinion.

Largely through the influence of Echizen, while resident at the palace during several months, the acts of the court were done in accordance with the policy suggested by the clans. In the deliberations of the men who formed the Government proclaimed January 3, 1868, Echizen, with his troops, being then guardian of the palace, this enlightened daimiô, besides pleading for union of all the political forces, old and new, without civil war or estrangement, urged above all things the necessity of a national parliament. Though the outbreak of war and the shedding of blood were keen disappointments to him, he persevered in the work of national unity and reconstruction. By an oath of the mikado (p. 349) the five principles of the new government which form this Constitution of 1868 and the basis of New Japan—expressed in their verbal form by Yuri Kinmasa, a samurai of Echizen, and pupil of Yokoi Héishiro—were published and established. In accordance with the promise that "a deliberative assembly should be formed, and all measures be decided by public opinion," the first parliament was opened in Kiôto in 1868, the representation being in the persons of samurai only, each clan, according to its numbers, sending one, two, or three members. When Yedo was made the kiô, or capital, and named Tôkiô, a second parliament of two hundred and seventy-six members, two hundred of whom were present, convened April 18, 1869. This new body was named Shiugi-In, or House of Commons. After discussing various questions, especially that of a new Constitution, and rejecting the proposition to relinquish the wearing of swords, this assembly died a natural death. It was, in the temper of its members, so far behind the needs of the time, and of the ideas of the progressive leaders in the Government, that it was likely to defeat the very ends proposed in its creation.

Although the petition of Gotô, Yuri, and others, in 1874, was rejected, and substitutes for a national assembly were supposed to exist in the Sa-In, or Senate so called, formed in 1871, its members being nominated by the premier, and in its successor the Genrô-In, also called a Senate, yet no decisive movement towards national representation was made until 1873, when a meeting of the governors of the prefectures was called in Tôkiô. Nevertheless, in the creation, in April, 1875, of the Genrô-In, or Senate, and the Dai Shin-In, or Supreme Court of Appeals, and the promise in the same decree to "gradually confer upon the nation a constitutional form of government," we see the first clear step towards the modern division of government into the executive, legislative, and judicial branches. In July, 1875, the promise to call a council of provincial officials "so that the feelings of the people may be made known, and the public welfare attained," was fulfilled. The seventy province-governors were addressed by the emperor, and Kido was made president. Actually more influential upon the people, however, than this too conservative body was the action of certain advisers of the governors coming up with them, who met in Tôkiô, and petitioned the Government for a national assembly based on popular suffrage. Adjourned in 1877, it was not in 1878 accepted as the boon desired by the nation, even though the foundations of local government by popular representation were laid in the decree of the emperor. Then followed two years of amazing activity in agitation for the long-desired parliament. Led by Itagaki, Ôkuma, Gotô, Soyéjima, and others, public opinion, to which nobles, gentry, and commoners contributed, compelled the proclamation of October 12, 1887, naming 1890 as the year of the national assembly.

While thus, on the one hand, the political education of the people in local affairs was provided for, so that the nation should have at least eight years of preparatory training in representative government, Count Ito Hirobumi was sent to Europe to study and compare the constitutions and laws of Western nations. Shortly after his return, in 1884, it became increasingly evident that the Constitution of 1890 would approach the German rather than the British model. In December, 1885 (p. 599), a long step forward was taken in the reorganization of the cabinet. During the next four years Ito and Inouyé were able guardians of the national policy. Especially were their abilities manifest during the protracted treaty negotiations, and the intense political excitement consequent upon the desire of the liberal agitators that English rather than Prussian principles should be emphasized in the new Constitution. The fears of the liberals led by Count Itagaki of Tosa were, however, confirmed by the remarkable imperial rescript of December 25, 1887, by which several hundred persons were ordered away from the capital.*

In April, 1888, a new body called the Privy Council was formed, of which Itô became president, while Kuroda filled the position of premier. In this body active debate upon the new Constitution began in May, and proceeded until February 11, 1889, when the long-awaited instrument was proclaimed.

Exactly to the day, almost to the very hour, thirty-five years after the American treaty-ships were in sight of Idzu, the emperor Mutsuhito took oath to maintain inviolate the government according to the Constitution, the documents attesting which he, before the

---

*A discussion of "Coercion in Japan," in *The Nation* of February 16, 1888, precipitated a violent newspaper controversy on both sides of the Pacific. Among other protests it was declared that the article had "a curious air of anachronism about it." Yet within two years, besides several futile attempts at violence or assassination, the lives of two cabinet ministers (Mori and Ôkuma) were assailed, the one by knife and the other by bomb; the ministry then in power was replaced by one more radical, while a strong reaction in public sentiment followed.

assembled audience of nobles, officers, and foreign envoys, handed
to Kuroda, the Minister-president of State. Extraordinary popular
demonstrations of joy and approval followed in the capital and provinces. For the first time in Japanese history the emperor rode beside
the empress in public. Posthumous titles of nobility granted to the
dead, illustrious rewards to the living, amnesty to prisoners, and other
marks of imperial favor carried joy to many hearts. The horrible blot
on the day's beautiful record was the assassination of the Minister of
Education, Arinori Mori, by a Shintôist fanatic.

The Constitution proper consists of sixty-six articles,* treating of
the emperor, the rights and duties of subjects, the Imperial Diet, the
ministers of state and the Privy Council, the judicature and finance,
with supplementary rules. With the laws proclaimed at the same time,
the articles number three hundred and thirty-two. In the first chapter
relating to the emperor the foundation-principle of the whole past of
the nation is reaffirmed. "The mikado's person is sacred and inviolable.
He combines in himself the rights of sovereignty, and exercises them
according to the provisions of the present Constitution." Japan is still
"the mikado's empire."

Hitherto the rights of the common people have never been
acknowledged, defined, or guaranteed. Chapter II is of immediate
interest to thirty-eight out of the forty millions of Japanese people.
Their status is to be determined by law. They have the right of abode

---

* See the writer's article in *The Forum* of April, 1889, entitled "Representative
Government in Japan"; the pamphlet containing the text of the Constitution
(Kelly & Walsh, Yokohama); *Commentaries on the Constitution of the Empire of
Japan*, by Count Ito Hirobumi, translated into English by Miyoji Itô, Tôkiô,
1889; and Prof. Basil Hall Chamberlain's *Things Japanese*, Tôkiô and London,
1890. This latter work is a mirror of contemporary Japan, and an encyclopædia
of valuable information. Also, the letters of J. H. Wigmore in *The Nation*, July,
and *passim*, 1890; and "Constitution of the Empire of Japan," Johns Hopkins
University, Baltimore, Md.

and of changing the same. Except according to law, they are not to be arrested, detained, tried, or punished. Trial is always to be by Judges determined by law. The right of domicile and freedom from search, the secrecy and inviolability of letters, the freedom of religious belief, and the liberty of speech, writing, publishing, public meeting, association, and petition within the limits of law, are guaranteed to every subject. Under the sun of Japan these are indeed new things.

The Diet assembles once a year, and is opened, closed, prorogued, and dissolved by the emperor, to whom the initiative of amendments to the Constitution belongs. Deliberations are public. The ministers of state may take seats and speak in either House, but are responsible to the emperor and not to the Diet. In the judicature exercised by courts of law in the name of the emperor the trials are public, and the judges are persons properly qualified, and irremovable except for offence. Expenses and revenue of the State require the consent of the Imperial Diet, but the fixed expenditures based by the Constitution upon the powers appertaining to the emperor, the organization of the different branches of the administration, and the salaries of all civil and military officers, such expenditures as may have arisen by effect of law, or that relate to the legal obligations of "the Government," shall neither be rejected nor reduced by the Diet without the concurrence of the Government. Expenses of the Imperial House do not require the consent of the Diet except for increase. The chief weapon of a hostile majority—the stoppage of supplies to the ministry in power—is thus removed.

The government of Japan, then, is organized on the basis of immemorial tradition, with modern features that follow the German rather than the English model. A definite amount of executive power is reserved to the emperor and the ministers who are responsible to him. Under the written lines of the Constitution are the watermarks of compromise, and the party lines are marked out by the instrument itself. Against the rushing stream of democracy, like their own mountain torrents, the conservatives will be the dikes (or *ja-kago*) to keep hard and fast the imperial prerogative. The progressives will at once begin to demand greater powers for the Diet, a broader electoral base, and greater control of the finances. Revolutions move but in one direction.

The Upper House, or (mixed) House of Peers, consists partly of hereditary, partly of elected, and partly of nominated members. Members of the imperial family, princes, and marquises sit for life. A certain number of counts, viscounts, and barons, elected by the members of their respective orders, serve for seven years. Men of ability and learning nominated by the emperor are life members. A novel and interesting feature is that from each of the imperial cities and prefectures a member (noble, gentleman, or commoner) elected by the fifteen highest tax-payers may serve for seven years. The combined number of nominated and elected men is not to exceed the number of members holding titles of nobility.

The House of Representatives consists of about three hundred members, at least thirty years of age, who pay national taxes to the amount of fifteen *yen*, or dollars, and serve four years. Electors must be twenty-five years old, and pay national taxes to the amount of fifteen dollars. The average number of representatives from each prefecture is not quite seven, the larger having from ten to thirteen members, and three cities (Tôkiô, Ôzaka, and Kiôto) twelve, ten, and seven, respectively. In 1887 there were 1,581,726 persons in the empire paying taxes to the amount of over five *yen*, of whom 1,488,700 had the right of voting for members of local assemblies. Of those paying over ten dollars in taxes there were 882,517, of whom 802,975 were eligible to vote, or sit after election in the local assemblies. In these local legislatures 2,172 members sat, the number of standing committees being 292. The electorate of the National Diet numbers probably 300,000.

With quietness and order the threefold election passed off in July, 1890, and we are now able to see the general complexion of the first Imperial Diet, and to form some idea of the eagerness of the Japanese to avail themselves of their new privileges. About eighty-five percent of eligible voters availed themselves of the franchise, and the number of candidates in each district varied from two to fifteen, there being in Tôkiô ninety-two applicants for the twelve seats, and in eighty other districts three hundred and thirteen.

For the House of Peers, so called, besides the nine members of the imperial family, ten princes, and twenty-one marquises, who sit by hereditary right, fifteen counts, seventy viscounts, and twenty barons, elected by members of their own orders (the nobles numbering nearly six hundred, and one-fifth of these electives being chosen), there were chosen out of the forty-five fully organized divisions of the empire, by the fifteen highest tax-payers in each, forty-five members, of whom thirty-three were *hei-min*, or commoners, eleven were of the gentry, and one was a noble. Other members are to be nominated by the emperor.

Among the successful candidates for the House of Representatives, a rough classification shows as great variety of political opinions as of occupations. In a word, all of the existing classes of the people are well represented. Without space to analyze the political parties, we may say that at present, far more than in Western countries, the so-called national parties are moulded by local and personal influences rather than by abstract questions of policy. "The Government" must confront a majority hostile in form, the election showing conclusively that the voting of the people is an expression of their own will, and not that either of the ministers in office or of the higher powers in authority. To be in any way connected with governmental employ was, in almost every case, to invite certain defeat; while on the other hand few of the old party leaders were chosen as standard-bearers in the new field. All things considered, the issue is most hopeful to the lover of humanity and well-wisher of the Japanese people.

In the reconstruction of her foreign policy Japan has endeavored to have the treaties revised in the interests of mutual justice, to secure the removal of the extra-territoriality clauses, and her treatment by the nations of Christendom as their equal. The long and weary question cannot here be discussed, but is probably not now far from solution. Since 1881 the new Criminal Code, based on the best principles of Western jurisprudence, has been in successful operation; and on the 22d of April, 1890, the new Code of Civil Procedure, and the first portion of the Civil Code, were promulgated. The fruit of fifteen years' labor of foreign and native experts in law are thus set forth. In both the letter of the documents and the spirit of their execution the sincerity of the Japanese in thus preparing to live up to what is expected of them by the world is clearly manifest. Contrariwise, the confidence of foreign nations is equally shaken when such relapses, on the part of "the Government," into the vices of despotism and feudalism as the issue of the so-called Peace Regulations of December 25, 1887, or when the excesses of the *so-shi*, such as the assassination of Arinori Mori, and the attempt by dynamite on the life of Ôkuma, October 18, 1889, chill the hopes of those who believe in the right of Japan to claim equality with Western nations.

For a solid basis to our hope in Japan's future we look to the large Christian community now increasing daily. In June, 1890, the churches of reformed Christianity had 34,000 members enrolled; those of the Roman form of the faith over 50,000 souls under their care; while 17,000 or more receive spiritual nurture according to the Greek method. These subjects of the mikado make in all a nominal household of a half-million who hold the promise of this life and of that which is to come through Jesus Christ. The celebration of the complete Bible in Japanese took place in Tôkiô, February 3, 1888. Already the fertilization of the native intellect by Christianity and the Bible is manifest in the new literature. Qualities utterly absent from the older writings are discerned in the essays, philosophy, history, fiction, and journalism. Christian men are leaders in thought and letters. The Japanese are even beginning to write critical history.

During these exciting years of 1889 and 1890, amid the ferment of politics, and the fierce discussion of treaty revision which has wrecked more than one ministry, a strong movement to preserve what is best in the national life, in language, art, government, and every department of achievement has been in progress. Such a movement naturally exhibited some phases interpreted by foreigners to mean reaction; but underneath much that is condemned by the best men of the nation there is a larger purpose that will command the sympathy and admiration of the world. No nation can be great that merely imitates and borrows. With wise selection the Japanese nationalistic movement means, we think, the proving of all things, the holding fast that which is good.

Strong in faith and hope of the prosperous future of this most interesting of Asiatic nations, and in undisguised sympathy with her noble purpose, we leave our inspiring theme of representative Japan. From no nation of Christendom will Japan receive more hearty good wishes than from that in which Matthew Calbraith Perry was born, and which of modern States first began its life and has longest lived under a written Constitution.

# Japan in 1894

Forty years ago the whistle of the American steamers awoke Old Japan out of her hermit sleep. On the 8th day of July, 1853, the four men-of-war arrived at Uraga. The signal rockets from the forts were answered by the rattle of cables and the splash of anchors, and Japan's new era began.

That 8th day of July prefigured the forty years of history which we now survey. The day was ushered in with fog so thick that the land was hidden. Only at intervals could the rocky outlines of the coast be discerned. Gradually through the sun-rent curtains of mist the mountains became visible. At meridian Fuji's glorious form loomed into view, and by mid-afternoon the whole panorama of the landscape and blue waters greeted the eye. At sunset the peerless mountain wore a crown of glory. From midnight until four o'clock A.M. appeared from the south-west a meteoric sphere of light that moved towards the north-east, illuminating the whole atmosphere, finally falling towards the sea and vanishing. The next day was one of sunny splendor.

So has it been with Japan, political and social. Foreigners in the morning of their life on the soil found themselves in a fog of ignorance. Everything Japanese seemed veiled in mystery. Hiding the real facts was "a vague embodiment of something which was called 'The Law'; but what that 'Law' was, by whom enacted, and under what sanctions enforced, no one could tell, though all seemed to stand in awe of it as something of superhuman efficacy; its mysteriousness was only equalled by the abject submission it received." No country was then less worthy of its numerous names, all making boast of the sun, of light, of radiancy. Japan was then the Land of Darkness.

Gradually the dawn broke, the fogs of mystery were riven, and the real Japan was discovered. Yet before the cloudless day was ushered in, that great meteoric movement from the south-west towards the north-east—the uprising of the great clans which made New Japan and seated the Emperor in Tôkiô—took place. Like the coming of the Sun-goddess out of her cave was the emergence of the mikado into the white light of public duty. The mystery-play was over. To-day Japan is worthy of her name—Sunrise. It is the 9th of July.

Now, information on a thousand subjects is freely furnished by the Government. Foreign scholars have penetrated the arcana of litera-ture, have challenged and dissected tradition, chronology, and claims even of the Heaven-descended dynasty. The Japanese themselves, applying Western methods of collection, comparison, classification, and research to their national treasures, land, language, and his-tory, are coming to self-revelation as never before. They are seeing themselves as they are. The process is not wholly safe to individuals, and freedom of speech and of the press are not yet what we count freedom. Yet there is at present probably as much liberty as can safely be enjoyed. One signal proof of the willingness of the Government to let light shine on what was once hidden, is its annual publication, *"Résumé Statistique de L' Empire du Japon."*\*

---

\* This manual for 1893, packed with figures skillfully tabulated, maps, diagrams, tables of weights and measures, comparatives, averages, totals, and other requi-sites for the student's eye, tells an eloquent story of Japan's progress. Area, popu-lation, agriculture and industry, commerce and public improvements, facilities of transportation by land and sea, private and public finances, education, religion,

Japan as wonder-land is as surprising in things vanished as in things created during these forty years. Gone are Tycoon, the duarchy, feudalism, the old codes, customs, ideals, personalities. In their places has come one government differentiated in three functions—executive, legislative, and judicial—with all the outward appliances of modern civilization. New social, industrial, and ethical systems are in process of formation. With much of the ancient and picturesque ignorance and superstition have disappeared some things that were worth keeping, yet in New Japan the new codes, ideals, and ambitions are vast improvements on those of the old days. The Japanese have determined to take their place not only among the nations of the world, but of Christendom, and to be found in the front rank. Nothing less than this will satisfy them. Already, the record of forty years is amazing, and the surprises are not all over.

Yet who have been the creators of New Japan? The natives or the foreigners? Would the Japanese of themselves have attained to the status already reached in this twenty-seventh year of Meiji? Are there not, apart from exterior influences, a power and a personality on the soil of the New that were not in the Old Japan? As secret, as concealed as leaven, were they not as potent?

Japan is not unique in history, not a case of entire self-reformation. Without the leaven from Christendom this oriental lump would not be as it is seen and felt to-day. The aliens employed by the Japanese have not told their story, yet, as Professor Basil Hall Chamberlain,

---

hygiene, charities, with details of justice, police administration, army and navy, and civil service at home and abroad, make a statistical appendix to this work of ours no longer necessary. This invaluable publication has for seven years been compiled and edited by Mr. Ishibashi, chief of the Imperial Bureau of Statistics in Tôkiô, author with Mr. E. Satow of a pocket dictionary of English-Japanese. I had the pleasure of first meeting Mr. Ishibashi when he was chief interpreter at the Foreign Office, in 1871, Mr. Térashima Munénori being then Vice-minister of Foreign Affairs.

in his "Things Japanese," says, "The foreign employé is the creator of New Japan." As certainly as on the foundation-stones of the Japan of the Meiji era belong the names of Rai, Sakuma, Yoshida, Yokoi, Fukuzawa, and a host of others who, while living, were unrewarded non-officeholders, so also should be inscribed those of the *Yatoi Tô-jin*, or "hired foreigners." Whether in Japanese pay or not, as hirelings, or as guests, or as forces healthfully stimulating, who from their own governments or societies received stipend, or self-impelled wrought for Japan's good, their work abides. The world may forget the singer, but the song is still heard.

For over a century the earnest thinkers of Japan went to school to the Dutch at Nagasaki. These Europeans, professing to be neither benefactors nor missionaries, but only merchants and physicians, gave their pupils a long object-lesson in civilization. Pilgrims thirsting for knowledge came from all over the empire to learn of the Hollanders, and dispersing homeward filled the country with centres of light. Maligned by their enemies in faith and by their rivals in commerce, the work of the Dutchmen for a century in supplying a hermit nation with books, science, and medicine, has been unknown or underrated. The Dutch laid the foundations of scientific knowledge of the Japanese and their country, secured the abolition of the insults to Christianity, and made the way easy for Commodore Perry and Townsend Harris. It would be hard to find a single native pioneer of progress in the early years of Meiji— statesman, diplomatist, military leader, physician, man of science, interpreter, author, preacher—who was not directly indebted to the Dutch.

Not, however, until the decade following the apparition of Perry did foreign influence become an overwhelming force and the foreign employé a permanent figure. Beginning probably with the American Professor Pumpelly, who wrote "Across America and Asia," the Japanese Government and individuals enlisted a great army of auxiliaries from

abroad. In what branch of science or friendly service are the makers of
New Japan not indebted? English scholarship as represented by Satow,
Aston, Chamberlain, McClatchie, Gubbins, and others, first rent the
veil from ancient Japan, and gave to native students the impetus to
that critical and comparative study of their own language and traditions which they are now beginning bravely to pursue. British experts
organized the navy and trained the lads that are now officers and
the junk-sailors that are now smart marines and skilful artillerists,
created and equipped the Ôsaka mint, struck the coinage of which
no Japanese is ashamed, and established the vernacular newspaper,
now the mighty power that even prime-ministers and Emperor must
reckon with. Frenchmen reorganized the army, codified the law, and
built the Yokoska dockyard. The Germans have directed the higher
medical education of the country. "Not less a feat than the reform of
the entire educational system was chiefly the work of a handful of
Americans." The posts, the telegraphs, the railways, the light-houses;
the trigonometrical, geological, and geodetic surveys; improved mining methods, prison reform, sanitary reform, cotton and paper mills;
manufactories of many kinds, chemical laboratories, water-works
and harbor-works, and a hundred other improvements which have
enriched the country, and which strike the eye and excite the admiration of the tourist—"all are the creation of the foreign employes of
the Japanese Government."*

---

* It is not probable that the future Japanese historian will deign to use as
important material for his narrative any of the little accordeon-like publications entitled *Yatoi Tô-jin* such as we have before us. While the throne and
the figure-heads and a multitude of names such as already clog the pages of
the Japanese annals will doubtless occupy vast space on the historian's page,
yet a glance at the little brochure giving names, salaries, and occupation of the
"hired foreigners," is like a visit to the power-house of an electric railway. Here
are the generating forces, and the wheels, belts, and motors, while to the outside world the brilliancy and speed of the moving trains astonish the spectator.

True type of the foreigners who not merely advised or inspected, but who wrought by example and precept, patiently teaching technical details, was the German Dr. Gottfried von Wagener, whose personal friendship the writer enjoyed while a fellow-worker in the Imperial University from 1871 to 1874. Dr. Wagener, born in Germany in 1831, was a master of applied science when, in 1870, he entered the service of the daimio of Hizen to improve the methods of porcelain manufacture at Arita, in which he happily succeeded so far as the resources of that province would then admit. One of his notable triumphs was in the introduction of coal as fuel. Besides his services in education at Tôkiô and Kiôto, he assisted materially in preparing the art exhibits of the Japanese at Vienna and Philadelphia. He established the Artisan's School in Tôkiô, revolutionized the *cloisonné*-enamel industry, and invented the famous *Asahi yaki* (Morning-sun faience), or pottery with varied colors under the glaze. The writer has never known a man who combined more nobly for the benefit of his fellow-men self-absorption in science with absolute self-effacement in disposition. He died at Suruga Dai in Tôkiô, November 8, 1892.

In the higher work of moral education and reform, the Christian missionary is a noble figure. The first teachers of language, literature, science, and philosophy; the first dispensers of medicine and healing, active in charitable relief, constantly stimulating to the Government and people by their hospitals, schools, colleges, preaching and advocacy of moral reforms; training tens of thousands of natives in the

---

Here are some of the names picked out at random: Pumpelly, Tracey, Hawes, Douglas, Cargill, Savatier, Verbeck, Brinkley, Brunton, Knipping, Capron, Antisell, Eldredge, Scott Wilson, Simmons, Geerts, Wagener, House, Divers, Gower, Lyman, Murray, Smith, Boissonnade, Palmer, Chamberlain, Müller, Hoffman, McCartee, Gowland, Milne, Mason, Clark, Clarke, Ingalls, Baelz, Conder, Miquel, Bertin, etc., etc., with scores of others who have during longer or shorter periods of time imparted the secrets of Western science, learning, or technical skill, and patiently shown the Japanese how to do likewise.

arts of self-government and parliamentary procedure; supplanting the old Confucian and Chinese codes of ethics with nobler ideals and practice, the teachers of Christianity have prepared the nation for the adoption of a higher form of civilization. Greater even than the wants of modern material forces and appliances, by the confessions of her own most thoughtful men, is Japan's need of moral power.

True types of the servant of servants, for Christ's sake, to the people of Japan, are Mr. and Mrs. J. C. Hepburn, who have done so much to break down the barriers between natives and foreigners. After thirty-three years of service in school, dispensary, home, and study, Dr. Hepburn left Yokohama for the United States in October, 1892. The story of the "American Missionary in Japan," of influences and results, and of native appreciation, has been modestly told in part by Dr. M. L. Gordon.* Since the reaction against everything foreign, which began in 1888, the Christian churches and schools have suffered. Yet the loss, or rather the retarded acceleration of progress, signifies "no real change of purpose in the national mind."

"Japan for the Japanese" does not mean more than healthy patriotism. Digestion and assimilation are as necessary as reception. Christianity, now rooted in the soil and no longer a mere exotic, can live its own life in the hearts and the minds of the people. Christian theology can live and grow expressed in terms of far-oriental as well as in Greek or Latin terminology. The Japanese Christians will create their own theology and adapt it to the national consciousness more healthfully, truthfully, and spiritually than can foreigners. In treating of "The Theological Movement in Japan,"* we have summed up our impressions as follows: "The Japanese genius, as vitalized by the Holy Spirit, tends to assimilation rather than to mere acceptance. Vigorously has the Christian consciousness of Japan cast off the sectarian and provincial creeds of

---

* *An American Missionary in Japan.* Boston. 1892.

merely English-speaking Christendom. Refusing the swaddling-bands of the Scotch, Yankee, and Anglican phases of the faith, it has sought the simplicity that is Christ.....They, with the Bible in hand, sought the shortest path to Christ." Already the record of independent native Christian life, work, and literature is a noble one. It shows clearly that the believers in Christ in Japan want the Christianity of Christ not in non-essential and accidental alien forms, but in its reality and purity as far as it can be apprehended and assimilated by them.

The statistics for the year ending March 31, 1893, furnished by Rev. Henry Loomis of Yokohama, show that the Christians of the Roman order number 44,812 in 244 congregations; those of the Greek order number 20,235 in 219 congregations; those of the Reformed order number 35,534 in 365 local churches. Baptisms for 1892 were: for the Roman, Greek, and Reformed phases of the one faith, 5324, 952, and 3731, respectively. Thirty-one organizations, usually called "Protestant," illustrate more of Christian unity than diversity, since five of these divisions comprise 33,390 Christians, all the self-support-ing native churches being affiliated with these groups. At present, the religion of Jesus in Japan is better represented by the parable of the leaven than by that of the mustard-seed. It is influencing the national life deeply, while not phenomenally increasing its superficial area. Buddhism, still the religion of the majority of the mikado's subjects, is being quickened into wholesome activity. It has yet to show whether it can hold the heart and intellect of New Japan.

Let us now turn to a survey of political history and see what has been the root and the offspring of the forty-years' movement. We shall inquire what is down at the bottom of the ceaseless unrest in national politics, especially in the long conflict, not between the people and the Throne, but between the people and the Government.

---

* "The Outlook" [*The Christian Union*], April 1, 1893.

The meteoric phenomenon of the night of July 8, 1853,* prefigured in its brilliancy, direction of movement, and apparent end the uprising of the two (or three) great clans which, since 1868, under every form of government, have ruled the mikado's empire. "It made its appearance in the southward and westward, and illuminated the whole atmosphere.... It pursued a north-eastwardly course in a direct line for a long distance, when it fell gradually towards the sea and disappeared."

So might a prophet have foretold the course of the coalition headed by the great Satsuma and Chôshiu clans, which we have described in Book I., Chapter XXVIII. Fifteen years after the meteor seen from the *Susquehanna*'s deck, the "*Sat-chô*" captured Kiôto and inaugurated New Japan. Twenty-one years more had to pass before the promise in the imperial oath to summon a parliament was fulfilled. To-day we write of the fifth session of the Imperial Diet—that august assembly representing the nobles, gentry, and people of the country ruled since 1868 by the Sat-chô. The story of the two elections and of the five sessions is that of a fierce and not wholly bloodless struggle between the Liberal parties and the Government, or, more exactly, of the people against the two mighty clans intrenched behind the throne.

The net results of four sessions seem at first almost trivial, and the story is soon told. In the first session of 1890–91, the hostility of the Opposition was against the cabinet led by Count Masagata. A reduction of the Budget to the extent of six and a half millions of *yen* was secured, and a collision on the very threshold of representative government was happily averted. The second session of 1891–92 opened even less hopefully for the Government, and, after a severe struggle, ended in dissolution. The Kai-shin and Jiyu parties were so joined in implacable opposition that the cabinet ministers soon found that the situation was beyond their control; and so invoking the Emperor's

---

* *Perry's Narrative.* Appleton's N. Y. edition, p. 272.

executive interference, they appealed to the country through fresh elections. How far active government influence was brought to bear unfairly to secure a more tractable temper in the Diet cannot be stated, yet it is evident not only that the estrangement between the popular and the official classes was increased, but that the Government was bitterly disappointed in results. The new Diet opened May 6th, 1892. Although in this third session the Budget was not considered, yet the Government escaped a formal, by receiving indirect, but real, censure. A new and eclectic cabinet, not yet the creation of the Diet, but chosen by the Emperor and made up of "all the talents," was now formed. It was led by the veteran Ito, "father of the constitution," and author of the best written commentary upon it, while Inouyé became minister of the Home Department. In the fourth session, the *Jiyu-tô*, or Radical party, whose favorite measure —the reduction of the land tax—had been accepted, manifested a desire to work with the cabinet. For months, however, so great were the forces of opposition, that the problem was one of either dissolution or compromise. A reduction in the Budget of nearly nine millions, or a grand total of less than eighty-four millions, was insisted upon. The Opposition appealed to the Emperor, who answered in a state paper of notable ability, in which party strife and politics were ignored, and the "fixed expenditures" reduced by three and a half millions, his Majesty ordering that one-tenth of his own income should be appropriated to secure the results desired. Peace came through the Throne, but the Kai-shin party is still implacable and continues agitation.

The battle ostensibly rages round the Budget, but the real questions at issue are these: Shall the government of the country be by party after the British model, or according to the Prussian method? Shall the Government be really responsible to the Diet, or nominally to the sovereign? Shall the power be in the hands of an oligarchy consisting largely of two clans, or shall the clan spirit be banished, and sovereign and people rule?

The roots of this difficulty go back to the days of the Taikô and Iyéyasu, to which rulers the great clans of Satsuma and Chôshiu never gave more than nominal submission. Proudly and sullenly they maintained their semi-independence, and waited over two centuries and a half for revenge. The coming of the alien in 1853 was the awaited signal to begin their work. While individuals were unselfishly con- secrated to patriotism, the clans masked self-interest under the plea of loyalty to the mikado, overthrowing in 1868 the shôgunate. If in Kiôto they devoured the prey, in Tôkiô they divided the spoil. No Benjamin or Saul in ancient Israel, no Fujiwara in mediæval Nippon, no American politician, ever so held their grip on the treasury, or excelled the Sat-chô in distributing offices to clansmen. The inside view as eye-witness which the writer enjoyed in Tôkiô during three years, over two decades ago, showed him how grandly the Japanese exceeded the American spoilsmen in nepotism. In this year of Meiji the 27th, the lists of government officers and employés show that the men of only two clans, Satsuma and Chôshiu, still fill a majority of the most desirable offices. In the many changes of ministries, it is "the mats and not the floor" that are rearranged. The Japanese political edifice for twenty-five years past has been an oligarchy cemented by clan spirit. This is the real meaning of the long struggle of the people against the Government, of the Lower House of the Diet against the Ministry. During the year 1893 the effort has been especially to reform the navy, which in *personnel*, declare the Kai-shin politicians, is virtually an organization of Satsuma men. Great as have been the services of the illustrious statesmen of the Meiji periods, it is evidently the deeply settled belief of the people that new times and problems demand new men, and that clan spirit is now an anachronism not to

be tolerated or excused. It is time for the meteor of July to fall into the
sea, so that the new morning of true national life may dawn.

The men of the Meiji era are now aging fast and passing away.
Sanjô Sanéyoshi, General Yamada, Yoshida Kiyonari, and Terashima
Munénori have "changed their worlds" since our last chapter was
written. Of some of those still in power and influence, like Ito and
Inouyé, it can be said that they have opposed the clan spirit, served
country and sovereign with pre-eminent ability and faithfulness, and
foreseen the needs of the nation. To such patriots, in and out of office,
belongs much of the credit of Japan's notable progress in wealth,
population, and prestige. For, despite all commotions, dangers, and
calamities, the increase is notably great. Whereas in 1872 the population of the empire was but 33,110,000, the census of 1892 shows a
total of 41,089,940 souls. There has been hopeful increase also of food
supply, savings, manufactures, mines, commerce and industry of all
sorts. The national wealth has doubled in ten years. Once Japan was
reckoned by Europeans as "hardly worth trading with." In 1892, the
total of exports (91,102,753 *yen*) and imports (71,326,079 *yen*) amounted
to 162,428,832 *yen*, the increase in one decade being one hundred and
fifty per cent. The United States, once having the least of the trade
with Japan, now leads every other nation as a buyer and seller, her
business aggregating in 1892 44,663,024 *yen*. Five-eighths of Japanese
trade is with English-speaking nations. It is from Anglo-Saxondom
that the leaders of thought and action derive their chief inspiration.
Resisting, for want of space, the temptation to prove and illustrate this
assertion, and to show the influence on religion, science, philosophy,
and literature, as well as upon politics and national development, of
the nations using English speech, we make passing reference to her
representation at the World's Columbian Exposition.

It was wholly fitting that Xipangu, the country which the Genoese,
in his Spanish caravels in 1492, was seeking, should join with the

world in honoring his exploit. The first Asian nation to send ships to America across the Pacific—a sailer to Mexico in 1573, and a steamer to California in 1860—was Japan. In the generosity of her financial appropriation, and the variety and interest of her contribution to the Chicago Exhibition, the mikado's empire was exceeded by only two other countries, while in the permanency and value of her gifts to Chicago she leads the world. Her total space occupied—falling far short of the desire of intending exhibitors—was about 150,000 square feet. Under the roofs of the halls of Manufactures and Liberal Arts, of Agriculture, Fine Arts, Horticulture, Forestry, Mining, Fisheries, and in the street devoted to entertainments, in bazaar and tea-house, her portable products of native industry and genius were visible. Yet, strange as it seems, the only permanent edifices, except the Art Exhibition building, that remain in Jackson Park after the White City has vanished, are the specimens of Japanese historical architecture on Wooded Island. Of the three separate buildings united so as to form to the uncritical eye a single structure, called the Hô-den, or Phœnix Palace, the centre and right and left wings represent three epochs. On the right the Fujiwara style (A.D. 1000–1200), before the days of nails, metal hinges, sliding partitions, but of silken corded and tas-selled curtains, such as Sei Shonagon could easily raise (p. 228), may be studied. On the left stands the house typical of the Ashikaga era (A.D. 1333–1579), when matted floors, papered walls and partitions, elaborate metal-work, and other luxuries came into vogue. The main edifice, with its greater number of roof-timbers and detail of decora-tion, follows the fashion prevalent in Tokugawa times (1604–1868). In its general ground plan the edifice follows the lines of the Phœnix Temple built in Uji in the year 1050.

While the United States has celebrated its first centennial of political union, and the four hundredth anniversary of the discovery of America by Columbus, Téi Koku Nippon proposes in 1895 to commemorate the millennial of Kiôto. A thousand years ago, in the castle of Héi-an, the mikado fixed his residence, and around him, as the fountain of authority, grew up the *Kio*, or "Blossom Capital."

The year 1894 opens in tumult and with portents that disturb the warmest friends of Japan, shaking their faith in the capacity of an Asiatic race for constitutional government or for participation in the comity of nations. The Diet opened November 25, 1893. The Budget, in six books, containing altogether 1,438 pages, estimated the revenue at 90,675,196 *yen* and the expenditures at 85,472,159 *yen*. The House of Representatives, in a spasm of political animosity, first proceeded to expel its speaker, Mr. Hoshi Toru, without any known charge against him as a presiding officer, and then attacked the Budget, hoping to compel a resignation of the Cabinet ministers. On the 19th of December the Government suspended the sittings of the House for ten days, apparently in order to consult what should be done—whether the Diet should be dissolved, or the Ministry either resign or set about reconstruction. Meeting again on December 29th, the House was, after a turbulent session, suspended for another ten days. On the next day the Diet was dissolved.

Thus far the people, as represented in the Diet, have steadily gained. The "military party" in the Government, that wants the reign of force continued, the Diet defied, and the Constitution rescinded, has been beaten. Men of moderate counsels have held control. With them a section of the Jiyu party, led by Count Itagaki, the unfaltering patriot and leader of a twenty years' campaign—peaceful campaign—is disposed to co-operate. They are willing still to wait and not precipitate a crisis. The Kai-shin party demands instant overthrow of clan government. The ten political coteries or groups ,in the House, differing seriously on minor points, are united in opposition to the Government, and in hearty hatred of that clan rule which, whatever be the political issue, seems doomed.

Meanwhile, awaiting with intense interest the solution of the problems of State and of Church, we note, in closing, the advent of the new book in New Japan and the literary movement so full of promise.* Now that the old literature based on feudalism and Chinese ethics no longer feeds the mind, it is cheering to see that fresh pens respond to the needs of the new age. After Bakin and Ikku have come Yamada, Tsubouchi, and Kotaro Han, in fiction; after Rai Sanyo appears Shimada Saburo in history; after Motoöri is Kumé; while in the other paths of thought and inquiry still walks many an earnest pilgrim. Besides embroidering the old annals with romance, there is a prodigious activity among native scholars, who now write their country's story on critical principles and in attractive literary form for the people. On the granite front of the Boston Public Library, in company with the hundreds of names of the literary torch-bearers of every age and country, stand those of Sugawara Michizané and Rai Sanyo. Recognizing the genius of the Japan that is past, Americans welcome gladly the dawn of a day so full of literary promise. Even in the morning of her life, Nippon was called Hi-no-moto (the day's beginning); to-day, in her larger and richer life, may Japan be the Land Where the Day Begins for all Asia.

---

* "The New Book in New Japan," *The Literary World*, May 6, 1893. "The Literary Movement in New Japan," *The Outlook*, January 27, 1894.

# The War with China

To most of the people of the three countries—China, Corea, and Japan—as well as to the world at large, the war of 1894, between Dai Nippon, a unit, and some fractions of the Chinese Empire, came like a lightning-bolt out of blue sky. To the rulers of the Middle and Sunrise kingdoms it was not altogether unexpected, for the relations between the governments of the two empires had become strained over the debatable ground of Corea. In attempting to explain the origin of the war, and in recounting the military and diplomatic movements, we shall endeavor to be impartial.

As we view the situation, China stood like a great giant, imposing to the world because of size, numbers, and claims rather than by inherent strength and simple truth. Trusting in antiquity, impervious to new ideas, contemptuous of every civilization except their own—never, indeed, dreaming that there was any other—the Chinese were in a chronic state of unreadiness. Japan, like an athlete, having all available powers in hand, was alert, vigilant, and prepared. Corea, like a pygmy, and without a government worthy of the name, stood between the jealous rivals soon to become hostile and combatant.

Strictly speaking, the war was provoked by a very few mandarins. The congeries of peoples called the Chinese Empire form in reality only a patriarchal state which has no real, but only a nominal, unity.

There is no such thing as China considered as a political entity, but there are various provinces, each having its own local government. There are also powerful viceroys, and a great central figure-head of parental authority in Peking, under whom is a bureaucratic administration. One of these powerful viceroys, Li Hung Chang, with patriotic motives, and desirous of stirring up the authorities at Peking to arm and equip for modern defence, to open the mines of coal and iron, to lay the railroad from the heart of China to its farthest frontier, to forestall Russian aggression, provoked the war of 1894. He and those who thought with him expected, with their superior ships to overpower the Japanese navy, and with his private, or at least provincial, army drilled by German officers, to beat back the troops of Japan from Corea. Thus would the two objects—of retaining Corea as a buffer state, and of exciting the Peking authorities sufficiently to secure appropriations—be secured. In Japan's intestine quarrels, the coveted opportunity seemed at hand. Deceived by surface indications, and not knowing the temper of the Japanese, China forced the war.

Those who during the past eight years have studied the behavior and aggressive advances of Yuan—China's, or, rather, Li Hung Chang's, envoy in Corea—know how well the servant obeyed his master, giving abundant excuse and justification to Japan, the United States, or some other power to interfere. The Japanese, having opened the once Hermit Nation to the diplomacy and commerce of the world, having created her modern trade and incipient industries, having interests outweighing and outnumbering those of all other foreigners within her borders, resented the action of China in virtually outlawing the treaties which Corea had made, and in practically keeping her subject and vassal to the Middle Kingdom.

On the other hand, Japan was internally nearing a political crisis in the virtual deadlock between the emperor's ministers and the lower and more important house of the Imperial Diet. It seemed as though something must be done to divert the attention of the people and of the too rapidly growing class of active politicians from intestine quarrels to some great national enterprise abroad. Further, the pressure of a population increasing at the rate of half a million a year has forced a colonizing nation like the Japanese to look longingly afield for expansion. A magnificent army and navy, superbly organized, drilled, officered, and ready for the severest trial of powers and patriotism, were awaiting only a signal. For twenty-five years the Japanese, oppressed by treaty, powerless under a diplomacy which they looked upon as galling and unjust, had apparently yielded only with and for the purpose of becoming victor in the end. Whether in time, had the provocation still remained, Japan would have outlawed the treaties made in her political childhood cannot be certainly affirmed; but of her desire to impress the world at large with her abilities as a military power, which her intelligent friends already knew she possessed, there can be no question.

Nevertheless, patiently biding the favorable time, knowing that China considered her as a traitor to Asia and to Confucianism, Japan kept herself ready to draw instantly the sharp line whenever and wherever patience should cease to be a virtue. Caring not a jot for the size, the numbers, or the reputed colossal resources and enduring powers of her giant rival, the athlete watched and waited. Jack and the Ogre, or rather Momotarô and the Oni's Castle, was to the Japanese an unforgotten childhood's tale.

In modern times, whatever forces have upheaved the Asiatic nations, stagnating in the dreaminess of Buddhism or the savagery of Confucian conceit, have been born of Christianity. In Corea the old elements and institutions of a society founded upon patriarchal and Confucian ideas had already been shaken. As far back as 1777 the first wind-wafted seeds of the Roman form of the faith began to germinate in Corean soil. By the year 1859 the wide-spreading and

deeply rooted tree was able to survive a prolonged storm of persecutions, the cruelty of which could be matched only in the annals of the
Inquisition. The bigotry that banned and the tortures that followed
were the direct result of a narrow Confucianism. A Corean scholar,
Choi, impressed with the convictions, zeal, and consecration of the
foreign priests and native Christians, withal astonished at their tremendous success, pondered deeply as to whether theirs might not be
the true religion. While thinking long upon the subject, he became
ill even to the point of death. In a trance he received a revelation
from God, whom he himself named, after the Roman Catholic title,
Lord of Heaven. Called, as he believed, to found a new religion,
Choi forthwith proceeded, from the elements of the three systems of
Confucius, Buddha, and Lao Tsze, to compose a sacred book, and
to write the prayer which his followers still daily repeat. Thus began
a great movement which, originating in religion, ended in politics,
in time degenerating into lawlessness. It caused a great uprising of
the most oppressed people on the face of the earth, which the feeble
government at Seoul could not suppress. It inflamed Japan and China
in war. Only by that new force in modern history, the Japanese soldier,
was the revolt quelled.

The name of this new sect or party is Tong Hak, or Eastern
Culture. Its Great Sacred Scripture, penned by Choi, combines what
he deemed best in the three religions already known to Chinese
Asia. In its literary features this cultus bears likeness at many points
to the Shin Gaku, or Heart-Learning movement, which, in Japan
in the first half of the nineteenth century, was started to cleanse the
abysses of Japanese immorality and irreligion. Eclecticism in doctrine,
earnestness of conviction, intensity of purpose, and practicality in
benevolence marked both movements. The Tong Haks took from the
Chinese classics the idea of the five relations governing human duty,
from the sutras and shastras the law of purity of life, and from the Tao

the rules for cleansing the body from lust and filth. One term for the so-called Tong Hak Bible combines the names of the three old religions, while in the title used for the Deity in the daily prayer we see the debt to Roman Christianity. The founder intended his scripture and work to be set over against So Hak, or Western Culture. In Japan the coming of Perry and the foreigners from Christendom paled the Shin Gaku as the sun drowns the taper's beams in daylight. To the hermits of Corea no such morning dawned.

Within six years persecution broke out, and the founder, Choi, was charged with being "a foreign-Corean" and "follower of the Lord of Heaven"—that is, a Roman Catholic Christian. After trial and torture he was beheaded, and his doctrines outlawed. Nevertheless, the new religion grew through a whole human generation, winning many followers. At a time of oppression and rapacity, extraordinary even in Corea, it was not astonishing that poor peasants should be goaded to rebellion. Nerved by their new zeal, they struck even against authority, though abominably misused, for enough freedom to make life tolerable. Early in 1893 fifty followers of the Tong Hak creed entered the Corean capital. On a table before the palace gate they spread a red cloth, and laid thereon a petition, praying that their martyred founder might be declared innocent, receive posthumous rank, be allowed a monument in his honor, that the ban on their religion be removed, and that they be put on a political equality with the Roman Catholics. The alternative, if their petition were rejected, was expressed in a threat to expel all foreigners from the country. The king refused their prayer. They were driven away, and some of their local leaders arrested.

No sooner had the snow of the next winter vanished than a widespread uprising in the southern provinces of Corea took place. The military sent from Seoul in April melted before the Tong Haks like frost in the sun. The civil magistrates were driven from their offices, swift vengeance in many cases following their horrible cruelties in the past. Instead of a few hundred zealots there were myriads of people in wild insurrection, bent only on destroying their oppressors. The May danger seemed to threaten the whole kingdom. The June moment was critical.

In Séoul the pro-Chinese faction at court, then vastly outnumbering their moderately pro-Japanese rivals, sent to Peking for a Chinese force to put down the Tong Hak rebels. According to the Chino-Japanese treaty of 1885 negotiated by Li and Itô, neither power was to send armed men into Corea without first notifying the other. In violation of this convention, the Chinese soldiers were first sent, and then the Government at Tôkiô was notified. On June 7th China sent a despatch which compromised not only Japan, but all the treaty powers which had acknowledged the sovereignty of Corea, by declaring her a subject country. "It is in harmony with our constant practice," declared this document, "to protect *our tributary states* by sending our troops to assist them.... General Yeh has been ordered to proceed at once to Zenra...in order to restore the peace of *our tributary state*." Thus China, against the world, reasserted her ancient claim of suzerain over Corea as a vassal state, and flung down the gauntlet to Japan, virtually bidding her to maintain her rights if she could. Treaties being usually held as sacred, the smaller country gained, even as the larger forfeited, the sympathies of the civilized world.

The Tong Hak match had fallen between two petroleum tanks that were already leaking. The whole Japanese people, through an extraordinary incident, which we shall recount, were at this moment on the point of combustion and explosion. The Chinese despatch fired both rulers and people of Japan to national conflagration.

Nine years before, the attempt of the Corean Liberals returning from America, Europe, and Japan, to effect a revolution in the Government in favor of modern civilization had failed. One of them,

Kim Ok Kiun, fleeing to Japan, received the same protection which, under the treaties, would have been granted to any foreigner. During his long residence he made himself extraordinarily popular, contriving, also, to elude his assassins. At last, in April, 1894, when lured to Shanghai by a false telegram and a forged bank draft, he was promptly murdered by a Corean emissary. With indecent haste, and with a barbarism that reveals the Chinese official character, the body of the murdered man was packed on board of a man-of-war to be delivered up to his real destroyers in Séoul, for public mincing, distribution, and exposure. The carrion was duly displayed at the capital and in the provinces, while the assassin gained gold and won official honor.

The news of this union of Chinese and Corean barbarism produced an extraordinary excitement in Japan. To Government and people it seemed as if China and her pupils in Corea had, with unnecessary ostentation, flouted and insulted the newly adopted civilization of Japan. It is not strange that the emperor and his ministers decided that, with China's forcible reiteration of her claim upon Corea, following a fresh outbreak of barbarism, and backed as it was by military force, the line of forbearance had been reached. The time for the wager of battle between two incompatible civilizations had come.

Down at the bottom this Chino-Japanese war meant, in its provocation and origin, the right of a nation to change its civilization. It is difficult for people in the Occident to understand the depth of pedantic polemic that underlies the estrangement between New Japan and unawakened China. For years the idea in Peking had been that Japan was not only a "neighbor-disturbing nation," but had been colossally wicked in discarding the Chinese calendar, and in turning away from Confucius and the civilization of the sages to adopt and assimilate that of Christendom. What the Chinese residents of Yokohama did in 1872—tumultuously engaging in public protest against that change of chronology, which in far-eastern Asia means also change in mental attitude, with repudiation of every suggestion of intellectual or political vassalage —the Chinese Government has been doing tacitly ever since. When, in 1879, Japan and China were on the verge of war over the question of the ownership of the Riu Kiu islands, the two governments, at the suggestion of General U. S. Grant, agreed to settle the matter by reference to a joint High Commission. Prince Kung, with colleagues, and Mr. Shishido were appointed as plenipotentiaries, and the conference began at Peking August 15th, 1880. On the 21st of October, by Chinese official notice, the Articles of Agreement were ready for signature. The commissioners indulged in mutual congratulations, and agreed to sign the instruments ten days later, when lo! on the 17th of November, sixteen days after the date fixed, the Emperor of China turned the whole affair into a burlesque. In a word, his majesty virtually cancelled the commission of the plenipotentiaries, transferring their function in a modified and incomplete form to "the Northern and Southern Superintendents of Trade." The profession which the Chinese Government made in conferring full powers upon any one but the emperor was an empty farce.

After such an experience, the Japanese statesmen were not likely to be lured into another similar humiliation. Furthermore, since in the unhappy Corean affair of 1885, in which the Japanese Legation guard of ninescore men had been attacked by fifteen hundred Chinese troops—one-half of the three thousand which had been encamped near Séoul—the mikado's ministers were fore-warned by experience not again to be caught napping. Hence, on the 12th of June, 1894, Japan, asserting her treaty rights, replied to China, announcing the despatch of a body of troops under strictest discipline to Corea.

The next step, five days later, was highly creditable to the government which had made the first treaty with Corea. It was an invitation from Japan to China to undertake jointly some needed reforms, financial and administrative, in the peninsular state, in order to preserve the peace of the East. This offer was curtly refused, China demanding the immediate withdrawal of the Japanese troops. Japan's reply was that, pending an amicable settlement of the questions in dispute, any further despatch of Chinese troops into Corea would mean war. China, having already chartered the *Kow-Shing*, a British transport, filled it with soldiers and despatched it to A-San, a well-fortified camp in a peninsula a formed by two rivers flowing into Prince Jerome Gulf, some forty miles southwest of Séoul. At the same time the Tartar forces in Manchuria began the march overland to Corea.

All this, through their spies, regular servants, and the telegraph, the Tôkiô Government knew well. Resolving once for all to settle the long string of questions inherited from the past; to break the power of Chinese insolence, and if possible shatter the old Chinese world of ideas, with its perpetual menace of implied or explicit claim of supremacy; to compel the elimination of Corea as a factor of disturbance in the affairs of the Far East; to assert her imperilled rights and dignity; to make proof of her duty and power to graduate from foreign tutelage and dependence; to reveal to her own people their power in union, and to impress the world with her ability to hold and maintain her place as equal among the great nations of the world, Japan called forth her military strength. With a secrecy, order, precision, celerity, and punctuality incredible, except to those who, as helpers and friends, had lived inside the country, away from the seaports, Japan landed first a brigade and then an army corps at Chemulpo. Her engineers completed in twenty minutes, a pontoon-bridge over the Han River. Within twelve days after orders received in camp in Japan a military cordon had been drawn around Seoul, in Corea. On the 23d of July, after a skirmish in front of the palace between the military escort of the Japanese minister, Mr. Hoshi Toru, and some pro-Chinese native troops, the question of Corea's independence and willingness to stand by her treaty was answered by the king in the affirmative.

On the water the Chinese were the first aggressors, the *Chen-yuen* firing on the *Naniwa*. The Chinese troops on the transport *Kow-Shing*, not knowing or unwilling to believe that the Japanese had adopted civilized rules of warfare, refused to surrender. After keeping his signals flying four hours, and these armed men refusing to surrender, the captain of the *Naniwa* quickly sank the transport. This was on July 25th. Four days later General Ôshima's mixed brigade moved out from Séoul, and after a battle at Song-kwan, in which the brave Major Matsusaki lost his life, A-San was occupied July 30th, and the Chinese driven back from their stronghold. The declaration of war came from the Japanese emperor on August 1st, in a document strikingly clear in phrase and temperate in tone.

The reinforcements despatched by way of Gensan, as well as Chemulpo, formed with the pioneer regiments the First Army. As "geography is half of war," it was matter of foreordination and necessity that the decisive battle should in A.D. 1894 be fought just where the decisive battles in Corean annals always had been fought—at Ping Yang. Here, three centuries before, Konishi had lost a battle and retreated southward before an overwhelming Ming and Tartar host. Now the pendulum of history, despite forty days' time for defence and fortification by the Chinese, was to swing to reverse effect.

The Chinese declaration of war—a new thing in the history of the Middle Kingdom, showing strikingly the progress of international law—was also dated August 1st, and was characteristic of mandarins who were not yet willing either to learn or to forget. From beginning to end the writing displayed utter ignorance of the enemy to be fought and the work to be done. It was declared that the Wo-jen, or pygmies (Japanese), had, "without any cause whatever," invaded "our small tributary;" that Japan had "violated the treaties," and was "running rampant with her false and treacherous actions," while "we [China] have always followed the paths of philanthropy and perfect justice."

The Chinese braves were called upon to "hasten with all speed to root the Wo-jen out of their lairs." A comparatively small number of really disciplined soldiers, armed and drilled in the European manner, was, with the usual mob of native military, hurried forward to Ping Yang, which, aided by the fugitives from A-San, they began to fortify.

China actually went to war without a hospital corps, or any organization of surgeons, nurses, or accommodations for the wounded or sick worthy of the name. Except detachments from Li Hung Chang's private army, very few of the Chinese officers or men had been educated in modern tactics. In their equipment all sorts of prehistoric accoutrements—flags, banners, umbrellas, and fans— were mingled with modern imported weapons, in a medley which resembled the diplomacy of Peking. On the other hand, besides a thoroughly well-officered, armed, drilled, equipped, and provisioned army of fifty thousand young men, the flower of the Japanese nation, the Tôkiô Government was able to call out for service a reserve of one hundred thousand strong and healthy. Patriots, burning with enthusiasm and familiar with the weapons, machinery, and practice of modern war. Furthermore, besides her numerous public and private hospitals, her splendid medical field-corps, her four hundred surgeons and pharmacists, and her fourteen hundred trained nurses, she had an efficient Red Cross society. Immediately both the nation and the government began the organization and consolidation of all public and private resources in order to strike as a unit. At home and abroad all sons and daughters of Nippon vied in diligence and sacrifice for the efficient carrying on of the war, and for securing the comfort of the soldiers at the front.

The secrets of Japanese success are patent to the student. In such a time as this, life for the average man in Nippon is worth living. With a flaming patriotism that surprises Europeans who have imagined the Japanese to be only average Asiatics and mere imitators, all classes, sexes, and ages rallied intelligently to the support of the national cause. A quarter of a century ago Japan was the hot-bed of caste, monopoly, and privilege. These seemed to crush out every germ of popular liberty and ambition. Even the proverbial politeness and submissiveness of the Japanese common people is in large part the result of ages of military despotism. To-day, with the soil virtually in the hands of the people who cultivate it; the courts open to all who seek even-handed justice; schools and education free to every one; military privilege no longer the prerogative of a special class; the existence of pariahs no more than a memory; government becoming more national and representative; democracy making strides every day, with little or nothing to hinder the advance of the individual in every line of human achievement, it is not strange to see a whole nation rising up in an outburst of intensest energy. Self-sacrifice, loyalty, and patriotism, with an unquenchable ambition to humble China, to impress the whole world, and to make their country great, characterize the Japanese of A.D. 1895. In this war they have irrevocably committed themselves to cosmopolitan as against Chinese or merely ethnic principles.

The sympathies of those who began, even twenty-five years ago, to help in making the New Japan have been from the first with the smaller country. Their seat of observation has not been the fence, in order to be sure, before applauding, which side would win. Seeing so clearly that the Japanese were triply armed in having their quarrel just, and knowing their earnestness, their former teachers and helpers not only, but Americans in general, have not been surprised at the swift success of the armies under the sun-banner. They have not wondered at the tenacity and staying power of the soldier-lads, or at the sustained ability and seriousness of statesmen and generals, and their power of mastering the secrets and applying the forces of Western civilization. In the campaign of 1894 the Japanese were no longer pupils. They went to war not only without foreign aids or advisers, but in clothes, arms, and ships made in large part by themselves.

Almost simultaneously the supremacy of Japan on both sea and land was demonstrated. The future historian will mark two days of September as the dates of battles that decided the future of Eastern Asia. On the 15th, at Ping Yang, General Nodzu, attacking in front, on the flanks, and in the rear, broke up the Chinese army. Within a fortnight every Chinese soldier had been driven out of Corea. Near the mouth of the Yalu River, on the 17th, the first great conflict between fleets of steel-armored ships took place. The cruisers of Japan, unevenly matched against the Chinese battle-ships and men-of-war from noon to sunset, so decided the issue that the dragon-flag was not again mirrored on the deep in presence of the sun-banner. Then followed the brilliant Manchurian campaign, in which the First Army won an almost unbroken series of victories, holding, in April, 1895, Chinese territory vastly greater in area than the Japanese Empire. Neither snow and ice nor exposure and hardship seem in any way to cool the ardor of the young Japanese conscripts.

The Second Army, under Field-Marshal Ôyama, was despatched to Port Arthur. This vast fortress had, after twenty years of toil, been fortified at a cost of two hundred millions of dollars. After bombardment by the fleet on the sea-front, and attack by the land forces in the rear, beginning before the dawn on the 21st of November, the town, forts, and ships were captured within ten hours. The glory of the victors was dimmed by an outbreak of cruelty, the reports of which, however, were highly exaggerated in the newspapers of America and Europe.

The Third Army was despatched to Wei-Hai-Wei, to reduce the fortress guarding the southern entrance to the Gulf of Pechili. After brilliant naval and land operations, this stronghold passed under the Japanese flag January 31st, 1895. The remaining ships of the Chinese northern fleet were captured, sunk, or destroyed. With both sea-gates defending the capital broken down, the Japanese fleet soon appeared before the Taku forts. Another expedition, despatched to Formosa, captured the fortifications in the Pescadores Islands, bombarded Tai-wan, and made a landing upon the main island.

From the first outbreak of the war, but especially after her multiplying reverses, China attempted, as suppliant, to secure sympathy, practical mediation, and direct help from the governments of Europe. This policy showed a vast change from that of ancient days, and a reverse of attitude that seems astounding. The inherent weakness of the geographical colossus was exposed. In area and population immense, a venerable patriarchal system but scarcely a political entity, the sham collapsed, and the truth about China is now known to the world. Neither mere bulk nor blind numbers, however great, are anything, and with her rhinoceros-crust of conceit pierced by the Murata rifle, it is to be hoped that China will be the gainer because of her bitter experience. Slow, however, in learning their lesson, the Peking mandarins tried to gain time and secure a favorable place in the line of indirection. In November, 1894, she sent a foreigner, Mr. G. Dietring, her faithful servant in the customs service, as peace envoy to Japan. As a matter of decency and of course the mikado's ministers did not receive him. Then, through offers of mediation from the Government of the United States, the Peking Government pretended to send two plenipotentiaries, Messrs. Chang and Shao, who, despite lofty titles, were in reality only very limited subordinates. They arrived at Hiroshima January 31st, 1895. Their credentials when examined showed that they had no powers to settle terms of peace. After her experience of China's behavior in the diplomacy of the Riu Kiu affair in 1879, Japan resolved not again to be duped. The two Chinese envoys with their suite of twenty-four other persons, including one honored American statesman and adviser, were politely sent home to their master. Throughout, Japan acted upon the principle expressed by Premier Ito, "The usages peculiar to China must give way to and be ruled by the canons of International Law."

In their third attempt to gain time, advantage, and peace the Tsung Li Yamen acted with honesty. The emperor, recalling from disgrace, real or nominal, Li Hung Chang, despatched him with full powers to Japan. At the historic city of Shimonoséki the peace conference was opened March 21st. The first request of Li was for an armistice, which at first was refused. On Sunday, the 24th of March, a fanatical *soshi*, attempting to assassinate the venerable Chinaman, fired a pistol, the bullet of which lodged in the cheek of the envoy. Thus again the old murderous spirit which has so repeatedly stained Japan's record—the same spirit in which the ruffian ronins used to cut down unsuspecting foreigners from behind, which has again and again butchered ministers of the Government, which has disgraced the nation in the eyes of the world by the insult and attempted murder even of the nation's guests, which has made a river of blood flow through her history, which is the exponent of one of her greatest dangers, and which may yet deluge her soil with an inundation of sanguinary anarchy— broke forth.

May 8th, the date appointed to exchange ratifications of the Shimonoséki treaty at Chifu, China, was an auspicious one. On that day in 1853 Perry's squadron lay at first morning anchor off Yokohama. On May 8, 1858, Townsend Harris and the shôgun's commissioners completed in Yedo the negotiations that opened Japan to light, science, and the gospel, introducing missionaries, teachers, physicians, and merchants, and making possible to Japan her new career. On this same day in 1895, in the era of Meiji, or enlightened appropriation of Western ideas, Japan obtained from China, as the results of her forty years' training and eight months' war:

The independence of Corea
Permanent cession of Formosa
Opening of China to manufactures and commerce
Cash indemnity to cover cost of the war

The question of the release of Manchurian territory occupied by Japanese troops was settled in such a way as to gain the good-will of Europe and avert war with Russia while satisfying China.

Formosa, first discovered and occupied by Japanese in the thirteenth and fourteenth centuries, is geologically and ethnically a part of Dai Nippon. Under Japanese rule, and probably within a generation, its interior will cease to be a lair of savages and its coasts a haunt of pirates, the whole island being opened to the world's commerce. Within four days of the signed treaty, the mikado appointed the military and civil administrators of Formosa. The island chain of Téi Koku Nippon now extends through nearly thirty degrees of latitude. Fronting Asia and its conquered nations, independent Japan now calls a halt to European aggression. Amid Spanish, British, French, Russian, and Chinese neighbors, she means to hold her own. Can she do it?

Aside from the extraordinary manifestations of popular joy called forth on account of the "silver wedding" of their imperial majesties the emperor and empress, the year 1894 will stand in history as that in which Japan received justice at the hands of Western powers. All the treaties allowing foreign trade and residence, except the one negotiated with Mexico in 1890, have been either based on, or debased from, that instrument made by Townsend Harris in 1858, who expected revision to take place in 1872. He, mourning over conditions then necessary and at first beneficial, but which when perpetuated became wrongs, but hoping to see justice done, died without the sight.* After twenty-two years of agitation and the wreck of three cabinets, Great Britain, in a new treaty signed August 26th by Lord Kimberly and

---

* See the biography and journal of his residence in Japan (1856–1862) in the book *Townsend Harris, First American Envoy in Japan*, by William Elliot Griffis: Houghton, Mifflin & Co., Boston, 1895.

Viscount Mutsu, virtually recognized Japan as an equal. The new American treaty received the signatures of Secretary Gresham and Minister Kurino November 22d, and was ratified by the United States Senate December 28th.

Whatever be the issues of the Chino-Japanese war of 1894–'95, probably the most significant in its influences of the Asiatic wars of many centuries, it is evident that after peace Japan's real difficulties begin and her greatest problems come up for solution. The conflict between clan government and the whole nation, and between the Ministry and the Diet is yet to be fought out. Furthermore, the trend towards democracy is unmistakable, and the perils of militarism are real. The impending revolution in industry is likely not only to modify, even to destruction, much of her beautiful landscape, but threatens to annihilate many things that are lovely and charming in the life of her people. The building of the factory, the introduction of machinery, and the rearrangement of industrial forces and combinations will sow seed for fresh crops of difficulty which only great wisdom and vast increase of moral power can overcome.

Yet, despite all the omens of evil and prognostications of gloom, there have been many signs made visible, even during the present war, of the increasingly serious purpose of the Japanese to persevere in their career of progress, and to seek to base this progress on education. Already earnest natives are raising warnings against the dangers which are sure to flow from excessive militarism and the intoxication of conceit. That great purifying and uplifting force, a belief in God, one and personal, is the expulsive power before which the fog and dreams of Buddhism and the agnosticism and paralysis of Confucianism are surely passing away. Japan has the great task before her of educating her masses and elevating her women. One thing seems certain, and that is that Christianity has taken root in the minds and hearts of the people. Japan will never be "converted" in the way that many old-fashioned folk hoped a generation or even a decade ago; but in the adoption and assimilation of the true spirit and real teachings of Jesus the Japanese are making steady advance. Despite so-called "reactions" and the tendency to "Japanize Christianity," we discern no real retrogression in the steady movement towards a Japan that knows but one Deity.

In ages that are past there could be and was a variety of civilizations, narrow, ethnic, defective. Now there can be but one civilization—that founded by Jesus. He fused the many ideals and inheritances into one. To his vision no one nation has yet fully attained or can attain. When all the families of the earth bend the knee unto the Father whom the Christ revealed, his ideas may be fulfilled in human history. Japan's best hope is that already some of her sons dwell in this open vision.

# The Testament of Iyéyasu

The Legacy of Iyéyasu" is a document whose authenticity is yet to be proved. It purports to be the testament of the founder of the last shôgunate; but a thoroughly critical examination of its claims has not, I believe, been made. It is certain that it was not popularly or generally known in Japan, nor ever reckoned as within the body of standard legal literature. It was translated into English (thirty-seven pages print) by Mr. J. F. Lowder, some years before its publication by him in Yokohama, in 1874. The title of the pamphlet read thus: "The Legacy of Iyéyasu (deified as Gongen-sama): a Posthumous Manuscript, in One Hundred Chapters, translated from three collated Copies of the Original," printed at *The Japan Herald* office.

Dr. Walter Dixon, also, in his work on Japan, gives (chapter VII) another version, with notes and comments. W. E. Grigsby, Professor of Law in the Imperial College in Tôkiô, in a paper read before the Asiatic Society of Japan, has given a scholarly analysis of the document, showing especially its similarity to most ancient law codes, such as those of Solon and Lycurgus, the Twelve Tables, the Mosaic, and the early Teutonic codes. He terms it "the most original monument which Japan has produced in the way of legislation," with which compare Dixon, pp. 269, 270. Whether authentic or not, it embodies the policy of Iyéyasu, is a mirror of feudalism, and is of great historic value.

The work consists of one hundred sections, in no logical sequence, and difficult to determine in the original. Of these, sixteen consist of moral maxims and reflections, which are quotations, or intended to be such, from Confucius and Mencius; fifty-five are connected with politics and administrations; twenty-two refer to legal matter's; and in seven Iyéyasu relates episodes in his own personal history. No sharp distinction is made in it between law and morality, between the duties of the citizen and the virtue of the man. The man who obeys the law is virtuous; he who disobeys it is vicious and low. It is the province of the legislator to inculcate virtue. All that we understand by law—all that embraces the main bulk of modern law, the law of contracts, of personal property, of will, commercial and maritime law—finds no place in this code. This arose from the fact that human life within the daimiôate was regulated by custom, not by agreement; and there was hardly any intercourse between the various daimioates, because the only property of any importance was land, and no will was allowed. On the other hand, great stress was laid on criminal law, the law relating to landed property, the law relating to the status of persons and classes, to etiquette and ceremonial, to tables of rank and precedence, and to political administration and government. On these points, especially the latter, minute details are entered into with a peculiarity which is striking, when compared with the poverty of the code in respect to those matters which seem to us most important in a system of law. Another of the many points of similarity to ancient codes of law, notably the Mosaic, is the elaborate provisions with respect to the avenging of blood and personal satisfaction for injuries done. The individual does not, as in more advanced societies, give up his right of private vengeance. Great stress is laid on caste distinctions, which are made more sharp and distinct by reducing them to writing, and thus perpetuating the unequal stages into which early society is divided.

Professor Grigsby further remarks that there is one great difference between this and all other early codes, viz., its secrecy. It was in express terms forbidden to be promulgated. The perusal of it was only allowed to the chief councilors of state (*rôjiu*). How can people obey laws if they do not know their nature? A parallel is found in the history of the Aryan race. In Greece and Rome, at the beginning of their history, the knowledge of the laws and their administration was confined to the aristocratic class, and the first struggle of the commons was to force this knowledge from them—a struggle which ended in these codes being reduced to writing and promulgated. The parallel is not complete in respect to writing. In the case of Greece and Rome, the laws were unknown because not written: in Japan, though written, they were yet to be unknown. In early communities, custom has absolute sway. The magistrates, as Iyéyasu says, are the reflectors of the mode of government; they interpret, not make, the law. Any additions to the old customs were to reach the multitudes by filtering down through the magistrates, who alone would be conscious that they were new. To the multitude they would only be slight modifications of the customs they had always observed. As a code of laws, this was the character of the testament of Iyéyasu, who claims merely to be a transmitter, not a framer, of the law. His work is a compilation, not a creation; a selection from old, not a series of new, laws.

The "Legacy" is invaluable in representing to us the condition of society in feudal Japan. The basis of Japanese life, the unit of civilization, is the family, which is a corporation, the most characteristic mark of which was its perpetuity. The head of the family held a power similar, in nearly all respects, to that of the paterfamilias at Rome, having complete power over the persons and property of his children, and doing as he pleased with both, fettered only by that custom which is the great hinderance to despotism in all early communities. But his liabilities were equally great with his rights. He was responsible for all the ill-doings of any of his family. A Japanese family was not, however, what we understand by the word. It was often not natural, but artificial. Persons whom we should exclude from the family were admitted into it, and those who with us are constant members were sometimes excluded from it. Adoption (*yoshi ni naru*) on the one hand, and emancipation, or the sending-away (*kandô suru*) of a son from the family, on the other, were in constant practice. In Rome, adoption was employed merely to enlarge the family; in Japan, solely to perpetuate it. The son adopted by a man having no male heir filled exactly the place of a natural child; and, in early times at least, he must take the name of the adopting parent. If the adopting parent had a daughter, the adopted son married her, becoming heir himself, in which respect the Japanese custom differed from the Roman, which held that the natural tie of brother and sister was formed by adoption, and hence their marriage was illegal. Only an adult could adopt; but if the head of the family were an infant, he could adopt. This practice was often resorted to in Japan for two reasons—the religious and the feudal; to prevent the extinguishment of the ancestral sacrifices, with the consequent disgrace to the family; and because the land, being held only on condition of military service, if a vassal died leaving no male children, the lands escheated to the lord. The second method which rendered the family artificial were the expulsion and disinheritance of a son from the family, which, however, were only effected when he was of an irredeemably bad character.

Marriage in Japan, which was allowed—rather, enjoined—in the case of a man at sixteen, of a woman at thirteen, was not a contract between the parties or a religious institution, but a handing-over of the bride to the family of her husband by her own family, she passing completely under the control of her husband, both as to person and property, subject to reference to a council of family relations.

So far the internal aspect of the family. Each family, however, was connected with other families, as in early Greece and Rome; and thus about fifty great clans were formed, of which the four principal were the Minamoto, Fujiwara, Taira, and Sugawara, all the families of which were, or claimed to be, descended from a common ancestor. Certain sacrifices were peculiar to each, and certain dignities confined to certain families. Thus the office of kuambaku was monopolized by the Fujiwara, and the shogunate by the Minamoto clans (the families in succession being, the line of Yoritomo, the Ashikaga, and the Tokugawa). This condition of society was analogous to that in Italy and Greece from 1000 B.C. to 500 A.D. But what is peculiar to Japan is that, with this primitive form of society remaining unchanged, we find a system that did not arise in Europe till about the eleventh century A.D. Thus the superstructure of feudalism was reared on the basis of the family—an incongruous social edifice, as it seems to our minds.

In Japan, then, at the time of the formation of the code, the mikado and the imperial court were above, and not included in, the theory of feudalism, at the head of which was the shôgun, and beneath him the daimiôs, each with a territory of greater or lesser extent, which he farmed out to the samurai, or vassals, in return for military service. In the greater daimiôates these vassals underlet their lands on the same conditions; in other words, subfeudation was common. A vassal not able, by reason of age or sickness, to perform this service abdicated in favor of his son. If a man died without leaving any children, natural or adopted, his property was retained for him by a legal fiction, for his death was concealed till permission was given by his lord for him to adopt a son, and only after such permission was given was his death announced. The necessity of having an heir, that the vassal's land might not escheat to the lord, but be kept in the vassal's family, greatly extended the practice of adoption. If the vassal proved faithless to his lord, both escheat and forfeiture were incurred.

The leading principles of Iyéyasu's policy are thus summarized: The position of the shôgun to the mikado was to be one of reverential homage. The shôguns were in no way to interfere with the mikado's theoretical supremacy, but to strengthen it in every way, and show all respect to the emperor's relatives, and the old court aristocracy. Secondly, toward their inferiors the shôguns were to behave with courtesy and consideration. All insult and tyranny were to be avoided, and the weight of power was not to press too harshly. The neglect of this principle, as shown in insolence to inferiors, was the rock on which the governments in nearly all ancient communities struck. This caution proves the consummate knowledge of human nature and the profound mastery of state-craft possessed by Iyéyasu. Another recommendation of Iyéyasu was, that the government of the lesser daimiôs should be frequently changed. The motive alleged for this was the prevention of misgovernment; but the real reason was, that they might not acquire local influence, and so endanger the power of the shôguns. This was similar in its purpose to the policy adopted by William the Conqueror, in portioning out the territories of his barons among several counties. In England the plan was completely successful; in Japan it failed, as we have seen, because the shôguns never dared to enforce the measure in the case of the greater daimiôs, who were the only ones to be dreaded.

# Notation of Time

The first systematic attempt at marking and recording time was in A.D. 602, when a Buddhist missionary from Corea, named Kuanroku, brought to Japan a Chinese almanac, and taught its use. From this time, the years, lunar months, and days arc counted, and the years named after the characters in a cycle of sixty years, which is made up of one series of ten, and another series of twelve, characters. The cycle of ten series is called from "the five elements," Wood, Fire, Earth, Metal, and Water, each of which is taken double, or masculine and feminine.

The cycle of twelve series is formed, according to the division of the zodiac, into twelve equal parts, to each of which the name of some Japanese animal is assigned. These are the Rat, Ox, Tiger, Hare, Dragon, Serpent, Horse, Goat, Ape, Cock, Dog, Hog.

By making a square, in which twelve lines are drawn horizontally, and ten perpendicularly, we have one hundred and twenty squares, of which sixty are used. Place the ten-series at the top, and the twelve-series on the left side, and the numerals from 1 to 60 in diagonal lines in the spaces from left to right, and from top to bottom. Thus the cyclical name of the year 1711 (see page 314) is "water"-"dragon," or the ten-series name, "water," and the twelve-series name, "dragon." The first year of the current cycle is 1864, and the cyclical name of 1877 is "fire"-"bull," the first belonging to the ten-series, and the second to the twelve-series cycle. (See diagram in Hoffman's "Grammar," page 156.) This method of reckoning time is still in use among the Chinese, Coreans, and the Japanese Buddhist world and priesthood. All Japanese literature is full of it, and it will be printed in the native almanacs for some years to come.

# *Enumeration of the Years by Year-periods*

From 645 A.D., under the mikado Kôtoku, the system of reckoning the years by chronological periods called *nen-gô*, or year-names, has been in use. In historical works, and in Japanese literature generally, these year-periods are always referred to, and formerly many natives committed the entire list to memory. Others used little reference-tables, kept in their pocket books or near at hand. No special rule or system was observed in changing the names, though the accession of a new sovereign, the advent of war or peace, a great national calamity or blessing, a profound social change or great national event, was made the pretext for adopting a new name. It thus results that from 645 to 1868 A.D. there have been 249 year-names, including those used by the "northern dynasty" during the period 1336–1392, treated of in Chapter XIX. The year-names are appointed by the mikado, and are chosen from sixty-eight Chinese words or characters specially reserved for that purpose. They are often very poetic and striking. (See in Dr. J. J. Hoffman's *Grammar*, page 157.) In the following list, it will be noticed that the same syllables recur often. The dates can not exactly correspond to our years, since the Japanese New-Year's-day was often as much as six weeks later than January 1st. A few years ago—1872—the Government fixed upon the year 660 B.C. as that in which Jimmu Tenno "ascended the throne," and Christmas,

December 25th, as the day. Hence, in the newspapers, official documents, and books printed since 1872, the time is expressed in "years of the Japanese empire," or "from the foundation of the empire," or "from the accession of Jimmu Tennô." These phrases have a value at par with the Roman "Ab urbe condita," the date of Jimmu's "ascension" being purely arbitrary.

| | A.D. | | A.D. | | A.D. |
|---|---|---|---|---|---|
| Taikua | 645 | Konin | 810 | Tenyen | 973 |
| Hakuchi | 650 | Tencho | 824 | Jogen | 976 |
| Sujaku | 672 | Jowa | 834 | Tengen | 978 |
| Hakuho | 673 | Kasho | 848 | Eikuan | 983 |
| Shucho | 686 | Ninjiu | 851 | Kuanwa | 985 |
| Taikua | 695 | Saiko | 854 | Eiyen | 987 |
| Taicho | 697 | Tenan | 857 | Eiso | 989 |
| Taiho | 701 | Jokuan | 859 | Shoréki | 990 |
| Keiun | 704 | Genkei | 877 | Chotoku | 995 |
| Wado | 708 | Ninna | 885 | Choho | 999 |
| Hoki | 715 | Kuampei | 889 | Kuanko | 1004 |
| Yoro | 717 | Shotai | 898 | Chowa | 1012 |
| Jinki | 724 | Engi | 901 | Kuannin | 1017 |
| Tempio | 729 | Encho | 923 | Chian | 1021 |
| Tempio Shoho | 749 | Shohei | 931 | Manjiu | 1024 |
| Tempio Hoji | 757 | Tengio | 938 | Chogen | 1028 |
| Tempio Jingo | 765 | Tenréki | 947 | Choréki | 1037 |
| Jingo Keiun | 767 | Tentoku | 957 | Chokiu | 1040 |
| Hoki | 770 | Owa | 961 | Kuantoku | 1044 |
| Téno | 781 | Koho | 964 | Ejo | 1046 |
| Enréki | 782 | Anwa | 968 | Tenki | 1053 |
| Daido | 806 | Tenroku | 970 | Kohei | 1058 |

| | | | | | |
|---|---|---|---|---|---|
| Chiréki | 1065 | Eiréki | 1160 | Enwo | 1239 |
| Enkiu | 1069 | Oyei | 1161 | Ninji | 1240 |
| Joho | 1074 | Chokuan | 1163 | Kuangen | 1243 |
| Joréki | 1077 | Eiman | 1165 | Hoji | 1247 |
| Eiho | 1081 | Ninan | 1166 | Kencho | 1249 |
| Otoku | 1084 | Kawo | 1169 | Kogen | 1256 |
| Kuanji | 1087 | Shoan | 1171 | Shoka | 1257 |
| Kaho | 1094 | Angen | 1175 | Shogen | 1259 |
| Eicho | 1096 | Jijo | 1177 | Bunwo | 1260 |
| Shotoku | 1097 | Yowa | 1181 | Kocho | 1261 |
| Kowa | 1099 | Juyei | 1182 | Bunyei | 1264 |
| Choji | 1104 | Monji | 1185 | Kenji | 1275 |
| Kajo | 1106 | Kenkiu | 1190 | Koan | 1278 |
| Tennin | 1108 | Shoji | 1199 | Showo | 1288 |
| Tenyei | 1110 | Kennin | 1201 | Einin | 1293 |
| Eikiu | 1113 | Genkiu | 1204 | Shoan | 1299 |
| Genyei | 1118 | Kenyei | 1206 | Kengen | 1302 |
| Hoan | 1120 | Shogen | 1207 | Kagen | 1303 |
| Tenji | 1124 | Kenréki | 1211 | Tokuji | 1306 |
| Daiji | 1126 | Kempo | 1213 | Enkei | 1308 |
| Tensho | 1131 | Jokiu | 1219 | Ocho | 1311 |
| Chosho | 1132 | Jowo | 1222 | Showa | 1312 |
| Hoyen | 1135 | Gennin | 1224 | Bumpo | 1317 |
| Eiji | 1141 | Karoku | 1225 | Genwo | 1319 |
| Koji | 1142 | Antei | 1227 | Genko | 1321 |
| Tenyo | 1144 | Kuanki | 1229 | Shochiu | 1324 |
| Kiuan | 1145 | Joyei | 1232 | Karéki | 1326 |
| Nimpei | 1151 | Tembuku | 1233 | Gentoku | 1329 |
| Kinjiu | 1154 | Bunréki | 1234 | Genko | 1331 |
| Hogen | 1156 | Katei | 1235 | Kemmu | 1334 |
| Heiji | 1159 | Rékinin | 1238 | | |

| SOUTHERN DYNASTY | | Eikio | 1429 | Manji | 1658 |
|---|---|---|---|---|---|
| Engen | 1336 | Kakitsu | 1441 | Kuambun | 1661 |
| Kokoku | 1340 | Bunan | 1444 | Empo | 1673 |
| Shohei | 1346 | Hotoku | 1449 | Tenwa | 1681 |
| Kentoku | 1370 | Kiotoku | 1452 | Jokio | 1684 |
| Bunchiu | 1372 | Kosho | 1455 | Genroku | 1688 |
| Tenjiu | 1375 | Choroku | 1457 | Hoyei | 1704 |
| Kowa | 1381 | Kuansho | 1460 | Shotoku | 1711 |
| Genchiu | 1384 | Bunsho | 1466 | Hokio | 1716 |
| | | Onin | 1467 | Gembun | 1736 |
| | | Bummei | 1469 | Kuampo | 1741 |
| NORTHERN DYNASTY | | Chokio | 1487 | Enkio | 1744 |
| | | Entoku | 1489 | Kuanyen | 1748 |
| Rékiwo | 1338 | Meiwo | 1492 | Horéki | 1751 |
| Koyei | 1342 | Bunki | 1501 | Meiwa | 1764 |
| Teiwa | 1345 | Eisei | 1504 | Anyei | 1772 |
| Kuanwo | 1350 | Taiyei | 1521 | Temmei | 1781 |
| Bunwa | 1352 | Kioroku | 1528 | Kuansei | 1789 |
| Embun | 1356 | Tembun | 1532 | Kiowa | 1801 |
| Owa | 1361 | Koji | 1555 | Bunkwa | 1804 |
| Toji | 1362 | Eiroku | 1558 | Bunsei | 1818 |
| Oan | 1368 | Genki | 1570 | Tempo | 1830 |
| Eiwa | 1375 | Tensho | 1573 | Kokwa | 1844 |
| Koréki | 1379 | Bunroku | 1592 | Kayei | 1848 |
| Eitoku | 1381 | Keicho | 1596 | Ansei | 1854 |
| Shitoku | 1384 | Genwa | 1615 | Manyen | 1860 |
| Kakei | 1387 | Kuanyei | 1624 | Bunkiu | 1861 |
| Kowo | 1389 | Shoho | 1644 | Genji | 1864 |
| Meitoku | 1390 | Keian | 1648 | Keiwo | 1865 |
| Oyen | 1394 | Showo | 1652 | Meiji | 1868 |
| Seicho | 1428 | Meiréki | 1655 | | |

# Index